BRUCKNER - MAHLER - SCHOENBERG
Revised Edition

Bruckner · Mahler Schoenberg

Revised Edition

DIKA NEWLIN

W · W · NORTON & COMPANY · INC ·

NEW YORK

Copyright © 1978, 1947 by Dika Newlin.

Published simultaneously in Canada by George J. McLeod Limited,
Toronto. Printed in the United States of America.
All Rights Reserved.

Library of Congress Cataloging in Publication Data
Newlin, Dika, 1923–
Bruckner, Mahler, Schoenberg.

Bibliography: p.
Includes index.
1. Bruckner, Anton, 1824–1896. 2. Mahler,
Gustav, 1860–1911. 3. Schönberg, Arnold, 1874–1951.
ML390.N55 1978   780'.92'2   78–8620
ISBN 0–393–02203–X

1 2 3 4 5 6 7 8 9 0

To my friends

MARIAN PASCHAL *and* HENRIETTE VOORSANGER

whose interest has made this work possible

Contents

BOOK THREE: SCHOENBERG AND BEYOND

Decades of Decision

Preface

THE IDEA of this book originally came to me during my years of study with Arnold Schoenberg in Los Angeles (1938–1941). At that time I was first introduced to the most "radical" works of Schoenberg—works virtually unknown in this country so far as public performances are concerned. I felt the need of a historical background which would explain the origins of the new style. It was this which brought me to a study of the works of Mahler and Bruckner; for Schoenberg's oft-expressed indebtedness to Mahler plainly indicated that the roots of Schoenberg's style might be found in Mahler's scores (however different Mahler's music might be in texture from Schoenberg's), and the relationship between Mahler and Bruckner seemed well established. Thence, it was but a step to the conclusion that Schoenberg is not only the heir of Bruckner and Mahler but also the heir of the great Viennese classical tradition, which they transmitted to him. It is this conclusion which I have tried to prove in the following pages; it has been my desire to portray Schoenberg's works as the culmination of several centuries of historical development, rather than as the products of a wilful iconoclasm. To this end, I have attempted to place Schoenberg in the Viennese cultural scene by analyzing, not only the musical background, but also the literary, artistic, and political background of his generation—a task which I have likewise performed for the period of Bruckner and of Mahler.

Such an extensive project could never have been carried out without the assistance and cooperation of those who were familiar at first hand with the milieu which I wished to reconstruct. Though space forbids detailed acknowledgments, I would like to express here some measure of my gratitude to all who helped me in any capacity—to Professor Paul Henry Láng and Dr. Erich Hertzmann, of the Department of Music, Columbia University, whose patient and painstaking guidance and unfailing encouragement were, from the beginning, of inestimable aid to me; to Dr. Herman T. Radin, who kindly furnished me with photostats and copies of unpublished Mahler material in his possession; to Mr. Leo Katz, for valuable commentary on the art-movements of the twentieth century; to Mr. Francis Aranyi, for the characteristic anecdotes relating to the première of Schoenberg's *Gurre-Lieder;* to all those who, by word or deed, stimulated my imagination to a more vivid conception of the period with which I dealt, or who made me acquainted at first hand with its musical manifestations—Rudolf Kolisch, Eduard Steuermann, Fritz Stiedry, Erika Stiedry-Wagner, Alma Mahler Werfel; and, inevitably, to the one whose work made this study not only possible but necessary, who is his own best critic, and whom I have allowed to speak in his own words wherever feasible—to Arnold Schoenberg.

New York City
1947

Preface to the Revised Edition

FOR A LONG TIME, both students and colleagues have been urging me to prepare an updated version of this book. At long last, the time and opportunity to do so have come.

Many things that I hoped for and predicted thirty years ago have come to pass. Bruckner's reputation has grown steadily in this country; Mahler has become a really popular composer; most of Schoenberg's major works have been recorded, and his two great religious works, insofar as he was able to complete them, have received American performances. More and more facts, insights, and interpretations concerning these three men have been brought to light, some by me, some by others. I have referred to many of these in newly added footnotes.

I have changed my mind about very little that I wrote thirty years ago. Today, my feelings towards Mendelssohn and Schumann, whom it was rather fashionable to denigrate in the '40s, have become much more positive. And I set much greater store by the religious element in both Mahler and Schoenberg. Other than that, I feel that time and events have confirmed most of the things I said.

The evolution continues—Schoenberg, Berg, Webern—the electronic composers—the chance composers—the minimalists. . . . As Mahler said, "There goes the last wave!"

Madison, New Jersey
August, 1977

The Continuity of Musical Tradition in Vienna:
Austrian Convention and Revolt

NO CULTURAL PHENOMENON, however isolated it may at first sight seem to be, can be presupposed without historical origin. This is as true of the work of the "neo-Viennese" school—Arnold Schoenberg and his disciples—as of any other manifestation of cultural life, yet curiously this fact has often been overlooked or has gone unrecognized. The reason for this is not hard to understand. At first sight —or hearing—nothing could seem further removed from a quartet of Haydn or Mozart than a quartet of the atonal Schoenberg. Yet the links between the Viennese school of the eighteenth century and that of our time are not merely present, they are manifold and, what is more, clearly traceable, even if not always visible to the naked eye.

Before speaking of the eighteenth century, however, let us take one step further back, to Vienna's high baroque. It was a time of Catholic domination, of Italian hegemony, and of operatic furore. In the splendor of her operatic productions, Vienna, the Catholic Hapsburg capital, more than held her own with the cities of Italy; even in an age whose keynote was magnificence, the Viennese production of Cesti's *Pomo d'Oro* (1668) was a high-water mark. Opera, in those times, was the accepted and inevitable concomitant of all imperial festivities. And it is well worth noting that underneath all the surface splendor might be found a solid core of honest, sturdy craftsmanship which did much to prepare for the coming of the Viennese school of the eighteenth century —and beyond. A man like Johann Josef Fux, doughty theorist and irreproachable technician of the theater, would never succumb to the blandishments of the more facile Neapolitan style. His fugal arias and elaborate choruses did not always convey as much unadulterated drama as could be found in the contemporary Italian opera, but the solidity and worth of his work, and hence its value for future generations, remained beyond question.

In a brief survey of the musical aspects of the high baroque in Vienna we may find much to point to the future. The direct influence of Italianism may perhaps be disposed of first; it is still very active in the eighteenth century, but becomes of practically no measurable importance in more recent times.[1] Insofar as the Italian influx stimulated the production of opera in Vienna, however, it is of the greatest importance for events to come. Standing at the threshold of the eighteenth century, we can look ahead exactly two hundred years to the time when the Vienna Opera House, under Mahler's direction, will be the focal point of Vienna's cultural life. And, in the twentieth century as in the seventeenth, the opera is the special joy of the House of Hapsburg, and the ornament of its festive occasions. In fact, there is even something faintly anachronistic in the spectacle revealed to us in the letters of Mahler, who was in so many ways the prototype of modernity, which tell of his grave preoccupation with the problems of arranging a gala opera evening in honor of the visit of the Shah of Persia. Opera, too, becomes of importance to the neo-Viennese school in still another way, for the entire period of late romantic flowering from which the school stems is under the aegis of the Wagnerian *Gesamtkunstwerk*. Wagner himself comes to Vienna and, thanks to the presence there of Hanslick, becomes the focal point of a dispute beside which even the most vitriolic episodes in the later controversies over Mahler, over Schoenberg, and over Schoenberg's pupils seem a little pale. Brahms, lured to Vienna by the pleas of friends, by the untenability of his somewhat anomalous situation in Hamburg, and by memories of Haydn, Mozart, and Beethoven, becomes, willy-nilly, an anti-pope set up against the Wagnerites. The Upper Austrian Bruckner, a curious baroque figure, falls under the spell of Wagner's music; he, too, comes to Vienna, and lives to regret it as he becomes an innocent victim in the Wagnerian controversy. Mahler, first in Vienna as a young conservatory student, returns at the height of his career, as a feted opera conductor, to play the part of high priest to Wagner with his unforgettable performances of *Tristan* and the other Wagnerian masterpieces. And Schoenberg begins his career thoroughly steeped in Wagner. Much later he says, "When I was twenty-five I had heard the operas

[1] One might possibly consider the "Verdi revival" popularized by Franz Werfel and Paul Stefan, represented by Werfel's novel *Verdi* and his edition (together with Stefan) of Verdi's letters, as a kind of renewal of Italianism for Vienna. However, the association is far-removed. Any musical results of such a revival have not been measurable, though it may be worth noting that Schoenberg had a well-developed admiration for Verdi. Mahler, of course, did full justice to Verdi as an opera-conductor, but any kind of Italianism in his music is practically non-existent. Actually, the Verdi revival was rather a conscious rebellion against Wagnerianism than a deliberate setting-up of Italian ideals.

of Wagner between twenty and thirty times each." [2] In view of all these facts, the citation of the beginning of *Tristan* in the last movement of Berg's *Lyric Suite* attains a more than passing symbolic significance. [3]

But of all the heritages from the baroque, one of the most significant and most problematic is the Catholic heritage. The Hapsburg monarchy was a stronghold of Catholicism in the baroque era and it remained so throughout its existence; the aristocracy, too, was strongly Catholic, and anti-Semitism was a force to be reckoned with in Vienna, in spite of the Jewish domination of a large proportion of the press. It is only through the entrenchment of Catholicism in the rural districts of Austria during the *Vormärz* (the period preceding the revolution of 1848) that a character like Bruckner, truly fanatical in his fervent Catholicism and in his submissiveness to established authority, can be explained. It has already been said that Bruckner was a man of the baroque. Indeed, it is not surprising that he should have been so, considering the environment in which he spent his formative years. The Abbey of St. Florian is one of the most majestic edifices in pure baroque style—"Jesuit style"—surpassed in Lower Austria only, perhaps, by Melk. And its magnificent organ inspired Bruckner to contrapuntal improvisations which bespeak the seventeenth-century soul in a man who was still alive when Schoenberg was twenty-one. Unlike Reger, he left no major organ works in the baroque tradition, but much of the essential nature of the baroque transmits itself to the monumentally orchestrated pages of his symphonies. In this sense, the baroque tradition passed to Mahler, but Mahler could never have been a man of the baroque in the sense that Bruckner was, for his faith was not Bruckner's. In his gropings for faith amid the mazes of Judaism, Catholicism, and pantheistic nature-worship we may discover the source of the pseudo-Catholic mysticism, a latent residue of romanticism, which animated men like Schoenberg and Werfel. The relentless probings of the conscience which their mystical speculations imply may even suggest to us the rigorous discipline of Loyola's *Spiritual Exercises*.

Passing to the eighteenth century, we find in Vienna a flourishing of eminent composers such as is unparalleled in her twentieth-century renaissance. Even the listing of their names is informative to us, for the presence of such names as Czernohorsky, Gyrowetz, Koželuch, or

[2] Arnold Schoenberg, "Art and the Moving Pictures," *California Arts and Architecture,* April, 1940.

[3] Later discoveries reveal that this citation also had an intimate personal significance for Berg.

Jiránek tells us that there was much Slavic blood in this so-called "Viennese school," a fact which may seem at first surprising. However, it must not be forgotten that it was the mixture of nationalities brought about by the aggrandizing policies of the House of Hapsburg which helped to create the style known to us as "Austrian." Vienna, as a brilliant musical center, was naturally a magnet to musicians from Austria's crown lands; but not to these alone, for some of Vienna's most renowned masters—men like Beethoven and Brahms—were no Austrians at all, but Germans. The factor of racial mixture, particularly when the Austro-Bohemian strain is taken into account, is of special importance because it brought about the introduction into the Viennese style of provincial folk elements. Such elements are much in evidence in the minuets of Haydn's symphonies, which often have the character of Austrian peasant dances. Here it is possible to trace a direct line of descent from the eighteenth century to more recent times. For the earthy scherzos of Bruckner's symphonies, too, spring directly from peasant soil. This is no fanciful analogy; it is a definitely established fact that Bruckner, in the insignificant Upper Austrian hamlets where it was his lot to teach as a young man, was much in demand as a fiddler at rustic entertainments. The spirit of the peasant dances was transferred to the scherzos of his symphonies, contrasting strangely with the grandiose organ-like passages of baroque inspiration. And it is not in Bruckner alone that this nineteenth-century Austrian version of the transfer of folk dance material to the symphony may be found. Mahler, too, utilized the rhythms and in some cases the melodies of Austrian and Bohemian folk song. In connection with what has already been said of the Slavic strain in the eighteenth-century Viennese school, it is well to remember that Mahler was born on Czech soil, in the little Bohemian village of Kalischt. In the slightly larger town of Iglau (Jihlava) to which his parents later moved he was exposed not only to folk music but also to the Austrian military music. At the age of four he is said to have known by heart most of the tunes played by the military band at the barracks in Iglau. This earliest childhood experience of music undoubtedly had something to do with the predilection of the symphonist Mahler for martial rhythms and tunes, though not nearly so much as some of his over-zealous biographers would have us believe. Specific instances can be pointed to, however: Ernst Křenek, for example, has commented on the identity of the opening horn motive of the Third Symphony with the first bars of a patriotic marching song well known to all Austrian school children.[4] This matter

---

[4] Bruno Walter and Ernst Křenek, *Gustav Mahler*, p. 193.

will be discussed again later with reference to other influences on Mahler; it is only mentioned here for the purpose of demonstrating the parallel between the influence of popular or semi-popular material on the Viennese style in the eighteenth century and in the late nineteenth and early twentieth centuries.

The Austrian popular music of the eighteenth century bore other fruit as well. In the Vienna of Mozart's time and before, one of its chief manifestations was the serenade, otherwise known as the cassation or divertimento. In its most artistic form it takes the shape of a finished masterpiece like Mozart's *Eine kleine Nachtmusik,* but it could be, and often was, of a much more informal nature. Thus its orchestration might consist merely of whatever group of instruments happened to be assembled at a given moment. However, in contrast with its North German relative, the dance-suite for wind and brass instruments, it is usually made up of winds or strings in a small chamber ensemble. Mozart wrote many such works, not only in the early part of his career (the B flat major divertimento for wind instruments) but also in his maturity *(Eine kleine Nachtmusik* and the string trio in E flat major). The divertimento or serenade does not end with Mozart. Beethoven's Septet, Op. 20, is a divertimento both in spirit and in the number of movements; the specific Austrian tone is notably evident in its minuet. A still later example of the divertimento is the Schubert Octet. These two compositions do not use the characteristic old names of "divertimento" or "serenade," and they exhibit truly symphonic proportions, but in view of what has already been said it is not surprising that at least one of the names continues to remain in use. Thus we must take into account Brahms' two Serenades for orchestra, concerning which Richard Specht's rather naïve words, in the light of the history we have just been retracing, seem to take on new significance: "It is as if Papa Haydn had been given a son. . . ." [5] It is the influence of the *genre* in more recent times that really concerns us, however, and here we shall find concrete evidence of the continuity of at least one Viennese tradition. Schoenberg's Op. 24 is entitled *Serenade,* and is set for seven instruments (clarinet, bass clarinet, mandolin, guitar, violin, viola, 'cello) and, in one movement, a baritone voice singing a sonnet of Petrarch—Petrarch, whose enervated lyricism seems so subtly appropriate to this Indian Summer of the Viennese serenade. The fallacy of the notion that the style achieved by the use of the twelve-tone row in composition must of necessity be a coldly impersonal one is indicated in the dance movements of this suite,

[5] Richard Specht, *Johannes Brahms,* p. 65.

which are specifically Viennese in tone, with their popular character emphasized by the use of guitar and mandolin. That the music happens to be atonal adds nothing to and detracts nothing from this well-defined character. The same tone may be noticed in the second movement (*Tanzschritte*) of one of Schoenberg's next-following works, the septet for piano, piccolo-clarinet, clarinet, bass clarinet, violin, viola, and 'cello; and, though the listener may not realize it on a first hearing on account of the atonal setting, the theme of the third movement (*Theme and Variations*) is, according to the composer, a "German folk song." [6] Given all that has gone before, such stylistic earmarks are not surprising, particularly as the Austrian tone is no stranger to the earlier works of Schoenberg. It creeps in, unannounced, in a *Ländler*-like passage of his *Pelleas und Melisande,*[7] in unmistakable fashion. Of the rather disconcerting appearance of "O, du lieber Augustin" in the second movement of his Second String Quartet there will be more to say later, in other connections.

The divertimento was by no means Vienna's only form of musical diversion in the eighteenth century. At least as popular an entertainment was the national *Singspiel,* with its merry medley of speech and music, its straightforward strophic songs, and its irrepressible Hanswurst, the comic figure *par excellence* of the Viennese public. Joseph II's official patronage of a national *Singspiel* theater in Vienna undoubtedly helped to raise the artistic standards of the *genre*—it could hardly have done otherwise when a Mozart was commissioned to write music for the new enterprise—but one feels that the Emperor's actions could have done nothing to increase or to abate the popularity of Hanswurst-Casperle, that irresistible buffoon. He was finally eliminated from Vienna's serious theater in 1772, when German actors took over the *Burgtheater* to play there the "legitimate" dramas of Goethe and Schiller, but he simply moved to the suburban theaters, where he continued telling his questionable jokes to the infinite delight of his Viennese followers and to the disgust of any North-German visitors who happened to be in the audience. His burlesques of Austria's non-Germanic racial types, too, amused an audience which was accustomed to the variety of national elements drawn from all corners of the polyglot Empire.

Some of the characteristics of this popular art may suggest to our minds the corresponding musical form of a later period in Viennese musical history—the operetta. True, the operetta is far inferior to the *Singspiel,* mainly on account of the commercialization which it under-

[6] It is Friedrich Silcher's *Ännchen von Tharau.*
[7] Pp. 32–33 of the full score, Universal-Edition.

went at the hands of composers like Franz Lehár and Oscar Straus. Johann Strauss was hampered in his efforts to create an artistically balanced operetta by the generally inferior quality of his libretti. Nevertheless, not only his operettas, but also his dances remain really great in their limited sphere. And to consider the Strauss waltz as the symbol of Vienna is not by any means to insult Vienna's "serious" composers. Schoenberg was not ashamed to call Strauss a "great composer." At first sight this type of music might seem to have very little in common with the lofty aims of the composers of the neo-Viennese school. However, it is a curious coincidence, if nothing more, that three of the school's most important composers got their start, in one way or another, through operetta. Mahler, barely twenty, fulfilled his first conducting engagements in the little spa of Bad Hall, conducting operettas and farces ("Possen"). Schoenberg, also in his twenties, had to abandon work on *Gurre-Lieder* in order to eke out a living by orchestrating second-rate operettas. And Alexander von Zemlinsky, Schoenberg's only teacher, was an operetta conductor—and, from all contemporary accounts, an excellent one—before he came to the Vienna Court Opera. Surely such association with operetta was no experience of unmixed pleasure for the composers concerned. But is it not possible that (especially in the case of Mahler) the necessary contact with this popular art was of importance to them later on, because it impressed upon them whatever had remained fresh and vital in it? We have already glimpsed the influence of Austrian folk song upon Mahler and Schoenberg; something of folk art was present in the operetta, too, though to a slighter and slighter degree as it underwent the commercializing process already referred to.

In speaking of the great number of composers in eighteenth-century Vienna, it was said that even a listing of their names could be very informative. Two of those names—Georg Matthias Monn (1717–1750) and Johann Christian Mann (1726–1782) are of special significance at this point because, thanks to them, we have an excellent opportunity of pointing out the continuity of Viennese musical life in still another way. The examples which we have so far cited of the influence of Vienna's earlier musical generations upon her later ones do not necessarily imply that the later composers were consciously affected by their predecessors. A truly vital continuity, on the other hand, could only be attained if the contemporary composers were really interested in the work of preceding generations, and made an active effort to keep it alive. Thus it is that Schoenberg's editions for the *Denkmäler der Tonkunst in Oesterreich* of a symphony, two harpsichord concerti, and a 'cello concerto by Monn, and a divertimento by Mann, assume more

than a passing significance, for they show that—though far from
musicologically-minded—he had a sincere interest in the art of Vienna's
past. Whether or not the principles on which he carried out the
basso continuo in these works are completely acceptable to musicologists is not in question here. The significant thing at this point is to
show that the revivifying of the works of their predecessors was apparently of some import to these composers. That this should be true
speaks much for the vitality of Vienna's traditions even if there were
no other evidence to support it.

To speak in detail of the importance of Haydn, Mozart, or Beethoven for the development of later Viennese composers is a task which
must be reserved for later chapters. All that is specifically a part of
the Viennese tradition, rather than of the international cultural heritage, in these men has been dealt with by implication in what was
said about the lesser musicians of the eighteenth-century Austro-
Bohemian school; and matters of broader significance must of necessity fall outside the scope of this introductory chapter. Thus we shall
have particular occasion to return to Beethoven when we discuss Mahler's choral symphonies. However, before leaving the eighteenth century it may not be amiss to point out an interesting historical parallel
between the activities of Viennese composers in foreign lands then and
now. The distribution of Austro-Bohemian composers during the eighteenth century is a matter of record; they might be found from Philadelphia to St. Petersburg. The so-called "Mannheim school" of pre-
classic symphonists was populated with these Austro-Bohemians; even
as Burney had cause to comment that Prague could not hold its native composers, so Vienna was to distribute her composers almost as
fast as she produced them. Now it is curious to observe the selfsame
phenomenon taking place in our time, when so many of the composers of the neo-Viennese school are political or religious exiles from
their own country. The historical parallel has gone further—the
present enforced distribution of the neo-Viennese school has led to
stylistic developments of international importance comparable to those
initiated by the widespread activities of the eighteenth-century Viennese school.

With Schubert an element enters the Viennese musical scene which
is thereafter to become of the greatest importance in the history of
the neo-Viennese school. This element is lyricism, and what is important for us to remember about it is that it finds its place at this
time not only in the romantically tinged *Lied*, where it might be logi-

cally supposed to belong, but also in the symphony, from which it had previously been far-removed. The natural result of this is a loosening of classical symphonic principles, form,[8] and idiom, coupled with the introduction into the symphony of elements drawn from the rich literary background of romantic lyricism. The full consequences of the latter step are not perceptible in Bruckner, who was immune to literary influences to a degree scarcely credible in the nineteenth century; but, as we have said, he was a strangely anachronistic figure. The most far-reaching results of this whole development in symphonic style may be witnessed in Mahler, from whose hands they pass to Schoenberg and his school, though not always used by these composers in the way that might have been expected.

It is when we reach the times of Schubert that we begin to get a more vivid conception of the vastness of the network of personal relationships between the generations of Viennese composers. Schubert, shortly before his death, desired to study with the renowned theorist and contrapuntist Simon Sechter, and would have begun to do so in earnest had he not been stricken, at that very time, with his last illness.[9] The presence of a man like Sechter, with his solid, albeit somewhat pedantic, knowledge, in the Vienna of this period shows that the sturdy strain which can be traced back to the baroque and to Fux had not died out; even more significant, in the same sense, is the desire of a finished master like Schubert to study with such a teacher. And when we find that Sechter was the most important teacher of Bruckner, and recall the line of direct descent which may be traced from Bruckner to Mahler to Schoenberg to Schoenberg's pupils, we begin to appreciate the true meaning of statements such as Felix Salten's remark that the relationship between Vienna's succeeding musical generations is often so close as almost to be perceptible as a living entity. The instance he gives to prove his point is the very one we have just mentioned, the connection between Schubert, Sechter, and Bruckner.[10] The citation of such instances, and the drawing from them of conclusions which sometimes outstrip the true facts, is nothing new, for much has been said or written on the subject of Viennese musical tradition, some of it rather superficial in tone, by writers more exclusively concerned with the modern period of Vienna's his-

[8] It must be constantly kept in mind during this discussion that the classical symphonic form is the true Viennese birthright, for the Viennese symphony *is* the classical symphony.

[9] Alfred Orel, *Wiener Musikerbriefe aus zwei Jahrhunderten,* pp. 29–30.

[10] Felix Salten, "Wien und die Musik," in Mengelberg, *Das Mahler-Fest,* p. 24.

tory. Paul Stefan's comparison of Schubert and Mahler is typical of this sort of discussion.

Schubert and Mahler sprang from the same source. It was their beloved Vienna, their blessed Austria, the melodies of the South-German borders, tunes in which sings so much that is strange and yet so much that is familiar. From this Austria they came. The experience of these masters began with everyday things—a street, a rustic garden, little brooks, paths between vineyards, a suburb of Vienna; it ended—differently, it is true, for each of them—ended in eternity.

Schubert lived isolated from his times and even from his city, lived only in the spirit. Mahler, at the turn of the new century, had all means at his command; he ruled over the greatest theaters and over concerts; he interpreted, he molded and formed artists, men, a public. . . . But basically he was just as childlike as Schubert. And just as demonic.[11]

The danger of such discussions as this, and of such remarks as Salten's, is that they are apt to lead to the formation of a certain kind of cliché in the criticism of modern Viennese developments. One of these clichés is the "Bruckner > Mahler" fetish, which has often been overdone. Between Mahler and Schoenberg—to take another example —there subsisted no such ideal relationship as has often been depicted by biographers too anxious to make their heroes into saints. In fact, it would be possible to pick flaws in any of the connections between Viennese composers of differing generations (and hence of differing points of view) here and elsewhere discussed. Many of the fallacies inherent in a system of classification which would represent the succession of generations in Vienna's musical history as a single smooth and uninterrupted flow will be dealt with later. What is important at this point is to realize that some such flow, though not always smooth or uninterrupted, did and does exist. It is only when we have grasped this basic idea that we can be sure of not losing our bearings when confronted with even the most surprising creations of the neo-Viennese school.

But, before this aim is completely fulfilled, there is one other basic idea which we must keep in mind. In the survey of musico-historical events just outlined one must perceive the latent functioning of a historical force which is a factor in every society and which is inevitably significant in the background of the Viennese composers under consideration. This force is the interplay and contrast of convention and revolt in the history of art, literature, music, and politics. It manifests itself in various ways: in the presence side by side of a conserva-

[11] Paul Stefan, *Franz Schubert,* p. 5.

tive faction and a radical faction, in the alternation of periods of reaction with periods of revolution, and in the presence of elements of
convention and revolt in the same party, or in the same individual.
Examples of these varying manifestations in Austria will immediately
occur to any student of history. One need only remember the irruption of the revolutions of 1848 into the stagnant Biedermeier period
of the *Vormärz;* or—to recall more recent history—the tragic contrast
dominating Austria before 1914, when the ageing Emperor Francis
Joseph, immured in the hereditary strict Catholicism of the Hapsburgs, failed to cope adequately with the disturbed conditions in
Austria's non-German crown lands. It is ironic that the very mixture
of national elements which in one way had been Austria's strength,
as we have seen in our brief outline of the development of the Viennese
musical style, should in another have proved the direct cause of her
downfall. This contrast seems no less significant than the fruitful
symbiotic relationship between convention and revolt of which Austrian history furnishes so many excellent examples. An anecdote which
illustrates this relationship most strikingly is recounted by Ludwig
Hevesi in his biography of Rudolf Alt, the great nineteenth-century
artist who did more, perhaps, than any other Austrian painter to im-
mortalize Vienna's architectural masterpieces and inimitable character-
types. It relates to the early days of Vienna's Secession, that militant
organization of ambitious young artists, as revolutionary as its name
implies.

When the Viennese Secession was founded in 1897, Rudolf Alt headed it
as honorary president. . . . Gloriously the aged man led a youthful band
which swore by principles of which he was perhaps unaware in theory but
which he had always followed in practise: the prime importance of the "artistic
moment," respect for nature, avoidance of academic clichés, loyalty to one's
self; artistic art and personal art, not commercial art for the public and the art-
dealers. It was a beautiful and touching scene, when, on a sunny afternoon—
April 27, 1898, the cornerstone of Olbrich's Secession Gallery was laid on a
site next to the Naschmarkt. . . . In the midst of the clutter of building materials sat Rudolf Alt, in a simple armchair which was decorated with a laurel-
wreath. When the cornerstone had been laid and our patriarch had dedicated
the building with the first strokes of the hammer, the laurel-wreath was plucked
to pieces; everyone present took a few leaves from this honored laurel in
memory of the first hour of a new age.[12]

Is there not something peculiarly symbolic in this dedication of the
"first hour of a new age" by the honored patriarch of an age gone by?

[12] Ludwig Hevesi, *Rudolf Alt,* pp. 148–49.

And is not something of the same symbolism intended by Paul Stefan when he begins his moving chronicle of the death of the old and the birth of the new in the Vienna of 1903–11 with the death of Rudolf Alt? [13] The feeling which this symbolism expresses is the natural consequence of the continuity of traditions in Vienna; and it is self-evident that this continuity exists not only in musical traditions but also in the traditions of all other forms of culture. Many further examples in proof of the same premise might be offered, but they would serve only to emphasize further what has already been said.

Under these conditions, the incorporation of elements of convention and revolt in the same faction, or even in the same individual, is quite understandable, and it is hardly surprising that convention and revolt could live together on very amicable terms in Vienna. In Schoenberg, for example, elements of both exist side by side, and their workings are quite consistent with one another. Thus, while his technique of "composition with twelve tones" [14] is revolutionary, his concepts of solid harmonic and contrapuntal technique, as inculcated in his teaching, are conventional, in the sense that they depend on vital traditions of the past. But this kind of conventionality has nothing to do with outworn academic formulae. Nothing could be less academic than Schoenberg's heartfelt admiration for Bach and Mozart. There is profound truth beneath the paradox in his statement, "I am a conservative who was forced to become a radical."

But convention and revolt do not always exist so amicably side by side, whether in the same person or in the same generation. Conservatism is often sterile academicism, and in that case it is urgently necessary that it be combatted by forces of revolt; but even conservatism of a worthy type is often placed in the position of having to defend itself against a revolutionary movement whose aims are equally worthy. Such an instance is the unfortunate Brahms-Wagner controversy, which manifested itself with particular violence in Vienna because of the presence there of Brahms on the one hand and Bruckner on the other. In this case, as in so many others, the conflict was aggravated by the zealous efforts of the partisans of both sides, a circumstance which led to much more ill-feeling than would otherwise have existed. One may recall still another controversy which, while in another sphere and of far less importance, illustrates the same kind of incompatibility between convention and revolt: the outbreaks of violence between op-

13 Alt died on March 12, 1905.
14 This expression is preferred by the composer to the much-misused term "twelve-tone scale," for reasons which will later appear.

posing factions when Mahler, the apostle of modernism in opera-production, was succeeded as director of the Vienna Court Opera by the well-bred conservative Weingartner.

Naturally, the continuous occurrence of incidents such as these led to the dissatisfaction of the more advanced Viennese intellectuals with Vienna, which they felt to exert a hampering influence upon their efforts for cultural independence. Austria was held to be insular, too much cut off from currents of world culture. The young Viennese artists and musicians of the turn of the century often looked towards Berlin as the home of intellectual modernity—an attitude expressed by Stefan in the opening chapters of *Das Grab in Wien,* and manifested by Schoenberg when he himself went to live in Berlin in 1901. Thus is engendered the "Austrian paradox," of which Ernst Křenek writes as follows:

The feeling of the approaching decay was growing throughout the later 19th century, when the inability of coping with the increasing political difficulties on the part of the representatives of the imperial idea became more and more evident. A most peculiar attitude of hedonistic pessimism, joyful skepticism touching on morbid sophistication, became the dominant trait in Vienna's intellectual climate.[15]

A most concise expression of the curious attitude of Viennese intellectuals towards Vienna is to be found in a letter of Schoenberg to Mahler. Sending his best wishes for Mahler's fiftieth birthday, Schoenberg expresses the hope "for all of us," that Mahler will soon live again—this time for good—in "our hated and loved Vienna"[16]—a phrase which expresses not only the paradox in Schoenberg's character, but also the paradox which was pre-war Austria.

And now that we must retrace our steps to the Austria of the first half of the nineteenth century—to the beginnings of the career of Bruckner—and proceed only by slow stages to the present day, it will help us to orient ourselves in the complex pages of cultural and political history we are about to traverse if we keep in mind the key phrases and the key concepts to the exposition of which this introduction has been devoted.

15 Walter and Křenek, *op. cit.,* pp. 198–99.
16 Mahler, *op. cit.,* p. 469.

BOOK ONE

ANTON BRUCKNER
CONSERVATISM AND CATHOLICISM

CHAPTER I

The Problem of Bruckner

IT IS A curious fact that, though more individual study has been devoted to the life and work of Bruckner than to that of Mahler, Schoenberg, and their followers, and though he has even attained to the status of a popular figure in Germany—a position which he still occupies because of his Wagnerian tendencies and his "Nordic" race—he still remains at least as enigmatic a figure as his successors. In fact, his appearance in the nineteenth century is in some ways a far more puzzling phenomenon than the appearance of a figure like Schoenberg in the twentieth. Schoenberg, with all his respect for the craftsman-ship of his predecessors, is in step with the age in which he lives, if indeed he does not outstrip it. Bruckner, on the other hand, for all his devotion to the Wagnerian ideals which were considered dangerously new in their day, is fundamentally oriented towards the past rather than towards the future. This is true, indeed, to a degree surprising in a man who lived almost to the threshold of the twentieth century.[1] In discussing the analogies between Vienna's musical culture in the baroque era and in the nineteenth and twentieth centuries, we re-ferred to Bruckner as a typical baroque figure, however anomalous that may seem in the nineteenth century. Some of the factors contrib-uting to the nature of his development have already been hinted at; these, and others, will be taken into account in the following chapters.

For such reasons as these, were it not for the fact that the ancestry of the neo-Viennese school can be traced from Bruckner through Mah-ler, one would be inclined to place him at the end of the preceding epoch rather than at the beginning of a new one. In almost every way he seems to differ from his successors. Unlike them, he was completely insulated from philosophical and literary influences because of the

[1] The same remark has often been made about Mahler, and criticisms levelled at his style often take this form. But it will become obvious that Mahler's orientation, though conservative in some respects, was far more directed towards the future than Bruckner's.

provincial environment in which he spent so many years—and also, no doubt, because the natural turn of his mind was in no way literary. His letters, with their naïve outpourings of grandiose epithets, usually totally unsuited to the rank and station of the person to whom they are applied, form a strange contrast with the Jean-Paul-like effusions of the eighteen-year-old Mahler and with the calculated paradoxes of Schoenberg's literary style. He is unlike Mahler and Schoenberg, too, in the excessive slowness of his musical development, for which, seemingly, psychological as well as historical causes must be adduced. Besides all this, problems of textual revision which are hardly to be encountered in the later composers have hampered seriously the work of propagandists for Bruckner.

Before the relationship of Bruckner to his successors can be properly appraised, the reasons for these problematic differences must be explained. While the facts of Bruckner's life have been thoroughly investigated by many writers and his works repeatedly analyzed, it is but rarely that an effort has been made to evaluate accurately his contributions to the future of music in Vienna and to separate them from those elements in his work which were only tributes to the past or which were for any other reason incapable of further fruition. It is this task which the following discussion proposes mainly to perform, and the available biographical and analytical conclusions will be used chiefly as a means to this end. Hence the chief emphasis, both in the presentation of biographical material and in the analyses of the works, will be on Bruckner's accomplishments in Vienna. However, before turning to this period of his life we must set the stage for it; that is, we must review the historical and cultural events taking place in Austria, and more particularly in Vienna, during the preceding decades, while glancing backward at Bruckner's own development during this period and correlating it with the contemporary historical and cultural conditions. To set the stage in this manner for Bruckner's appearance in Vienna will be the aim of the following chapter.

CHAPTER II

Backgrounds for Bruckner

IN THE FIRST CHAPTER ("Years of Youth") of his *Bruckner: Eine Lebensgeschichte,* Ernst Decsey writes:

> From the point of view of time, Anton Bruckner originates in the sphere of influence of the Emperor Francis. It is the epoch of the *Vormärz,* medievalism grown old and grey, fearfully shut off from Europe, held motionless in intellectual stagnation. The word "freedom" smacks of high treason; life is closely regulated, authority weighs heavily on all forms of existence. Children address their parents formally, with "Sie"; but members of the commonalty, whether teachers, organists or gardeners, are addressed by their spiritual ruler with the condescending "Du." The *Handküssen* is the accepted form of intercourse between those of low and high degree; and the humanity of Austria is divided into "sheep and goats," into aristocrats and non-aristocrats. . . . And
> . . . Emperor Francis ruled over the whole state (held in an artificial trance by Metternich) like a kind of Viennese landlord, looking out of his palace windows in dressing-gown and nightcap, regarding his peoples as tenants; sometimes mean and petty, and then again rich in favors—that is, so long as the masses do not start to make trouble, but behave themselves and leave him in peace.[1]

This description of pre-revolutionary Austria forms a suitable starting-point for our discussion of the background of Bruckner, particularly as Decsey himself goes on to remark how important all this is for the spiritual attitudes of the mature Bruckner. However, the picture requires some expansion in detail. It is true that Bruckner was not the man to be profoundly shaken by political or literary occurrences. The occasional abnormal interest which he took in this or that historical event—as witness his concern with the Austrian polar expedition and with the fate of Maximilian in Mexico, described by many of his biographers, but by none with a deeper impress of personal experience than by Friedrich Eckstein, Bruckner's one-time pupil, in his *Erinnerungen an Anton Bruckner*—seems to have been akin to the fixations which sometimes tormented him, during which he imagined

---

[1] Ernst Decsey, *Bruckner: Eine Lebensgeschichte,* p. 14.

a compulsion to count the stars in the sky, the windows of a tall building, or the ornaments on a dress. That is to say, he experienced such
interests with a curious intensity and in speaking of matters connected
with them often gave way to excessive mental excitement. Such psychological phenomena have nothing to do with a lasting interest in
historico-cultural events such as might have had a measurable influence upon Bruckner's music. But even some of the elements which
most puzzle us in his personality and his work—and especially the anachronistic elements, paradoxical as that may seem—can be partially accounted for by the times in which he lived. In itself, pre-revolutionary
Austria was an anachronism. In fact, anachronistic elements prevailed
in Austria till the very expiration of the Dual Monarchy. Is it surprising that an artist who was the product of his environment to the extent that Bruckner was should have been, to our way of thinking, an
anachronism in the nineteenth century?

Bruckner's youth was spent in the humblest of circumstances. Like
Mahler, he was born in a small village; like Mahler, too, he was the
eldest of a large family, for he had ten brothers and sisters, most of
whom died early in life. There was music in the child's environment,
but it was mostly of a rather elementary nature, consisting mainly of
the conventionalized school-training of his father, who, though doubtless competent enough, was not very advanced in musical theory. A
little later, the boy showed enough promise to commence studies with
his cousin, Johann Baptist Weiss, a church-composer; but it was not
until his thirteenth year, when his father died and he moved to St.
Florian, that he began to come in contact with a somewhat wider field
of music. During all this time, he had not displayed signs of precocity
or genius; nor had he seemingly any other ambition than to become
a schoolmaster as his father and grandfather had been—for that, too,
was a part of Austrian tradition.

As we have already observed, the keynote of Austrian history during
the period we are about to examine is repression. This in spite of the
revolutionary movement of 1848, for that uprising suffered from the
lack of training of its leaders, members of the peasant and bourgeois
groups whose initiative had been so long suppressed by the rigid
Hapsburg absolutism that, when the reins of power were placed in
their hands by the accident of revolution, they were not properly prepared for the task of taking over the reform of the state. Besides, the
nationalistic aspirations of revolutionary groups of differing racial
backgrounds were so disparate as to make a unifying work of reform
difficult, if not impossible. Each nationality was preoccupied only with

its own problems. Hence it could come about that ". . . from the first moment of the constitutional concessions the old absolutist militarism and police system lay in wait in order to annihilate the new liberties of the peoples and to restore the old autocracy." [2] To what kind of system this meant a return may be judged from a description of the imperial reign immediately preceding the Revolution, that of Ferdinand I (1835–48). Jászi does not exaggerate in his statement that "Austria lived medieval days in a time when the third French Revolution was rapidly approaching," [3] a statement in which we may note again the stress laid on the *anachronism* of Austria. During the reign of this feeble-minded emperor, the Jesuit spirit penetrated every form of cultural life, and the alliance of clericalism and absolutism attained to overwhelming strength. The influence of the Roman Catholic Church in these times can be likened only to its hegemony in the heyday of the Spanish Hapsburgs. Its power remained, in fact, well-nigh unabated until the end of the Dual Monarchy, supported not only by the aristocracy but also by a vast Catholic front of sincere peasant and middle-class believers, from which the clergy drew much of its strength.

That it is possible to write in a similar vein of events in 1914 and 1848 shows how little fundamental difference the revolution made in the dynastic attitude and hence in the military and clerical absolutism. It is fateful that the young Francis Joseph should have first occupied the throne in the midst of the revolutionary turmoil of 1848, because these first terrifying experiences of the vacillations which imperial power could undergo did much towards conditioning him to the hereditary, inbred conservatism of his dynasty. It is small wonder that his reign of seven decades was not distinguished by anything resembling a progressive, forward-looking policy, or even by a real plan for the future. Thus the old Metternich system, supposedly smashed in 1848 with the downfall of its founder, simply reappeared in new dress as the "System Bach" (1849–60). This systematization of absolutism founded by the supposedly "liberal" Minister of the Interior, Alexander Bach, was marked by such refinements as a police system so all-embracing that it could bring its own leader under supervision and censure his actions. The *Concordat* of 1855 in effect handed over the whole educational system, the whole spiritual production, and the whole matrimonial jurisdiction to the representatives of Rome. [4] The importance of the continuous renewal of clericalism for the life not only of Bruckner but also of Mahler and Schoenberg can scarcely be

[2] Oscar Jászi, *The Dissolution of the Habsburg Monarchy*, p. 87.
[3] *Ibid.*, p. 85.   [4] *Ibid.*, p. 101.

over-emphasized; hence the stress laid upon it in this introductory historical sketch.

Innumerable instances of the effect of the repressive dynastic policy upon literary and artistic manifestations might be cited. It goes without saying that any intellectual movement even mildly revolutionary was frowned upon, but it could also come about that a person of indubitable patriotism would find himself in ill repute with the government as the result of even the most innocent action. Let us consider, for example, a few typical cases from the career of Grillparzer, whose long life (1791–1872) encompasses the decades under discussion. Characteristic was the fate of his Austrian historical drama *König Ottokars Glück und Ende*. It was first performed at the Vienna *Burgtheater* on the 19th of December, 1825—but it is only by the merest chance that it ever reached the stage at all, for the manuscript narrowly escaped being lost forever to posterity. When the work was completed, Grillparzer, in accordance with regulations, submitted it to the public censor. Two years elapsed, during which he heard nothing concerning its fate. The unfortunate author inquired at office after office, was shunted from pillar to post, and finally located his play through the intercession of the Empress (brought about by an almost coincidental chain of circumstances). It was not until some years after the performance of *Ottokar* that an incident occurred which, for Grillparzer, threw some light on the reasons for the long disappearance of his play, and, for us, throws some light on what the censorship meant in nineteenth-century Austria. Grillparzer, asked by an official of the censorship bureau whom he had casually encountered why he wrote so little,

. . . answered, that he, as an official censor, ought to be in a sufficiently good position to know the reason. "Yes," was his reply, "that is the way with you literary men. You always imagine the censor engaged in a conspiracy against you. When your 'Ottokar' was held up for two years you probably believed that a bitter enemy of yours prevented its performance. Do you know who kept it back? I myself, and the Lord knows I am no enemy of yours." "But, my dear court councillor," I answered, "what was there in the play that seemed so dangerous to you?" "Nothing at all," said he, "but I thought: After all, one can't be sure"—and this the man said in a tone of utmost friendliness, showing that the official in charge of literary matters had not the faintest conception of literary property rights. It never entered his mind that the work of a poet might have as good a claim to appreciation and compensation as that of an official or an artisan.[5]

Unfortunately, this was not the only experience of the sort in Grillparzer's career. Some years later he became, quite unintentionally, the

[5] Quoted in Gustav Pollak, *Grillparzer and the Austrian Drama*, pp. 118–19.

center of a real anti-dynastic literary revolution. During a serious ill-ness of the crown prince, Grillparzer expressed his sentiments con-cerning this young man (afterwards the Emperor Ferdinand) in a short lyrical poem. In so doing he had no intention of criticizing the prince, for, as he himself says in discussing the affair, "My devotion to Austria was part of my very being. . . . My love of country I trans-ferred only too easily to the reigning family, as its representative. Little reason as I had hitherto had to be grateful to any member of that family, I was exceedingly slow in condemning one of them." [6] However, when we bear in mind what has already been said of the mental capacities of Ferdinand, it is not surprising that he was not particularly pleased with the following verses:

> *Mayhap about thy prince's crown bright gleaming*
> *We'll once behold the gifts of brilliant mind;*
> *We look not to a future distant-seeming,*
> *Since now we know at least that thou art kind.*[7]

Through the tactless action of the literary censor, this poem, which Grillparzer had never intended to be published, was submitted to the higher authorities. Permission for its printing was, of course, refused, but at the same time it was distributed in innumerable written copies, and achieved such a wide circulation as to inspire scurrilous replies which were also distributed in written copies. Under such circum-stances as these, it is small wonder that, however innocent Grillparzer may have been in the matter, Ferdinand bore him a grudge for a long time as a result of this affair. What the effects of such a grudge might be on the poet's career is easily imagined. But imagination is not nec-essary here, for his own words, "Despotism has ruined my life, at least my literary life," [8] are sufficiently eloquent. They take on an added pathos when we recall that, in spite of his hatred of despotism, he refrained from taking active part in the Revolution of 1848 because he feared lest it might destroy his beloved fatherland.

One would expect to find a similarly undemocratic situation pre-vailing in the musical world, and indeed such was the case. It is true that the year 1848 brought manifestations of a would-be democratic spirit in Austrian musical life as well as in other cultural spheres. These sometimes took rather curious forms, as, for example, the vig-orous opposition of the opera-going public of Vienna to the opening

---

[6] *Ibid.*, p. 250.

[7] *Ibid.*, p. 252.

[8] Franz Grillparzer, *Recollections of the Revolution of 1848*, quoted in Pollak, *ibid.*, p. 327.

of an Italian opera season in April, 1848. Signor Balocchino, who managed the Italian *Stagione* of the *Kärntnerthor-Theater,* had planned to open this season with a production of Verdi's *Ernani.* But scarcely had the posters announcing this event been put up when they were all defaced or torn down, and Signor Balocchino himself received so many threatening letters that the Italian season had to be abandoned and the troupe of singers rapidly dispersed in all directions. How ironical that the composer whose name was to stand as a symbol of Italian liberation should be the victim of an anti-aristocratic mob demonstration! Yet there were logical reasons for this apparent paradox. The opening of the Italian season, which generally occurred on Easter Monday, had always been a gala event for Vienna's most elegant society. In the lives of these people, the opera was an aristocratic divertissement, of no greater cultural significance than the Easter Monday promenade in the Prater. What was more natural than that democratic feeling should rebel against an institution which had been so outspokenly aristocratic in its spiritual tendencies! Add to this the resurgence of strong German (and hence anti-Italian) feeling occasioned by the revolution, and the paradox is explained. It is all of a piece with the changing of the titles of actresses and singers, as printed on theater programs, from "Madame" and "Demoiselle" to "Frau" and "Fräulein."

But what was the result of all this praiseworthy democratic agitation? Perhaps more than he meant to say can be read into Hanslick's comforting sentence, "After the storm of the revolutionary year had abated and peace had returned not only to the streets of Vienna but also to men's minds, the ardent desire for relief and reconstruction through art, and the need for music and theater, began once more to be felt." [9] In other words, things returned bit by bit to a more normal and less democratic state. The *Theater nächst dem Kärntnerthor* became the *Hofoper;* its repertory, while quite extensive and varied, was not progressively oriented on the whole—for example, it did not produce *Tannhäuser* in 1857 because the strict censorship, revivified by the reactionary state of affairs in the fifties, forbade any such performance to take place. Even in the revolutionary period music had, as often happens, failed to keep pace with politics. Hundreds and thousands of patriotic songs had been written and it had been hoped that a "German Marseillaise" might be discovered among them—but who remembered any of them two years later? As Hanslick says, "Thousands of such works were produced . . . during that national

[9] Eduard Hanslick, "Musik," *Wien 1848–1888,* v. 2, p. 309.

awakening—not one note of them has become part of our folk heritage." [10]

Conservative elements had the upper hand in the concert-hall, too, though it cannot be denied that the programs of the post-revolutionary period in Vienna, at least as soon as the situation there became sufficiently settled so that musical matters could be properly handled, represented an improvement over what had gone before. In the Vienna of pre-revolutionary days, the inveterate concert-goer might hear, if he were so inclined, 120 to 130 concerts during the course of a season. Most of these were, however, virtuoso concerts, like those that Liszt and Thalberg had introduced in Paris; operatic potpourris were the rule, for the performance of a piano sonata was still a rarity in public. If the concert-goer tired of hour-long virtuosity and what Hanslick calls "Flitterkram" (the endless round of bravura variations, Italian arias, and so forth), he might attend an orchestra concert— one of the *Gesellschaftsconcerte,* perhaps, or one of the *Spirituelconcerte.* Here, however, he would find little to please him, if he were a serious-minded musician interested in new developments in German music. These concerts were directed and organized by dilettantes, and gave little or no attention to the more progressive trends of the times. According to Hanslick, the names of Schumann, Gade, Hiller, Loewe, Franz, and Wagner were hardly known by Vienna; and while we may smile at seeing Gade named in the same breath with Wagner in such a matter-of-fact way, we must recognize the truth of the basic premise that modernity was not a welcome guest in Vienna—any more than, in different guise, it was to be in later years.

While duly noting, with Hanslick, that the situation improved later, thanks to the vigorous efforts of Josef Hellmesberger and, subsequently, of Johann Herbeck as director of the orchestra of the *Gesellschaft der Musikfreunde,* to the activity of Karl Eckert, Otto Dessoff and Hans Richter as successive directors of the Vienna Philharmonic, and to the fine chamber-music concerts given by the Hellmesberger Quartet and other organizations of comparable quality, we must admit that many of the conservative tendencies in Viennese musical life still remained. This fact must be constantly kept in mind, for, as has been emphasized (and often over-emphasized) by the eulogists of Bruckner, Mahler, and Schoenberg, it was because of these very tendencies that the composers whom we consider the most typical representatives of modern Viennese music often won their reputation in practically every other musical center before being recognized in Vienna, where

[10] *Ibid.,* p. 305.

they all resided. Even though some writers have emotionally over-stressed this conflict, it is impossible to go very far in the cultural history of nineteenth- and twentieth-century Vienna without encountering it at every turn. A concrete example of the extremely conservative orientation of the post-revolutionary concert-going public is provided by Hanslick when he says,

> In the beginning, the introduction of new, modern elements was a slow and difficult process. The majority of the public was definitely unfavorable to these elements and would only recognize the validity of Haydn, Mozart, and Beethoven. So it came about that the managers of the *Gesellschaftsconcerte* were hesitant about Schumann for a very long time; until late in 1854 the *Gesellschaft der Musikfreunde* had not performed a single work of this great master, who had been revered for nearly twenty years in Germany! [11]

For Hanslick it was self-evident that Schumann was now (1888) a popular favorite, and he could refer to the exceptional conservatism of those concert-goers of 1854 who were distinctly cool towards Schumann's C major symphony. But how consistent was this feeling with the position which he maintained in his own times—with his attitude towards Brahms on the one hand, and towards Wagner and Bruckner on the other? The attitude of an earlier Viennese public towards Schumann was typical of conservative elements in Viennese musical feeling; but Hanslick's attitude towards Bruckner, whether expressed directly or indirectly, is equally typical. In his article on music in Vienna from which we have quoted throughout this section—written, be it remembered, after Bruckner had lived twenty years in Vienna—he mentions Bruckner twice. Once Bruckner is referred to as an outstanding virtuoso of the organ, which is certainly true enough, but seems rather beside the point when we consider what Bruckner had accomplished as a composer by this time.[12] He is again mentioned, in the postscript to the main body of the article, as one of the "competent composers and notable talents" which "our musically epigonous age" has brought forth in Austria. The list is indeed an enlightening one. The name of Bruckner appears, without any attempt to single it out, among the following names: Carl Goldmark, Ignaz Brüll, Robert Fuchs, Hugo Reinhold, Anton Rückauf, Richard Heuberger, Julius Zellner, Richard v. Perger, Carl Nawratil, Kremser, Grädener, Stocker, and Bachrich. Do more than two or three of these names mean anything to the non-Austrian reader? [13]

The account of Bruckner's personal conflicts must be reserved for

---

[11] *Ibid.*, p. 327.   [12] *Ibid.*, p. 330.
[13] *Ibid.*, p. 342.

a later place, but we have now touched upon the Wagner-Brahms controversy; and, though its genesis and nature have been described many times before, it is necessary to describe them again here. In picturing the Austria of the *Vormärz* we have set the stage for Bruckner's formative years; in describing the musical life of post-revolutionary Vienna we have attempted to set the stage for his arrival there in 1868. (Hence the title "Backgrounds for Bruckner." The depiction of a single background would not be sufficient; and if the Viennese background has been stressed more than the others, it is simply because this is the history of a development whose nerve-center was in Vienna itself, not merely the history of the careers of individual composers.) As the Wagner-Brahms conflict is one of the most important elements in the latter stage-setting, or, to put it more accurately, is the chief component of the dramatic situation into which Bruckner entered when he stepped upon the Viennese scene, we must introduce a brief exposition of it at this point, even if we cannot say anything new about it.

The hostility of Hanslick, dean of Viennese music critics and high priest of Brahmsian conservatism, to Wagner's musical ideology had not always been in evidence. As a matter of fact, Hanslick had, in his youth, been a great admirer of Wagner's early works, and had expressed this admiration to Wagner. But with the passage of time his attitude had changed, and at the time of Wagner's visits to Vienna in 1861 and 1862 Hanslick's feelings towards the composer and the man were distinctly cool. It must be admitted that Wagner had done little to conciliate the critic, whom he usually treated like a perfect stranger, or, at best, a superficial acquaintance, when he met him at social functions. Friends of Wagner, such as Dr. Joseph Standhartner, the *Burgtheater* director Heinrich Laube, and the singer Louise Dustmann who had won such a success as Elsa in the Vienna Opera's *Lohengrin* performance of May, 1861 (the first that Wagner ever heard), made well-meant attempts to reconcile the two men, but these always resulted in failure. There was, for example, the dinner-party given by Laube in the autumn of 1861 [14] at which Newman says Wagner completely ignored Hanslick. That this statement is slightly exaggerated is shown by Hanslick's own account of the affair, in which

[14] According to Newman, *The Life of Richard Wagner*, III, 198. Hanslick, in the second volume of *Aus meinem Leben* (pp. 3 ff.), places the event in 1862, in which year he says Wagner came to Vienna for the *Lohengrin* performance. Apparently Hanslick confuses the two occasions, 1861 and 1862, when Wagner came to Vienna for the purpose of studying *Tristan* (later abandoned) with the singers of the Vienna Opera, among them Louise Dustmann and Aloys Ander.

he describes a conversation with Wagner during which the famous parody of *Tannhäuser* (given with Nestroy and other well-known actors in the *Carltheater* at the time of the Viennese première) was discussed. However, he goes on to say that, although Wagner was much interested in what Hanslick had to say about the *Tannhäuser* parody, his demeanor in general was rather unfriendly. Afterwards, Laube explained to Hanslick that this was because Wagner had heard (he did not read musical criticism himself) that Hanslick's attitude towards *Lohengrin* was much less favorable than it had been towards *Tannhäuser*. Quite so, says Hanslick, and, now writing as of 1894, elucidates his reasons for preferring *Tannhäuser*. He finds that pieces such as Tannhäuser's first dialogue with Venus and the relation of Tannhäuser's pilgrimage possess a dramatic power quite missing in *Lohengrin*, which he dismisses rather contemptuously as "the favorite opera of all emotional ladies." [15]

Then there was that unhappy affair at Dr. Standhartner's in November, 1862, when Wagner read the *Meistersinger* libretto before a gathering of invited guests of whom Hanslick was one. In spite of Wagner's affectation of surprise that Hanslick should find anything offensive about this occasion, we can easily imagine the critic's feelings; for—whether Wagner used the name during this particular reading or not, and he may well have done so—were there not dozens of people in Vienna who knew that the character now called Beckmesser was, in the first version of the play, called Hanslich? It is true that the first sketches of the Beckmesser character were made before Wagner had any desire to lampoon Hanslick; but it is equally true that some little touches which could refer only to Hanslick were added later.[16] It is noteworthy that Hanslick makes no reference to any unpleasant aspects of this affair in his memoirs. He praises Standhartner as an amiable and tolerant man, refers to his generally favorable impression of the play and its subject-matter, and quotes from the review of the reading which he wrote at the time for the *Neue Freie Presse*. He said in 1862 that Wagner had better be a Meistersinger to the German nation than a Nibelung, and finds that the attitude of the public in 1894 merely corroborates his view. It is known that he also preferred the *Meistersinger* music to that of other mature works of Wagner.

No favorable impression of the moment, however, could really bring Hanslick and Wagner closer together. When Newman says that Ander,

15 Hanslick, *Aus meinem Leben*, II, 92.
16 Ernest Newman, *The Life of Richard Wagner*, III, 199.

the tenor who was supposed to take the lead in the Viennese première of *Tristan*, "kept supplying the journalists unfriendly to Wagner with inside information calculated to damage the prospects of the work," [17] we are not surprised to read, in Hanslick's memoirs, of Ander's running to him to say, "Oh, *Tristan* will go over fine; we know the second act almost by heart now, but we've forgotten the first one again!" [18] Of course, Hanslick's attitude towards Wagner was well known and he was the logical person to whom to make such remarks. It seems very strange for him to say, immediately after recounting the above story about Ander, that the cancellation of the *Tristan* première in Vienna (*Tristan* was not performed there until after Wagner's death) was not due to intrigues against Wagner!

And what of the place of Brahms in all this? What was his personal attitude towards Wagner and the Wagner question, and how did anti-Wagnerites feel towards him?

Perhaps a hint at answers to all of these questions may be found in Hanslick's remarks on Brahms which follow directly upon his previously quoted discussion of Wagner in the section "Richard Wagner und Joh. Brahms 1862" of *Aus meinem Leben*. The juxtaposition of Brahms and Wagner as opposites is self-explanatory here, and reading Hanslick's views about the two men in direct sequence is extremely helpful in gaining a perspective view of the situation as it was in these years before Bruckner came to Vienna. Here, then, is part of what Hanslick has to say about Brahms (still living at the time he wrote these lines) in his memoirs.

When we heard his B flat major sextet (in 1862) in the evening after Wagner had conducted various fragments of the *Ring* and *Tristan* in the afternoon, we felt that we had been transported into a pure world of beauty—it sounded like a revelation. Just as their music was completely different, so was the personal appearance of the two men. Brahms would approach the piano or podium with a kind of awkward diffidence; he would respond with the greatest reluctance to the stormy applause and could not disappear fast enough afterwards, while Wagner would use every excuse for one of his famous addresses to the public. Brahms spoke but little, and never about himself. . . . Tirelessly he aided gifted young composers in their difficult beginnings, with word and deed. Often I heard him defend Wagner vigorously, when narrow-mindedness or stupid, crude conceit delighted itself with contemptuous expressions of scorn for the latter. He knew and appreciated fully the brilliant aspects of Wagner, while Wagner speaks with but little respect of Brahms, whose significance, according to him, consists of "not wanting to make any effect." Nevertheless, it is incorrect to speak of Brahms as an *"admirer* of Wagner" as was recently done in a jubilee article. How could that be possible!

[17] *Ibid.*, III, 202.   [18] Hanslick, *op. cit.*, II, 95.

When could he, of all people, feel a need for Wagner's music! Brahms, who allows nothing important to escape his scrutiny, knows the Wagner scores quite thoroughly; however, he has probably not heard the operas in the theater more than once. He could never be persuaded to attend the Bayreuth festivals. There was only a short and superficial personal association between Brahms and Wagner, which was chiefly connected with the circumstance that Wagner, through Frau Cosima, had asked for the return of several Wagner autographs belonging to Brahms.[19]

Hanslick mentions this "short and superficial personal association between Brahms and Wagner" in a very casual manner; yet the incident deserves further attention, as it sheds some light not only on Brahms' attitude towards Wagner but also on the character of both men. Tausig, the celebrated piano virtuoso, who had obtained Wagner's original manuscript of the Venusberg scene of *Tannhäuser* (Paris version), possibly at the time when Wagner gave it to Cornelius to copy during his stay in Vienna, had for some reason turned it over to Brahms. For a long time Wagner did not even know where it was, but when he found out, in 1865, he tried to persuade Brahms to return it to him, on the ground that Tausig had not had the right to make a present of it to anyone. This Brahms refused to do, as he felt that Wagner did not really need the score, and that he himself had a perfect right to it. Cornelius and Cosima Wagner bombarded him with letters on the subject, none of which he ever answered. Finally Wagner was able to recover his score, but only by sending Brahms a copy of the de luxe edition of *Rheingold,* in return for which Brahms was to let him have his manuscript back. This was ten years after Wagner's original request for the manuscript![20] Of course this incident would not necessarily furnish proof of a personal animus against Wagner, for in all his dealings with other people Brahms liked to display a studied rudeness which, some say, only served to hide an uncommonly sensitive soul. But then there was the affair of the *Putzmacherin* letters. These were a group of letters written by Wagner to his *Putzmacherin* (milliner) Bertha Goldwag, in Vienna, during the years 1864–65. It was from her he ordered the silken dressing-gowns, white tulle, blond lace, flowered moiré, artificial roses, grey ruching, pink satin, and so many other things which he felt he needed in order to create the proper atmosphere for his work. Naturally, letters such as these would be a gold-mine for scandalmongers, and, in fact, they were printed in the *Neue Freie Presse* during Wagner's lifetime (1877) by one Daniel Spitzer, a journalist who was a colleague of Hanslick,

[19] *Ibid.,* II, 14–16.   [20] Newman, *op. cit.,* III, 471.

and who seems to have felt much as he did about Wagner. At the time it was not generally known how Spitzer had happened to get hold of these letters, but later, thanks to a brochure of Ludwig Karpath [21] and to an article of Brahms' friend Hugo Wittmann,[22] the truth of the whole matter came out. It seems that Bertha Goldwag's husband, Louis Maretschek, had stolen these letters, and had then presumably sold them to the autograph-dealer Kafka. Kafka immediately showed the letters to Brahms, who was highly delighted with them, read them to his friends, and told Kafka that he must get Spitzer to buy them. They were actually bought by the editor of the *Neue Freie Presse,* Michael Etienne, but were then turned over to Spitzer to do with as he saw fit. What he did, we have already seen. The subsequent history of the letters is not of special importance here—except that it is interesting to note that, after many vicissitudes, they are now in the Library of Congress—but the story up to this point must make us realize even more vividly the tremendous tension that was developing between the opposing forces in musical Vienna.[23]

In a conversation with Richard Specht, Brahms is supposed to have said, "I once told Wagner that I'm the best Wagnerian alive. Do you think that I'm so narrow-minded that I, too, can't be charmed by the gayety and greatness of *Die Meistersinger?* Or so dishonorable as to keep it a secret that I think a few measures of this work are worth more than all the operas written since? And they want to make an anti-pope out of me? It's too stupid for words!" Nor does he "keep it a secret" that as of 1897 he understands Wagner's work better than any other musician, "at least better than any of those so-called disciples of his who would just love to poison me." [24] One would like to know when and where he told Wagner that he was the best Wagnerian, and what Wagner thought of the statement. Was it before or after Bruckner came into the picture? In any case, it is interesting to note how Brahms and Hanslick agree in praising *Die Meistersinger.* This is one of the instances which tend to prove that perhaps the failure of Hanslick to understand Brahms, which is so often deplored by Wagnerians, was not so great as they like to imply.[25] Certainly, too, some of these Wagnerians, then and now, did not realize that men of the artistic worth of Brahms and Wagner could not waste much time

21 Ludwig Karpath, *Zu den Briefen Richard Wagners an eine Putzmacherin,* Berlin, n.d. (1907?).

22 *Neue Freie Presse,* May 10, 1908.

23 Newman, *op. cit.,* III, 567–69.

24 Max Kalbeck, *Johannes Brahms,* III, 2, 409.

25 For an example of this see Max Graf, *Wagnerprobleme,* p. 20.

playing at pope and anti-pope. That sort of thing was largely left to
the hangers-on of both sides; it was thanks to their efforts that the
tension in Vienna grew to such an intolerable pitch. And, though
many of the opposing elements were later reconciled, in a way the
controversy never died. But we must reserve the discussion of its further manifestations for a later time. It is now necessary for us to take
a closer look at the forty-four-year-old Anton Bruckner who entered
this arena of strife in 1868, and to find out what he brought with
him as defense against the hostile air of Vienna.

CHAPTER III

Bruckner Comes to Vienna

IT IS indeed unfortunate that among the letters of Bruckner which have been preserved we possess no document which tells us of his first impressions of Vienna, of his first reactions on going to the place where he was to spend the remaining twenty-eight years of his life. Of course, Vienna was not new to him in 1868, but in the letters we seek in vain for any description of the impressions made upon him by the great musical city during those earlier visits which he made for the purpose of studying with Sechter, or of submitting himself to one of those "qualifying examinations" before a jury of experts which he was always so fond of arranging.

This seeming lack of reaction on Bruckner's part is but a symptom of a curious inarticulateness in intellectual and spiritual matters, an inarticulateness which will stand in our way again and again when we try to analyze Bruckner's personality or to draw conclusions about his work from his own comments. It is this quality of mental isolation which makes the approach to Bruckner through Austrian cultural history so much more difficult than is the case with Mahler or with Schoenberg, both men whose contacts with wider cultural circles were numerous and fruitful and who were, if anything, over-articulate about their own work and about the concepts and individuals with whom their experiences brought them in touch. This is why the letters of Mahler and the memoirs which have been written about him prove to be a source not only of interesting personal material but also of valuable data for an integrated cultural history of the last decades of the nineteenth century and the first years of the twentieth in Austria, whereas the letters of Bruckner and such memoirs of him as those written by his pupils Max von Oberleithner and Friedrich Eckstein are more likely to interest the Bruckner biographer than the student of cultural history. Yet, in order to understand the way in which Mahler and his successors follow Bruckner, it is necessary to integrate

the life and work of Bruckner with the cultural picture presented by
Vienna during the years in which he was active there in so far as it is
possible to do so. The best way to do this is to determine with a reason-
able degree of accuracy the influence which Vienna, as a musical and
cultural center, had upon Bruckner. It is just at this point that testimony in his own words as to his first impressions received from
Vienna would be of value. But, given the personality of the man, this
is something that we cannot expect to have; and, even supposing that
he had left such testimony, it is highly likely that the intellectual
inarticulateness already spoken of would have resulted in posterity's
being presented with something no more valuable than his famous
description of the finale of his Eighth Symphony as "the meeting of
the three emperors." Therefore, we must try for another approach to
the problem.

It is stylistic analysis which may help us to determine the relationship between Bruckner and Viennese tradition. Here, however, great
care must be exercised. Were we to take the year of Bruckner's permanent settlement in Vienna as a starting-point for our stylistic investi-
gations, we would not arrive at satisfactory results. The Bruckner who
came to Vienna to live and teach was a mature man who had already
composed his three great masses, three symphonies (including the C
minor, now known as the First, and two earlier "trial flights" not
included in the numbered nine), and a variety of other works. That
his other eight symphonies were composed while he was residing in
Vienna is a matter of small import, for it could not possibly be claimed
that the symphonist Bruckner was influenced in any way by the proximity of the symphonist Brahms (except in so far as the vigorous
opposition of the Brahms-Hanslick circle contributed to his becoming disturbed about his own works and revising them frequently and
radically). The heading "Bruckner Comes to Vienna" is an essential
one for our study, but its importance has more to do with the influence Bruckner exerted in Vienna than with that which he received
from it during the years of his residence there.

What we must look for, then, is a possible source for genuine
Viennese influence on Bruckner. Here the name of Simon Sechter at
once springs to mind, and so it becomes necessary to point out how
true a representative of Viennese classical "tradition" Sechter was,
what his doctrines were, in what form they were transmitted to Bruckner, and how Bruckner assimilated them. A wealth of material lies
ready to hand for this study; for not only are Sechter's treatises available, but we have also the correspondence between Bruckner and

Sechter, and a great variety of documents to prove the thoroughness with which Bruckner assimilated Sechter's particular brand of musical thought. From many of the Bruckner pupils, but from Eckstein in particular, we receive a vivid picture of Bruckner's teaching method, so firmly grounded upon the Sechter theories; Eckstein even enriches his little monograph with excerpts from the harmony exercises which he did under Bruckner's direction.[1] We find it touching, and at the same time slightly disconcerting, when we read in various sources how Bruckner used occasionally, when composing, to adorn his measures with the numbers of the fundamental harmonic root-progressions as a little sign to himself that he was proudly and faithfully obeying Sechter's rules of harmony. But Sechter will only help us with a small part of our problem. We must explain the part that Wagner plays in the Bruckner style, without being disturbed by the fact that Wagner could scarcely be termed a "Viennese influence," or led astray in our stylistic judgment by the beautiful Bruckner-Wagner legend. From the point of view of our history, nothing could be more dangerous than to label Bruckner, as has often been done, a mere Wagner epigone. This terminology automatically obscures the idea of any new development made possible through Bruckner, while, on the other hand, by directing our attention to the harmonic and orchestral coloring of Bruckner's works—to such items of superficial interest, for example, as the "Wagner Tubas" in the Adagio of the Seventh Symphony—it distracts our attention from their form. And yet the matter of form is of prime importance, for, in determining the effect of Viennese musical trends upon Bruckner, not the least of our concerns must be the direction in which Bruckner oriented the symphony. If any one form may be called the birthright of Vienna it is the classical symphony; therefore, it is necessary to discover what Bruckner learned from its masters, particularly from Beethoven and from Schubert. With what attitude did he approach the Viennese classical symphony? What stimulation did he receive from its masterworks? Where did he carry the form that he found?

In answering these questions—even in posing them—we find ourselves for the first time perilously close to a tragic apparition which stalks through the declining century and into the twentieth, following Bruckner, Brahms, Mahler through their brilliant careers like a dark shadow. It is *The Decline and Fall of the Classical Symphony.*

[1] Ernst Schwanzara's detailed class-notes are also of great importance (see Bibliography).

CHAPTER IV

Concepts of Symphonic Style

WHY, one may ask, is it necessary to restate the principles of the "symphonic form" as we find them in Haydn, Mozart, and Beethoven? The nature of the "classical sonata form" has been described so many times that every music student knows it by heart!

Unfortunately, this statement is quite true. Every music student who has completed a first-year course in analysis knows that the "sonata form" consists of an "exposition," a "development," and a "recapitulation." The "exposition" must contain "two themes" (why only two?), a "main theme" in the tonic and a "subordinate," "subsidiary," or "melodic" theme in the dominant. The "development" consists of a "free fantasia-like treatment" of the thematic material and the "recapitulation" is a repetition of the "exposition" with the "melodic theme" in the tonic. So far, the conventional handbook of analysis. The average student, confronted with this kind of explanation, which leaves stylistic questions utterly out of account, unconsciously acquires the habit of measuring works in "symphonic" or "sonata" form against an artificial standard, and of rating them according to the closeness with which they conform to that standard. Thus, a Mozart sonata-movement in which some of the thematic material is omitted in the recapitulation may seem "less good" to him than one in which the recapitulation is complete. When he composes in "sonata form," he will conscientiously fill out a pattern imposed from the outside, and will compose "two themes," in the tonic and in the dominant as prescribed, with little thought as to whether the all-important element of contrast is present in the motivic material itself.[1]

---

[1] It is true, nevertheless, that the "sonata form" *can* be taught to students for compositional purposes without leading to such deplorable results. Arnold Schoenberg's approach to the problem in teaching is a shining example of the way such problems should be handled and usually are not. In explaining the rough scheme of the classical sonata form to students, he takes great pains to emphasize that this outline is merely a "school-form" which will never be found in a pure state in any true classical

For it is this element of contrast, this dynamic principle, which is the life-blood of the symphonies of the classical Viennese school; it is a symphonic "style" rather than a symphonic "form." And that is what it remained through Beethoven's time, until the theorists began to abstract from the living works of art what had been a vital principle operating from within and to convert it into an artificial pattern applied from without. The romanticists, who considered Beethoven their spiritual leader, naturally took over the symphony as their representative instrumental form, and it was in the course of their effort to adapt this large-scale form to their own lyrical world that they found themselves obliged to create rules which the true classicists had never needed. Misled by this procedure, minor composers of the nineteenth century thought they were imitating Beethoven, when they were merely feeding on a sort of bloodless extract of the classical Viennese school. Talented musicians could still imitate the classic gestures of their great forebears, but the gestures had lost their meaning, as we see plainly in the stereotyped padding of the first movement of Berlioz' *Symphonie fantastique.* This is why, in the realm of the symphony, years had to elapse after the Beethoven-Schubert era before the achievements of Brahms, Bruckner, and Mahler; for the symphonies of Schumann cannot stand on their own feet from a stylistic-formal point of view, while those of Mendelssohn are polished in form and idiom, but not significant in content, and certainly do not point the way towards any novel achievements in the symphonic field. As for the "minor" symphonists of those days, their music has disappeared from our concert programs, if only to be replaced by that of their contemporary counterparts.

Three great musical figures like Brahms, Bruckner, and Mahler, confronted with this problem, could not simply ignore it and go on creating in a vacuum. Each one had to come to grips with it in his own way, and each one, as befitted his temperament and background, chose an entirely different way. None of them composed as he would have done if the problem had not existed, that is, if the classical symphony had not gone into a decline. That, of course, is a commonplace

---

masterpiece, as it was abstracted from the music by theorists and *not* prepared by the theorists for the composer to obey blindly! He discards the conventional terms of first and second "themes" in favor of "thematic groups," which explains the real structure far more accurately.

Schoenberg is, of course, not alone among progressive musical thinkers in discarding the outworn academic concept. Roger Sessions, for example, quotes Virgil Thomson's dictum that "the sonata-form was invented by Vincent d'Indy for use in the Schola Cantorum."

statement; as well say that Beethoven, living and writing in 1900, would not have written as he did in 1800. Yet it is a necessary statement; for, in the case of each of these composers, attitudes which they assumed as a direct result of the age in which they lived have been held against them as proof of lack of originality, lack of formal sense, or even (as in the case of Bruckner) lack of intellect. As each of these men showed unmistakable intimations of musical genius, such accusations seem rather pointless; but uncritical acceptance of all their works as of equal value will not do, either. At least, however, we can advance beyond the narrow partisan viewpoint (still upheld, unfortunately, in so recent a book as the monumental nine-volume life of Bruckner by Goellerich and Auer) which sets up Bruckner, the apostle of Divine Inspiration, against Brahms, the exponent of arid formalism; or, vice versa, as Hanslick would have said, Brahms, the rightful heir of the Viennese classicists, against Bruckner, the crazy Wagnerian. Both points of view are, or should be, equally outmoded, and today we may enjoy with a clear conscience both Brahms and Bruckner.

At this point it may not be amiss to state just what solution each of the composers in question was searching for so that the intention of specific analyses which will occur later may be better understood.

Brahms, who of our three symphonists met with the most general acceptance in his lifetime, has also fared the best with posterity. Quite aside from questions of merit, there are several good reasons for this. Purely economic motives, such as the necessity of hiring many extra musicians to satisfy the requirements of their large scores and the commercial impracticability of devoting an entire program to one work, have certainly not worked in favor of Bruckner and Mahler, whereas Brahms can be performed readily without the outlay of either extra money or time. Among the public, Hans von Bülow's unfortunate remark about the "three B's" (one of those misconceptions for which the writers and readers of the program-book style of musical literature seem to have a special affinity) has done its work effectively, for the variation "Bach, Beethoven, Bruckner" does not seem to have "caught on" outside of Germany, even if Wagner did call Bruckner "my third B." It may, on the other hand, be questioned whether the public, once lured to the concert-hall by the presence of an outstanding conductor or soloist, finds Brahms any "easier to listen to" than Mahler or Bruckner; in fact, one might even expect the reverse. The question of absolute length does not enter here; it may not be susceptible to proof, but it is a matter of personal experience that a composition seems "long," i. e., too long, only if too large a proportion of it is composed of superfluous padding, or of "dead spots" where nothing happens. That is, if a form which was intended to encompass only a certain length of time—always approximately speaking, of course—is expanded, padded, swelled beyond its normal length, we feel that the resultant work is "too long," a feeling which has nothing whatever to do with its *absolute* duration in time, but only with its *relative* duration as compared with the time in which the form could have been adequately encompassed and the musical material sufficiently developed without excessive padding. On the other hand, if the musical materials exclusive of padding are so extensive as to *require* a broader formal layout, i. e., a longer duration of time, for their logical development, we will not feel excessive length, whatever the absolute duration—within physical limits of endurance, of course.[2]

These may seem like superficial reasons for the enduring popularity of a composer, but they must nevertheless be taken into account, for it is often possible that even such trivial causes may determine which work shall survive and which shall not. We shall now touch upon a reason which brings us closer to the heart of Brahms' conception of the symphonic style. The survival and influence of musical works, after all, must partly depend on their finding sympathetic and understanding interpreters, not only in their own time, but also in future generations. Now, musical interpreters, because of the training which they receive, are more than likely to be of a "traditionalist" turn of mind, and to devote their performing talents to the recreation of a more or less faithful record of the intentions of classical composers. It is at this point that the serious-minded interpreter finds himself strongly drawn to Brahms. For it was Brahms' ambition to preserve a jealously guarded classical tradition within himself, and to perpetuate it carefully in his works. It is this conscious and conscientious reverence for something past and done which we treasure in Brahms' symphonies; that is what they mean to us today.

Brahms did not, of course, preserve the classical edifice intact, and no one will ever take a Brahms symphony for a Beethoven symphony, whatever Bülow may have meant by calling Brahms' First "Beethoven's Tenth." What he did was to take the classical building-stones

---

[2] Thus no one would seriously maintain that from an esthetic point of view Bach's *St. Matthew Passion* is "too long," even though its uncut performance takes over four hours. The force of musical logic in determining one's feeling of duration is strong enough to make some people assert that they actually "feel" uncut Wagner performances to be shorter than cut ones. This was strikingly experienced in Vienna, where, says Paul Stefan, Weingartner's productions of cut versions not only *seemed,* but actually *were* longer than Mahler's productions of the uncut scores!

and erect with them a sanctuary for himself, built in his own time, but built with its portals facing the setting sun. That is why one never thinks of Brahms as the beginning of a new road—but here again is our Austrian paradox of "Convention and Revolt"; the "Neo-Viennese" all pay homage to Brahms—Schoenberg even characterizes himself as having been, in his youth, a "Brahms fan" rather than a "Wagner fan." Strange words from the man who wrote *Verklärte Nacht,* which he always regretted that Brahms did not live to hear. . . . One wonders what Brahms would have said of it.

Bruckner's approach was a different one. As we have already said, he, too, was fundamentally oriented towards the past; yet when he looked backward, he did not look with the eyes of a Brahms. Brahms looked upon the classics from the vantage point of a solid cultural background buttressed with elaborate musicological studies of his own. Bruckner had none of this. He was not so uncultured and musically ignorant as some of his opponents have liked to claim, but neither can he be proved to have possessed a really inclusive knowledge of musical literature—at least the contents of his musical library would not seem to indicate this. The circumstances under which he grew to maturity explain this fact sufficiently. In isolated spots like Ansfelden, Kronstorf, Windhaag, and even St. Florian there was little opportunity, to say the least, for becoming acquainted with masterpieces of symphonic literature. When the youthful Bruckner first went to Linz to enter what would nowadays be called a "teacher training course," those in charge of the education of the young candidates did not encourage such worldly activities as concert-going and theater-going. When, in later years, he commenced going to Vienna for lessons with Sechter, he was always too busy with the actual work that brought him there to have time for concert-going. Apparently he did not become acquainted with Beethoven's piano sonatas until introduced to them by Otto Kitzler (later an opera-conductor at Brünn) with whom he studied in his last Linz years. Certainly he knew not one note of Wagner before that time. When he finally settled in Vienna for the rest of his life, he went to concerts but little, being, like most mature composers, much more interested in his own works than in those of other composers. He did not even go to hear Wagner very often (in Vienna, that is; for he was an ardent participant in the yearly Bayreuth festivals).

Bruckner's musical gods were Bach, Beethoven, Schubert, and, of course, Wagner. He possessed an enthusiasm for Bach hardly shared by his university colleague and arch-enemy, Hanslick, to whom Bach's music was only of antiquarian interest, if that, though it is true that Bruckner was certainly not familiar with the great bulk of Bach's works. His deification of Wagner has been so much discussed that it need not be described here. His adoration of Beethoven, too, knew no bounds; he was wont to submit movements of Beethoven symphonies to the most minute periodic and harmonic analysis on Sechterian principles. Schubert (with whose four-hand music he was especially familiar) was dear to him, doubtless for the Austrian tone and atmosphere which appear with such felicity in his music and which Bruckner used with equal delight, as well as for the *expansion in duration* which he had permitted the classical Viennese symphonic form to undergo, and which Bruckner was to carry to even greater lengths.

Bruckner's attitude towards the symphony is, in a sense, one of compromise. Thus, he preserves the customary four movements, and, while enlarging the classic orchestra along Wagnerian lines, envisions nothing approaching the Mahlerian choral symphony. (The story that he wanted his *Te Deum* to be performed at the end of his Ninth Symphony if he did not live to complete the Finale will be dealt with later.) A classic periodicity of even numbers of measures is highly valued by him, yet he introduces so much varied thematic material into his expositions as to give them almost the aspect of developments. He modulates frequently and boldly, yet never loses sight of a hard-and-fast tonic—the foreshadowings of atonality which we may feel in Mahler are not yet present here.[3] Cheek by jowl with "Wagnerian" harmonies or "endless melodies" we may discover passages which would do credit to any text-book of harmony; for example, the "choral" subordinate theme in the Finale of the Seventh Symphony.[4] A particular feature of these passages, as of Bruckner's method of musical development in general, is the consistent use of sequences, which are often highly effective in modulation even though their frequency may sometimes make us feel that Bruckner should have been informed of Mattheson's *bon mot,* "A good sequence is not bad."

One would think that Bruckner, with so many conservative elements in his makeup, would logically have appealed to the traditionalists as much as Brahms, though in a different way. Hanslick, who had originally met Bruckner in Linz, was at first quite friendly with him and anxious to have him come to Vienna, apparently as a coun-

[3] But note the roving harmony and the long postponement of the tonic's appearance in the opening measures of the second movement, First Symphony.

[4] *Eulenburg's Kleine Partitur-Ausgabe,* pp. 128–29 (mm. 65 ff.).

terpoise to Wagnerian agitation.[5] This shows that he appreciated the traditional elements in Bruckner and, as an astute propaganda-maker, was quite ready to turn them to his own purposes. But when Bruckner sided with Wagner, and, more annoyingly still, insisted on becoming a "lector" (lecturer of non-professional rank) at the University against his "friend" Hanslick's wishes, then the die was cast. Bruckner always used to say that Hanslick turned against him when he, Bruckner, refused to marry a niece of Hanslick's. But that story cannot be proved, and, in any case, has no bearing on the real issues involved. The upshot was that Bruckner was championed by all the enthusiastic young people who sneered at the didactic opinions of Hanslick, handed down by him, priest-like, in the cathedral of the *Neue Freie Presse*. The partisans of the conservative camp now stressed Bruckner's destructive modernist tendencies instead of examining his conservative background. They realized, too, that he approached the classic form from an empirical, rather than a scholarly, viewpoint, and converted this realization into the accusation that Bruckner "lacked a sense of form." But this statement is hardly tenable in view of what we know about his anxious care with respect to regular periodicity and the like. As a matter of fact, the modern feeling might be that Bruckner was, at times, too anxious about "form" in the abstract, too concerned with filling out a predestined pattern. The Viennese classicists did not compose "forms," and neither did Bruckner at his best. But when he is at his worst, as in his earliest symphony, the so-called "School Symphony" in F minor which he wrote under Kitzler's tutelage and which is not included among his numbered works, one feels that it is because he is filling a preconceived form without having a very clear idea of the true dynamic relationships of the several parts. His real stylistic feeling matured only later.

It is Mahler who, of all the composers in question, developed the most independent concept of the nature of the symphony. Paradoxically enough, none of his "symphonic innovations" were new; the use of the chorus and of the solo voice, the increase in the number of movements, were all devices which had been used frequently before him. Needless to say, he was thoroughly familiar with the classical symphonic literature (though hardly in a musicological sense) and no one could have been more aware of its implications than he. His ap-

---

[5] In connection with this one recalls Brahms' efforts to induce Dvořák to teach at the Vienna Conservatory in 1896; "obviously," Stefan says (*Anton Dvořák*, p. 249), "to counterbalance Bruckner." But this last statement seems highly exaggerated. Bruckner was no longer teaching in 1896 and was known by everyone to be a dying man. (The incident took place only six months before his death.)

proach to the problem of form is completely different from Bruckner's; no anxious counting of measures or tabulating of harmonic progressions here. He is not concerned with the filling-out of a pattern, or with the reconstruction of a classical monument. An oft-quoted remark of his: " 'Symphony' means to me the building of a new world," characterizes his attitude with epigrammatic succinctness. When one builds a "new world," one constructs in conformity with the materials one has chosen, and does not violate the nature of these materials by shaping them in an inadequate form. We shall find that, in some ways, Mahler's most problematic works are those in which he consciously follows the "classic pattern" instead of the principle—a rather indefinite one, to be sure—which he enunciated himself. Such works are the First and Fourth Symphonies, which contain many remarkable features but are hardly on the original level of the Eighth Symphony or the *Lied von der Erde*. In each case, a "classical" symphonic pattern has been recognizably followed, and in the first movement of the Fourth Symphony this procedure almost produces the impression of a "pseudo-classicistic" style (though if we look more closely we shall see that Mahler's intention here was at least partially humoristic).[6]

We have spoken of the dynamic contrast inherent in the nature of the classical Viennese "sonata form." Let us return to this question, and discuss the most important element in that contrast, the character of the "symphonic theme" itself.

The classical "symphonic theme" should, perhaps, not be called a theme at all, but rather a motive. For in itself it may be quite insignificant, incapable of standing by itself as a melody, or, rather, as a musical entity. In that case, it is only the way in which it is developed, elaborated, interwoven with other motivic threads which makes it important. Even so, it has a shape and a style of its own, which render it peculiarly fitted for this sort of development. It is usually short, sharply defined in its boundaries, and strikingly rhythmicized. Often it will assume the form of a rising broken chord, the so-called "Mannheim skyrocket," as in Beethoven's Op. 2, no. 1:

---

[6] Such strictures can hardly be applied to the Sixth Symphony, which, though it outwardly preserves the "classic form" even to the double bar at the end of the exposition of the first movement, is nevertheless one of Mahler's most powerful (and least popular) works.

The ideal example of such a motive, the kernel of the work which is, more than any other, the epitome of what we call "symphonic style," is, of course,

So far, we have mentioned only "principal themes." It is usually taught that the "subordinate theme" must be of a more outspokenly lyrical character; this is true, within certain definite limitations. That is to say, the subordinate theme should not be of such a lyrical nature that it cannot be logically associated with the principal theme—yet a distinct contrast is necessary. This is a problem which all the classical Viennese composers had to face. Haydn, for example, had his difficulties with it, as we see in some of his symphonies where the incongruity between principal and subordinate themes is plainly to be seen; yet, in other works, he achieved the homogeneity of the monothematic exposition, in which the contrast is attained simply through the opposition of tonic and dominant.

Now, it was precisely on the rock of the subordinate theme that many a romantic symphonist foundered. It was only natural that the romanticist should give most attention to composition-types in which lyric feelings could be expressed in extended melodies. How could this attitude be adapted to the frame of classical symphonic logic? If the composer tried at all to follow a classical pattern—which he was likely to do in his desire to copy Beethoven, the "father of romanticism"—one of two things was bound to happen. Either the subordinate theme became a thing-in-itself, and, enclosed in its own lyricism, was incapable of development or of association with the principal theme (as is the case in the Finale of Mahler's First Symphony), or the lyrical character of the subordinate theme invaded the principal theme itself, changing it from the short, insignificant, but utilitarian motive that it used to be into a long melody quite capable of standing on its own feet, but enormously unwieldy to handle in further developments. These stylistic changes would have been justifiable if no attempt had been made to preserve a form into which they could not be made to fit. As the form was preserved, however, there came about that discrepancy between materials, means, and models which made the term "symphony" a dilemma for historians, critics, and composers alike. Here was a problem which could never be solved absolutely, but only more or less well according to the genius of the individual.

At this point there must arise the question of when we are, and when we are not, justified in applying the stylistic (*not* formal) standards of the Viennese classic era to any work called "Symphony." In cases where the classical "form" has been consciously adopted and followed, criticism according to classical stylistic criteria seems justifiable. If, in a work of this kind, we feel that the nature of the thematic material is such that the principal and subordinate thematic groups are placed in mere *juxtaposition* instead of in dynamic *opposition*, we have the right to consider this a defect in "symphonic style," insofar as it is not concealed or made convincing by the composer's technical skill. (For example, Brahms is able to conceal with his high technical accomplishment the fundamentally "unsymphonic" nature of the main theme in the first movement of his Fourth Symphony, which is in reality tremendously long and unwieldy. Schumann, confronted with the problem of handling "unsymphonic" material "symphonically," failed both structurally and stylistically.)[7] On the other hand, we have to remember that "symphony" can be a term of many meanings, and that it would be manifestly absurd to single out one of those meanings as the only correct one and to criticize, on such a basis, any work named "symphony" which cannot be explained by that single valid definition. In its original Greek signification, a "symphony" is simply a "coming together of sounds," i. e., an interval. Later, the word takes on all kinds of meanings. J. S. Bach's three-part inventions are "sinfoniae," the overture of a seventeenth-century opera is a "sinfonia"—to give only two well-known examples. Now we come upon such phenomena as Mahler's Eighth Symphony, which is really a miniature music-drama, and his *Lied von der Erde*, a song-cycle which is expressly called "Eine Sinfonie" by the composer. And then we have the designation "symphonic poem" arising to bring more confusion into the picture. But can we measure these works by a standard which pertains to *one* definition, and one alone, of the versatile word "symphony"? Obviously not. If one definite conclusion must come out of such questions, it is this: the sooner the concepts of "symphony" and "sonata form" are separated from one another, the better it will be for historians and composers alike.

Brahms' symphonies are so familiar, and the critical attitude towards them has become so detached and unbiased, that a detailed analysis of them does not seem necessary in this work. Bruckner and Mahler, however, present a different problem, inasmuch as their symphonic

---

[7] Bruckner—so often criticized for lack of stylistic and structural sensitiveness—felt this defect in Schumann keenly. He always used to call Schumann's symphonies "Sinfonietten."

oeuvre has always been analyzed either by fanatical disciples or by eager opponents—for dispassionate observers of the Viennese scene are rare indeed. Therefore, the development of each of them as a symphonist will be set forth separately and in detail at the proper place, always, of course, with reference to the general principles and concepts explained in this chapter. However, it must be borne in mind that this work is not a history of the "declining symphony," but a description of a certain period of Viennese musical culture as expressed in the lives and works of its outstanding figures; so, before we discuss Bruckner the symphonist, we shall examine other phases of his creation, and other elements in his background.

CHAPTER V

Sources for Bruckner's Theory of Harmony

BRUCKNER'S views on the teaching of harmony cannot be classified as part of his creative activity. Nevertheless, they must be discussed at this point for several reasons. In the first place, Bruckner's influence as a teacher in Vienna, apart from his influence as a composer and as an outstanding musical personality, can be examined accurately only if we understand his attitude towards theoretical problems; for he never taught composition, but only harmony and counterpoint, and even forbade his pupils to compose while studying with him. In the second place, an examination of his extremely conservative theoretical approach will help us to understand conservative elements in his composition, which must be explained and reconciled with the more "modernistic" elements. And in the third place, while looking back to the sources of Bruckner's theory we shall have an opportunity to study a little more closely a man whose mastery of abstract harmonic and contrapuntal problems makes us think of Fux's, and whose influence as a theoretician can be traced as far as Schoenberg's *Harmonielehre* and beyond.

We speak advisedly of the mastery of "abstract" problems, for Simon Sechter (1788–1867), Bruckner's predecessor at the Vienna Conservatory, was anything but a creative talent. One may easily convince oneself of this by reading over those versets and fugues of his which were painstakingly copied into bound manuscript-books by Konrad Max Kunz (1812–75) in 1836. The sixteen volumes of manuscript contain, besides compositions of Bach and his sons, Albrechtsberger, Clementi, Hummel, and others, the following compositions of Sechter: a set of five versets (short imitative compositions) in four voices, a set of thirty-two two-voice versets for the organ, Op. 22, and three organ fugues, Op. 2, in G major, D major, and G minor.[1] Further samples of Sechter's immense contrapuntal skill may be studied in his manuscript treatise *Introduction to Strict Style*,[2] which contains endless

---

[1] Ms. in New York Public Library.
[2] *Einweihung in die gebundene Spielart*. Ms. in New York Public Library.

canons in augmentation and contrary motion, with or without the addition of free middle voices, a crab canon in contrary motion, and other similar pieces. All these compositions and examples bespeak the master theoretician; they are carefully worked out, and faultless from the point of view of contrapuntal technique. They are, however, quite innocent of anything even remotely resembling musical inspiration. The characterless Sechter "fugue" is an example of what happened to the fugue after it became a "form" instead of a "style"—need one insist further on the connection between this historical phenomenon and what was said in the previous chapter regarding the "decline of the symphony"?

It is obvious that Sechter the composer need not detain us longer. We are concerned with Sechter the theoretician only, for it was he who taught Bruckner and whose doctrines exercised a lifelong spell over that composer. For the purposes of this discussion, his most important work is the first volume of *Fundamentals of Musical Composition,* entitled *The Correct Sequence of Basic Harmonies; or, the Fundamental Bass and its Inversions and Substitutes.*[3]

The most important terms in this title are obviously "basic harmonies" and "fundamental bass," and their presence here indicates that we have to do with a theoretical offshoot of Rameau's harmonic principles. For it was Rameau who first propounded the theory of the *basse fondamentale,* which became the foundation for all harmonic investigation after his time. Before Rameau, chords had been reckoned *from the actual bass alone,* so that what we would today call "the first inversion" of the C major triad was considered to be constructed in a completely different manner from the same C major triad in "root position." Rameau changed this concept when he examined harmonies from the acoustical viewpoint and showed that every triad possessed a root (fundament) and a fifth and third generated from this root according to the overtone system, and that the mutual relationship between the root, the third, and the fifth is always the same, regardless of which of these tones may happen to be in the lowest voice. A C major triad will, of course, perform different *functions* according to whether its root, its third, or its fifth is in the bass; but its *structure* will always remain the same, i. e., its root will always be C, its third E, and its fifth G. Harmonic progressions can, therefore, be equally well designated as "root-progressions" (*Fundamentschritte*), and the Roman numerals affixed to harmonies in anal-

---

[3] *Die Grundsätze der musikalischen Komposition;* v. I, *Die richtige Folge der Grundharmonien, oder vom Fundamentalbass und dessen Umkehrungen und Stellvertretern.* Leipzig, Breitkopf & Härtel, 1853.

ysis abstract the root-progression from the chords, showing us, with no reference to the melodic progression of the bass voice, what position the root of each chord occupies in the scale of the given tonality. This is the ultimate realization of the *basse fondamentale* theory.

Once the fundamental nature of the root-progressions was understood, it was only natural that thoughtful theorists should try to find out whether some root-progressions were stronger than others, and if so, why. This is exactly what Rameau's German followers Kirnberger and (later) Sechter attempted. They were confronted with the fact that, according to the theory on which they were building, the three most important chords in any given tonality are I, IV, and V. It is with these three chords that every perfect cadence is built. Now, the root of IV lies a perfect fifth below that of I, just as that of V lies a perfect fifth above. Given these circumstances, the next logical step was "to extend this fundamental motion of the bass, the fifth-leap downwards (V–I), even further, by traversing the entire diatonic scale of fundamental basses in a chain of such successive leaps—beginning, for example, with the dominant, following it with the tonic, the subdominant, the seventh degree, and so on, always descending by fifths until the dominant-tonic cadence is reached." [4]

This attitude naturally led to a rating of root-progressions as "strong" or "weak." Sechter, in his list of requirements for good four-part harmonic writing, makes the following very clear statement on this point:

Two successive chords ought to have a natural relationship with one another, and it happens that the relationship between some is closer than between others. Two chords are well connected together when the fifth of the second chord is prepared; this case occurs when the root-progression is a descending third or an ascending fourth, which is identical with a descending fifth. When the root-progression is an ascending third or fifth (i.e., a descending fourth) the octave of the second chord is prepared. In some cases this makes for a good connection, but oftentimes, as we shall see later, it is not sufficient. [5]

Sechter illustrates this with the following harmony example, wherein the root-progressions are all descending fifths, i. e., ascending fourths:

He explains, further, that this arrangement is good because the fifth of each following triad is prepared by the root of the preceding chord.

[4] Eckstein, *Erinnerungen an Anton Bruckner,* pp. 28–29.
[5] Simon Sechter, *Die richtige Folge der Grundharmonien,* p. 15.

So far, we have seen how the system works when applied to root-progressions of fourths and thirds. How can it be made to apply to progressions stepwise? Here, Sechter uses the idea of imaginary intermediary roots. He propounds the theory that when we play or hear a chord-succession such as

we hear, between the first and second chords, an imaginary fundament G which would convert the root-progression into the following:

(The black notes, not actually sounded, represent the "understood" root-progression.)

Sechter does not stop here with the use of the concept of imaginary roots, but turns it to good advantage in his discussion of the diminished seventh chord, which he always calls "the dominant ninth chord with root omitted." According to him, the progression (in A minor)

must be understood with the following root-progression:

All other diminished seventh chords are explained in the same way.

Such, in brief, was the harmonic theory which Bruckner inherited from Sechter, and to which he clung faithfully in his teaching and even in his composition. It is true that he added a few pedagogical devices of his own; for example, he always used black notes to designate the root-progressions, and insisted that his pupils do likewise. (This device is not used in Sechter's own examples.) In the main, however, he adhered strictly to the rules which his revered master had set down, and passed them on in turn to his pupils.

Now, from an abstract point of view it may be quite possible to find flaws in this theory of Sechter's as it was adapted by Bruckner and, as we shall see later, by others of note. Some of these flaws are pointed out by George Capellen in his self-styled *Streitschrift* entitled *Is S. Sechter's System a Suitable Point of Departure for Theoretical Analysis of Wagner?* [6] This work is directed not only against the Sechterian theory in itself, but also against attempts to apply it to the harmonic analysis of Wagner. The first of these attempts had been made in 1881, when Carl Mayrberger, professor of music in the state teachers' training course at Pressburg, published his analysis of the inner significance of Wagnerian harmony according to Sechter's principles. In his dedication of this work to Wagner, Mayrberger wrote: "As a theorist, I take my stand on Sechter's system and am thoroughly convinced that this system and this system alone (purified, of course, and developed to a point where it is capable of explaining modern music) can explain your harmonies as the product of the deepest musical art, by means of truly logical analysis." [7]

This profession of faith is not surprising from the man who had already published, in 1878, the first part (*Die diatonische Harmonik in Dur*) of a *Lehrbuch der musikalischen Harmonik in gemeinfasslicher Darstellung,* in which he shows himself a most faithful follower of Sechter, as he indicates in the preface: "Since the author is a pupil of the Imperial Kapellmeister Gottfried Preyer, who in his turn was privileged to be instructed by the famous harmonist and contrapuntist Simon Sechter, it is easy to understand why this book agrees for the most part with Sechter's work 'The Correct Sequences of Basic Harmonies: or, the Fundamental Bass. . . .'" [8]

It was not the work of Mayrberger, however, which was directly responsible for Capellen's polemic pamphlet. The gifted Bruckner pupil Cyrill Hynais had just been turning his attention to Sechter's theories, and putting them into practical application in Wagner analyses, in some articles published in the *Neue musikalische Presse* in Vienna. It is needless to say that Hynais' attitude towards Sechter was distinctly favorable. Capellen, for his part, expresses his regrets at the turn that Wagner studies seem to be taking, in these terms: "It is not very heartening for modern theory that the study of Wagner has gone back to a textbook which was already in print in 1854, and which would be a suitable basis for Wagner studies in spite of its age if the scholarly thoroughness and the logic of Sechter's explanations were not founded, at important points, on false premises." [9]

6 George Capellen, *Ist das System S. Sechters ein geeigneter Ausgangspunkt für die theoretische Wagnerforschung?* Leipzig, Kahnt, 1902.

7 As quoted in Capellen, *ibid.,* p. 5.

8 Carl Mayrberger, *Lehrbuch der musikalischen Harmonik,* p. VII.

9 Capellen, *op. cit.,* p. 35.

Capellen's chief objection to the Sechter theory pertains to its basic thesis that the descending fifth is the simplest, most natural root-progression. In his application of this fundamental idea, Sechter gives the root-progression of a diminished fifth the same value as that of a perfect fifth. Thus, in the first four measures of an example already cited, we see that Sechter uses the diminished fifth in exactly the same way as the perfect fifth:

etc.[10]

Eckstein defends the validity of this procedure, saying that the cumulative force of the sequence in fifths, especially if it is of long duration, has the effect of equalizing the diminished fifth and the perfect fifth, as far as their harmonic implications are concerned.[11] Capellen, however, refuses to accept the equality of diminished and perfect fifth, and cannot understand why Sechter did not accept stepwise progressions without postulating imaginary intermediary roots for them, since a simple stepwise progression is in any case far more natural than a progression by diminished fifths. He also questions the logic of Sechter's explanation of the origin of the diminished seventh chords. And he dismisses Sechter's statement that "a diatonic progression must be the basis of every chromatic progression"[12] with his own counter-assertion: "Sechter's view that every chromatic progression is derived from a diatonic one is not correct in every case; on the contrary, exactly the opposite is often true."[13] It is obvious that, if this were true, Sechter's theory would be completely unfitted for an analysis of Wagner's harmony; and that is, of course, exactly what Capellen wished to prove.

Such theoretical arguments as this have, however, only an academic interest if they are not correlated with the living music of their time. In determining the merits of a theoretical system, it is not so important to find out whether it is flawless from a technical viewpoint as to assess the influence which it has had upon the creative intellects of succeeding generations. In this respect, we must rate Sechter far above his opponents. It is not every contrapuntalist who can boast of having been the chosen teacher of a Schubert and the idol of a Bruckner. Whatever may have been superimposed upon the theoretical foundations laid during Bruckner's years of intense study with Sechter, it was these which prevented him from losing himself when his musical

10 Sechter, *op. cit.*, p. 13.   11 Eckstein, *op. cit.*, p. 29.
12 Sechter, *op. cit.*, p. 128.   13 Capellen, *op. cit.*, p. 22.

imagination was turned loose on the harmonic world of Wagner. That the Sechterian principles were not a mere basis for Bruckner's method of teaching, but also sustained him actively in composition, we have already seen. And, as Bruckner imparted these principles to his pupils, they did not die out with him. None of his actual pupils became composers of world renown, although men like Kamillo Horn and Max von Oberleithner gained fame at least in Germany and Austria; but fine musicians like the pianist August Stradal and the conductor Franz Schalk exercised a wholesome influence wherever they worked. Mahler, though not a Bruckner "pupil" in the strict sense, associated with Bruckner in his youth and was schooled in the traditions which Bruckner represented. So, in these men, the influence of Sechter, too, lived on.

But to appreciate fully the effect which Sechter's theories can have on a modern creative intellect, we must look ahead to the year 1943, and to the words of a man who is, in the public eye, the foremost apostle of "modernity" in music. For Arnold Schoenberg, in the glossary of his *Models for Beginners in Composition,* expounds a theory of root-progressions which is, in effect, a transposition of Sechter into his own terms. It was Decsey who, in his life of Bruckner, first drew attention to the kinship between Sechter's theories and Schoenberg's theories as expressed in *Harmonielehre.* However, he mentioned this phenomenon only in passing, and did not make a detailed comparison. That part of Schoenberg's theory which is a continuation of Sechter will be discussed later in its chronological place. We refer to it here only as another indication that the man whose influence extended to our very day was no ordinary dry-as-dust schoolmaster. And let it be remembered that Bruckner idolized this man almost as much as he did Wagner!

CHAPTER VI

Bruckner as Church Composer

IT HAS sometimes been averred that Bruckner's achievements in the realm of church music are of far greater importance than his achievements in the field of the symphony, and that his churchly compositions display much more originality and mastery of form than do his symphonic works. Such a statement demands attention and examination.

To begin with, we must face the fact that, today, church music is not a living art. There are several reasons for this. In the first place, the completely artificial standard of what is and is not "churchly" in music has led to the continued composition of a sweetly sentimental variety of church music which is a mere imitation of what was written in the same vein by minor nineteenth-century composers. It is ironical that this erroneous notion of an "ecclesiastical style" should have been indirectly fathered by Palestrina. Baini, Palestrina's romantic biographer, gave to posterity the legend of a Palestrina who was completely immersed in unworldly thoughts, and whose smoothly flowing, emotionless music was the epitome of seraphic bliss. Thus was born the "Palestrina myth," which was to cause untold damage in the field of church music. Not the least destructive result of neo-Palestrinianism was the "a cappella ideal," which arbitrarily cut composers off from the wealth of orchestral resources placed at their disposal by the eighteenth and nineteenth centuries.

The most representative manifestation of Palestrinianism in the nineteenth century was Cecilianism. The *Cäcilienverein*, founded by Franz X. Witt (1834–88) in 1867, had as its avowed aim the propagation of works in the so-called "Palestrina style," and the suppression of instrumental church music. "Away with the instrumental Masses of the Viennese school!" exclaimed Seydler,[1] including in his condemnation the Masses of Beethoven, Schubert, Cherubini, Hummel, and

[1] Anton Seydler, "Geschichte des Domchores in Graz von den Zeiten Erzherzogs Karl II bis auf unsere Tage," *Kirchenmusikalisches Jahrbuch,* (1900), p. 34.

Weber, to say nothing of Haydn and Mozart, for whom he has only words of pity: "It is really a shame that even such illuminated spirits, such pure, noble artists and such pious men as Haydn and Mozart were led astray into a blind alley of weakened, denatured church music." [2]

The Cecilians may be forgiven for having produced no great composers; we can only smile when Anton Walter, the devoted biographer of Witt, speaks of the "fame and worth, the greatness and immortality" of his compositions, and further describes them as "brilliant, dazzling, glittering . . . phenomena in the heaven of art." [3] What they cannot be forgiven, however, is their setting up of a false ideal of church music which still continues to befuddle historians and stands in the way of a true church art.

Since this ideal has been set up, it has become increasingly difficult to write of the church music of Haydn and Mozart without stating categorically that it is indeed unchurchly or arguing vigorously that it is churchly when no argument at all should be necessary—for why should these composers have belied their own natures and written in an artificial, stiff, "churchly style" when, as yet, there was no *Cäcilien-verein* to tell them how they must compose? Thus Alfred Schnerich, the enthusiastic defender of the Viennese instrumental Mass, has to go out of his way to prove that Haydn was justified in writing festive *Kyries*.[4] Then, paradoxically enough, Max Auer, who, as an ardent admirer of Bruckner's instrumental Masses, could hardly be called a Cecilian, questions Schnerich's justification: "Jollity must be considered especially unsuitable for a Kyrie. If jolly Kyries may be found in Haydn and Mozart, Schnerich's excuses are not sufficient for these cases." [5] And he goes on to excuse the gayety of some Mozart Masses on account of the composer's youth!

It is partly, if not entirely, because of this attitude towards church music that most of our churches today are unable or unwilling to muster sufficient instrumental and vocal forces to give even remotely adequate performances of the great ecclesiastical works of either Protestant composers (Bach) or Catholics (Bruckner, Liszt). But the church is not entirely to blame for this. Certain Catholic works written by Protestants, such as Bach's B minor Mass, because of their dimensions, cannot possibly be made to fit within the frame of the church service without being cut to an extent that would destroy them as works of

[2] *Ibid.*
[3] Anton Walter, *Dr. Franz Witt*, p. 136.
[4] Alfred Schnerich, *Messe und Requiem seit Haydn und Mozart*, pp. 20–21.
[5] Max Auer, *Anton Bruckner als Kirchenmusiker*, pp. 34–35.

art, let alone the liturgic ban that they would incur if a single word of the codified text were to be omitted. There remains the possibility of a "concert performance" of such Masses, and that is in itself an anomaly. Given these facts, it is easy to see why the "grand tradition" of German church music as represented by Bach and Beethoven, and in a completely different way by Liszt and Bruckner, has failed to gain ground in our day. There is no suitable place left for its cultivation.

However, to find out why Bruckner's religious compositions, which form such a large proportion of his work, exerted so little lasting influence on the "neo-Viennese" composers, we must look not only to practical, but also to psychological causes. It must not be forgotten that Bruckner, reared in the shadow of the church during the *Vormärz,* was Catholic to an extent that we can hardly imagine today. His religion was the foundation of everything he said and did, and the same pious spirit which breathes from his Masses also imbues his symphonies, so much so that he even introduced reminiscences of the Masses into the symphonies. It is true that he wanted his *Te Deum* to be used as the finale of his Ninth Symphony in case he did not live to finish the instrumental finale. We have sketches in his own hand which may represent a transition from the Adagio of the Ninth to the *Te Deum.* This has nothing to do with any carrying-on of the misunderstood tradition of Beethoven's Ninth in the spirit of Wagner; Bruckner's selection of the same key, D minor, for his last symphony was either purely coincidental or else dictated by a quite subconscious associative pattern. We know he admired Beethoven's Ninth so tremendously that he used to say he felt "like a little dog" before it. But, after all, he had been exposed to the influence of Wagner's ideal of the human voice for years, and if it had stimulated his creative imagination he would have experimented with the voice in previous symphonies. This contention is borne out by the fact that he actually did make sketches for a purely instrumental Finale for the Ninth, but was physically and mentally too weak to carry them out. No, the addition of the *Te Deum* to the symphony cannot be understood otherwise than as a profession of faith. After all, had not Bruckner expressly dedicated both works to God?

But Bruckner's successors could no longer recapture his simple and naïve faith. Here the racial factor enters into the picture, for the spiritual leaders of Vienna's musical life after Bruckner, first Mahler and then Schoenberg, were both of Jewish extraction. They could interest themselves in Catholicism and mysticism, but their attitude towards religion would always be one of restless groping and searching, not one of childlike faith such as Bruckner's. It is perfectly natural that neither of them ever composed a Mass; this must not be attributed to unfamiliarity with the traditions of Viennese ecclesiastical music, for Mahler had conducted Bruckner's D minor Mass and *Te Deum* in Hamburg with great success. A friend once asked Mahler why he had never composed a Mass, and he replied that the idea sometimes came to him but that he would never be able to set the *Credo,* as he could not bring himself to such an affirmation of faith. But later Mahler said to this same friend, when speaking of the Eighth Symphony, that gigantic music-drama of human faith which is spiritually a continuation of the *Aufersteh'n, ja aufersteh'n* of the Second Symphony: *"This is my Mass!"*

Granted that under such spiritual conditions Bruckner's religious works could not be very influential in succeeding generations, it is still necessary for us to examine them as an important part of his *œuvre.* In doing this, we shall confine ourselves to the major works of his maturity, the three Masses and the *Te Deum;* for the little Masses and other small ecclesiastical works written at St. Florian and other places before he attained artistic maturity were intended only for immediate practical use, and are only of biographical, not of musical, interest. Later ecclesiastical pieces of smaller dimensions, like the *Ave Maria* for harmonium and alto and the 150th Psalm for chorus, orchestra, solo soprano and solo violin, are fine both in conception and in execution, but teach us nothing about Bruckner's technique which we cannot learn from the larger works.

First of all, since we have already spoken in a general way about Bruckner's attitude towards the classical "sonata form" as expressed in his symphonies, we must determine his attitude towards the classical "Mass form." Max Auer has already attempted this in his work *Anton Bruckner als Kirchenmusiker,* but as his discussion is inaccurate in several respects the problem must be examined anew.

In general, Bruckner's attitude towards the classical Mass is the same as his attitude towards the symphony. In each instance, he is very much aware of his classical models, although he does not take over their form-patterns intact, but expands them to suit his own needs. Here we touch upon a possible reason for the intrinsic superiority of Bruckner's Masses to his symphonies from the formal point of view. When he tried to expand the classical symphonic form he showed himself original but was not always successful, for the result was neither the classical symphony reincarnated nor the complete rebuilding of the symphonic structure to suit the needs of the new material, as prac-

tised by Mahler. In his Masses, however, the preservation of a pattern
did not hamper him, for this pattern is set by the divisions of the
liturgical texts and could not be broken without destroying the integrity of the Mass. It is not the procedure alone which is more or less
fixed in the Mass; through the centuries, certain stock modes of expression have almost become the rule for some liturgical text-passages.
Thus "et unam sanctam catholicam et apostolicam Ecclesiam" is tra-
ditionally set in unison, "descendit de coelis" is represented by a
descending passage, and so on. Bruckner carefully respects such traditions as these.

"The Kyrie," says Auer, "is, in Bruckner's works, tripartite, in duple
time, and through-composed in one piece." [6] In other words, the sections *Kyrie, Christe, Kyrie* are woven together instead of being treated
as entirely separate compositions, as is, for instance, the case in Bach's
B minor Mass. The second *Kyrie* is always a kind of varied repetition
of the first. In the D minor and F minor Masses, Bruckner introduces
solo voices in the *Christe* section, a practice long sanctioned by classical usage, though not invariably observed. Although the *Christe* section is not markedly different in texture from the *Kyries* in Bruckner,
it usually has its own motivic pattern.[7]

The composition of the *Kyrie* in duple time represents a departure
from Viennese classical tradition. Haydn's *Kyries,* for example, are frequently in triple time, and the same metrical construction characterizes
those of Schubert. This keeps the duple rhythm fresh for the *Gloria,*
where it is always used. Bruckner, however, attains his contrast by
tonal rather than metrical means. Although his *Kyries* and *Glorias*
are both in duple time, the *Kyrie* is always in minor and is invariably
followed by a *Gloria* in major, whereas in the Viennese instrumental
Masses of the eighteenth century the *Kyrie* was more likely to be in
major than in minor. A notable exception to this is the *Kyrie* of
Haydn's Nelson Mass, a stern piece in D minor, whose opening invocation in all voices:

strongly suggests certain passages of Bruckner which are marked by a
powerful descending octave; for example, the fugue theme of the 150th
Psalm:

6 *Ibid.,* p. 33.

7 A glance at the scores demonstrates that Auer is mistaken in saying that, contrary
to classical tradition, Bruckner uses no independent motives in his *Christe* sections.

Al - les was O - dem hat, Lo - be den Herrn.

We know that Bruckner was familiar with the Nelson Mass as its score was catalogued among his effects after his death.[8]

Here it must be remarked that it is quite idle to argue whether rhythmical contràst is a better way to distinguish *Kyrie* from *Gloria* than tonal contrast, or vice versa. Both ways are valid, and if Haydn's or Mozart's Masses are superior to Bruckner's it is not because Haydn and Mozart scrupulously wrote their *Kyries* in 3/4 time and their *Glorias* in 4/4.

Bruckner's *Glorias* are divided into three parts according to the classical pattern: a slow section begins at "Qui tollis," and the recapitulation at "Quoniam." This corresponds exactly to the practice of Haydn. All three *Glorias* end with a fugue on "Amen"; in the F minor Mass, the fuller text "in gloria dei Patris, amen" is used. This would not be worth commenting on if Auer had not called it "a deviation from the classical model, which customarily uses the words 'cum Sancto Spiritu' for the fugue." [9] Haydn's Nelson Mass, with which we know Bruckner was familiar and which Auer himself tells us may have furnished the inspiration for the sombre spirit of his *Kyries,* displays a regular fugue on "in gloria dei Patris, amen." Bruckner also owned a score of Haydn's so-called "Heilig-Messe" in B flat, the *Gloria* of which ends with a double fugue on "in gloria dei Patris, amen." Surely the use of a fugue on these words is not so unfamiliar as Auer's statement would seem to imply!

In the *Credo,* Bruckner employs a structural device not used by Haydn, but familiar in the F major and G major Masses of Schubert. This is the introduction of a recapitulation at "Et in Spiritum Sanctum" (Schubert, often lax in liturgic propriety, makes the text read "Credo, credo in Spiritum Sanctum.") After the fashion of Haydn, Bruckner uses the same key for both *Credo* and *Gloria.* However, in discussing Bruckner's *Credos* there are other important features to be taken into consideration which show the extent to which he clings to classical ideals. For it is in the representation of the Resurrection and the Last Judgment that he shows himself not only a church composer, but a true dramatist; and we should recall that the composers of instrumentally accompanied church music, from Scarlatti to Mozart, were dramatic composers. (This is also true of Haydn and Bee-

[8] Auer, *op. cit.,* p. 35.   [9] *Ibid.,* p. 39.

thoven, even though opera was not their strong point.) Instead of merely hinting at the tremendousness of the Resurrection with a radical change in mood, tempo, and key, as Haydn does in the Nelson Mass, Bruckner chooses to represent the event realistically, as a dynamic unfoldment. This method is different from the symbolic use of contrast which characterizes this section in the Viennese classical Masses (even Beethoven's *Missa Solemnis*). Obviously, both the classical masters and Bruckner visualized the scene almost operatically; the difference between them lies in the changed concept of what constitutes the dramatic in music. To many it may still seem like sacrilege to mention Mass and opera in the same breath, but those who are so easily shocked forget, firstly, that it was direct contact with the works of Wagner through Kitzler which brought the composer Bruckner out of his cocoon and that the Masses and the First Symphony were the immediate outcome of this new-won artistic maturity, and, secondly, that in Catholic Austria the celebration of the Mass still retained the baroque splendor, well-nigh operatic in its vividness, which had belonged to it in the seventeenth century and which had lived, too, in classical works like Haydn's *Pauken-Messe*. As Auer says:

> Bruckner took literally . . . the words of the author of the Psalms: "Praise ye him with drums and cymbals." He displays a splendor and brilliance in his orchestral and choral color-combinations which is comparable to the glow of the glorious colors in Rubens' paintings. In this sense we recognize in Bruckner's Masses (with the exception of the E minor) the *direct descendants of the Viennese school*. They correspond perfectly to the elaborately and imaginatively organized ceremonies of the Catholic service. Altars shining in brilliant light, priests in gold vestments, flying banners, incense, ringing bells, processions on high feast-days; then again utter humility, the penance of fast-days and of advent, quiet meditation in gloomy corners of the church illumined only faintly by the roseate glow of "eternal light"; all this we experience in Bruckner's music.[10]

It is a far cry from the eighteenth-century *opera buffa* to the Wagnerian music drama, but the motives which led Haydn to incorporate the idiom of the one into his Masses are not different from those which influenced Bruckner to capture some of the vividness of the other in his. Both Haydn and Bruckner were simple, naïve, devout in the way that, perhaps, only the rural Austrian Catholic can be. Both of them felt on friendly and intimate terms with God; Haydn is said to have averred that his heart leaped up with joy whenever he thought of holy things. And if his heart leaped with joy, why should not his music? Why should he exclude the beloved *opera buffa* ele-

[10] *Ibid.*, pp. 86–87.

ments from his Masses when he had already used them with such stimulating effect in his symphonies and chamber works? In the age of the classic symphony, opera was everywhere, fertilizing everything it touched, forming the very backbone of the new symphonic style, lending to it all those stylistic earmarks which would later become its clichés. Of course Haydn wrote his Masses in the style which pleased him best and which he felt would please God best, too. As for Bruckner, what finer tribute could he pay to his God than to offer up to Him the results of the study of Wagner's music, which, to him, was nothing less than a divine manifestation?

This must not be understood in the sense that Bruckner was a mere imitator of Wagner, as has been so often and so erroneously asserted. Those who speak of a bodily transplantation of the principles of the *Gesamtkunstwerk* to the symphony or to the Mass are describing an impossibility, for these forms can make no use of a catalogued system of *leitmotivs* or of "endless melody," to say nothing of the philosophical principles which underlie the music drama and which have no validity in absolute music. The testimony of many who knew him must convince us that Bruckner's appreciation of the music-dramas was purely musical. He never seems to have had a clear idea of the plot of the *Ring* or to have taken any interest in its muddled philosophy. Some of the more empyrean spirits of the *Wagnerverein* must have found it rather trying to discuss Wagner with him on purely musical terms; his lack of appreciation of the non-musical elements in Wagner's work has been tacitly excused on the basis of his lack of literary culture. But we do not need to excuse Bruckner in this way, for in disregarding Wagner's pseudo-mythical trappings and going right to the heart of things, to the music, he showed himself much more sensible than those who tried to set up Wagner's involved plot-constructions as the model of perfect drama. Instinctively he chose the only aspect of Wagner's *Gesamtkunstwerk* which could possibly have had any meaning for him, and concentrated on it. In no other way could Wagner have been palatable to him, for his religious nature would have been revolted, had he ever seriously thought about it, by the gross immoralities inherent in the theme of the *Ring* and by the pseudo-religion—"Christianity arranged for Wagnerians" as Nietzsche called it—of *Parsifal*. This explains why, though he often toyed with the idea of writing an opera himself, he was never able to do so. And we may be thankful that he did not, for in the field of the music-drama he might have been betrayed into a too facile imitation of Wagnerian precepts; and his opera, while it would undeniably have possessed interest from a historical viewpoint, might have to be regretfully consigned to the rubble-heap of music-dramas that we call "post-Wagnerian." Instead, his nature forced him to originality, so that he gave us Masses and symphonies which owe something to Wagner without being overpowered by Wagnerianism. Strangely enough, we are often intrigued by finding in his works so-called "Wagnerian clichés" which prove, on examination, to have been written by Bruckner before they were written by Wagner. Auer gives an example of pre-*Parsifal* "Grail Sixths" from a composition of Bruckner's St. Florian period, the *Tantum ergo* in E flat (1846). The passage is:

Auer makes a great point of explaining that Bruckner, in 1846, could not have known the famous passage in Mendelssohn's Reformation Symphony and could not have heard the responses sung at Dresden's *Hofkirche* which were the source for both Mendelssohn and Wagner.[11] But it seems a little futile to make emphatic claims for the originality and novelty of a simple passage in parallel sixths like this. Parenthetically, it may be remarked that Bruckner also used the Grail motive *after* hearing *Parsifal,* and reproduced it quite accurately, as, for example, in the Gradual *Virga Jesse* (1884).

But the use of such a motive by Bruckner cannot be accounted plagiarism, particularly as the Grail motive is, in a sense, common property. Besides, we must remember that in each musical era there are certain stock locutions which, while they may have been originated by one man, belong more to the time than to the man, and pass into the musical speech of his contemporaries without effort. We are familiar with the stock locutions of the baroque and of the classic era, and accept them as common property, not crying out "Plagiarism!" when we hear in Beethoven an operatic unison passage which we

11 *Ibid.,* p. 52.

may have previously heard in Mozart or in Haydn. But we are still too close to the nineteenth century, and particularly to Wagner, to realize that certain of his clichés—for example, the ubiquitous "Wagner turn" as in *Rienzi:*

do not belong to him alone, but to the whole century, and that their appearance in works of his contemporaries and his successors has nothing to do with questions of plagiarism or of originality.

Leaving these considerations, let us now dwell a little longer on Bruckner's treatment of the *Credo,* and see how he goes about building up his dramatic *Resurrexit* scenes. For this purpose, we shall analyze the greatest of them all, the *Resurrexit* of the F minor Mass.

The actual technique of this "scene" is very simple. We shall find its like in many other works of Bruckner; the opening of the *Te Deum* comes to mind by reason of its motivic similarity, and so do many passages from the symphonies which are built upon *tremolo sostenuto, ostinato,* or pedal-point motives. But while in the symphonies these passages occasionally impede the flow of thematic development and seem out of place from a formal point of view, here the pedal-point and the *ostinato* have tremendous dramatic value. Beginning with a pianissimo roll on the low E of the kettledrum, supported by pizzicato tones of the 'celli and basses, Bruckner introduces the viola figure:

Six measures of steady crescendo over this *ostinato* motive (an old operatic-dramatic standby) ensue before the chorus enters on a brilliant E major chord with its "Et resurrexit." The pedal-point remains on E for twelve measures, then shifts to A for ten; after this, there is no pedal-point, but the eighth-note *ostinato* figure continues unabated in all the strings for 74 more measures—that is, till within two measures of the end of the "scene," which embraces the Resurrection and the Last Judgment. Thus, all told, there are 102 measures during which the *ostinato* figure proceeds remorselessly, gathering additional strength with each repetition. The broad plan of this one section is partially, but not entirely, explained by the grand proportions of the F minor Mass; upon the structural necessity was superimposed Bruckner's wish to present a vivid, naturalistic Resurrection scene. Hearing this music, it does not require too much imagination for us to visualize the trembling of the earth and the rows on rows of souls marching to the seat of the Last Judgment.

Bruckner does not deviate from his classical models of form in the construction of the *Sanctus* and the *Benedictus*. In the D minor and F minor Masses, he employs for the *Sanctus* the structure already used by Haydn (in which a slow, solemn opening is succeeded by a rapid *Pleni sunt coeli*) and also follows classical example in choosing for the key of this movement the tonic major. In all three Masses, the *Benedictus* is characterized by that intimate, subjective lyricism which beautifies the slow movements of his symphonies and which won for him the epithet "Master of the Adagio." This lyricism, however, never oversteps the bounds of liturgical "propriety," by which is meant that it does not fall into the sentimental tone which characterizes such pseudo-liturgic music as Gounod's Masses. Lyricism receives its most poignant expression in the orchestral introduction of the *Benedictus*, a feature missing in none of the Masses. The idea of such an orchestral introduction is not new with Bruckner; it, too, was part of the classical tradition, as a glance at the *Benedictus* of Beethoven's *Missa Solemnis* will show.

Bruckner's treatment of the *Agnus Dei* is of interest because of its similarity to his treatment of the symphonic finale. It was a time-honored tradition that the last section of the *Agnus*, the *Dona nobis pacem*, should represent a return to the mood and often to the thematic material of the opening *Kyrie*. Bruckner was not, however, satisfied to use the *Kyrie* alone, but enriched this section with thematic references to other sections of the Mass; thus, in the finale of this large form, he was already using the same technique which he was later to turn to such good advantage in the finales of his symphonies. While we may admire the skill with which he handles the principles of cyclic form, we certainly cannot credit him with originality in using it; "cyclic form," in one shape or another, is as old as the *Tanz* and *Nachtanz*.[12] And it would be impossible to agree with Auer's statement that Bruckner's use of motives from several different parts of the Mass in the *Dona* is an adaptation of Wagner's *leitmotiv* technique to the Mass form.

Thus, in the final pages of the *Agnus* of the F minor Mass, we witness a veritable *stretto* of previously heard motives; the choir sings

[12] To say nothing of the primitive origins of that combination. See Sachs, *World History of the Dance*, pp. 274-75.

"dona nobis pacem" to the motive of the fugue "In gloria Dei Patris" from the *Gloria*, the oboe plays the main theme of the *Credo* which is then taken up by the voices, and even the last two measures contain a final reference to the *Kyrie* theme in the solo oboe. This uniting of all the motives undeniably makes for an impressive close; but Auer once more outstrips the actual facts when, playing on the texts of the Mass-sections involved, he writes, "In this combination is expressed Bruckner's conviction that *only he who believes and trusts* finds true peace and the glory of the Lord." [13] Auer, who recognized the analogy between the cyclic technique in the *Dona* and in the symphonic finale, might, in this instance, have more profitably confined himself to a purely musical explanation of musical phenomena.

Turning from the three great Masses to the *Te Deum* (1884), we shall not find any startling changes in Bruckner's approach to ecclesiastical music during the years which had elapsed since the completion of the last Mass, the F minor. Bruckner was already a mature man when he wrote the Masses, and, even if they were the first great works of his artistic maturity, they display the true "Bruckner style" as we know it. Therefore, the *Te Deum* bears all those stylistic earmarks which we have noted in the Masses; a strong feeling for scenes of dramatic pomp and vigor, manifested in the opening "Te Deum laudamus" and in the final fugue "In te, Domine, speravi—non confundar in aeternum—"; a penchant for meditative romantic lyricism which finds striking expression in the tenor solo "Quos pretioso sanguine"; a fondness for motives centered around the basic progressions of fourth, fifth, and octave, exhibited in the theme

Te De-um lau-da-mus! Te Domi-num con-fi-te — mur.

The relationship between the *Te Deum* and the Ninth Symphony has already been referred to above, and so that discussion will not be recapitulated here. In the proper place, more will be said about the whole problem of the choral finale in all its aspects.

We have already observed the close connection between Bruckner's ecclesiastical music and that of the Viennese classical school. It still remains for us to compare and contrast Bruckner's attitude towards church music with that of his great contemporary, Liszt, and also with that of the Cecilian Society.

[13] Auer, *op. cit.*, p. 166.

In his short essay *On the Church Music of the Future* (written in 1834 when Bruckner was a child of ten) Liszt found words to describe his ideal "humanistic music" which read like a description of Bruckner's Masses. He wrote: "Let this music (which we might call, for want of any other name, humanistic [*humanitaire*]) be devout, strong, and forceful; let it unite, in colossal proportions, theater and church; let it be at one and the same time dramatic and holy, resplendent and simple, solemn and serious, fiery and untamed, stormy and peaceful, clear and intimate." [14]

The important element in this description is the union of theater and church. We have already seen dramatic elements introduced into Bruckner's Masses in idealized form, and Liszt's Masses likewise display dramatic qualities. Yet Liszt's conception of this union was more literal, as well as more literary, than Bruckner's. This we see plainly in the construction of his two oratorios, *Saint Elizabeth* (1862) and *Christus* (1866–67). Liszt's strong words must not lead to misunderstanding, for it was never his intention that these oratorios should be staged, as has sometimes been done. However, the very fact that Bruckner never attempted an oratorio should tell us that, in spite of certain striking similarities, we should not seek for the identity of his conception of church music with Liszt's. Liszt's literary and philosophical interest in the problem of dramatic church music is shown by the fact that he could first write an essay about it and then produce the oratorios which exemplified the principles expressed in the essay. Bruckner's approach, on the other hand, was purely musical and religious.

It is interesting and valuable to compare the attitudes of Bruckner and of Liszt towards the use of Gregorian elements in modern church music. As is generally known, Liszt made more consistent and conscious use of these than did Bruckner. *Saint Elizabeth*, to give but one characteristic example, derives its motivic material from several of the ancient chants, but uses this material in a thoroughly modern way, without any attempt at an archaistic style or any suppression of the emotional current of the drama. It is paradoxical that Liszt, the fighter for musical progress, should have been influenced at all by the conservative trends of the Gregorian revival and of Cecilianism, yet it is undeniable that he was so influenced. As Ursprung puts it, "Extremes met once more in the aims of Liszt and in those of Cecilianism: a radical principle of progress and strictly limited historism, the most finely chiseled scores and primitive, almost columnar chord-

[14] Franz Liszt, *Gesammelte Schriften*, II, 56.

successions, the most individual art of expression and colorless banality." [15]

And it is Ursprung, too, who, remembering the great traditions of the Netherlands school, compared Liszt to Obrecht: "When Liszt uses Gregorian themes, he becomes, *mutatis mutandis*, another creator of the type of Obrecht, insofar as his vivid emotional experiences soon lead him away from the Gregorian chant and even out of the liturgical expressive sphere." [16] An element of deliberation, of thought about musical problems which may take a literary or philosophical turn before it expresses itself musically, has always to be taken into account with Liszt, and in one sense justifies Ursprung's statement that Liszt and Bruckner present the greatest possible contrast as composers for the Catholic Church—this although, as we have already seen, there are certain positive similarities between them.

As we might expect by this time, Bruckner, when he used the Gregorian chant, had no thoughts of forcible reform of church music. As a church organist, he was thoroughly familiar with the chant, which he had to accompany at services, and so it is only natural that he used it in smaller liturgical compositions such as the antiphon *Tota pulchra es Maria*. But it is significant that, whereas Liszt utilized Gregorian thematic material in his Masses, as, for instance, in the *Gloria* of the Mass in C minor for male chorus and organ, Bruckner never employed such material in a single one of his great "symphonic" Masses, although, in the E minor Mass, he bowed to Gregorian tradition in beginning the composition of the *Gloria* with "Et in terra pax" and of the *Credo* with "Patrem omnipotentem," thus allowing the traditional intonation of the preceding words by the priest to take place.

Bruckner unavoidably had contact with the Cecilians; but, whereas we can trace the positive results of such contact in Liszt's works, in Bruckner's case its most interesting result was a rather amusing incident which, though it has already been related by several writers, may well be retold here, as it throws a striking light on the musical *mores* of the Cecilians. Bruckner, asked to contribute an original work to Witt's periodical *Musica Divina*, sent in an *a cappella Tantum ergo* in the Phrygian mode. The final cadence of this piece contained a striking suspension of the ninth, of which Bruckner was particularly fond. Therefore, his consternation can be imagined when, receiving

[15] Otto Ursprung, *Restauration und Palestrina-Renaissance in der Katholischen Kirchenmusik der letzten zwei Jahrhunderte*, p. 52.
[16] Otto Ursprung, *Die Katholische Kirchenmusik*, p. 273.

his printed copy of the work, he found that Witt had quietly corrected the offending ninth into a harmless octave! He was naturally indignant, and the copies of the piece in the possession of several of his pupils and friends, wherein the composer's blue pencil definitively restored his original ninth, bear ample testimony to this indignation.

We have now compared and contrasted Bruckner's attitude towards ecclesiastical music with that of the Viennese classical school and that of his contemporaries, the Cecilians and Liszt. Before closing our discussion, however, we must touch on a point which does not strictly pertain to Bruckner's church music, but which has some bearing on his feeling in religious matters. Also, it is a phenomenon which is not confined to Bruckner's music, but which reappears strikingly in the works of Mahler and his successors, and thus offers a contrast to the unfortunate circumstance that Bruckner's great compositions for the church proper have not become as widely known as they deserve to be. We refer to the use of the so-called "chorale" in Bruckner's symphonies.

The qualifying expression "so-called" is used advisedly, for it must be kept in mind that Bruckner never, in any of his works, used a real Protestant chorale. In fact, given his ardent Catholic sympathies, it would have been spiritually impossible for him to do this. The chorale-like themes which occur so frequently in his symphonies are not expressions of a creed, but rather of an idealized religiosity.[17] This is expressed in a more personal way by citations of the thematic material of the Masses in the symphonies; these never take on the importance of Mahler's use of themes from his songs in his symphonies, but are nevertheless clearly present. The chorale-like tunes, however, give us a greater impression of universality. As they appear at the close of a movement, in triumphal garb, they have often suggested to commentators, and may also suggest to the imaginative listener, the idea of a militant and triumphant Catholic Church. Hence it is really misleading to call them "chorales," though they often superficially resemble the old chorale-type in their melodic structure. The music of César Franck, a Catholic and a mystic like Bruckner, presents a parallel case; his "chorales" are not chorales at all, but solemn chordal pronouncements.

Mahler's use of similar chorale-like melodies—one need only recall the so-called "Dies irae" theme in the Second Symphony—was doubt-

[17] They might have been influenced by the traditional Catholic *Wallfahrtslieder* (songs of pilgrimage and procession) which Bruckner certainly knew.

less conditioned by Bruckner's. Like Bruckner, he never used a real chorale melody; also like Bruckner, he wishes his melodies to express a feeling of mystical universality above and beyond their purely musical value, though a narrowly Catholic religious interpretation would have been quite foreign to his spirit. It may seem a far cry from the idealized chorale themes of Mahler and Bruckner to Berg's programmatic use of the Protestant chorale "Es ist genug! Herr, wenn es Dir gefällt,/So spanne mich doch aus." in the finale of his violin concerto. Yet, when we consider the line of descent of Bruckner > Mahler > Schoenberg > Berg, does it seem so unlikely that this is another example of the spiritual bond between successive generations of Viennese composers?

CHAPTER VII

Bruckner's Chamber Music

IT HAS frequently been remarked that composers of the romantic era tended to specialize, rather than to universalize, their gifts. Thus Chopin concentrated on the production of piano music, Wagner on that of music-dramas. Bruckner and Mahler, too, were specialists—specialists in the symphony (this despite Mahler's rich production of finely chiselled orchestral songs, for the composition of which Berlioz had set a precedent). Of all the great figures in German music of the latter half of the nineteenth century, Brahms alone was able to achieve equal stature in the field of chamber music and in that of the symphony. Bruckner's single string quintet comes, then, as an exception, not only in his own work but in the trends of the times. Let us examine the historical reasons for this.

Chamber music in the latter half of the nineteenth century was entering upon the second round of the great cycle which is its history. There had been a period in the first half of the eighteenth century when it was difficult, if not impossible, to determine where orchestral music left off and chamber music began; the string quartet, already weaned from orchestral literature, was not yet clearly distinguished from the divertimento on the one hand and the symphony on the other. Riemann called the trios of Johann Stamitz (1717–57) "orchestral trios," and justifiedly· so; for their musical expression belongs to the symphonic sphere—the C minor trio, indeed, already foreshadows Beethoven's Fifth—and we possess documents to show that they were performed with great effect by the world-renowned Mannheim orchestra.

This state of affairs changed, however, as chamber music became freed, bit by bit, from its moorings and drifted towards independence. The Serenade (second movement) of Haydn's string quartet Op. 3, no. 5 is still in the divertimento manner, but the string quartets of the mature Haydn are purified of all extraneous stylistic and instrumental accretions. Here, a new style has been created, the new "instrumental ensemble polyphony," a happy blend of homophonic and polyphonic elements which turned out to be just what chamber music needed. This style reached its highest perfection in Haydn's and Mozart's quartets, and here we may say that the historic cycle of chamber music had reached a balance point, a point of rest. But it was not to remain there long. Already we see signs of disturbance in Mozart's string quintets, which, though they still remain within the sphere of chamber music, reach out towards symphonic expression with the addition of a fifth instrument to the string quartet. As for Beethoven, he became so acutely conscious of the problem that he stopped composing quartets for years, only to return to them at the end of his life. We understand why he had to stop when we consider the first theme of the F minor string quartet, Op. 95. Here we stand at the very threshold of quartet and symphony, and feel that only a few more steps would carry us out of the realm of chamber music altogether.

After Schubert, the speed with which the cycle revolves is almost frightening, for this time the *rapprochement* of orchestral music and chamber music threatens to destroy the latter. No wonder, for the age was dominated by Wagner, who stood for the very opposite of all that the world of chamber music represents. It is true that this world maintained itself in the Mendelssohn-Schumann-Brahms circle, but the signs of struggle were manifest even there. Mendelssohn, consciously holding himself aloof from musical strife and revolt as always, produced euphonious, beautifully constructed chamber music which moves with gracious ease, though at times it skims lightly over the surface of musical thought. The very fact that he wrote a string octet is in itself significant; for the octet (or double quartet) is a direct consequence of that *rapprochement* between chamber music and orchestral music which was expressed in far less artistic form by Spohr's double quartets and *Quatuors brillants* wherein virtuoso effect reigned supreme. Schumann's difficulties with the symphony are duplicated in his works of instrumental chamber music, in which he is most successful when he can rely on the brilliant and triumphal effects of his favorite instrument, the piano. We qualify "chamber music" advisedly with the adjective "instrumental," for in Schumann we see how the spirit of chamber music, momentarily uprooted from its natural soil, has borne a new and lovely bloom: the romantic song. It is not meant to suggest that the *Lied* as practised by Schumann did not have an ancestry all its own, but rather that the nineteenth century found in the *Lied* the field for intimate expression which it had lost in the string quartet. Even the *Lied* was, however, to be swept away by the irresistible trend, and to end up in Mahler, Strauss, and Schoenberg as the orchestral song. Brahms, a bulwark of tradition in chamber music as well as in the symphony, created in this field more works that will endure than did any of his contemporaries; yet elaboration, often forced, filled his pages with so much music that euphony, a prime requisite of true chamber music, was greatly endangered. Thus is betrayed to us the appreciable weakening of the classical tradition of chamber music. The tremendous struggle that preceded Brahms' first string quartet bears eloquent testimony to his awareness of the magnitude of the conflict.

It might have been hoped that the piano would serve as a refuge for chamber music; it may fairly be said to have served this purpose in the characteristic short piano pieces of Schumann, Chopin, or Brahms. But piano music was not to remain immune from the general trend. It either strove for orchestral effects (Liszt's *Années de pélerinage,* Brahms' piano sonatas) or degenerated into salon music, the kind of weak imitation of Mendelssohn or Chopin of which even Bruckner left us a pathetic example in his *Erinnerung,* a brief piano piece reprinted by August Stradal.

Of paramount importance in the weakening of feeling for chamber music in the nineteenth century was the practice of transcription. Transcription is nothing new in musical history, for the earliest singer to add a *vox organalis* to the Gregorian chant was, in effect, a transcriber or arranger. Nor is transcription necessarily an evil practice, as is proved by Bach's sixteen concertos for multiple harpsichords, which are all transcriptions of Vivaldi but are so convincingly done that, until the research of modern musicology brought the truth to light, they were believed to be Bach's own work, and are still performed as such on many a concert program. Transcription becomes vicious, however, when, as it did in the nineteenth century and is still doing today, it destroys or displaces a portion of the legitimate repertory. On the one hand, the practice of chamber music and the feeling for it were seriously impaired by the endless orchestrations of Beethoven's piano sonatas and quartets. This sort of thing was going on as early as Habeneck's day (1828); the proportions which it reached even among serious musicians can best be gauged by the fact that as fine a musician as Mahler thought Beethoven's Op. 95 quite flat as a quartet, and deemed it necessary to perform it with string orchestra, something that Toscanini was to do in our time with other quartets. Though we have already seen that Op. 95 does, in fact, stand at the very threshold of symphonic music, to perform it in any other medium than the one for which it was intended is a violation of the composer's intention, and cannot be justified by precedent. Mahler's action excited a great deal of opposition, but it is interesting to note that his fast friend, Natalie Bauer-Lechner, writing of the event in her diary, finds no word of protest,[1] though she was herself a member of the Soldat-Roeger string quartet and, as such, presumably familiar with the traditions of classical chamber music. It is to her diary, also, that we owe the revelation that Mahler thought one violinist completely insufficient for the Bach violin sonatas.[2] Whatever he had in mind, the remark in itself is interesting insofar as it throws light on the rather standoffish attitude towards chamber music which was characteristic of the times. Perhaps it helps to explain, too, why Mahler, who had written several chamber music works in his youth, destroyed them all[3] (even as Brahms had destroyed his early quartets) and why, though he began by writing songs with simple piano accompaniment, he veered to the orchestral song. The influence of Mahler is probably the explanation for Schoenberg's orchestrations of two Bach chorale preludes and of Brahms' G minor piano quartet—works which seem to be at odds with the rest of his historical development, since his career lies on the path of the upward swing of the cycle of chamber music which began, in the Viennese school at any rate, shortly after the turn of the century.

While, on the one hand, orchestrations were destroying the feeling for the legitimate literature of chamber music (and, to a certain extent, of the piano), on the other hand, piano reductions of orchestral works were invading the concert stage and displacing the pianistic literature. The making of piano reductions of large orchestral works is far more justifiable than the making of orchestral transcriptions, for the piano reduction is a valuable tool for home study. Its place is, however, in the home, and not in the concert-hall. It is quite understandable that Bruckner's symphonies received many performances in the versions for one and two pianos; in the earlier years of the Bruckner movement, orchestral performances were few and far between, and the composer's ardent disciples naturally wished to familiarize a larger public with his work as best they could. On the other hand, it is questionable how much the cause of any composer is served by performing his orchestral works publicly in piano arrangements, no matter how skilful these arrangements may be.

---

[1] Natalie Bauer Lechner, *Erinnerungen an Gustav Mahler*, p. 111.

[2] *Ibid.*, p. 157.

[3] The first movement, and a Scherzo fragment, of a piano quartet (1876) survive. This material was published in 1973 by Musikverlag Hans Sikorski, Hamburg (ed. Peter Ruzicka). See also Dika Newlin, "Gustav Mahler's Piano Quartet in A Minor," *Chord and Discord*, 1963, pp. 180–184.

Chamber music, then, was decidedly being relegated to a secondary place. Neither Liszt nor Wagner found their way to it; Berlioz, though he had indulged in song-writing (a typical romantic manifestation), had written no instrumental chamber music. Every composer is entitled to at least one venture into this field (cf. Verdi's string quartet); however, in the midst of an epoch of musical history the dominating tendencies of which were grandiose rather than intimate, the appearance of a solitary work of chamber music [4] by Bruckner is indeed a matter for wonder, even if it can be accounted for on a practical basis by Hellmesberger's request for a quartet. Bruckner's early songs and piano pieces can be dismissed as the immature works of an apprentice, but it is not so easy to deal with the quintet, which is a product of the composer's maturest art. Commentators on Bruckner have followed three different lines of thought in discussing it. The anti-Bruckner faction views it as an erratic spark struck off by the collision between chamber music and the Wagnerian colossus. The Brucknerites, however, either deny indignantly that the work contains any orchestral elements or, taking the opposite mode of attack, point with pride to its truly symphonic character. It will easily be seen that none of these ways of looking at the problem is logically justifiable. In the first place, given the history of nineteenth-century chamber music in general and Bruckner's background of large-scale orchestral writing in particular, it would not only be surprising, but even a little disconcerting, were we to observe in the quintet a complete absence of all instrumental elements loosely referred to as "orchestral." The argument that such symphonic elements do not exist here is a purely defensive one, and has no historical validity. Were the internal evidence not enough to prove this, we should have only to point to the undisputed fact that Bruckner, asked by Hellmesberger to write a *quartet* for his organization, obliged them with a *quintet*. The addition of an extra instrument to the quartet has always, as we remarked in the case of Mozart, represented a reaching-out of chamber music towards the symphonic sphere. While the chamber work will still retain its intimate character, a certain symphonic element will be incorporated into it. We may observe a broader layout of the thematic material in the first section; we may, too, find, as in Mozart's quintets (particularly the C major quintet), that the fifth instrument, coupled now with its upper and now with its lower partners, causes us to feel at times that more than five instruments are actually participating in this play of alternation.

---

[4] Bruckner did compose a string quartet in C minor in 1862, during his studies with Kitzler. It was first performed by the Koeckert Quartet of Munich on a RIAS, Berlin, broadcast of February 15, 1951. A critical edition by Leopold Nowak appeared in 1955 as part of the *Gesamtausgabe* (see Bibliography).

But if we have established that the addition of another instrument to the string quartet makes demands of sonority on the composer which are greater than those of the string quartet, we will find it unhistorical to praise or discredit Bruckner for using "orchestral elements" in his quintet. The presence of these elements is not at all a matter of praise or blame, but simply part of a historical process which was also functioning in the chamber music of composers far different from Bruckner. The duty of the impartial historian in this case is not to bestow adjectives, but to find where the "orchestral elements" occur, and how they are used.

Looking at the simplest factor of all, the instrumental layout of the piece, we see at once that Bruckner has followed Mozart's example and made a second viola his fifth instrument. As in Mozart's quintets, this immediately opens up innumerable possibilities of enriched instrumental effect; the viola, an instrument of middle range, is far more mobile than a second 'cello would be, since it can be coupled with either the upper or lower parts. Many varied effects are produced by such couplings, but an examination of the score will not introduce us to any novel procedures. There is nothing in all Bruckner's coupling of various parts and systems which does not belong to the very essence of chamber music.

If we want to find truly orchestral elements in the quintet aside from the increased number of possibilities admitted by the presence of a fifth instrument, we shall be well-advised to break the work down into its formal elements, and to find the places which correspond to those parts of the symphony where Bruckner liked to deploy his full orchestral forces. The most obvious places to look will be the portions of the composition in which a dynamic climax is called for, as, for instance, the ends of movements (especially of the first movement and of the finale) and the points at which transitional sections reach the utmost harmonic concentration immediately before the introduction of subordinate themes. Now in Bruckner's quintet we do, in fact, find at these points an instrumental texture which contrasts strikingly with the discreetly spaced writing of other sections. There are passages which, while they are quite playable by the instruments to which they are assigned, certainly suggest symphonic *tutti* in every detail. They do, however, "sound," as anyone who has listened to the quintet may attest, and it would be a mistake to assume that Bruckner was not aware of the character of the sonorities which he employed. This misconception has been far too frequent, even among admirers of Bruckner, as Loewe and Schalk made only too clear when, under the impression that a simple country schoolmaster transplanted to Vienna could have no feeling for the miracle of modern orchestration, they

radically revised his scoring for publication and thus got rid of some
of his most original ideas. With the best will in the world, they
wronged their revered master in exactly the same way that Rimsky-
Korsakoff wronged Moussorgsky when he revised *Boris Godunov;* and
we would be making precisely the same error if we accused Bruckner
of not knowing what a piece of chamber music should sound like. He
must have been well aware that certain passages of his quintet had a
definitely orchestral tinge; but, according to the standards of his time,
there was no reason why he should have thought this wrong. When
many of the most influential composers of the age produced no chamber music at all, when its most distinguished exponent, Brahms, was
the one composer who could have no influence whatsoever on Bruckner, and when Bruckner's own background had never included any
real participation in chamber music and his profession had not en-
tailed any familiarity with its literature, we may be surprised that the
quintet is marred by so few lapses into a truly orchestral speech. But,
when we see such lapses, we will do better to lay the blame where it
really belongs, on the ideals of the neo-German school of Liszt and
Wagner rather than on Bruckner himself.

It is quite in keeping with the spirit of chamber music that Bruckner has laid out the quintet on a perceptibly smaller scale than the
symphonies. This is noticeable in all the movements; the first movement is 273 measures long, the Scherzo 282, the Adagio 173, and the
Finale a mere 197 measures. The brevity of the Finale is all the more
surprising as it is this movement that Bruckner customarily allows to
bear the greatest weight of the symphonic form. It is rather the Adagio
which serves as fulcrum here, for in spite of its comparatively small
number of measures, its extremely slow tempo makes it the longest of
the movements. In his symphonies Bruckner always tended to stress
the Adagio particularly, but never to the extent of making it the focal
point of the symphony. That the Adagio finally coincided with the
Finale, in the Ninth Symphony, is only because Bruckner did not live
long enough to complete the work. It remained for Mahler to elevate
the coincidence of Adagio and Finale to a constructive principle, in
his Third and Ninth Symphonies.

As the movements of the quintet are smaller in dimensions than
those of the symphonies, we do not find so many extensions of the
classical formal boundaries here as in the symphonies. In particular,
there is not room for nearly so much "padding"; after all, the comparative paucity of such instrumentally inspired non-functional ma-

terial is a characteristic of chamber music, one of the most important stylistic traits setting it apart from truly symphonic music.

Considering Bruckner's background, ideals, and environment, and the age in which he lived, it is indeed remarkable that, in spite of the occasional use of orchestral idiom, he was able to create a work which is, on the whole, comparatively sound in its use of the chamber-music style. It is ironic that, of all Bruckner's contemporaries, not his beloved Wagner but Brahms, his bitterest rival, should have been the only one capable of such a performance. Nevertheless, chamber music was not really Bruckner's field; and it is in his true element—symphonic composition—that we shall see him next.

CHAPTER VIII

Bruckner the Symphonist

AT LAST, we stand at the threshold of Bruckner's real life-work, his symphonic creation. Many preparatory steps were necessary to reach this point, but we shall find that each of them helped us to gain a better understanding of the problems which we now approach. It will not be our aim here to analyze each of Bruckner's symphonies in all its wealth of formal detail; rather, we shall attempt to make a stylistic abstract of the content of the symphonies, and to determine if any changes take place in Bruckner's concept of symphonic style between the First and Ninth Symphonies.

At the outset, we must guard against a variety of errors. First and foremost, if we wish to gain an accurate idea of Bruckner's musico-formal intentions, we must exercise the greatest care in our selection of musical texts. For about the accurate reading of the symphonies there has raged a battle which would be taken as a matter of course if the music concerned involved abstruse problems of a possibly ambiguous medieval modal notation or of pitchless neumes, but which is well-nigh incomprehensible in connection with the works of a composer who died at the threshold of our century. The whole situation is a confusing one, but out of the welter of prefaces, replies, accusations, and counter-accusations, there seem to emerge the following clear-cut facts:

1. The texts of the symphonies printed during Bruckner's lifetime vary greatly from the texts which a study of the manuscripts establishes as representing his original intent.

2. Bruckner made so many revisions of each symphony that each of the several manuscripts which he may have written for a given work displays a different set of revisions.

3. We know in some cases, and suspect in others, that the changes introduced into the original printed score were not made by Bruckner's own hand. In some instances, these changes were made with his consent (sometimes willing, more often reluctant); in others, it is impossible that he can have had anything to do with them.

The picture presented by these facts is a bewildering one. How is it possible that mangled editions of a composer's work can be published during his lifetime without his protest? If he himself made several different sets of revisions, what justifies us in taking his original conception, rather than the revised version, as the most complete expression of his creative will? If we wish to follow the *Internationale Bruckner-Gesellschaft* party line and maintain that Bruckner made his late revisions under the influence of well-meaning but misguided friends, how shall we determine where outside influence begins and leaves off? If we repudiate the late revisions, is it consistent to accept the so-called "Viennese version" of the First Symphony on equal terms with the original "Linz version," as is done in the first volume of Haas' edition of the complete works, and must we perform the Fourth Symphony with the almost unknown finale of 1878 instead of with the far superior finale of 1880? [1]

To obtain final answers to such questions, we should have to go far afield, even delving into the hinterland of psychology to find an explanation for Bruckner's attitude towards his own works. Though we may not follow those explorations here, we may and must present their end-results; these seem to justify acceptance of the *Urtext* as a basis for research wherever it is available, with due allowance made for the far wider distribution of the old versions. Bruckner's attitude is understandable if we remember his excessive humility caused by his upbringing during one of the most absolutist periods in Austrian history. He was always a little frightened by Vienna, always the provincial in awe of the big city; and when his energetic young friends and admirers managed to convince him that his symphonies would make a better public impression if cuts were introduced, he complied, though not always gladly. (In fact, he finally grew to resent the activities of his most busily revising disciples, the Schalks and Loewe.) From his letters we know that, if cuts proved advisable in performance, he still insisted that the printed scores and parts should remain complete; from the old scores themselves, we know that this wish was not always granted.

When we compare the *Urtext* of a Bruckner symphony with any other printed edition, we suddenly find it necessary to discard certain stock criticisms of Bruckner which are based on the old printed texts but which lose their meaning when confronted with the *Urtext*. There is, for example, the accusation of "lack of formal balance." In most cases this fault must be laid at the door of the editor, not of the composer

[1] For an updated commentary on the complex problem of the Bruckner editions (made even more complex by the Robert Haas *vs.* Leopold Nowak controversy), see Bibliography.

for, in fact, the cuts which occur, admittedly or tacitly, in the old editions are quite sufficient to throw the form off balance. Bruckner's broad expositions and developments urgently require full recapitulations and strongly affirmative codas to give them the proper weight; yet it is precisely in the recapitulation that the most startling cuts usually occur. For instance, let us look at the Finale of the Second Symphony in a typical reprint of the old edition, an Eulenburg miniature score. In the recapitulation we find a cut which, if observed in performances, would eliminate all the recapitulation except the coda.[2] How is formal balance to be achieved under these conditions?

If we analyze the rumor about Bruckner's "Wagnerian orchestration," we shall find that it, too, stems from unfamiliarity with the *Urtexte*. While Bruckner himself liked to contrast woodwinds, strings, and brass in pure groups, somewhat after the fashion of organ-registers, his editors retouched this orchestration to suit the taste of the time, mixing colors and doubling parts in the various choirs so that the whole took on a much more Wagnerian aspect. (This is not to say that Bruckner's orchestra does not owe much to Wagner, particularly in the added mobility and brilliance of the brass choir and in certain technical devices such as the introduction of the main theme under a long string *tremolo*.)

Because of these and other considerations, we shall base our discussion of the symphonies on the *Urtexte* in all instances where they are available. In the Third (Wagner) Symphony the only available orchestral text, as reprinted in the Eulenburg edition, obviously displays inadmissible cuts; for a clearer idea of the form, we must turn to the four-hand piano reduction made by Mahler, which stems from the period when Mahler, a young student, was in direct personal contact with Bruckner, and exhibits an earlier version of the symphony in which the illogical cuts have not yet been made. Finally, for a study of the Seventh Symphony it was necessary to rely entirely on the Eulenburg text, which doubtless contains many deviations from the *Urtext*.[3] It is particularly unfortunate that the *Urtext* of this work should not yet have been made available,[4] for it was the Seventh which first won international fame for Bruckner so that even the Viennese were forced to recognize what a great master they had in their midst.

Once the textual question has been settled (if, indeed, it can ever be satisfactorily settled) we must immediately guard against another pitfall. If we take literally the designation of the first C minor symphony

2 *Eulenburg's Partitur-Ausgabe*, pp. 139–53.
3 In fact, fewer than might be expected.
4 It is now available, of course; see Bibliography.

as "First Symphony," we are, at first, apt to be a little surprised at the maturity and consistency of its style. But to give way to this feeling would be to overlook certain incontrovertible historical facts. In the first place, Bruckner was a mature man of forty-two when he completed the Linz version of the symphony, and the more familiar Vienna version is a product of his sixty-seventh year. In the second place, the so-called "First Symphony" was actually preceded by two other symphonies, as well as by a number of other orchestral pieces in which the late-maturing composer tried his wings; he later (and justifiably) repudiated the two immature symphonies, which are commonly known as the "School Symphony" (F minor) and the "Symphony No. O," or "Nullte" (D minor). The existence of these preparatory essays in symphonic form partially explains the lack of "progress," in the customary sense of the word, between the First and Ninth Symphonies. By the time he arrived at the stage of the First Symphony, Bruckner's mental habits had become fixed, and not even such a great external change as the move to Vienna could affect them seriously. His technique became more skilful but acquired no new elaborations; the spiritual content of his works deepened but remained essentially the same. It would be unfair to call the symphonies "stereotyped," but so persistent are certain stylistic traits in all of them that we cannot deny occasionally feeling that it would be an easy matter to exchange movements, or even individual themes, between them. Though at first we may find this characteristic a defect, it is also possible to think of it as a symptom of a higher unity among the works in question. Bruckner himself lends credence to our view when he deliberately intercalates quotations from one work into another; thus measures 180–185 of the Andante of the Second Symphony are a direct citation from measures 98–103 of the *Benedictus* of the F minor Mass, and a famous passage of the Adagio of the Ninth Symphony (measures 181–184) quotes the *Miserere* of the D minor Mass (measures 100–103 of the *Gloria*). This latter quotation is introduced into the Adagio in especially skilful fashion, for the phrase in question:

is, besides being a quotation from the *Miserere,* an inversion and augmentation of the first four notes of the subordinate theme of the Adagio:

These citations tell us that Bruckner's mind was dominated by religious thought but they also speak to us of that higher unity which was not unfamiliar before Bruckner's time, as Beethoven had already welded his last quartets into one great cyclic form. Richard Wickenhauser, in his book *Anton Bruckner's Symphonien—ihr Werden und Wesen,* has called attention to the "secret bond" uniting all of Bruckner's creation. Many of his parallels represent pure coincidence and can be dismissed as exhibiting similarities no more striking than those normally to be expected in the work of a single composer; but the idea of a certain interrelationship is, nevertheless, plausible.

It is rewarding to glance into the score of the First Symphony and observe how many of those style-characteristics are present which are later to become familiar to us as typical "Brucknerisms." The opening measures already display certain highly distinctive stylistic features. The beginning of the first movement,

consists of two elements: an *ostinato* bass figure *a* and a dotted rhythmic motive *b,* which is the most important constructive particle of the first theme. Though the "theme proper" does not begin till the second measure, we shall first give our attention to that opening measure in which, apparently, nothing happens. For it is this type of beginning which is to become one of the most characteristic earmarks of Bruckner's style. Looking at the openings of the nine symphonies, we invariably find a harmonically static beginning characterized by a *tremolo* or *ostinato* figure over which the theme unfolds itself.

Obviously, such a beginning is a far cry from the succinct opening of the classical symphony *in medias res.* The difference calls for some kind of explanation. Many German writers on Bruckner have followed the lead of August Halm in providing a mystical-philosophical elucidation of the phenomenon. Halm writes:

Before the motive, "that which moves," originates, we experience something like a moment before time, something almost timeless; there, time and events themselves seem to be doled out to us gradually.

For the first time in Bruckner we feel completely the holiness of the fundamental; we think we are inhaling something like the breath of creation, when we are enveloped in the first tones of his Seventh, Ninth, or Fourth Symphonies. We feel it; it is not just a piece of music which begins here, but music itself commences.

The classic composers are able only to lead us into the specific piece of music of the moment; in rare instances, they give us at least a hint of a real musical beginning. They themselves felt this lack from time to time, and then tried to make up for it by means of an introduction.[5]

This conception became widespread, and was popularized in such pictorial language as that of Max Auer:

The beginning of almost [sic] every Bruckner symphony with a soft tremolo or some other characteristic fundamental motion resembles the dawn of a glorious day on the mountaintop, whose gray is ever more brightly underlaid by the first rays of the sun until its glowing countenance arises in all its majestic glory. It is a mighty crescendo with which the thematic structure, always regally proud, with its far-gazing span, raises itself out of nothingness. A mighty "Let it be!" rings forth to us from it.[6]

Auer is careful to lead us out of this wilderness of metaphors by providing a footnote which informs us that "all these pictures are always to be conceived only as symbols, in no way as real pictures; rather, they are intended to signify the psychological happenings within us, an awakening from unconsciousness and darkness to light and clarity."[7] Even with this enlightening explanation, however, we have doubtless begun to feel that such a symbolic, mystical description does not meet the requirements of musicological research, which prefers to deal with accurate style-criticism and established facts. We shall, therefore, be well-advised to turn our attention to a historical explanation of Bruckner's unusual symphonic beginnings.

We must avoid confusing the technique employed in the opening bars of these symphonies with that used in the introduction of the classical symphony. Bruckner himself has given us the clearest indication that they are different when, after the fifty-bar slow introduction to the first movement of the Fifth Symphony (the only symphony in which he uses such an introduction), he still deems it necessary to precede his main theme with four bars of his customary *tremolo*. After such a long introduction, what purpose does the *tremolo* serve? Alfred Orel, whose book *Anton Bruckner; Das Werk—Der Künstler—Die Zeit* deserves a place of honor in Bruckner literature for its unrhetorical tone and analytical approach, has made an interesting suggestion

[5] August Halm, *Die Symphonie Anton Bruckners,* pp. 42–43.
[6] Max Auer, *Anton Bruckner, Sein Leben und Werk,* pp. 423–24.
[7] *Ibid.*

about the function of the *tremolo* accompaniment in Bruckner. Taking note of the extremely rhythmical nature of the greater number of Bruckner's principal themes, he concludes that Bruckner's purpose in using the *tremolo* or *ostinato* type of accompaniment so consistently may have been to set off the emphatic rhythm of the main theme against a background of more neutral tone, so that the hearer's attention would be concentrated on that one theme. Orel's theory has much to recommend it; we shall return to it a little later when we proceed from the study of the thematic accompaniments to that of the principal themes themselves.

Although the *tremolo* and the long orchestral introduction serve different purposes, it is still possible to compare them; for the musical ethos of both belongs, in reality, to another art-form—to the opera. This is true in the technical, as well as in the esthetic, sense. While the slow introduction of the classical symphony can be traced back to the slow-fast form of the Lullian French overture, the Bruckner *tremolo* is born of Wagner's music-dramas; one need only recall the opening of the overture to the *Flying Dutchman:*

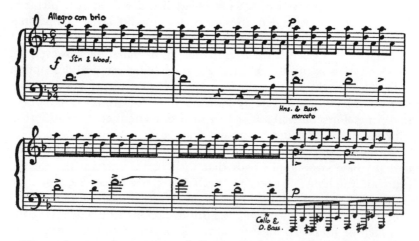

Not only are these two techniques derived from actual operatic practices, but the musical spirit which vivifies them is truly dramatic. The classical introduction, with its grave character which oftentimes verges on foreboding, and its occasional hints at the thematic material of the main body of the symphonic movement, seems literally to speak of things to come, and in this dramatic sense justifies its derivation from the overture. The *tremolo* has been used ever since Monteverdi's day to heighten dramatic tension; Orel's abovementioned suggestion may easily lead us to the conclusion that, in the beginning, Bruckner presents the theme for its own sake (not as a scrap of musical material whose significance will only appear in the course of the symphonic development) and concentrates the attention of the listener upon it, even as in truly dramatic music our attention will be focussed upon the human voice and what the orchestra does will only serve to heighten the total dramatic effect.

At this point it becomes necessary for us to look more closely at the nature of the Brucknerian principal theme. Once again, we may begin by citing the theme of the First Symphony, for we shall find its traits in subsequent works as well:

The periodic structure of this sixteen-measure phrase is quite clear; it consists of an antecedent (a), a consequent (b), and an extension of the consequent which leads to a final flourish somewhat reminiscent of the "Mannheim skyrocket." What interests us more, however, is its character. It still possesses something of the *élan,* the urgency which characterizes the classical symphonic form; the movement is march-like, and the melody, far from being a single *cantabile* flow, is in reality hammered together out of constant repetitions of the rhythmic particle ♪. ♩. Its unfoldment as a complete theme is gradual, however, and does not culminate till the final note.

This technique of slowly evolving the complete theme is one of Bruckner's most characteristic devices. Such a theme as this is far from being a mere imitation of the Wagnerian "endless melody," but represents a synthesis of the Wagnerian melos with the "motto technique" of the classical symphony (as represented by Beethoven's Fifth Symphony—not to be confused with Brahms' different application of the technique in his symphonies). These disparate elements are not always perfectly balanced; sometimes one preponderates, sometimes the other. Thus, the first theme of the Second Symphony, though comparable to that of the First, is already far more outspokenly melodious; individual motivic particles (including a characteristic dotted rhythm) may still be picked out in it, but the cesurae which would indicate a larger periodization are no longer distinct. The third of Bruckner's C minor symphonies, the Eighth, also displays a thematic structure similar to that of the First. In comparison with the Second, the purely melodious element has retreated into the background; a dotted rhythm is, however, still a prominent feature. The cesurae here are so sharply marked that the theme gives an impression of fragmentariness until, looking more closely, we discover that the phrases are carefully graduated so that each one ends on a final note higher than that of the preceding phrase. Thus, through the effect of a climax attained with effort, and by degrees, Bruckner gives his theme ideal unity.

There exists a further category of Brucknerian principal themes which, while taking over certain significant characteristics from the class of themes already described, is still distinct enough to warrant being considered separately. For want of a better name, the themes belonging to this category may be figuratively styled "trumpet themes," since they are without exception enunciated by a brass instrument. The most typical example is the famous theme from the Third (Wagner) Symphony, which inspired Wagner to refer characteristically to its composer as "Bruckner, die Trompete":

A more concise formulation of a basic idea could scarcely be wished for. It is true that this idea immediately receives a continuation in the horn which is in its turn continued in the woodwinds, so that the whole first section of the theme is twenty-six measures long. This method of building on to the original theme with extensions was already observed in the previously discussed themes. The difference is, however, that, whereas in the First, Second, and Eighth Symphonies the true theme was only revealed when we counted up the sum of numerous particles, here the very first measures give us a complete motive to work with. In typical fanfare fashion, this motive centers on the tonic and dominant of its basic tonality, which is to say on the melodic intervals of octave, fifth and fourth. The falling fifth is of particular interest to us, for, as we learned in the chapter on harmony, the harmonic progression which it represents (V–I) is a fundamental or "strong" root-progression in the Sechterian theory—as, indeed, in any tonal harmonic system. That, as a melodic progression, it should appear prominently in some of Bruckner's most important themes only serves to demonstrate once more how deeply ingrained was his harmonic and tonal feeling.

Even better known than the trumpet theme of the Third Symphony is another motive which exhibits the same characteristics, the opening theme of the Fourth ("Romantic") Symphony (see score). The simple motive of the falling and rising fifth has often been compared with the famous theme of Beethoven's Fifth Symphony. Theodor Helm, writing a memorial article on the occasion of Bruckner's death, places the two citations side by side, and suggests that the Bruckner theme is in compactness and pregnancy the equal of Beethoven's. August Halm, however, goes much further, and claims that Bruckner's theme is superior because it contains more developmental possibilities; this statement is in direct line with his idea of Bruckner as the man who, in the field of the symphony, completed and perfected what Beethoven had given us only "imperfectly." It goes without saying that such statements are not deserving of serious consideration; we can appreciate Bruckner's true merits without indulging in such absurd comparisons.

The nature of the "trumpet theme" is preserved intact at the beginning of the Ninth Symphony (see score). This theme, the successive motivic particles of which gradually build up to an overwhelming climax on C flat, is closely related to some of the more purely "melodic" themes of the first category which likewise rely on a "particle" construction. On the other hand, Bruckner's predilection for big intervals, fifths and sixths, in the "trumpet" themes is sometimes also reflected in the themes of the first category which usually deal with smaller intervals. (The Sixth Symphony gives us an example of the interpenetration of the two types.)

We have not yet spoken of the first theme of the Seventh Symphony. That is because it occupies a place apart in Bruckner's creation, for

in it there remains no single trace of the classic symphonic urgency
which is symbolized by dotted rhythms or martial I–V–I fanfares.
Here the ideal unity which held together the motivic particles of the
previously discussed themes is translated into tone, for during the
first nine measures there is not a single pause. This is the very type
of the smooth, broadly flowing "romantic" theme (see score).

One of the most striking ways in which Bruckner's subordinate
themes differ from his principal themes is in the manner of accompaniment. Whereas the principal themes were sharply set off against
a background of neutral *tremolo,* the subordinate themes tend to be
double or even triple themes; that is, they are made up of two or
three concomitant melodies of equal or nearly equal value, and these
melodies are sometimes in double counterpoint. This is not always
true; the two very similar subordinate themes of the first and last
movements of the Second Symphony, for example, are simple melodies
superimposed on an equally simple *pizzicato* accompaniment.

However, to these simple themes are later added countermelodies
which, while they do not exactly attain to the dignity of thematic
development, still have a little melodic life in their own right. The
countermelody is more significant in the subordinate theme of the
first movement of the First Symphony. Note here the prominence of
the melodic interval of the sixth, particularly in comparison with the
two themes just cited:

Examples of this nature can be found in almost every Bruckner
symphony; a special place should be assigned, however, to the famous
"Chorale-Polka" combination which is the subordinate theme of the
Finale of the Third Symphony. Bruckner, once asked what the inner

meaning of this combination was, pointed out to his interlocutor the
contrast between a house which they were just passing, where a dead
man lay in state on his bier, and the sounds of gay music heard not
far away. Thus, he said, in his Third Symphony the "Polka" was supposed to represent the joy of life, while the Chorale pictured life's sorrow. We need not take this explanation too seriously; for Bruckner,
an absolute musician at heart, was sometimes given to inventing programmatic explanations (for his own amusement or his friends' edifi-
cation) which had really nothing to do with the matter in hand. He
used the "double-theme" technique often enough without any such
elaborate program! In any case, here is the musical example (score
reduced to the essential themes):

To conclude our discussion of this thematic type, we shall take note
of two examples—very simple ones, to be sure—wherein double counterpoint plays a part in the conception of the theme. The passages in
question occur in the first movement of the Third Symphony, three
measures after D and three measures after E respectively (Eulenburg
edition). "Double counterpoint" is perhaps too pretentious a name
for so simple an exchange of parts, which belongs to the realm of self-
evident devices of instrumental ensemble polyphony rather than to
that of contrapuntal invention. With no intention of minimizing
Bruckner's skill as contrapuntist, we may sincerely say that many of
his German admirers overshoot the mark when they cite such ele-

mentary devices as a shining example of the Master's unparalleled contrapuntal knowledge.

Bruckner has often been credited with introducing a "third theme" into the exposition of the symphonic sonata-form. This statement must be subjected to much qualification. The codetta section which, following the subordinate theme-group, closes the exposition of the classical sonata, is quite likely to have an independent theme or motive of its own, though that is not always the case. Such an independent codetta theme may be seen in the first movement of Beethoven's sonata Op. 14, no. 2:

(D Major)

It is true that this little theme is not greatly extended. This gives us the clue to a more correct formulation of our statement about Bruckner's codetta themes. We may assert that, here as elsewhere, Bruckner did not invent a new symphonic conception but rather expanded the classical frame. It goes without saying, however, that the ideas he expressed always became completely his own by reason of the force of his artistic personality and will, whatever their historical sources may have been. Thus, the *tutti unisono,* which was originally a stock operatic gesture and as such passed into the classical symphony, in Bruckner's hands becomes the hallmark of the codetta theme, which is of energetic, forceful character, and which (again following classical tradition) is likely to be related to the principal theme. A typical example of such a codetta theme occurs in the first movement of his Fifth Symphony, measures 199 ff. After introducing a powerful motive of this kind, Bruckner likes to close his exposition in a thoughtful, meditative mood, for contrast. Illustrations of this technique may be seen in measures 173–192 of the first movement of the Fourth Symphony, and in measures 196–210 of the Finale of the Fifth (immediately after the famous chorale theme which in its turn follows upon one of the abovementioned unison passages).

We shall reserve our discussion of the development and recapitulation sections until we examine the conception of the finale in Bruckner. Let us turn now to the interior movements of the symphony, the Adagio and Scherzo. The order is immaterial, for Bruckner arranges them in both of the possible ways; however, we shall begin with the Adagio, since it comes first in the majority of the symphonies.

From examining first movements we have seen that it is fairly easy to generalize about Bruckner's symphonies, and the Adagios will not cause us to change our opinion. All of them are laid out on broad lines, are of an extremely expressive character, and exhibit moods ranging from pious devotion (Second Symphony) to passionate longing succeeded by resignation (Ninth Symphony). It is especially the Adagios of the Eighth and Ninth Symphonies which bear comparison with the best of Beethoven's late slow movements—were, indeed, strongly influenced by them—and which won for Bruckner the name of *Adagio-Komponist.* The title is not misplaced, for Bruckner's pronounced lyrical gifts found their fullest expression in the slow movements, and in that framework appealed more readily to those musicians who found them disconcerting in the "sonata form." His feeling for tragic expression, too, finds its most satisfactory outlet here; at the beginning of the Andante of the Fourth Symphony, for example, and also in the opening measures of the second movement of the Fifth Symphony, which depicts a mood of extreme desolation.

In connection with what we have already said about Bruckner's methods of theme-building, it may be noted that he introduces both of these Adagio themes in a way which corresponds very closely to the manner of introduction of the principal themes of his first movement. Instead of the *tremolo,* which Bruckner was the first to use so consistently as a means of expressing "symphonic" agitation, we have, in each of these cases, an *ostinato* figure which deadens movement instead of releasing it; this *ostinato,* however, sets off the melodic and rhythmic features of the theme superimposed on it, just as we have seen that the *tremolo* does. The four-measure *ostinato* phrase which begins the Adagio of the Fifth Symphony is unusually long; Bruckner generally prefers two-measure *ostinato* phrases such as we see in the introduction to the first movement of the Fourth Symphony and also in the opening of its Adagio.

We have already said that it is difficult to assume "progress" from the First to the Ninth Symphonies. The beginning of the Adagio of the Ninth Symphony, in which the tonality is not definitely established till the seventh measure, seems to indicate a gradual loosening of tonal bonds; but a parallel passage from the beginning of the slow movement of the First Symphony already exhibits similar tendencies. Surely such examples must support our contention that Bruckner's nine mature symphonies represent a homogeneous style-group in which no great forward leaps occur. We do, however, observe that certain changes set in during the interim between the composition of the First

and Second Symphonies. To understand these we must once again re-
fresh our memories of Bruckner's personal psychology and of conditions in the Vienna to which he came after the composition of the
First Symphony. He did not attain true freedom as a composer until
he had put behind him his period of apprenticeship with Otto Kitzler,
the period during which he produced the rather dreary F minor Symphony. Only then could he let his imagination take flight. And this
imagination, which had waited forty-odd years for its final release,
found expression in the First Symphony, which Bruckner himself always considered one of his most radical works. Fondly, he used to
refer to it as " 's kecke Beserl," a favorite expression of Viennese students designating a bold young girl. But what happened between the
composition of this work and that of the Second Symphony? Bruckner
came to Vienna, was thoroughly overawed by the conditions there,
and, in the face of the prevailing conservatism, began to worry lest
his beloved *Beserl* should turn out to be a little too forward for Viennese tastes. That is why we feel a marked return to a more conservative manner in the Second Symphony. When the chaste and simple
harmony of the opening bars of the Adagio is compared with the tor-
tuous paths followed in the Adagio of the First Symphony the difference will immediately be felt. After the Second Symphony, Bruckner
slowly finds his way back to a transfiguration and clarification of the
earlier, more "advanced" style. The final results of this process are
apparent in the Adagio of the Ninth Symphony.

Strangely enough, it is possible to trace a definite line of progress
in Bruckner's scherzos from the First to the Ninth. As a class, these
scherzos are among his most successful compositions—successful in the
sense of popularity, that is. While the public enjoyed them for their
Beethovenian humor expressed in heavy-footed rhythms and melodies
typically Upper-Austrian in their turn, the more conservatively inclined musicians preferred them to Bruckner's larger movements because, being smaller in scope, they offered less room for harmonic and
motivic fantasies of the type condemned by followers of both the
classicistic and the modern camp.

The character of the typical Bruckner scherzo is immediately established in the third movement of the First Symphony, with its heavy
accompaniment in accented quarter-note chords and its folk-dance-
like melody:

and Bruckner, having found this vein, does not abandon it. The quint-
essence of the type of music represented by the Scherzo of the First
Symphony is to be found in the well-known "Hunting Scherzo" of the
Fourth. It is curious that this piece should have been an afterthought
in the symphonic plan, for Bruckner had originally composed another
scherzo for this symphony. But perhaps this fact is reflected in the nature of the composition; unlike most of Bruckner's symphonic movements, it stands apart from the other movements of the symphony to
a sufficient extent that one feels it would lose nothing in being performed as an independent piece of music. In itself, it is a genre picture
of a most charming kind. The Scherzo proper, with its gay horn fanfares in E flat, clearly intended to portray a band of hunters galloping
through the forest, while the Trio in G flat, as described by Bruckner
himself, represents a moment of rest, when the hunters dismount from
their horses and stop to take refreshment (to the accompaniment of
typically Austrian dance-strains). This is as close as Bruckner ever
comes to writing real program-music, and the program is plainly of a
rather naive and obvious kind, far removed from the mystical connotations which certain over-enthusiastic Bruckner disciples wished to
give their master's music.

After the culmination of what we may call the "Austrian dance
type" of scherzo has been reached in the Fourth Symphony, Bruckner
begins an interesting period of experimentation with the scherzo. He
does not abandon the motives of the Austrian dance, but combines
them with other elements and in various ways sublimates them. The
first hint we have that Bruckner is seeking a new function for the
scherzo comes in the Fifth Symphony. We have already mentioned the
accompaniment

at the beginning of the Adagio. For the Scherzo, Bruckner transforms
his slow six beats into quick 3/4 time—

and superimposes a new melody:

Here Bruckner enriches the symphonic concept with a technical device familiar to us not from the classical symphony, but from the old *Tanz* and *Nachtanz* (or Pavane and Gaillard) of the sixteenth century. Bruckner does not carry through his use of this device to the point of changing from duple to triple rhythm or vice versa; however, his use of a musical technique which suggests the early baroque rather than the classic period is of particular interest when compared with Brahms' similar employment of a baroque form, the passacaglia, for the Finale of his Fourth Symphony. All such phenomena are inseparable from the whole mixture of tradition and revolution which is the very essence of Viennese musical history.

Continuing his experimentation, Bruckner next tries, in the Scherzo of the Sixth Symphony, the effect of a lighter texture. In spite of the clearly marked rhythm, we are here a long way from the *marcato* beginning of the Scherzo of the First Symphony, and the greater subtlety of orchestral means and motivic combinations shows us that we are dealing with a definite stage of progress on Bruckner's part. He does not, however, confine this progress to a steady development in one, and only one, new style. Thus, in the Seventh Symphony, he introduces into the Scherzo a bold trumpet theme similar to those which he is so fond of using as main themes for his first movements:

but it must not be forgotten that the Scherzo of the Third Symphony already displays a trumpet-like motive which is clearly derived from the main theme of the first movement. As for the Scherzo of the Eighth Symphony (the sublimation of the Austrian dance-spirit, embodied in a symbolical-mythological figure, *Deutscher Michel*, who is the personification of the hard-working, hard-headed Austrian peasant), it exhibits no stylistic innovations—unless one wishes to count as such Bruckner's first use of the harp, an instrument of which he was never fond.

It is in the Scherzo of the Ninth Symphony that we see vividly the tremendous progress made by Bruckner since the days of the First Symphony. He has not belied his nature in this last expression of his symphonic character; one need only look at the passage beginning at measure 43 (one measure before letter A in the *Urtext*) with its heavy unisons of brass and strings, to realize that the spirit of the Austrian dance still lives intact in this music. But something new has been added to it, not only in an instrumental but likewise in a harmonic sense. The single chord on which the first twelve measures are built has invited as much discussion as anything in  Bruckner's entire work. It was the eminent theoretician Heinrích Schenker, at one time a pupil of Bruckner though never a very great admirer of his master, who found the logical explanation for this harmony when he called it a diminished seventh chord in which the expected G natural had been altered to G sharp. The harmonic structure would then be

This analysis is borne out by the resolution of the chord, which proceeds to a D major sixth-chord in the thirteenth measure, just as an unaltered diminished seventh chord naturally would. The much-debated harmony occurs in an even more interesting form one measure after letter A, where it is superimposed upon a pedal-point on D.

Turning our attention to the orchestration of this last Scherzo, we discover in it a lightening of texture. There was a tendency in this direction as early as the Sixth Symphony, but it is in this Scherzo, and especially in the Trio, that the new style reaches fulfillment. The technical means by which Bruckner obtains the desired light touch are simple. For the first forty-one measures, all of the stringed instruments are played *pizzicato* and are supported, at first, only by soft sustained harmony in the oboes and clarinets; when the trumpet is added in the thirteenth measure, it enters inconspicuously, in triple piano. Even when a gradual crescendo begins in the twenty-third measure, no more instruments are added, and as a result of this judicious economy the sudden change to *pesante* and *fortissimo* (*tutti*) at letter A comes as a stunning surprise. The Trio, which is to be played at a slightly faster tempo than the Scherzo, displays Bruckner's mastery of varied orchestral techniques in even more striking fashion, and is highly to be recommended to those who think of Bruckner's musical imagination only in terms of the trumpet theme of the "Wagner" symphony. The beginning of the Trio, with the staccato accompaniment in the violin, viola, and 'cello softly supported by the double-bass *pizzicato*, and the *spiccato* melody in the first violin, ornamented with a light figure in the first flute, shows us a Bruckner whose existence we would not have suspected in the Scherzo of the First Symphony. Some commentators on this work have compared it to the *Queen Mab* Scherzo of Berlioz, and, in truth, the lightness of Bruckner's texture brings this composition closer to the popular ideal of

"French music" than anything else he ever wrote—though it should be needless to reiterate that his scherzos never wandered too far afield from the Austrian dance.

We have spoken of the "gradual progress" in Bruckner's scherzo style. Are we justified in calling the change which occurs between the First and Ninth Symphonies "progress"? The increase in harmonic subtlety and complication may certainly be so termed in the historical sense at least. Whether or not the changes in orchestral conception which we have mentioned can rightly be considered progressive is not so easily determined, especially since the lightened orchestration in the Scherzo of the Ninth does not involve soloistic treatment. But it does convince us that Bruckner, even in his last years, possessed greater versatility than he is often credited with, and it is important for us to know this in making a fair estimate of his merits as a symphonist.

We now approach the weightiest problem in Bruckner's symphonic creation, his treatment of the finale. In our discussion of this problem, we shall examine only those symphonies in which the characteristic principle of cyclic form has been carried to its final consequences. All of Bruckner's symphonies display interrelationship of movements to some degree; therefore, we are justified in assuming that the ideal fulfillment of this relationship was one of the goals of Bruckner the symphonist. We can safely say that Bruckner's ideal finale is one in which all that has happened in the preceding movements is synthesized. Such a synthesis is symbolized in the citation of themes from previous sections of the work; so we shall study those finales in which such citations are most numerous, for these will surely furnish most significant examples of Bruckner's ideal of cyclic form.

Let us look at the introduction to the Finale of the Fifth Symphony. Even its graphic appearance at once suggests some interesting comparisons, for the basic idea of this passage is plainly derived from the beginning of the Finale of Beethoven's Ninth Symphony, wherein one theme after another (drawn from the preceding movements) is tried and then discarded before the entrance of the main theme of the movement. Bruckner's admiration for this work was so boundless that we are only surprised that he did not copy this particular formal device more often. Though nearly all the symphonies display cyclic tendencies of one sort or another, this is the only finale wherein the technique of Beethoven's Ninth has been taken over literally. Bruckner has, in fact, copied the letter, rather than the spirit, of the music which inspired him here; his brief references to preceding movements, all of which are compressed into the space of twenty-nine bars, are rather schematic, and fall short of Beethoven's dramatic effect. Beethoven prepares the entrance of his main theme through ninety measures, and thus resolves the problem of this type of introduction more successfully than Bruckner has done. Since Bruckner and Franck—both mystics out of touch with their time—have been so frequently compared by musical commentators, it is not without interest to note that Franck, likewise a devotee of cyclic form, also copied the introduction to the Finale of Beethoven's Ninth much as Bruckner did, in the Finale of his string quartet.

With the beginning of the real body of Bruckner's Finale, a three-measure fugal theme of intense rhythmical vigor is set forth (measure 31) in the 'celli and basses. Already we divine that Bruckner is planning a movement wherein polyphony and homophony will be blended into that "instrumental ensemble polyphony" which was the triumph of the classical Viennese school whose descendant Bruckner is. In fact, this particular movement can be compared in this sense only to such consummate elaborations of the principle as the Finales of Mozart's *Jupiter* Symphony and K.387 string quartet. Bruckner, finished master of counterpoint, reared in the stern school of a Sechter, has here reached the point of being able to take up or to leave his fugal texture at will without incurring the charge of amateurish and superfluous fugato-writing which has so often and so justly been brought against hosts of composers from Carl Heinrich Graun to the present day. Bruckner, master of the fugue in the Finale of his Fifth Symphony; Brahms, master of the passacaglia in the Finale of his Fourth—they belong side by side, and nothing will ever bring us closer to the realization that we must value not Brahms *or* Bruckner, but Brahms *and* Bruckner, than the comparison and contrast between these two works.

The mixture of homophonic and polyphonic elements is clearly audible when the continuing fugal exposition in the strings is set off by blocks of accented chords in the winds, brass, and kettledrums; later (measure 67) the fugue retires in favor of the lyrical subordinate theme, wherein "counterpoint" is confined to free dialogue-like imitation between the first violin and the melody-bearing second violin. Following a broad exposition of this material, there appears the usual Bruckner "third theme," a powerful unison motive which is related to the first theme through its most characteristic interval, a descending octave. All of this thematic work differs in no way (except in the fugal exposition) from what we customarily find in Bruckner's first movements. The "chorale" theme, intoned ponderously by the brasses at measure 175, is in no way surprising, for Bruckner often likes to use a chorale-like motive as a contrast to his "third theme." The *pianissimo* ending of the exposition is also typical of what we have already seen.

Now, however, we are to be introduced to something which we have not previously studied—Bruckner's art of development, complicated in this instance by the demands of the cyclic form and the necessity of fugal elaboration. After a brief passage of "preludizing" on the chorale motive (I to K in the *Urtext*) a new fugal exposition begins, this time using the chorale motive as its theme. Once more, the actual fugal exposition takes place in the strings while the winds add free figuration, and later double the strings at important thematic entrances. The inversion of the chorale theme appears immediately before the fugal texture subsides during six bars of pedal-point on F. Throughout these six bars, the rhythm of the first theme is heard in the 'celli, and may lead us to suppose that the recapitulation is being prepared; the harmonic character of the passage also helps to substantiate this impression. Bruckner, however, is as yet far from the recapitulation. That he returns to the tonic here, in the middle of a development section where modulatory harmony is expected, may surprise ùs, and we must seek for an explanation. Perhaps we should accept it as an indication that the fugal, contrapuntal element was of more importance to Bruckner in this movement than was the harmonic, symphonic element. In any case, there now begins a double fugue which must surely be accounted one of the finest passages in Bruckner's *oeuvre*. The two themes (the main theme of the movement and the "chorale theme") are carried forward relentlessly in all parts, and Bruckner's fluent counterpoint never flags; nor does he fail to exploit the possibilities inherent in the inversion of both themes. By the time the F major pedal-point is reached (measure 363) we are in the presence of a fugue which recalls the contrapuntal mastery of the great baroque composers.

At measure 374 sonata-form reasserts its rights in the recapitulation; it is combined with the chorale theme, which we have already learned to know as the counterpoint of the main theme, played *fortissimo* in the brass section. As most of the possibilities of this combination were already exploited in the development, the recapitulation of the first theme is of token length. After only twenty-four measures we are reintroduced to the subordinate theme, which had not been used at all in the development. Bruckner shows fine harmonic sense when he eschews the customary recapitulation of the subordinate theme in the tonic, preferring instead to state it in the key of the dominant, F major, as a welcome contrast to the unusual amount of pure tonic harmony in the development. (In the first section, this theme was stated in D flat, the lowered third degree of B flat major.)

After a full-length recapitulation of the lyrical subordinate theme, the martial "third theme" makes its appearance in the tonic at measure 460. And now, for the first time since the noteworthy introduction, the force of the cyclic form begins to assert itself. Bars 462–63 contain a quotation from the main theme of the first movement, set forth in the woodwinds. A little phrase

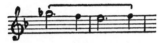

(except for the slightly altered rhythm, an exact transposition of the Second Symphony theme:)

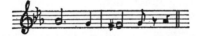

serves as a counterpoint to the imitative repetition of this main theme in horns and trumpets; it is also accompanied by thematic material belonging to the Finale alone—the scale-figure of the "third theme" in the violins and violas, and the rhythm of the principal theme in horns, trombones, and kettledrums. The entire coda section is built up on such combinations as these. Bruckner no longer resorts to fugal treatment but takes advantage of every combinational possibility, and crowns the climax (measures 583 ff.) with the "chorale" in augmentation.

In spite of its great length (635 measures) this Finale does not fall apart from lack of structural relationships. The homophonic and polyphonic elements (fugal texture and symphonic form) have been blended with a sure hand, and, with the exception of the curiously unconvincing introduction, the cyclic form is well integrated. It may fairly be said that the Finale of the Fifth Symphony represents the summit of Bruckner's symphonic composition up to that time—in fact, perhaps of all his work, for never again did he crown a symphony with a gigantic double fugue. Even so, Beethoven had created, in his Fifth Symphony, what was probably (in spite of the great symphonies that followed) his most intense symphonic work.

Bruckner's handling of cyclic form when contrapuntal elements are not involved may most profitably be studied in the Finale of the Eighth Symphony. As this composition differs in significant respects from the Finale of the Fifth (though in still other ways the two movements are worthy counterparts) it, too, deserves detailed analysis.

We immediately observe that Bruckner has abandoned the cyclic introduction as a useless appendage, preferring to introduce cyclic elements into the coda in a more organic manner. The exposition proceeds along fairly conventional Brucknerian lines. A bold opening "trumpet theme," which, interestingly enough, does not assert the tonic C minor positively till its thirty-first measure, is developed through sixty-seven measures. The characteristic rhythm of the accompaniment remains unchanged throughout the theme; this sort of rhythmic pedal-point, frequent in Bruckner, also reminds us strongly of Schubert. In the sixty-eighth measure there is one of Bruckner's typical general pauses, followed by a double subordinate theme which is introduced without previous transition or modulation. The unison "third theme" appears in measure 135 and is enriched with chorale-like episodes (the basic motivic material of which is derived from the seventh through tenth measures of the subordinate theme) as well as with varied restatements of the initial "trumpet theme."

The formal construction of the development section may be schematically outlined as follows (according to the *Urtext* edition):

Letters S–U (measures 273–305)—rhythmical variants of measures 75–78 of the subordinate theme.

Letters U–V—inversion of the third theme (letter I).

Letters V–Z—combination of first and third themes.

Letters Z–Aa—first theme treated imitatively to the accompaniment of quarter-note triplets in the winds and horns.

Letters Aa–Ee—first theme accompanied by rhythmical variant of third theme. Gradual retransition to

Ee—Recapitulation.

This brief survey is sufficient to show that the development is thematically dominated by the first, or "trumpet," theme. Nevertheless, Bruckner treats this very theme at great length in the recapitulation, devoting to it a full 110 measures as compared to the 68 which it occupies in the exposition. In all this long passage, however, Bruckner never once recapitulates the first theme in its "tonic form" as it was first stated in measures 31–39. This suggests that Bruckner may have intended this portion of the recapitulation to be an organic continuation of the development, a supposition which is strengthened by the fact that the beginning of the recapitulation is joined to the end of the development without pause.

Curiously, the recapitulation of the subordinate theme occurs in the same key—the sixth degree (A flat)—in which it appeared in the exposition. The reason for this seems clear when we recall that the development contained no allusions to the motivic contents of this theme; thus, the repetition in the identical key cannot have an effect of monotony. In any case, by the time the "third theme" is reached Bruckner has returned to the expected tonic. A thirty-measure pedal-point on the dominant leads to the final coda, and to the consumma-tion of the cyclic form. At measure 717 the Scherzo theme, "Deutscher Michel," appears in augmentation in the four horns in unison; at measure 725, it appears in imitation at the half-measure, also in the horns. It is not until measure 735 that the combination of the main themes is introduced; the scherzo theme is played in the flutes, clari-nets, and first trumpet, the theme of the first movement in the bas-soons, fourth horn, trombones, 'celli and basses, and the theme of the Adagio in the first and second horns. This combination has often been praised as a masterpiece of contrapuntal ingenuity. Such claims are exaggerated, for the combination of three themes all of which are centered about the tonic triad presents no great problems, and it is to be noted that the main theme of the first movement is not even quoted in its original form, being remodelled into the tonic-triad pat-tern. However, a strictly contrapuntal treatment of the combination is hardly necessary in a movement which, in contrast to the Finale of the Fifth Symphony, is definitely constructed along symphonic rather than fugal lines.

Having now studied two distinct types of Bruckner finales, we must still discuss one more "finale problem"—that of the Ninth Symphony. Although we have already made some remarks on this subject, it will be advisable to recapitulate them here, with certain additions, for the sake of completeness and clarity.

The case of the Ninth Symphony must not be likened to the case of Schubert's *Unfinished* Symphony. In the latter instance, Schubert actually began to write a third movement, but was probably deterred by the realization that the two movements which he had already com-posed were complete in themselves. Bruckner, on the other hand, had already finished three movements of his symphony and was only pre-vented from completing the Finale by his serious illness. When he realized that he probably would not live, he is said to have requested the performance of the *Te Deum* in place of the unfinished Finale. But we possess Bruckner's sketches for the Finale,[8] and the extent to which he carried them out indicates that he would not have wished the *Te Deum* to be performed in place of the Finale unless it was unavoidable. The fact that he wrote "Te Deum" over some sketches the motivic material of which strongly resembles the accompaniment figure of the opening *Te Deum* chorus does not necessarily prove that he intended these sketches to serve as a transition to the *Te Deum;* the words were probably an expression of devotion, like his touchingly naïve dedication of the Ninth Symphony to "dem lieben Gott." Besides, this particular motive occurs very frequently in Bruckner's works, not in the *Te Deum* alone. The conclusion to be drawn from these facts is plain, and in stating it we shall also be making a most necessary summary of Bruckner's contribution as symphonist. He was not interested in extending the symphonic field by introducing vocal elements, though he would have been no innovator in this respect, but would merely have been following in the footsteps of Beethoven as interpreted by Wagner. It was not his concern to build new symphonic worlds as Mahler did; yet his attitude towards form was not the severely classical one of a Brahms, and despite his many conservative tendencies it was he who was selected to bear the banner of the ultra-modernists. Both Brahms and Bruckner stem from Beethoven. But there never could have been a Brahms without Schumann and Mendelssohn, and without Schubert there could never have been a Bruckner. In Brahms, we find the synthesis of North-German and Austrian musical tendencies; in Bruckner, the chief link between the Viennese classicists and their modern counterparts. Bruckner reinterpreted the spirit of Beethoven in the musical language of his time; now it was up to his successors to do so in the language of theirs. Here was a task fit for Bruckner's greatest immediate successor, Gustav Mahler.

[8] Reprinted by Alfred Orel in V. 9 of the *Gesamtausgabe*.

BOOK TWO

MAHLER

CHAPTER I

Mahler, Bruckner, and Brahms

THE VIOLENT partisanship which seems to characterize all discussions of the controversial "neo-Viennese" composers has not failed to enter into the consideration of whether or not Mahler was a true Bruckner disciple. Some tend to link Mahler and Bruckner rather too closely; this tendency is exemplified by the Bruckner Society of America, which propagandized the work of the two composers with little, if any, discrimination between them.[1] Others vigorously deny that Mahler had any real comprehension of Bruckner's work, citing in proof of their theory his "cut" performance of Bruckner's Sixth Symphony in Vienna, and his failure to subscribe to the fund for the erection of Tilgner's Bruckner monument (for which he gave the excuse that he did not want his name to appear on the same subscription list as the names of those who had not cared for Bruckner in his lifetime but made a great fuss over him after he was dead). Naturally, this tendency was most extreme among the admirers of Bruckner in Hitler's Germany, who made due obeisance to the humble disciple of Wagner but could not tolerate Mahler, the Jew.

Actually the truth of the matter lies somewhere between the two points of view just expressed. Ernst Křenek, although perhaps too much inclined to see the relationship between Bruckner and Mahler as a completely idyllic one, has yet given us an interesting appraisal of the similarities and differences in their musical thought, in the following passage:

Both composers have in common . . . the propensity for the monumental simplicity of the fundamental themes, the sense of the magnitude of gesture. . . . To Bruckner, the Catholic of age-old tradition, his faith was unproblematical, like the air he breathed. To Mahler, who later underwent religious conversion, relation to the Supreme Being was a matter of endless concern and ever-renewed discussion. The actual sphere of common interest for Bruckner and Mahler was undoubtedly their admiration for Wagner. Bruckner had enough confidence in his young friend to entrust him with the preparation of the piano arrangement of his Third Symphony which he had dedicated to

---

[1] Later, it included the name of Mahler in its official title.

the master of Bayreuth. [N.B. We have already seen that this reduction represents a more genuine version of Bruckner's original thought than the later
"cut" version.] Mahler acknowledged the significance of his intercourse with
the elder composer in a beautiful statement answering the moot question as to
whether he should be considered Bruckner's disciple. He also manifested his
esteem for Bruckner actively as soon as he could, by including Bruckner's compositions in the programs of his concerts.[2]

Křenek has shown his understanding of the importance of the association between Mahler and Bruckner by devoting a whole chapter
to this question. But, though he tells how Mahler, after two years in
the Conservatory of the *Gesellschaft der Musikfreunde,* came to the
University of Vienna, where Bruckner was lector in 1877, and permits
himself to wonder "with what feelings the elder musician, wrestling
with ever unconquerable symphonic difficulties, looked upon the nervous, talkative Jewish boy from Bohemia,"[3] he has not adduced certain original sources which would contribute materially to our knowledge of the subject. For example, there is a letter written by Mahler
to Bruckner on the sixteenth of April, 1892, on the occasion of performing his *Te Deum* in Hamburg:

Honored Master and Friend!
    At last I am so fortunate as to be able to write you that I have performed
a work of yours. Yesterday (Good Friday) I conducted your splendid and
powerful *Te Deum.* Not only the whole public, but also the performers were
most deeply moved by the mighty architecture and the truly noble ideas, and
at the end of the performance I experienced what I consider the greatest
possible triumph of a work; the public remained silently seated, without even
so much as moving, and it was not until the conductor and the performers had
left their places that the storm of applause broke loose.
    You would have been happy about the performance. I have seldom seen a
group of performers work with such enthusiasm as yesterday. The reviews, on
account of the holidays, will not appear for several days; I shall not fail to
send them to you.—"Bruckner" has now made his triumphal entrance into
Hamburg. I squeeze your hand most heartily, honored friend, and I am, in the
true sense of the word, *your*

Gustav Mahler.
Anna Street, 10/III.[4]

A letter written to Bruckner by his admirer Wilhelm Zinne describes
the same occasion glowingly and affords a check on the sincerity of
Mahler's own words.

Honored Herr Professor!
    On Good Friday your forceful *Te Deum* was performed for the first time

[2] Bruno Walter and Ernst Křenek, *Gustav Mahler,* pp. 164–65.
[3] *Ibid.,* p. 162.
[4] Anton Bruckner, *Gesammelte Briefe,* II, 329–30.

here in Hamburg, in the City Theater under Kapellmeister Mahler's inspired leadership. . . . As I found out from personal association with Mahler, he is a true admirer of your works. Besides, a pupil of yours rehearsed the chorus for this performance—Herr William Sichal, chorus-master at the City Theater, and known in Vienna as one of the best students of piano. In any case, he went about his task with enthusiasm and conviction. While Mozart's *Requiem* (doubtless because it was presented with nervous haste) did not make any very great impression, your work was positively enkindling, particularly because of its final chorus, moving with irresistible force.

The great applause was spontaneous and hearty, but for that very reason all the more pleasing to those who already admired and knew the work.[5]

When Mahler expressed himself in the most intimate circle of his family, however, he was likely to give vent to feelings quite different from those which we have observed in these letters. Citations from letters written to his wife in 1904 may surprise us with their somewhat slighting treatment of both Brahms and Bruckner, composers whom we are accustomed to think of Mahler as admiring. In an undated letter he writes, for example,

I have now gone through all of Brahms, more or less. Well, I must say that he turns out to be a measly little fellow, rather narrow-chested to boot. My God, when such a tempest from the lungs of *Richard Wagner* rushed by him! Of course Brahms had to be economical, in all his poverty, in order to survive! Not that I want to tread on his toes, you know. But where he falls down most— you'll be amazed when I tell you—*that's in his so-called development sections!* It is rare indeed that he knows what to do with his themes (often very fine ones). Anyway, that art was mastered by Beethoven and Wagner alone.[6]

And in the next letter he says, "After going through all of Brahms, I went back to Bruckner again. Strange mediocre men. The former was a bit 'overcooked,' but the latter hasn't been put in the oven yet. Now I stick with Beethoven. Only *he* and *Richard* exist—otherwise, there's nothing! Mark it well!" [7]

These opinions contrast strangely with the picture we had formed of Mahler as a sincere admirer and disciple (if not pupil) of Bruckner; yet there is no cause for accusing Mahler of insincerity, inconsistency, or double-dealing. In the years which had elapsed since the writing of the letter to Bruckner—years during which Brahms and Bruckner had both died—Mahler had matured artistically, and had developed a musical language which, while it owed something to both these composers, was personal and independent. Now, a master in his own right, and no longer bound to the older generation by ties of living friend-

[5] *Ibid.*, II, 387–88.
[6] Alma Mahler, *Gustav Mahler: Erinnerungen und Briefe*, p. 302.
[7] *Ibid.*, p. 303.

ship, he could afford to speak freely of the weaknesses of Brahms or of Bruckner, without sacrificing his essential respect for them.

In connection with the subject of Mahler's personal relationship with Bruckner, a word about his relations with Brahms seems in order. In his personal life, Mahler demonstrated admirably the essential futility of the Brahms-Bruckner controversy, which had once seemed a matter of such tremendous importance to the proponents of both sides, by keeping on good terms with both composers. Brahms may not have been entirely convinced of the ultimate value of Mahler's compositions, with their Wagnerian undertones; it is significant that he and Hanslick headed the jury for the Beethoven Prize which rejected Mahler's earliest preserved work, *Das klagende Lied*.[8] He did, however, admire Mahler's capacities as conductor. The story is told of how Brahms, invited to a performance of *Don Giovanni* in Budapest, grumbled all the way to the opera-house that no one could ever conduct that particular work to suit him. But after the first act he was in ecstasy, exclaiming to all who would listen, "That's the right *Don Giovanni* for me! This man really knows what he's doing!" The conductor so highly honored was Mahler.

Richard Specht has left us an entertaining description of the last meeting between Brahms and Mahler, which illustrates beautifully the ever-present conflict between older and younger generations, and helps to explain the somewhat petulant tone of Mahler's abovementioned remarks about Brahms. He says:

Gustav Mahler visited Brahms in that last summer [1896—Ischl] and they had a . . . conversation during a walk on the banks of the Traun. Brahms again spoke of the decline and fall of music, but Mahler suddenly took his arm and pointed down to the water with his other hand, exclaiming,—"Just look, doctor, just look!"—"What is it?" Brahms asked. "Don't you see, there goes the last wave!" It was a good symbol for the eternal movement in life and in art, which knows of no cessation. But I seem to remember that it was Brahms who had the last word, thus:—"That is all very fine, but perhaps what matters is whether the wave goes into the sea or into a morass."[9]

There can be no doubt that Mahler had a real appreciation of the artistry of Brahms in spite of their disagreements. Walter says, though without quoting any specific statement, "He admired with all his heart the *Haydn Variations* of Brahms and was fond of explaining what a high conception of the idea of variation Brahms had shown in that composition."[10] This opinion is of particular interest, for the *Haydn*

---

[8] Walter and Křenek, *op. cit.*, p. 167.

[9] Richard Specht, *Johannes Brahms*, pp. 352–53.

[10] Walter and Křenek, *op. cit.*, p. 103.

Variations is one of Brahms' most formalistic works, replete with the North-German spirit which seems at first glance so incompatible with the more cosmopolitan Austrian nature. The variation device proper was used only once by Mahler, in the Adagio of his Fourth Symphony, and then rather in the sense of "variations on two themes" as employed by Beethoven in the Adagio of his Ninth Symphony. In these facts lies much food for thought. We may discount the incompatibility of North-German and Viennese temperament, for, after all, they were more or less reconciled in Brahms himself, even though his personality was a strangely divided one as a result of the disparate elements within it. Mahler's respect for the traditional art of the *Haydn Variations* bespeaks the deep feeling for tradition which we have pointed out in our historical discussion of Austria's musical generations. But the fact that Mahler did not imitate or copy the variation form tells us what should have been self-evident from the beginning: Mahler was a great and independent artist who, like all other human beings, had his roots in time and place and his connections in the past, but who, in the manner peculiar to the outstanding individualist, possessed something quite his own which momentarily elevated him beyond the accidents of present time and location and of cultural ancestry. Too often, when we discuss "schools," and "influences," and "musical borrowings," we tend to lose sight of this individual quality.

We may say that the relationship between Mahler and the Brahms-Bruckner generation (it is indicative of a subtle change in values and viewpoint that Brahms and Bruckner are now classified together) is a typical case of old *vs.* new combining with old *plus* new—in other words, a characteristic example of the symbiosis of Convention and Revolt of which we have spoken before and which we shall have occasion to mention later in connection with the similar relationship between Mahler and the generation of the young Schoenberg.

In general, it may be said that Mahler's harmonic and melodic speech is closer to that of Bruckner than to that of Brahms. This is not surprising; for Bruckner, in spite of his fundamental conservatism, was always considered (and in many respects really was) more "modern" than Brahms, and hence was more likely to appeal to the "revolutionary" sensibilities of the young Mahler. Particularly is this true because of Bruckner's close connection with Wagner, whom Mahler (as we have already seen) considered the world's greatest composer next to Beethoven. The exceptionally ardent admiration for Beethoven, together with its symbolic representation in the cult of the nine symphonies, also draws Mahler closer to Bruckner, although Mahler was most deeply interested in one particular aspect of the Beethovenian symphony—the choral finale of the Ninth—which influenced Bruckner's composition not at all in the outward sense.

Bruckner was secure in his religion. Mahler, whose restless search for faith finally ended in a Catholicism of convenience, reached out for support, whether consciously or unconsciously, to Bruckner's most shining symbols of belief, the chorale and the trumpet fanfare. No single composition of Mahler's could illustrate this more vividly than the Second Symphony, which is filled with such passages. The opening invocation of *Urlicht* and the beginning of the *Aufersteh'n* chorus are unthinkable without the previous work of Bruckner in this stark choral style. These examples may suffice for the time being to indicate Mahler's strong inward relationship to Bruckner; our next task will be to essay a portrait of the complex personality of the young Mahler, which will serve as a key to his mature work.

CHAPTER II

Portrait of Mahler as a Young Man

Puszta-Batta, June 17, 1879

Dear Steiner!

Please do not be angry that I have left you so long without an answer; but everything is so desolate around me, and behind me the branches of a sterile and withered existence are breaking. Much has happened within me during the time I did not write to you. But I cannot tell you of it. Or, rather, only this much, that I have become another being; whether or not a better one I do not know, but in any case not a happier one. The highest ecstasy of the most joyous strength of life and the most burning desire for death: these two reign alternately within my heart; yes, oftentimes they alternate within the hour— one thing I know; it cannot go on this way! Since the dreadful force of our modern hypocrisy and insincerity has driven me to dishonor, since the unbreakable connection with our way of art and life was able to fill my heart with scorn for everything that is holy—art, love, religion—what other way out is there than suicide? Violently I break the bonds that chain me in the sickening hollow dump-hole of existence; with the strength of distress I cling to sorrow, my only consolation. Then the sun smiles upon me—and the ice has melted from my heart, I see the blue heavens once more and the quivering flower, and my scornful laughter dissolves in the tears of love. And I *must* love it, this world with its deception and light-mindedness and eternal laughter. O, that some god might tear the veil from before my eyes, so that my clear glance might penetrate to the very dregs of the earth! O, I would like to gaze upon it, this earth, all laid bare without decoration or adornment, as it lies open before its Creator; then I would step before its spirit. "Now I know thee, oh liar, thou hast not deceived me with thy hypocrisy, hast not blinded me with thy gleam! Oh, behold! A man, enlaced by the most cunning nets of thy falsehood, struck down by the most frightful blows of thy scorn, yet unbowed and strong! Let fear smite thee where thou hidest thyself. From the valleys of humanity it rings on high, up to thy cold and lonely peak! Canst thou comprehend the unspeakable misery which has piled itself into mountains through the eons down there below? And on the peaks of those mountains thou reignest; and laugh'st! How wilt thou excuse thyself one day before the Avenger, thou who knowest not how to still the sorrow of a single tortured soul?

June 18

. . . Oh my beloved earth, when, oh when, wilt thou take the abandoned one unto thy breast? Behold! Mankind has banished him from itself, and he flees from its cold and heartless bosom to thee, to thee! Oh, care for the lonely one, for the restless one, Universal Mother! [1]

[1] Gustav Mahler, *Briefe 1879–1911*, pp. 5–9.

THESE LINES were penned by a lad of eighteen who was spending the summer on a Hungarian *Puszta,* where his comparatively light duties of keeping his employers musically entertained and teaching piano to the boys of the family left him much time for intense thoughts. This is the young Mahler, and it is through such literary utterances as these that we must make the acquaintance of his personality during these formative years, for the conscientious artist later destroyed nearly all his immature musical works. In this very letter, for example, he speaks of an opera which he had written some time before, *Ernst von Schwaben.* How much we would like to know an opera by Mahler![2] But, since composers create or destroy according to their own will and not according to the convenience of the next generation of investigators, we must content ourselves with such material as we can assemble. We should not lose sight of the fact that the conclusions which we draw about Mahler the young man are of the utmost importance in our assessment of Mahler the mature composer. The informed reader may already have noticed a remarkable parallelism between the portion of the letter written on June 18, 1879, and the poetry of the second movement of *Das Lied von der Erde.* This alone would tell us that Mahler at eighteen had already entered into the spiritual realm where he was to dwell all the rest of his days. We cannot but admire this consistency of character; it shows us that no matter how mercurial and temperamental he may have appeared to outsiders, he was always true to himself—a trait which we have already had occasion to observe in Bruckner.

It is not surprising that the young man who could write such rhetorical letters also tried his hand at poetry. The following lines, sent to his close friend Anton Krisper on March 3, 1880, are a good example of the kind of literary attitudinizing that every German youth of the romantic or post-romantic period—including many far less gifted than Mahler—seems to have had to go through at one time or another:

Vergessene Liebe

Wie öd' mein Herz! Wie leer das All'!
Wie gross mein Sehnen!
O, wie die Fernen Tal zu Tal'
sich endlos dehnen!
Mein süsses Lieb! Zum letzten Mal!?

---

[2] The major portion of the libretto which Mahler wrote for his opera *Rübezahl* (never completed) survives. For an account of the vicissitudes of its history, see Dika Newlin, "Mahler's Opera," *Opera News,* March 18, 1972.

Ach, muss ja ewig diese Qual
* in meinem Herzen brennen!*
Wie strahlt' es einst so treu und klar
* in ihren Blicken!*
Das Wandern liess ich ganz und gar
* trotz Winters Tücken!*
Und als der Lenz vergangen war,
Da tat mein Lieb ihr blondes Haar
* wohl mit der Myrthe schmücken!*
Mein Wanderstab! Noch einmal heut'
* komm aus der Ecken!*
Schliefst du auch lang! Nun sei bereit!
* Ich will dich wecken!*
Ich trug es lang, mein Liebesleid,
Und ist die Erde doch so weit,
So komm, mein treuer Stecken!

Wie lieblich lächelt Berg und Tal
* in Blütenwogen!*
Kam ja mit seinem süssen Schall
* der Lenz gezogen!*
Und Blumen blühn ja überall—
Und Kreuzlein steh'n ja überall—
* die haben nicht gelogen.*[3]

Another poem of this period, the *Ballade vom Blonden und Braunen Reitersmann,* is of more than passing interest because, though Mahler never set it to music after all, it was originally intended to serve as the first part of *Das klagende Lied.* We shall discuss this work in the next chapter.

The combination of Byronic pessimism and Hoffmannesque grotesquerie which dominates the spiritual expressions of Mahler at this time is characteristic of his generation to an extraordinary degree. Certain morbid tendencies seemed to be inescapably bound up with the times; it is not without its unpleasant significance that Mahler's three closest school friends, Anton Krisper, Hans Rott, and Hugo Wolf, all died insane, and at a comparatively early age. But, in Mahler's case, family history and previous experiences contribute even more to his tortured state of mind than does the *Zeitgeist.*

It is Alma Mahler who has revealed most clearly the causes of Mahler's life-long melancholy. She tells of his miserable childhood in a family of twelve children, most of whom died in early years; of the constant and bitter quarrels between his brutal, ambitious father and his gentle, patient mother; of his unhappy days in the Grünfeld home in Prague, where he was systematically mistreated and robbed of his

[3] Hans Holländer, "Unbekannte Briefe Gustav Mahlers," *Die Musik,* XX. Jahrgang, Heft 11, p. 810 (August, 1928).

belongings; of the eccentricities of his brothers—the sickly Ernst, the morbid Otto (who eventually committed suicide) and the fantastic Alois. Then there were the student years of poverty in Vienna, when the young man, unable to afford proper food, wrecked his digestion in such a way as to cause him trouble for the rest of his life. It is small wonder that, subjected to such experiences, and by nature inclined to melancholy, he tortured himself into a mental state wherein he actually had visions of his body lying dead on a bier in the room before his living self. That he kept his sanity at all is certainly a tribute to the strength of his coördinating intellect.

Though so much of the music of the early years was destroyed, we still have the cantata *Das klagende Lied,* and several groups of songs. It is to the former that we shall now turn, as the first preliminary to our study of Mahler the mature symphonist.

CHAPTER III

Das Klagende Lied

G UIDO ADLER, in the chronological table appended to his brief book on Mahler, gives the following concise information about the origin and outcome of the first of Mahler's important works to be preserved for posterity. "1880. 'Das Klagende Lied.' Poem and music, begun in 1878, finished in 1880 (first version). Revised in 1898, published in 1899. Orchestration revised in the years after 1900." [1]

Thus, we see that work on this composition was spread over more than twenty years of the author's life. However, in its essence, it remains a conception of his youth, and hence it is logical to study it first among his works.

The musical type represented by *Das klagende Lied*—a cantata with legendary background—was no stranger to German romanticism; it is interesting to note that a later member of the neo-Viennese group, in a composition of his youth, was also to leave us a work in this genre —though, to be sure, a much more extensive one. It is Schoenberg with his *Gurre-Lieder* who comes to mind here, although the two works rest on different premises.

Mahler had originally planned a more extensive format for his work. This is easily deduced from the ballad which he includes in a letter to his friend Anton Krisper and which was evidently intended to form the first part of *Das klagende Lied*.[2] The opening stanzas of the poem are as follows:

Ballade vom Blonden und Braunen Reitersmann

> *Da war eine stolze Königin*
> *Gar lieblich ohne Massen.*
> *Kein Ritter stand nach ihrem Sinn,*
> *Sie wollt' sie alle hassen.*

[1] Guido Adler, *Gustav Mahler*, p. 97.

[2] This first part was, in fact, composed by Mahler under the title of *Waldmärchen;* the score has since come to light and has been the subject of extensive discussion. See, in particular, Jack Diether, *"Das klagende Lied*—Genesis and Evolution," in "Notes on some Mahler Juvenilia," *Chord and Discord*, 1969, pp. 3–65; also Donald Mitchell, *Gustav Mahler: The Wunderhorn Years*, pp. 56–69. The vocal score of *Waldmärchen* was published in 1973 by Belwin-Mills.

O weh, du wonnigliches Weib,
Wem blühet wohl dein süsser Leib!?

Im Wald eine rote Blume stand
So schön wie die Königinne;
Welch Rittersmann die Blume fand,
Der konnt' die Frau gewinnen.
Nun ach, du stolze Königin,
Nun bricht wohl bald dein stolzer Sinn.

Zwei Brüder zogen zum Walde hin,
Sie wollten die Blume suchen.
Der junge hold, von mildem Sinn,
Der andere wollte nur fluchen.
O Ritter, schlimmer Ritter mein,
O liessest du das Fluchen sein!

Als sie so zogen eine Weil',
Da kamen sie zu scheiden;
Das war ein Suchen nun in Eil'
Im Wald und auf der Heiden.
Ihr Ritter mein, in schnellem Lauf,
Wer findet wohl die Blume auf?

Der Junge zieht fröhlich durch Feld und Heid',
Er braucht nicht lang zu gehen,
Bald sieht er von Ferne bei der Weid'
Die rote Blume stehen.
Die hat er auf den Hut gesteckt,
Und dann sich zur Ruhe hingestreckt.[3]

The conclusion of the story is obvious; the elder brother finds the younger one sleeping, kills him, steals the red flower from his hat-band, and so wins the hand of the queen. Thus is the stage set for the opening of *Das klagende Lied*.

The orchestral introduction to the first section is characterized by a persistent *tremolo* pedal-point on C, and by a number of march-like themes which adumbrate symphonic motives of the mature Mahler. Following this introduction, a narrative passage wherein alto and tenor alternate in the exposition of the tragic tale (an interesting fore-shadowing of the alternative technique in *Das Lied von der Erde*) leads to the first utterance of the refrain *O Leide*, which thereafter appears in varied forms. The choral sections of the first division are written with care, though they do not attain the grandeur of the choral-symphonic expressions of the later Mahler. Typical of the young composer's well-developed color sense, which was to become even more refined later on as he gained experience through conducting, is the giving of such detailed technical directions as "whispering with head-

---

[3] Hans Holländer, *op. cit.*, p. 808.

tones" to the tenors. The orchestral interludes, which make liberal
use of pedal-points, *tremoli,* and persistent rhythmical figures attribut-
able to the influence of Bruckner, are already couched in the harmonic
and emotional language of the mature composer; the tell-tale directions *Etwas drängen, Immer noch drängend,* which bespeak the personality of the author so vividly, may be found in the score of any
Mahler symphony.

The second division begins with a spirited orchestral introduction,
filled with trumpet calls. There follows a majestic chorus, opening
with a spacious phrase sung by the basses, and containing some curiously unvocal lines, the result of rather naïve word-painting. The
dramatic tension grows steadily until the moment—prepared by an
orchestral interlude including effects for off-stage orchestra which suggest those of the Second Symphony—where the king, disturbed in the
midst of his wedding festivities by the importunate minstrel with his
flute, finally puts the bone from the body of his murdered brother
mockingly to his lips. Thereupon the following mournful phrase, noteworthy for its delicate nuances of metrical structure, is heard:

and rises to a passionate pitch of accusation in an extravagant melodic
curve:

Plainly, the immense range and mobility demanded of the female
voice by Schoenberg in such a composition as *Herzgewächse* are not
without precedents in the Viennese school! However, in this particular instance, the handling of the vocal line is partly, at least, due to
youthful inexperience, for such lines as these are not found in Mahler's later choral works.

The drama proceeds to its inevitable catastrophe—a "Liebestod." The betrayed queen falls to the floor in a swoon, the gay trumpets and drums of the wedding festivities cease to play, the terrified knights and ladies flee this accursed place as the ancient walls of the castle crumble into nothingness. "Ach Leide," whispers the soprano, reiterating for the last time that phrase which, whether as verbal refrain or musical *leitmotiv,* has served as one of the principal elements of formal and emotional unity of the work; and the orchestra, too, participates in the disintegration as the composition draws to a close.

Undoubtedly *Das klagende Lied* is in some respects immature. The verse, although in general well-written and fluent, relies heavily on the clichés of German folk-romanticism; the music displays unassimilated influences of Bruckner and Wagner. But the dramatic spirit with which the work is imbued, and its youthful verve, make it a worthy predecessor of Mahler's mature creations. Certainly, it does not deserve the neglect with which it has met.[4]

[4] The work has since become better known through recordings. That by Boulez (Columbia M 2 30061) includes the *Waldmärchen.*

CHAPTER IV

Literary Influences on Mahler

IT IS EASY to see that Mahler was a young man with definite literary ambitions of his own. His literary style and manner of thinking were strongly conditioned by E. T. A. Hoffmann and Jean Paul; nor had he escaped the infection of the Wagnerian *Stabreim*—for Wagner was, after all, capable of exerting a literary influence as well as a musical one. And there was another influence upon him even more profound than these, even more pervasive in his work—the collection of lyrics known as *Des Knaben Wunderhorn*. It would not be accurate to say that Mahler's discovery of this volume, in 1888, changed all his conceptions of lyricism. Already, in his first song-cycle, the *Lieder eines fahrenden Gesellen* (1884), he had used texts of his own devising, the idiom of which is very close to that of the *Wunderhorn*.[1] But in the *Wunderhorn* he found for the first time a supply of this folk-material organized and ready to hand for all his musical needs; and so, for him, the "magic horn" truly became a "horn of plenty."

It is not essential, for the purposes of a study such as ours, to be familiar with all the details of the planning of the *Wunderhorn*; however, it is well to know something of its history. The work was compiled by those two famous authors of the romantic period, Ludwig Achim von Arnim (1781–1831) and Klemens Brentano (1778–1842). They first became acquainted in the summer of 1801, and were soon fast friends, but it is not till 1805 that we begin to find definite references to a projected collection of folk songs in their correspondence. Once conceived, this plan was rapidly executed, for it was towards the end of 1805 that the first volume of *Wunderhorn* poems appeared.

The Brentano-Arnim collection is a typical product of the romantic *Zeitgeist*, with its stress on the simple, artless life of the "little people" and on the glamor of bygone days. Hence it is small wonder that

[1] Many writers profess to see here a proof of the composer's "prophetic gifts"— surely a far-fetched assumption, since the lyrical tone of these poems can scarcely have been unfamiliar in Mahler's environment.

it attracted much attention in the literary world, drawing comment from even so distinguished a personage as Goethe—all the more reason for us to be surprised that its immediate repercussions in the musical world were not greater. We do find settings of *Zu Strassburg auf der Schanz* and *Morgen muss ich fort von hier* by Friedrich Silcher; but neither Schubert, nor Beethoven, nor Mendelssohn, nor Schumann [2] seems to have paid much heed to this rich treasure of lyricism accessible to all of them. One is tempted to suppose that these great *Lieder* composers were afflicted with that same shortsightedness which, in a different way, afflicted the *literati* (the classic example of this is Goethe's preference of Zelter's settings of his verses to those of Schubert). The situation changed, however, with Mahler's appearance on the musical scene; for, whatever isolated *Wunderhorn* poems were used by composers before Mahler's day, it was he who really "discovered" them for music. Though many composers followed him along this path, he always made a point of his priority in the field.

Much more will be said about the *Wunderhorn* in our chapters on *Mahler the Lyricist* and *Mahler the Symphonist*. Now, however, our attention turns to one of the brightest lights on Mahler's literary horizon—Nietzsche. It is in his *Birth of Tragedy* that we find the quintessential expression of a philosophy which guided Mahler throughout his life. Nietzsche, in this work, set up a contrast between the calm "Apollonian" world and the ecstatic "Dionysian" world, and glorified the artistic results of the fusion of these two worlds—a fusion of which *Tristan,* according to him, was the most perfect example. Never, he said, would the German nation find itself spiritually until it followed Dionysian impulses freely. It is clear from Mahler's life, music, and writings that this exaltation of the Dionysian viewpoint made a profound impression on him. It may be that when he used the folk poetry of *Des Knaben Wunderhorn* he unconsciously remembered Nietzsche's dictum that folk song is the *perpetuum vestigium* of a union of Dionysian and Apollonian, and as such highly to be prized. This cannot be proved; but the direct way in which the more flamboyant aspects of the Dionysian idea appealed to Mahler's dramatic nature can easily be seen. Nietzsche's influence affected not only his literary tastes and, perhaps, his manner of literary expression, but also, and far more significantly, the very heart of his music. He himself recognized this plainly when, writing an account of his life to Dr. Richard Batka, at that time editor of the *Prager neue musikalischer Rundschau* (1896), he was inspired by his irritation over the frequent performances of

---

[2] Schumann did compose four *Wunderhorn* texts. Brahms composed six original *Wunderhorn* songs and made arrangements of tunes written to the texts of several others. I do not know whether Mahler was acquainted with any of these songs. He definitely considered himself, though, a pioneer in this area.

the *Blumenstück* from the Third Symphony (without the other movements!) to the following illuminating commentary:

That this little piece (more of an intermezzo in the whole thing) must create misunderstandings when detached from its connection with the complete work, my most significant and vastest creation, can't keep me from letting it be performed alone. I have no choice; if I ever want to be heard, I can't be too fussy, and so this modest little piece will doubtless . . . present me to the public as the "sensuous," perfumed "singer of nature."—That this nature hides within itself everything that is frightful, great, and also lovely (which is exactly what I wanted to express in the entire work, in a sort of evolutionary development)—of course no one ever understands that. It always strikes me as odd that most people, when they speak of "nature," think only of flowers, little birds, and woodsy smells. No one knows the god Dionysus, the great Pan. There now! you have a sort of program—that is, a sample of how I make music. Everywhere and always, it is only the voice of nature! . . . Now it is the world, Nature in its totality, which is, so to speak, awakened from fathomless silence that it may ring and resound.[3]

It is doubly significant that the Third Symphony, which Mahler is discussing here in terms of a Nietzschean conception, should be the very one into which he introduces a poetic excerpt from *Also sprach Zarathustra*—additional proof that Nietzsche's influence on him was more than a passing phase. The deep concern with the fate of the universe and of all mankind which was characteristic both of Mahler and Nietzsche is reflected in the words which Mahler has given to the contralto voice in the fourth movement:

> *O man! Take heed!*
> *What saith deep midnight's voice indeed?*
> *"I slept my sleep—,*
> *From deepest dream I've woke, and plead:—*
> *The world is deep,*
> *And deeper than the day could read.*
> *Deep is its woe—,*
> *Joy—deeper still than grief can be:*
> *Woe saith: Hence! Go!*
> *But joys all want eternity—,*
> *—Want deep, profound eternity!"* [4]

It is plausible to trace back Mahler's preoccupation with Nietzsche to his student days at the University of Vienna—more specifically, to his friendship with a talented young writer who had already been powerfully drawn into Nietzsche's orbit and who had, indeed, composed a drama, *Prometheus Unbound*, which had impressed Nietzsche deeply. This young man had many things in common with his younger friend Mahler; he, too, was of Jewish extraction, and, like the *Deutschböhme* Mahler, came from a part of the Empire not predominantly

---

[3] Gustav Mahler, *Briefe 1879–1911*, pp. 214–15.
[4] Friedrich Nietzsche, *Thus Spake Zarathustra* (Modern Library), p. 322.

German—in this instance, Galicia. Physically he was hardly prepossessing—quick and gnome-like in his movements, high of forehead, gleaming of eye. Yet, probably under the influence of Nietzsche's hypothetical *Übermensch*, he was highly egotistical; and his manners can never have been winning, for Nietzsche and (under his wife's influence) Mahler broke with him on personal grounds.

This strange character, Siegfried Lipiner, is almost entirely forgotten today, promising though he seemed in his youth. Yet he wrote works of some interest, the most significant of which for our purposes is the curious poem *Der Musiker spricht,* a tribute to Mahler on his fiftieth birthday. Its oddly turgid and involved style makes little sense in a literal translation; the piece may, however, be paraphrased in prose as follows:

Let the world be shut out, and the gate shut! I am weary of light, my eyes and my ears are weary of light. How noisy is this light! How it wells up and smashes into shards, into the shard-heap of the world! Now darkness encloses the room, sweeps about it, enfolds it, and the room is no more.

Come, darkness, thou from whose bosom light burst forth once a long time ago—why dost thou delay, oh darkness!

Light is not silent; its sounds no longer press upon ear and eye—and yet light is not silent! It is not to be seen, and nothing in it is to be seen; yet it wells up and echoes—oh horror, what horror! And slumber slips softly into the soul, a silence deep as the deep dark of the sea. And the one who sits there in the brain worrying and muttering, and the one who hammers in the heart, they are both silent.

Light is not silent! Though the night may envelop it, yet there is no night which will extinguish this glow. And the night itself—listen, how it resounds with the eternal light which quivers in its bosom. It trembles, it glows—and the soul is drawn into the warm glow, basks there. . . . Those are not beams, nor yet glowing sparks! Those are voices—voices! That is living light! . . .

But what rises there, like the dawn; above the whirlpools in its bright path? The *melody!* Just as upon a still pond the swan's neck bends and sways so gracefully, here and there describes many a soft curve, then rises straight up, shimmering whitely; even so dost thou, caster of spells from a strange land, not sent *by* the spirit, but *to* the spirit itself! Thou wonder, that took love from the lips of God Himself to relieve all pain! How it divides itself, and reunites itself, and entwines itself in lovely arabesques, and sanctifies the changing play of time! . . .

O melody, what is it that draws thee upward? What does that cry of power promise? Whatever it may be—away, away with thee, O thou leader of the dance of the spirits! Along the echoing path of sunbeams—I, too, a dance! And I, too, a song! [5]

Obviously the writer of these lines was no man of ordinary caliber; eccentric he may have been, but there are certain moments when his

[5] Siegfried Lipiner, "Der Musiker spricht," as quoted in Hartmut von Hartungen, *Der Dichter Siegfried Lipiner* (1856–1911), pp. I–IV.

eccentricity smacks of genius. Hartungen, dissecting his life-work in cold blood, is of the opinion that Lipiner lacked creative originality, and that his work was incapable of influence on the German literature either of his own time or of future generations.[6] His distinguished contemporaries certainly felt quite differently about him. That Mahler, no mean judge of style and thought, valued his friend's contribution to literature very highly, is evidenced everywhere in his correspondence with the poet, but nowhere more strongly than in the following letter, with its strong overtones of Nietzsche:

June 1898

Dear Siegfried!

Only a few lines to let you know that I just received your *Adam*. What a joy—at last!—I've just finished the first act—a storm from the south has been raging outdoors, and it was amazing how that storm mingled with your drama —always blowing in right on its cue!

That is a really Dionysian work! Believe me, no one living can understand that except me. In the *Bacchantes* of Euripides I find a similar tone, except that Euripides always talks too much about things instead of really bringing them to pass. *What* is it, then, that gives life to the force of Dionysus? Wine intoxicates and exalts the drinker! But *what* is wine?—Representational art has never yet succeeded in giving us what is found as a matter of course in every note of music. In your poetry *this* music storms! Really, it is unique in the whole world. It does not tell of wine or describe its effects—but it *is* wine, it *is* Dionysus! Furthermore, it seems to me that, with the ancients, the figure of Dionysus represented *Life-Urge* in that mystical, grandiose sense in which you have conceived it. There, too, it drives its victims out to the animals, with whom they become *as one*. Many thanks, dear Siegfried, I want to honor your work—but how fortunate it is that *I* have it!

Cordially,
Your
Gustav [7]

Manifestly, it would be impossible to consider that every poet or literary work with which Mahler came in contact exerted a lasting influence upon him. Certain musical settings of verse testify only to an unusually strong momentary impression. Such is the case in the Finale of the Second Symphony. Mahler, who had previously sought through all of world literature (including the Bible) for a text suitable to his musical and philosophical conception of this music, heard a setting of Klopstock's *Auferstehung* [8] sung at Bülow's funeral and immediately realized that this was the poetry he was seeking for his symphony. But

---

[6] Hartungen, *op. cit.*, pp. 80–81.

[7] Mahler, *op. cit.*, pp. 279–80.

[8] The text is found in Klopstock's *Geistliche Lieder* (Vol. VII of his Collected Works, Leipzig, 1804, pp. 133–34); Donald Mitchell reprints it, together with Mahler's version of the text, in Appendix C of *Gustav Mahler; The Wunderhorn Years*, pp. 416–18).

this does not mean that Klopstock exercised a permanent influence upon the composer. Nor, in spite of Mahler's fondness for the delicate and slightly affected lyrics of Rückert, can we seriously aver that Rückert made a basic contribution to Mahler's *Weltanschauung*.

Mahler's intellectual relationship with Schopenhauer furnished him with a philosophical groundwork which he valued deeply. Talking one day with his friend Arnold Berliner, the Hamburg physicist, Mahler remarked that what Schopenhauer had written about music in *Die Welt als Wille und Vorstellung* was the most profound elucidation of the true nature of music which he had ever come across; and on other occasions he said that the only writing about music comparable with it in scope and intelligence was Wagner's article on Beethoven.[9] Schopenhauer's philosophy of music was a source of inspiration for Mahler, though it cannot be too much emphasized that, the philosophic background once established, Mahler proceeded to create his scores on purely musical terms, without being hampered at every turn by a cumbersome "program" literally followed. It is remarkable to see how Mahler is capable of welding together Schopenhauerian philosophy, thematic material both symphonic and lyric, German folk-poetry, and the abstruse expression of Nietzsche into a unified work of such vast proportions as the Third Symphony.

Our discussion of literary influences on Mahler would not be complete without the name of Goethe. The very fact that Mahler chose the visionary final scene of *Faust* as the textual basis for the last movement of what is perhaps his most grandiose work, the Eighth Symphony, shows the special importance of Goethe's masterwork to him.[10] Mahler's personal concept of Goethe's ideas might not stand up under the strain of logical examination; the important thing, however, is to realize how much Goethe and the other writers we have discussed meant to Mahler, and how deeply they could—and did—influence the direction of his musical creativeness.

[9] Mahler, *op. cit.*, p. 126.
[10] In a letter to his wife (1909) he has given an elaborate commentary on the all-important mystic final lines of the scene.

CHAPTER V

Mahler the Lyricist

ALL OF MAHLER'S published songs are posterior to the first version of *Das klagende Lied*. The songs making up the three volumes of *Lieder und Gesänge aus der Jugendzeit* were composed from 1883 to 1892, while the first of the great song-cycles, *Lieder eines fahrenden Gesellen*, was written in 1884; these were succeeded by the two books of *Wunderhorn* songs, the *Sieben Lieder aus letzter Zeit*, and the *Kindertotenlieder*. Studying these works in the order of the composer's development, we shall begin with the *Lieder und Gesänge*, which, though their composition spanned nearly ten years, may conveniently be considered as a unit.

A number of examples of Mahler's mature style immediately present themselves to view in these three volumes. The earliest songs, those of the first book, are naturally the weakest—that is to say, the least individualistic—although among them are charming pieces like the *Serenade* from Tirso de Molina's *Don Juan* with its guitar-like accompaniment, and the bright, folk-like [1] dance song, *Hans und Grete*.[2] But in the other two books we find songs that are at least equal to the twelve *Lieder aus "Des Knaben Wunderhorn"* which were composed somewhat later. The first song of the third book, *Zu Strassburg auf der Schanz* (based on two *Wunderhorn* texts) is full of those trumpet-calls which over-imaginative biographers have liked to attribute to the influence of the military barracks near which Mahler spent his childhood, but which might also be accounted for by the influence of Bruckner's symphonies—though the universality and grandeur of Bruckner's horns and trumpets have here been transported into an earthier, more human sphere. It is interesting to see how in the accompaniment of this simple song the piano is always reaching out for orchestral effects. Thus the introductory phrase for piano is distinctly

[1] Though the text of this song is indicated as a "folk-song" in all editions, it has been definitely proved that it was written by Mahler alone. See Fritz Egon Pamer, "Gustav Mahlers Lieder," *Studien zur Musikwissenschaft*, XVI, 120–21.

[2] This song appears also to have been part of Mahler's unfinished opera *Rübezahl*. See Dika Newlin, "Mahler's Opera," *Opera News*, March 18, 1972.

marked "Wie eine Schalmei." And, as a footnote to one interlude-figure, we find this hint to the interpreter: "In all the low-register trills the sound of muted drums is to be imitated with the help of the pedal." Mahler's conductorial imagination betrays itself at every turn, and yet there is nothing unpianistic in the writing, even when the piano is asked to imitate the "Alphorn" so conveniently mentioned in the text. The orchestral allusions are meant to stimulate the imagination of player and singer alike; they must not mislead us into thinking that the piano was inadequate for Mahler's intentions here, or that he was handling the unfortunate instrument in a makeshift manner. Mahler, be it remembered, was also an excellent pianist, trained by Julius Epstein at the Vienna Conservatory (he had even won a prize one year for his performance of a Schubert sonata—history tells us the "A minor," without disclosing which). We shall hardly accuse him lightly of not knowing how to write for the instrument.

Mahler's art of vocal writing has progressed a long way since the linear extravagance of *Das klagende Lied*. The vocal melody here is economical to the point of sparseness, yet expressive in the extreme by virtue of this very restraint. Clearly, Mahler the composer was learning much from the melodic structure of the German folk-song, even as Mahler the writer had borrowed the phrases and the concepts of its poetry. Pamer has shown that there is an unmistakable family likeness between the folk-melodies associated with the verses of *Zu Strassburg auf der Schanz, Scheiden und Meiden* (*Drei Reiter am Tore* in the *Wunderhorn*), and *Nicht wiedersehn!* (*Herzlieb am Grabe*, a folk-song from the neighborhood of Kassel), and the melodies of Mahler's settings.[3] For examples, the relationship between the opening phrase of *Zu Strassburg auf der Schanz* and a folk-song of Hesse-Darmstadt, *Le Deserteur*, seems clear.

Mahler's music, because it so often uses the simple harmonic and melodic means of the folk-song, has frequently suffered the accusa-

---

[3] The same holds true for *Der Schildwache Nachtlied* (a Westphalian melody, "Ich kann und mag nicht traurig sein") and *Trost in Unglück* (*Husarenliebe*). See Pamer, "Gustav Mahlers Lieder," *Studien zur Musikwissenschaft*, XVI, 122–23, and Erk-Böhme, *Deutscher Liederhort*, I, 606; II, 560, 561, 568; III, 261, 281.

tion of banality. But a deeper study of the issues involved should have shown that, though Mahler borrows the strength and substance inherent in the simplicity of the folk-song, he more often than not infuses this "raw material" with a subtlety that is all his own—witness the way in which he ends *Zu Strassburg auf der Schanz* on the subdominant instead of the tonic, as though the last complaint of the dying soldier were to remain forever unanswered. If one wants to assay the quality and originality of Mahler's treatment of folk-material, one need merely compare it with the work produced by some of his successors and imitators in the field of *Wunderhorn* song-writing. As previously mentioned, Mahler's musical "rediscovery" of the *Wunderhorn* started a new vogue for this *genre. Die Woche,* a Berlin popular periodical, stimulated the trend with its announcement (1903) of a prize contest for "Lieder im Volkston." The "best" of the songs entered in this contest (and we are told that the number of entries exceeded all expectations) were then printed in two volumes and were subjected to popular vote. Among these select specimens of the "New Berlin School" we find *Wunderhorn* songs by Ludwig Thuille, Humperdinck, Viktor Holländer, and that fiery virtuoso and pedestrian opera-composer Eugen d'Albert, in addition to an *Abendlied* from Herder's *Stimmen der Völker* written by Friedrich Gernsheim, a composer whom Mahler admired greatly for reasons somewhat obscure today. Few can look at these faded album-leaves of an artificially revived folk-art without feeling that, with negligible exceptions, they are miserably tawdry imitations of "the real thing." Only Mahler— and, in a quite different way, Brahms—could truly revivify the folk-art, by reliving with sincerity, and expressing through their own strong individualities, the emotions which had inspired it.

One of Mahler's most beautiful essays in the *genre* of the *Wunderhorn-Lieder* is the touching song *Nicht wiedersehn!,* likewise from the third book of *Lieder und Gesänge,* which may be compared and contrasted with *Zu Strassburg auf der Schanz.* Here, the element of grim and sardonic irony which is the emotional basis of the latter song is supplanted by simple yet deeply moving pathos. While in *Nicht wiedersehn!* Mahler has not resorted to the practice of giving hints for a sort of "mental orchestration" to the performers, we still feel that symphonic possibilities lie hidden in the simple song. Mahler had already used just such a bass as that of the fourth measure, with its heavy-falling fourth, in the third movement of the First Symphony; and let us not forget that the interweaving of song and symphony had already begun with the *Lieder eines fahrenden Gesellen* and the First Symphony, and that a song from the very volume which we are discussing, *Ablösung im Sommer,* was to become the Scherzo of the Third Symphony. The opening phrase of *Nicht wiedersehn!,* in its stark simplicity, sets the tone for the whole. However, the greatest poignancy is reached in the refrain, which already on its first appearance embodies that striking C♮–C♯ contrast so reminiscent of Schubert's bold juxtapositions of major and minor, but which attains the highest pitch of expression in its final form, with which the song closes.

The *Lieder eines fahrenden Gesellen,* which follow immediately (1884) upon the first book of *Lieder und Gesänge,* are remarkable and interesting for several reasons. We have already referred to the fidelity with which Mahler caught the spirit of true folk-poetry before he had become acquainted with the contents of *Des Knaben Wunderhorn.*[4] The romantic circumstances under which he composed the cycle, after the breaking-off of his love-affair with the soprano Johanne Richter in Kassel, are intriguing insofar as they link the music to his own personal life.[5] However, the cycle is chiefly important because it furnishes the thematic material and spiritual background of the First Symphony. The implications of this statement are of great significance, but will not be examined until we discuss the symphonies themselves.

The story told by the *Lieder eines fahrenden Gesellen* is a simple and tragic one. A young man, scorned by his sweetheart who has married another, is driven from his native place by the force of his grief and shame, and now wanders aimlessly over the countryside singing of his turbulent emotions, the various aspects of which are successively represented in the four songs of the cycle, *When My Love is Wed* (*Wenn mein Schatz Hochzeit macht*), *As I Wandered o'er the Fields* (*Ging heut' Morgen über's Feld*), *I Bear a Burning Dagger* (*Ich hab' ein glühend Messer*), and *The Blue Eyes of My Love* (*Die zwei blauen Augen von meinem Schatz*).

The first song presents an interesting rhythmical scheme which distinctly shows the influence of Bohemian folk-song and dance (e. g. the

[4] Indeed, more than the spirit of this poetry is reflected in the first song of this cycle, which contains verbal reminiscences of a well-known folk-song, *Horch, was kommt von draussen rein,* of a folk-song from Posen (*Blümlein blau*) and even of a *Wunderhorn* poem, *Wenn mein Schatz Hochzeit macht.* However, Pamer is doubtless right in saying that we need not assume that Mahler made the acquaintance of the *Wunderhorn* collection earlier than has been previously supposed, since he could have known the poem from other sources.

[5] For interesting details on the affair, see the flawed but fascinating biography by Henry-Louis de la Grange, *Mahler,* Vol. I (1973). For further commentary on the song-cycle, see Mitchell, *Gustav Mahler; The Wunderhorn Years,* pp. 91–113, 119–126.

furiant) in its consistent alternation of duple and triple rhythm.[6] This simple alternation lends not only musical piquancy but genuine emotional poignancy to the basically simple harmonic background. Noteworthy in this song is the variety in unity which Mahler attains by building successive new motives after the pattern of the original motivic germ-cell

which characteristically returns to the point at which it began:

The original motive itself returns persistently throughout the song, both in sixteenth-notes and in eighth-notes. However, it scarcely overshadows in emotional content the highly expressive interval of the sixth which appears four times, each time at significant cadences, with great effect.

An ending, not in the expected D minor but in G minor, provides the logical upbeat to the beginning (in D major) of the next song, *Ging heut' Morgen über's Feld.* Later on, we shall have opportunity to compare the thematic development of the song with that of the symphonic movement which it engendered; for the present, however, a few general observations will suffice. The theme itself, which begins with the prominent interval of a fourth that already played a significant part in the opening of the first song, seems eminently suited to the voice, though, as we shall see, it is easily adaptable to the purely instrumental idiom. Carrying out the precedent established in the first song, Mahler ends this one in F♯ major rather than in D major. This principle of progressive, rather than concentric, tonality is not only strictly adhered to in each of the songs of this cycle, but also subsequently becomes an important constructive element in the symphonies. The historical significance of such an attitude towards tonality will become apparent in due course.

6 Such alternation is also found (as Pamer shows in examples chosen at random) in German folk-songs which Mahler probably knew. See Pamer, *op. cit.,* XVII, 109.

Cyclic, indeed almost symphonic, form-principles determine the interrelationship of these four songs. We have mentioned the importance of the interval of a fourth in the first two songs. That the stress laid on this interval—which is to become the cornerstone of the First Symphony by virtue of the prominent position which it occupies in the theme *Ging heut' Morgen über's Feld*—was no mere coincidence is proved by the emphatic accentuation it receives in the introduction to the third song, *Ich hab' ein glühend Messer.* And the motivic significance of the fourth is vigorously underlined in the phrase

which is later recalled over a visionary *tremolo* on G. The climactic phrase of the song, in E flat minor (in which tonality the song ends), is related to the phrase "Hab' ich meinen traurigen Tag" of the first song through the highly expressive inflection of a minor sixth. Of all four songs, this one surely bears least resemblance to folk-music, and it gains all the more in dramatic impact because of the contrast between it and the other three.

The last song, *Die zwei blauen Augen von meinem Schatz,* is again a source of material for the First Symphony (third movement). The typically Mahlerian direction *Durchaus mit geheimnissvoll schwermüthigem Ausdruck (nicht schleppen)* sets the stage for a mysterious march-like beginning, likewise typically Mahlerian, which is surprisingly in E minor—surprisingly, because each of the other songs began in D major or minor. Mahler's tonal sense doubtless led him to choose E minor as the most violent possible contrast to the E flat minor immediately preceding. The occasional introduction of a 5/4 measure into the predominating regular 4/4 metre subtly recalls the alternation of 4/8 and 3/8 with which the cycle began. Once more, too, there is a faint reminiscence of the phrase "Hab' ich meinen traurigen Tag." The ever-significant interval of the fourth plays its part not only in melodic construction, but also in the formulation of a characteristic accompaniment-figure which later underlines the poignant word "Ade" in a passage that reminds us strongly of the treatment of that same word (already referred to) in the song *Nicht wiedersehn!* The song ends with a striking application of that juxtaposed major-minor principle which Mahler learned from Schubert and proceeded to make his own, even to the point of using it in condensed form as a motto theme in the Sixth Symphony. Consistent with his scheme of progressive rather than concentric tonality throughout the cycle, Mahler has led the final song from E minor to F minor. The resultant tonal progression of the entire cycle, D minor to F minor, is of more than passing significance since it probably suggested the tonal scheme of the Finale of the First Symphony, which progresses from F minor to D major.

The *Twelve Songs from "Des Knaben Wunderhorn,"* written between 1892 and 1895 [7] and published in two volumes, display further development of the lyricism already found in the earlier *Wunderhorn* songs of the *Lieder und Gesänge.* Two of the songs in this group, *Urlicht* and *Es sungen drei Engel,* are taken directly from the symphonies (Second and Third Symphony respectively); still another, *Des Antonius von Padua Fischpredigt,* served as source-material for the Scherzo of the Second Symphony. The remaining songs are of many types. Grace and playfulness (*Rheinlegendchen*), the macabre (*Wo die schönen Trompeten blasen*), satire (*Lob des hohen Verstandes*), grim tragedy (*Das irdische Leben*)—all these are vividly portrayed in Mahler's music. Some of the poems—*Der Schildwache Nachtlied, Lied des Verfolgten im Turme*—are in dialogue form, giving the composer an opportunity for sharply defined dramatic characterization. Military motives, so beloved of Mahler in song and symphony alike, play a prominent role (*Der Schildwache Nachtlied, Wo die schönen Trompeten blasen*).

Obviously it is impossible to cite all, or even a large proportion, of the striking features of this music. However, a few especially characteristic passages may well be mentioned here. For example, the introduction to *Wo die schönen Trompeten blasen* exposes in a simple and masterly way the harmonic, melodic, rhythmic, and expressive possibilities inherent in the permutations of a single tone, *A.* A grotesque animal imitation in *Lob des hohen Verstands* foreshadows some of Schoenberg's extravagant vocal lines, and similarly exaggerated effects of vocal line enhance the ghastly undertones of *Das irdische Leben,* with its eternally agitated accompaniment in sixteenth-notes grimly moving towards an inevitable end. Of course, such references as these are completely insufficient to give the reader a rounded picture of the lyrical art of Mahler. They should, however, stimulate his interest in music which has been far too little heard on the programs of singers in this country. It is not clear why the songs of Strauss and Wolf should be permitted to overshadow these highly original creations, a

---

[7] Later manuscript discoveries reveal that *Lied des Verfolgten im Turme* and *Wo die schönen Trompeten blasen* were composed in July, 1898. *Lob des hohen Verstandes* was composed in June, 1896. Cf. Mitchell, *op. cit.,* p. 140.

knowledge of which is essential to an understanding of Mahler the symphonist.

The *Sieben Lieder aus letzter Zeit* were written, as the title implies, somewhat later than the *Wunderhorn* songs just discussed. Two of them, *Revelge* and *Der Tamboursg'sell*,[8] were composed about 1899. Both of these are *Wunderhorn* songs with a military motive, similar to other songs of the type which we have already studied. With the five other songs of this series, however, we enter upon a different field; for all of them are based upon poems by Friedrich Rückert, author of the *Kindertotenlieder*. Perhaps it is difficult to determine what attracted Mahler to the rather pallid romanticism of Rückert which seems always to be vacillating between sincere pathos (*Kindertoten-lieder*) and intellectualized word-play (*Ich atmet' einen linden Duft*). However, it is not hard to see that Mahler made the most of the musico-lyrical possibilities of Rückert's verse. The playful "Look not, Love, on my Work Unended" (*Blicke mir nicht in die Lieder*) is not one of Mahler's most significant creations; but a briefer song, "Lov'st Thou but Beauty" (*Liebst du um Schönheit*), is charming in the painstakingly purified simplicity of its melodic and harmonic contours, and the splendid closing pages of "The Midnight Hour" (*Um Mitternacht*) show that Mahler could, when he wished, turn the hymnic ending to as good advantage in his songs as in his symphonies. The finest of the seven songs is, perhaps, *Ich bin der Welt abhanden gekommen;* in its mood of tender resignation, it is like a preliminary version of the famous *Adagietto* of the Fifth Symphony, which was written at about the same time (1901–02).

But none of these songs reach the level of intensity of the *Kinder-totenlieder* (1900–02), which represent the culmination of Mahler's intimate lyric art. Since the *Lieder eines fahrenden Gesellen,* he had eschewed the song-cycle proper (even though all his subsequent collections of songs are unified, poetically at least—*Wunderhorn-Lieder, Rückert-Lieder,* etc.); now he returns to it, and the differences between the *Kindertotenlieder* and the *Lieder eines fahrenden Gesellen* show vividly the great progress made by Mahler the composer in sixteen-odd years.

There are five *Kindertotenlieder,* all of which treat, in varying degrees of emotion, of the same subject—the death of beloved children and the grief of the bereaved parent. Rückert wrote the verses (selected by Mahler from a much larger group bearing the same title) after the death of his own two children from scarlet fever. Imaginative com-

---

[8] Composed in August, 1901 (Mitchell, *op. cit.,* p. 142).

mentators have made much of the fact that Mahler's own little daughter Maria Anna later died of scarlet fever and diphtheria at the age of four (1907); Mahler himself, in a moment of grief, said that he must have foreseen the tragedy when he wrote the songs. (Yet he did not, for Alma Mahler writes that once, when he was working on the orchestration of the last songs at their summer home, she asked him how he could bear to handle so sad a subject when his own two children were playing happily outside, and he replied that it made no difference.)

The sameness of subject and tone throughout the cycle invites the danger of monotony, but Mahler has skilfully avoided this pitfall, thanks to the extreme subtlety of the emotional gradations of his music. He uses few climaxes of a purely dynamic character, with the result that those which he does use come with far more powerful effect. The intensity of emotion is rather inwardly experienced than outwardly expressed. The opening lines of the first song, "Once More the Sun Will Dawn so Bright" (*Nun will die Sonn' so hell aufgeh'n*), already set the tone of powerfully repressed grief which is common to the whole cycle. The second song, "Oh, Now I Know Why Flames so Darkly Glowing" (*Nun seh' ich wohl, warum so dunkle Flammen*), is more openly sentimental and passionate. A passage of concentrated expressiveness leads to the high tone F (the highest so far appearing in the vocal line) and drops back again in a curve logically and beautifully constructed.

The folk elements already observed in previous songs of Mahler appear to a certain extent in the *Kindertotenlieder* as well, although, it is true, in a more refined and subtle form. They are particularly in evidence in the third and fourth songs, "When Your Mother Dear" (*Wenn dein Mütterlein*) and "Often I Think They've Only Gone a Little Way" (*Oft denk' ich, sie sind nur ausgegangen*). Of all these songs, the most passionately externalized in expression is the final one, "In Such a Tempest" (*In diesem Wetter*). The words lend themselves to tone-painting of a striking kind; the instrumental introduction, with its dark coloring, foreshadows the mood of the opening lines, "In such a tempest, in such a storm, Ne'er would I have let the dear children roam!" All the more impressive, when it finally comes, is the contrast of the final verse, "In such a tempest, in such a storm, They rest as in their mother's arms . . . " and of its instrumental epilogue, filled with all the intimate tenderness of a *Hänsel and Gretel* episode.

Up to this point we have discussed exclusively the piano versions of these songs of Mahler. It is, however, necessary to mention their orchestral versions, too. (The term "orchestrations" is avoided, since Mahler did not simply arrange a piano part for orchestra, but actually *rewrote* the song in the orchestral medium.)[9]

The very existence of a song with orchestral accompaniment (exclusive of opera or dramatic aria) would at one time have been considered a paradox. In the days of Schubert the *Lied* was the most intimate form of expression, intended for the home, not the concert-hall. Romantic expansiveness, however, soon forced the *Lied* out of the sphere of chamber music. Here we are permitted to view the reverse of the process whereby—as we shall later see—the song invades the field of the symphony. The accompaniment of the erstwhile simple *Lied* now takes on all the trappings of the full symphonic orchestra. It is fitting that Berlioz, who gave lyricism a predominating place in symphonic structure, should likewise have composed orchestral songs. Thus the penetration of orchestral elements into the field of the *Lied* was complete by the time Mahler arrived on the scene.

Some of Mahler's songs are frankly painted in the most vivid orchestral colors, with an instrumental complement which yields nothing to that of the symphonies in size and variety. A brilliant example of this type is the military song *Revelge,* which is well outfitted with trumpets and military drums and uses every effect of the modern symphony orchestra (e. g. the *col legno*) to underline the dramatic significance of the words. Such a song can be performed as a simple *Lied* with piano accompaniment, but it loses much in such a performance. Side by side with songs of this type, there appear others of a very different instrumental complexion which indicate another trend. As the new century dawned, the post-romantic tendency towards constant expansion of material means of performance began to reverse itself. The chamber orchestra started coming into vogue—and Mahler, creator of monumental orchestral structures which are the complete embodiment of super-romantic expansion, made a noticeable contribution to the new style. Anton Schaefers is quite correct in remarking in connection with the special historical importance of the *Kindertotenlieder* because of the chamber-music-like treatment of the orchestra:

The history of orchestration in the nineteenth century shows a steady increase in the means of orchestral expression. About the turn of the century, . . . a change of direction occurred—the reduction of orchestral means and a definite trend to the chamber orchestra. Two causes, one outward and one inward, seem to have shared joint responsibility here: one is sociological [the financial problem inherent in assembling large orchestral forces] and the other purely musical. The latter, grounded in an altered conception of music,

[9] For the chronology of piano and orchestral versions, see Mitchell, *op. cit.,* and de la Grange, *op. cit.*

seems to have been the decisive one. Arnold Schoenberg's "Chamber Symphony for Fifteen Solo Instruments" is considered an epoch-making work in this new development, and is at the same time radical for its period. [10]

The moment has not yet come to analyze what Schoenberg did with the new trend towards which he found encouragement in Mahler's work. Our more immediate task, since we have already glanced at orchestral elements in the history of the song, is to investigate the reverse of that process, the incursion of the song into the symphony. The results of this investigation will furnish a significant part of the next chapter.

[10] Anton Schaefers, *Gustav Mahlers Instrumentation,* pp. 22–23.

CHAPTER VI

Mahler the Opera Director: Mahler the Symphonist

W E ARE NOW approaching the focal point of all Mahler's creative activity—the symphony. We touch here upon some of the most problematical musical questions of our time. Bruckner's symphonies were already written in a time when "symphonic form" and "symphonic style" were becoming definite and disquieting problems. Mahler's approach to the symphony, however, precipitated a crisis which was to be decisive for modern music.

But, before we proceed to a study of the music itself, let us look for a moment at a phase of Mahler's career which may be appropriately discussed at this point because it ran parallel to his career as a symphonist and in many ways influenced the course of his compositions. In fact, Mahler the opera director was oftentimes, in the public eye, a far more important figure than Mahler the symphonist, whose works some dismissed as mere "Kapellmeistermusik"—the spare-time creations of a conductor who composed on the side.[1]

Mahler found no easy path to the top, either as conductor or composer. His conducting career began in a summer-resort and brought him only gradually to better positions—Prague, Leipzig, Budapest, Hamburg—until he finally secured the coveted directorship of Vienna's Imperial Opera House, in 1897. However, at the age of thirty-seven, he could flatter himself that he had attained a most important position for a comparatively young man; and, without holding any brief for the Austro-Hungarian Empire or its institutions, it may be said that the appointment of a Jew to so high a post indicated a racial tolerance which one might not have expected in court circles (this even though Mahler found it advisable to profess Catholicism as a matter of form).

The decade of Mahler's regime in the Vienna Opera was really a cultural era in itself, and was regarded as such by those who were

[1] See de la Grange, *Mahler,* for a more detailed account of Mahler's operatic career.

fortunate enough to live through it. It was not just the quality of each individual singer or even of each individual performance that made the Vienna Opera what it was during that time; it was the over-all coördinating direction of a single great intellect bent on making the opera-house a true temple of art rather than a mere place of amusement. Just as every symphony which Mahler wrote was regarded by him as a separate world with, as it were, its own special laws of gravity, even so every opera had to be a living, breathing world as well—not a mere "concert in costume," as Mahler used to say. It was his high moral concept of the function of the ideal lyric theater, a concept that expressed itself in a rigorous and relentless perfectionism overlooking no detail of a performance, which set the tone for the ethical ideals of a whole generation of Vienna's musicians and artists.

Although Mahler introduced to the Viennese public novelties of varying national background, including Charpentier's *Louise* (dubbed by a Viennese cartoonist of the day "as flat as lemonade") and Smetana's stirring glorification of the Czech past, *Dalibor,* his organization of the repertory was based on the supremacy of German opera, beginning with Gluck, and extending through Mozart, Beethoven, Weber, and Wagner to Strauss and Pfitzner. Mahler intended to present a complete and unified cycle of operas worked out on this basis, but his departure from the Vienna Opera in 1907 prevented the consummation of this scheme. Some of the works which he presented often are quite forgotten today; among these is one of his favorites, Goetz' *Taming of the Shrew,* which he apparently viewed as a minor classic of German opera, but which seems rather negligible now.

As might be expected, Mahler laid great stress upon the works of Wagner in the repertory; furthermore, he insisted that they be presented without cuts—a reform which even Hans Richter, good Wagnerian as he was, had not instituted, and which was abandoned by Weingartner when he became Mahler's successor at the Vienna Opera. Mahler was fortunate in having many excellent Wagnerian singers, of whom some had been members of the Vienna personnel before his time, while others were added during his directorship. Chief among these was the incomparable tragic actress Anna von Mildenburg, later the wife of the Austrian writer Hermann Bahr. She had been a very good friend of Mahler's in Hamburg, and had, indeed, served her apprenticeship in opera under him. Her teacher, Rosa Papier-Paumgartner, who had been most helpful in the negotiations that finally brought Mahler to Vienna, was instrumental, too, in securing a position for Anna there; and from then on her presence lent added lustre to such productions as that of *Tristan und Isolde.* There were those who felt that her acting was considerably better than her vocal technique, and the same was said of Marie Gutheil-Schoder, also a favored singer during the Mahler regime. But such criticisms did not perturb Mahler; he would rather people his stage with intelligent actors and actresses than with exponents of a flawless *bel canto* who were unable to enter into the ensemble spirit of opera. Mahler and Strauss used to have many amiable arguments on this subject; but, later, their viewpoints underwent complete reversal, for Mahler, under the influence of the Metropolitan Opera (which, during his New York stay, offered him vocal material of a higher calibre than anything dreamed of in Vienna), became more and more enamored of the *bel canto,* while Strauss fell to writing operatic parts especially designed for singers like Anna von Mildenburg.

It was not merely Mahler's productions of Wagner, it was his entire conception of opera in general which was conditioned by Wagnerian ideals. This is shown in many ways, but particularly in his treatment of other operas, as, for example, his curtailment of the final scene of Smetana's *Dalibor* for a reason which has to do with the drama as such, not with the music. Since the laws of drama are completely different from the laws of opera, few opera libretti—and Wagner's are not among the few—can stand on their own feet as plays. But, in altering operas for dramatic reasons (and *Dalibor* was not the only case of this kind), Mahler showed that he was under the influence of that Wagnerian theory which would give drama the supremacy over music.

During the latter half of his Viennese regime, Mahler had an outstanding collaborator who displayed a real understanding of his wishes and who, at the same time, influenced him to innovations. This was Alfred Roller, his stage designer. The theatrical conceptions of both Roller and Mahler were strongly conditioned by their knowledge of Adolphe Appia's book *Die Musik und die Inscenierung.* In that work, Appia, all of whose ideas were based on the assumption that Wagner's *Musikdrama* was the dramatic form of the future, had propounded the thesis that present-day staging, even as conceived by Wagner himself, was completely inadequate for the realization of Wagner's grand design. Too often, the conventional stage was merely a pretty picture which had little or nothing to do with the activities of the singing actors upon it, and which impeded, rather than assisted, their efforts to create an illusion. Appia maintained that the singing actor was the most important single element upon the stage and that all other elements must be, not necessarily subordinated to him, but correlated with him. To this end he proposed such reforms as the elimination of the false perspective of painted backdrops and a general minimizing of the role of painting in favor of that of functional lighting. Similarly, Roller's stage ideas tended to stress architecture more than flat painting. There were, for example, the four famous towers of the Roller-Mahler production of *Don Giovanni*, which dominated every scene of the opera. These towers were condemned by many, and even Mahler and Roller themselves were not too enthusiastic about them in the long run. But then, as Mahler said, they had been used merely as an experiment, and another experiment could be tried the next time, for was not experimentation the very life-blood of the theater?

Mahler never wanted his opera productions to degenerate into routine; yet, in a theater which had to give performances every day, it was impossible to maintain indefinitely the high standards of a festival. It was this, as much as anything else, which caused Mahler to become dissatisfied with work in the theater, and which drove him to inward revolt against theatrical conventions long before his actual resignation from the Vienna Opera. Gradually he came to realize that such perfection as he dreamed of could not possibly exist on the lyric stage—not even in Vienna, which, he admitted, had offered him more resources than he could have found anywhere else. Nothing would satisfy him but a theater in which each performance was just as fine as the preceding one; and that was an unattainable ideal. He could not achieve it; none had achieved it before him and none could achieve it after him. Besides, affairs of censorship, such as that which had prevented his presentation of *Salome* in the Vienna Opera, were profoundly depressing to him; and his interests as opera-director and as composer came into conflict more and more often—indeed, it was an argument over the question of whether or not he was entitled to a leave of absence for the purpose of conducting his own compositions which was the immediate cause of his resignation.

Considering the many difficulties of Mahler's double career, one might wonder whether his labors as opera-director were detrimental to his accomplishments as a composer. Insofar as his directorship took up a great deal of time, so that only the summers could be devoted freely to composition, such a question would have to be answered in the affirmative. But, on the other hand, his conducting career gave him added routine and knowledge of orchestral effects which showed to brilliant advantage in his symphonies, and his operatic conceptions definitely influenced his symphonic thinking. These things will become clear in our discussion of Mahler the symphonist.

It is easy to be misled in the study of Mahler's symphonies by circumstances which belong to the era in which the music was written, not to the music itself. Even as Bruckner was led, partly by the powers of suggestion of his disciples and partly by his own naïveté, to provide inappropriate programmatic backgrounds to his symphonies, so Mahler was influenced by the spirit of the times to imagine detailed programs for his symphonies—notably the First, Second, and Third—so that they might be more easily understood by those who required a specific literary program to stimulate their musical thinking. But such an idealist was bound to find this procedure unsatisfactory in the long run, particularly since those who were sensitive enough to understand the music had no need of the program, while those for whose benefit the program was written tended to be absorbed in the program to the detriment of the music. Naturally, Mahler expressed himself frequently and at great length on this vital subject, so that we cannot possibly remain in doubt as to his views. For example, he writes to Max Marschalk in connection with the very sympathetic review which the latter gave to an all-Mahler concert (including the First Symphony) in Berlin on March 16, 1896:

There is some justification for the title [of the First Symphony] ("Titan") [after Jean Paul Richter] and for the program; that is, at the time my friends persuaded me to provide a kind of program for the D major Symphony in order to make it easier to understand. Therefore, I had thought up this title and explanatory material after the actual composition. I left them out for this performance, not only because I think they are quite inadequate and do not even characterize the music accurately, but also because I have learned through past experiences how the public has been misled by them. But that is the way with every program! Believe me, the symphonies of Beethoven, too, have their inner program, and when one gets to know such works better one's understanding for the proper succession of the emotions and ideas increases. In the end, that will be true of my works also.[2]

In the third movement (funeral march) it is true that I got the immediate inspiration from the well-known children's picture [after Callot] ("The Huntsman's Funeral.")—But in this place it is irrelevant what is represented—the only important thing is the *mood* which should be expressed and from which the fourth movement then springs suddenly, like lightning from a dark cloud. It is simply the cry of a deeply wounded heart, preceded by the ghastly brooding oppressiveness of the funeral march.[3]

Six days after writing these words, Mahler wrote to Marschalk again on March 26, 1896. What he has to say in this letter is even more directly concerned with the problem of the validity of the "symphonic program." He wrote:

Just as I find it banal to invent music for a program, I find it unsatisfactory and unfruitful to try to give a program to a piece of music—this in spite of the fact that the *immediate cause* of a musical conception is certainly an ex-

[2] Such ideas were later to be carried to absurd lengths in the literary interpretations of Beethoven by Arnold Schering and the *Neue Deutung* school.

[3] Mahler, *Briefe 1879–1911*, pp. 185–86.

perience of the author, that is to say a fact which is surely concrete enough to be described in words. We stand now—I am sure of it—at the great crossroads which will soon separate forever the two diverging paths of symphonic and dramatic music in plain sight of those who have a clear conception of the essence of music.—Even now, when you put a symphony of Beethoven and the tone-pictures of Wagner side by side, you will easily detect the essential differences between the two.—It is true that Wagner appropriated the *means of expression* of symphonic music, just as now in his turn the symphonist will be justified in helping himself to the new possibilities of expression opened to music by Wagner's efforts and in using them for his own means. In this sense, all the arts, even art itself, are united with nature. But no one has thought sufficiently about this as yet, because no one has as yet achieved a perspective view of the situation.—Besides, I have not constructed such-and-such a system for myself and then based my creative work upon it; but, after composing several symphonies (with real birth-pangs) and always running into the same misunderstandings and problems, I have finally come to this view of things as far as I personally am concerned.

All the same, it is good when, during the first period when my style still seems strange and new, the listener gets some road-maps and milestones on the journey—or, rather, a map of the stars, that he may comprehend the night sky with its glowing worlds.—But such an explanation cannot offer more.—Man must make the association with something *already known*—otherwise, he is lost.[4]

In the light of this statement it is possible to interpret the detailed "program" for the Second Symphony, which comprises the rest of this letter to Marschalk, as a suggestion of the content of the music rather than a precise map of the territory to be traversed. Indeed, this is the only way to interpret such programs as they apply to Mahler's music. The difference between his and Bruckner's programmatic interpretations is one of intent. While Bruckner let himself be led into fanciful descriptions out of a naïve desire to please and to be up-to-date, Mahler concocted his programs deliberately to lure a certain type of listener into appreciation of his music. Let it not be thought, however, that Mahler was consciously insincere when he worked out such a literary program. He simply had a very keen awareness of how much—or how little—it was worth. Surely it is obvious how different his approach to this whole problem was from that of Strauss, who used the kaleidoscopic musical material of his tone-poems to create concrete pictures and tell a definite story. Mahler used to say that he and Strauss were like two miners who dig into a mountain from opposite sides—only to come out at the same place. The "place" can be considered the same only in a sense of absolute ideality; Mahler felt that Strauss was working towards the ultimate aims of music, as he himself was, but in an entirely different way. (As a matter of fact, the mutual esteem between Mahler and

[4] *Ibid.*, pp. 187–88.

Strauss was not on as high a level as this one remark would seem to indicate.)

Mahler did not want to turn the symphony into an animated accompaniment for extra-musical phenomena. He also did not want to cling to the codified school-form which had given Bruckner so much moral support. What, then, was his conception of the purpose of the symphony? In a previous chapter we learned that, for him, each symphony was a separate world with a law and order all its own which must be built up afresh with every new symphonic composition. One so literary-minded as Mahler would hardly have left posterity without more than one reference to so important a theme, and so we find in his letters many significant passages such as the following:

Imagine a work so great that the whole world is actually reflected therein—one is, so to speak, only an instrument upon which the universe plays. But I have explained it to you so often already—and you must accept it, if you really understand me. You see, everyone must realize this in order to live with me. In such moments I no longer belong to myself. . . . The creator of such a work must suffer dreadful birth-pangs, and much absent-mindedness, self-centeredness and renunciation of the outside world must of necessity precede the mental processes of organization, construction and inspiration. . . . My symphony will be something which the world has never heard the like of before! All Nature is endowed with a voice there, and tells secrets so profound that we can perhaps imagine them only in dreams! I tell you, I sometimes have the strangest feeling in many passages, just as if I hadn't written them.[5]

And again:

My music is, everywhere and always, only a sound of nature! It seems to me to be this which Bülow once designated significantly, in a conversation with me, as the "Symphonic Problem." I do not recognize any other sort of program, at least not for my own works. Although I have given them titles now and then, it is just because I wanted to indicate where emotion should become transformed into imagination. If words are necessary for this purpose, the articulate human voice is there to fulfill the boldest ambitions—thanks to its association with the revealing word![6]

Later, to Willem Mengelberg:

I have just finished my Eighth Symphony—it is the greatest thing I've done yet. And so original in content and form that it absolutely cannot be described! —Imagine the universe beginning to ring and resound. It is no longer human voices, it is planets and suns revolving.[7]

Such romanticized descriptions of Mahler's musical intent give some idea of the problems posed by the music itself; these problems could not be understood without previous knowledge of the basic conceptions,

[5] *Ibid.,* pp. 162–63. [6] *Ibid.,* p. 215.
[7] *Ibid.,* p. 332.

however exaggerated they may have been, which guided Mahler in symphonic composition. [8]

In the First Symphony we are confronted with a "symphonic problem" of the first magnitude; for, more than any other orchestral work of his, this symphony is saturated with thematic material from his own songs—in this case, as we have already seen, the *Lieder eines fahrenden Gesellen.* The importance of such procedure on Mahler's part can hardly be over-emphasized. Lyrical elements had been penetrating the symphony for a long time, and in many different directions—as witness the operatically-inspired "singing allegros" of Mozart (e. g. the first movement of the great E flat major Symphony) and the incursion of the human voice into the symphony with Beethoven. Schubert had set a precedent for introducing his own song themes into instrumental works with the *Forellenquintett,* the quartet *Death and the Maiden,* and the fantasy in C major for violin and piano which contains variations on *Sei mir gegrüsst;* such lyric elements were used by him in conformity with the classic symphonic principles. Mahler was the first to use song-themes structurally in the symphony, and this fact is of great significance as an indicator of late nineteenth-century trends.

We have spoken before of the "decline of the classical symphony." By this phrase has been understood the steady growth of lyrical elements in the symphony to the detriment of that dramatic contrast between principal and subordinate theme-groups and tonalities which had been the basis of the classical symphonic style. In a sense, the expansion of lyrical elements in the symphony began with the moment of their appearance in the subordinate theme-group; certainly it would be a mistake to assume that their expansion began only with the romantic period, as we can already see a full-blown lyricism in the principal theme of the first movement of Mozart's E flat Symphony. But during the romantic period lyricism became ever more prominent until, in extreme instances, it blotted out that thematic contrast which had given the classic symphony "form." Insofar as we are justified in using the term "decline of the classical symphony," it is in connection with such phenomena as the symphonies of Schumann, which fall in an uncomfortable period of transition when the expanding lyricism has not yet created a new form to fit its needs.

Bruckner and Mahler were both profoundly affected by this "decline," but this does not mean that we should criticize their works by

---

[8] The Critical Editions of Mahler's symphonies often differ in details from the scores on which these analyses were based. The reader is advised to consult the Critical Edition, wherever possible, for comparison.

comparing them with classical symphonies and finding fault with them at every point in which they differ from the classical model. To recapitulate for a moment what was said in an earlier chapter: we must remember that the mere word "symphony" itself has no abstract meaning of its own but can be made to cover a multitude of concepts, and that it is quite impossible to measure the concept of Mahler with the completely different concept of Mozart, although Bruckner may be more fairly measured with his forebears since he was consciously bound to a previously used form. Besides, the abovementioned classical model proves, on closer examination, to be practically non-existent; for, while there are certain principles of theme-building which seem to be common to all symphonies of a certain era (for which "classical" merely happens to be a more or less convenient name), the ways in which these principles are used by Haydn, by Mozart, or by Beethoven—so often and so handily lumped together—are all radically different from each other.

One generalization is, however, possible; in the classic symphony (or sonata or quartet), the real song elements are confined to those movements which are not in sonata form. One thinks of Haydn's variations on the Austrian hymn, as well as the abovementioned song-movements of Schubert and countless other variations on song-like themes written by Haydn, Dittersdorf, Rosetti, and others. These were relics of the old divertimento, which still lived in Mozart's well-known A major piano sonata (wherein "sonata" form had no rights at all, for the first movement was a set of variations). Therefore, it was Mahler who first used a real song-theme (not to be confused with a "singing allegro" theme) in any of the major movements of a symphony; and this new expansion of lyricism finds its parallel in the new enlargement of the lyric field—from the simple song with piano accompaniment to the elaborate orchestral song.

While it would probably be going too far to say that any formal insufficiencies we may feel in Mahler's First Symphony are caused by the dominance of a song-theme in the first movement, it is doubtless true that he had not yet completely learned the art of handling his lyrical materials symphonically. Small wonder, for this was his first mature symphonic composition, and, what is more, it was conceived at a most turbulent period in Mahler's emotional life, when his mind was dominated by everything that the *Lieder eines fahrenden Gesellen* stood for. If, therefore, we feel at certain moments that the First Symphony might have been more accurately named "Fantasy on Themes from *Lieder eines fahrenden Gesellen*," we must recall that in some ways this symphony is atypical of Mahler's subsequent work. But to say this is not to belittle the symphony, for—to name but one of its many outstanding features—the third movement is absolutely original in the musical literature of its time, creating a mood of bitter irony which had not been previously expressed in music but which was later to find continuation in Schoenberg.

It is not just the themes of the *Lieder eines fahrenden Gesellen* which give the First Symphony its distinctive tone, but the symbolic extract of those themes, the interval of a fourth. The whole introduction of sixty-two measures (all over a pedal-point reminiscent of Bruckner's symphonic beginnings) is based on permutations of this basic interval disguised variously as a cuckoo-call or a military trumpet-signal. The second movement contains none of the song-themes, but is dominated by the ever-present fourth nevertheless. The exposition of the "Frère Jacques" theme in the third movement is accompanied by a thirty-six measure pedal-point on D–A in the tympani, while the fourth is prominent in the "parody" section which, according to Mahler, imitates Bohemian village musicians. Finally, in the last movement, the characteristic interval conditions the outlines not only of the sturdy marching principal theme (which was already in evidence in the first movement), but also of the triumphal D major apotheosis of the entire symphony.

This preoccupation with the interval of a fourth inevitably reminds us of Bruckner's fondness for themes based on the primary intervals of fourth and fifth—for example, in the Romantic Symphony. Here is an unquestionable case of Bruckner's influence on Mahler; Mahler could not deny it himself, even when he castigated his former master's "underdone" music; nor can Mahler's critics deny it by saying that he could not comprehend Bruckner because he performed Bruckner's Sixth Symphony with excessive cuts.

Once the long pedal-point introduction of the first movement is over, the theme proper is introduced. Here, then, we can begin to compare the development of the symphonic movement with that of the song on which it is based. As might be expected, the actual melodic sequence of the song can be literally repeated in the symphony for a comparatively short period only. As a matter of fact, only the first eight-and-a-half measures of the vocal melody remain unaltered at the beginning of the symphony. Whereas the phrase "Ei du! Gelt?" in the song ends with a whole note followed by a whole rest, in the symphony it is immediately treated in sequence-style. Three neutral measures then lead to a transposed version in A major of measures 4–33 of the B major portion of the song, beginning with the text-words "Und da fieng im Sonnenschein." The order of the original materials of the song is altered in the symphonic exposition, for the next section, beginning with the statement of the principal theme in the 'cello, is a direct transposition from the earlier D major section of the song, "Auch die Glockenblum' am Feld'."

Thus far we have come across singularly little symphonic development of song materials; they have merely been rearranged—a sign that Mahler was not quite sure as yet how to handle such materials. This impression is strengthened by the remarkable fact that, instead of going on to new forms of thematic development and new modulations, Mahler simply begins his elaboration section with an open return to the introduction and its pedal-point on A. As a beginning after the manner of Bruckner, or as a piece of *Naturstimmung*, this introduction was highly effective at the opening of the symphony, but when recapitulated so soon it seems to lose in effectiveness, even though the recapitulation is not literal. The pedal-point, indeed, shifts from A to F; but this makes little difference, for Mahler is soon back to D major again (at number 15 in the full score). In fact, he then continues in D major so long that it is impossible to be sure whether he actually intends to have a development section or not. Stiedry has referred to this portion of the movement as a "second exposition" in his explanatory notes written for the Boosey and Hawkes edition of this symphony; but, since Mahler eventually comes to the point of modulating in a manner consistent with symphonic elaboration, and even of introducing a new theme (the principal theme of the finale), such a change in terminology seems unnecessary. One wonders, however, why Mahler felt the necessity of dwelling on the tonic so long in the section of elaboration. Bruckner sometimes did the same thing, but usually as a counterbalance to extensive modulations in the exposition; Mahler, on the other hand, remained so close to tonic and dominant in this exposition that such an explanation cannot be admitted. With due respect to the symphonic mastery (in a very special sense) of the mature Mahler, it seems impossible to attribute this particular procedure in his first symphonic composition (aside from the unknown *Nordische Symphonie* which he destroyed) to anything else but an uncertainty leading to formal and stylistic inconsistency; for there is not even an external justification for it in the literary program. The best proof that immaturity is the correct explanation is the fact that Mahler never resorted to such a mode of procedure again in the same way.

Concerning the recapitulation of this movement—a vivid and fresh piece in spite of all its inconsistencies—it may be remarked that Mahler has, as in the exposition, failed to follow that almost stereotyped scheme of Bruckner wherein at least three themes, each of a specific and easily definable sort, are stated at length and are recapitulated at equal length, only to be followed by a coda of vast proportions. Mahler's coda here is only thirty-five measures long—of almost classical brevity, indeed. Here it must be reiterated that, just as Mahler was not a devotee of the ready-made vast form in the way that Bruckner was, his themes are not so automatically typified or so easily interchangeable. As in the case of any composer with a definite, original style of his own, it is possible to find thematic characteristics common to many themes of Mahler, but it would be difficult to catalogue Mahler's themes in the same orderly fashion as Bruckner's.

The second movement [9] of the First Symphony may be passed over briefly, for it presents no novel stylistic features. Of all the movements, it is closest to the style of Bruckner (and also of Schubert), especially in the *Ländler*-like Trio. Mahler shows a fine psychological sense of the values of performance when he follows this uncomplicated and direct movement with the "stage-direction," "make a rather long pause here before the next movement (No. 3) begins." In no other way could he have shown how clearly he felt the contrast between the two movements; for the third movement, while outwardly not complicated, is psychologically—as cannot be too often reiterated—one of the most subtle delineations of bitter irony in the whole of musical literature, and, in fact, the first of its kind.

There is no need to quote the familiar "Frère Jacques" motive with which this movement begins, and the long pedal-point over which it is stated has already been referred to. Harmonically simple though this section, centering around tonic and dominant, may at first seem to be, it contains dissonant passages which are far more than mere contrapuntal curiosities.

"On the street there stands a linden-tree; there for the first time I lay at rest." This is the theme of the middle section, "sehr einfach und schlicht wie eine Volkweise," which is based on the final section of the song *Die zwei blauen Augen von meinem Schatz.* The treatment of the song material differs from that of the first movement; whereas the order of the individual motives was arbitrarily reversed in the first movement, the section "Auf der Strasse steht ein Lindenbaum . . . Lieb', und Leid, und Welt, und Traum!" is simply transposed from F major to G major here, without any change in the

[9] Recently, the original second movement, *Blumine,* of the symphony's first, five-movement version has been discovered. See Jack Diether, *"Blumine* and the First Symphony," in "Notes on some Mahler Juvenilia," *Chord and Discord,* 1969, pp. 76–100. The score of *Blumine* is published by Theodore Presser; a performance of the five-movement version of the First Symphony by the New Haven Symphony Orchestra under Frank Brieff is available on Odyssey Records.

order of its individual segments. In accordance with the dynamic indication this section in the original song, "Soft till the very end" (*Leise, bis zum Schluss*), everything in this part of the symphony happens within a dynamic range of *p* to *ppp*.

It is after this G major section that Mahler indulges in one of those tonal subtleties which were to be so characteristic of his later work. We have already remarked that he considerably lessened the effectiveness of the long introduction to the first movement by repeating it, *in the same key*, at the beginning of the elaboration section. But when he did not have to cope with the problems of moulding song material into sonata form, his fine harmonic sense came to the fore and guarded him against such a mistake. Here, the beginning of the recapitulation of the "Frère Jacques" theme in E flat minor, following upon the final G minor of the "Lindenbaum" section, is of striking effectiveness, all the more so as the theme enters *ppp*. The return to D minor is prepared for by the introduction of the "parody" theme in a B flat major which can be understood either as the dominant of E flat minor or as the sixth degree of D minor. The actual modulation back to D minor in the recapitulation is accomplished by a simple sequence, which is executed by the first violins divided into three equal parts and playing *col legno* (a direction which Mahler, fearful lest his special effect be overlooked, underlines in a frantic footnote: "Note for the conductor: No error! To be bowed with the wood").

From here on there is a gradual *diminuendo* until the end of the movement, which closes in *ppp*. This is another of Mahler's carefully contrived theatrical effects which prove repeatedly how large a part the concepts of the lyric theater play in his symphonies. After a brief fermata, he begins the Finale, "Stürmisch bewegt," with a crashing chord *fff*. He himself used to tell with pride how, at the first performance, one startled lady jumped from her seat and dropped all her possessions when this chord jarred the audience out of its complacent listening. Such tricks had been indulged in by composers ever since Haydn; but, knowing Mahler's theatrical tendencies, one may be tempted to conclude that this is a case of the introduction of the spectacular for its own sake. Such excesses seem to be more characteristic of Mahler's earlier works than of his more mature creations; although the love for violent contrasts remained with him always, he was later able to motivate them more convincingly. The two principal themes of this Finale display a contrast which has been dramatically conceived but not completely integrated from a musical point of view. The martial first theme has but little to do with the tender, lyrical second theme, which is worked out on its own level and is, as it were, insulated from the surrounding storm. This theme is developed almost in the fashion of a separate lyrical piece and its differentiation from the rest of the thematic material is symbolized by the fact that it is not developed at all in the section of elaboration. Because of this differentiation, we may be troubled by the feeling that, in spite of its intrinsic beauty, the theme is not an organic part of the symphonic structure, but has been deliberately inserted for the sake of calculated contrast. In Mahler's other symphonies we shall occasionally find a single movement which stands in the same relationship to the rest of the movements as this lyrical theme to the surrounding thematic complex—for example, the *Andante grazioso* of the Second Symphony (second movement) and the *Adagietto* of the Fifth Symphony (fourth movement).

Of all the movements of the First Symphony, it is the Finale which displays most originality of construction. Particularly significant in this respect is the tonal scheme of the movement; surprisingly, it begins in F minor, only to end in D major, the basic tonality of the entire symphony. The idea of using such a tonal scheme for the Finale may well have been suggested to Mahler by his consistent use of the same device in the *Lieder eines fahrenden Gesellen* on which the symphony is based; but one cannot be sure whether or not he consciously used it as a link between the two works in the same sense as, for example, the thematic links. In any case, it is this tonal scheme which largely determines the structure of this movement. During the exposition, Mahler confines himself to F minor and its related keys, with, as has already been noted, a subordinate theme in D flat major. It is, then, in the region of D flat that the elaboration begins; a section of roving harmony (cue numbers 22–25 in the full score) leads to a positive C major section (25–28) which is followed by a C minor passage designed to culminate in the all-important modulation to D major. Mahler, once more displaying his sure and keen dramatic instincts, remains strictly in C minor until the last possible moment, and accomplishes his striking modulation with the fewest possible chords. There is no academic way of accounting for the effectiveness of this modulation. Not even the Schoenbergian idea of "strong steps" as developed from Sechter's theories explains it adequately; for the final and decisive step from B flat to D is actually, according to this theory, a "weak" root-progression because a weaker tone in the first chord (the third) becomes the root of the second chord. And yet this modulation, for all its abruptness, is peculiarly and immediately convincing. However, it confronts us with an immediate problem. If Mahler proposes to end the whole movement in D major, how is he to accomplish the feat of bringing, at once as a surprise and as a convincing ending, a final D major which has already been anticipated by the D major here in the section of elaboration? At first sight, he does not appear unduly concerned with this problem; for he not only dwells on D major in an almost coda-like manner during the elaboration, but he also returns to the thematic material of the introduction to the first movement in D minor. The retransition to the recapitulation takes place during this D minor episode; the pedal-point on D proceeds downward chromatically via D flat to C, where it remains to serve the expected function of an upbeat-dominant to F minor or major. What follows, however, is unexpected. The recapitulation begins with the second theme, in F major, and the first theme makes its appearance only after the second theme has been allowed its full melodic development. Here is a device which is unusual and which has certainly been taken note of by Mahler's admirers (cf. the recapitulation of Schoenberg's *Kammersymphonie* No. I).

The first theme is now being recapitulated in F minor. How is Mahler to return to D major without anticlimax, since he already has exploited so many of the possibilities of D major in the elaboration? He accomplishes this by a remarkable crescendo (already used in the first movement) of comparatively simple harmonic background, compounded of rhythmic subdivision and thematic liquidation. Taking the third measure of the principal theme,

Mahler transfers it to the bass, inverts it,

and then uses it as an *ostinato* **bass:**

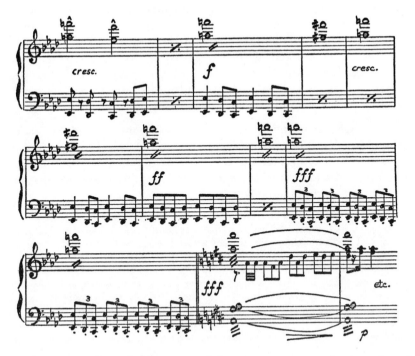

The turn to D major here certainly comes as a surprise in spite of the emphasis on D major in the elaboration. This is not only because D major was approached in quite a different manner in the elaboration, but also, perhaps, because of certain psychological phenomena associated with dramatic music. We have already said that Mahler's symphonic music has strong dramatic tendencies, and that its spirit is often close to that of the Wagnerian music-drama. Now, key-consciousness in dramatic music, at least in dramatic music of the nineteenth century (for the profound and detailed key-symbolism of the *Magic Flute* is quite another matter) is of far less importance than in symphonic music. This has nothing to do with the question of atonality; it simply means that the composer, on the one hand, is much less likely to be concerned about the possible effect of several different returns to the same key in an operatic scene than in a symphonic movement, and, on the other hand, that even the intensely musical listener is, by the same token, equally unlikely to observe such returns to a given key or to notice whether a scene begins and ends in the same key. This kind of nineteenth-century "operatic" tonal conception plays its part, not only in Mahler's composition *per se* but also in our perception of it, so that a tonal procedure which would have seemed unnatural, amateurish even, in a classical symphony, is perfectly understandable in Mahler. And, even if we had any doubts left, the triumphal and affirmative D major close seems to wipe out all recollection of them. So, in this optimistic and positive vein—not unlike the happy ending of Jean Paul's *Titan* which was its partial inspiration—closes Mahler's First Symphony.

It is fitting to introduce the Second Symphony with Mahler's own programmatic explanation of it, but only on the condition (as Mahler himself says) that we take the program only as an *Andeutung* and not as a literal description of everything which happens in the symphony. He writes to Max Marschalk:

> I have called the first movement "Funeral Pomp," and, in case you want to know, it is the hero of my D major symphony whom I bear to his grave there, and upon the clear reflection of whose life I gaze from a higher vantage point. At the same time there is the great question: "Why hast thou lived? Why hast thou suffered? Is all this only a great and ghastly joke?"—We *must* solve these problems in one way or another, if we are to continue living—yes, even if we are to continue dying! He in whose life this call has once resounded must give an answer; and I give this answer in the last movement.
> The second and third movements are designed as an interlude; the second movement is a recollection—a sunny scene, calm and untroubled, from the life of this hero.
> It must have happened to you once—you have borne a dear friend to his grave, and then, perhaps on your way homewards, there suddenly appeared before you the image of a long-past hour of happiness, which now enters into your soul like a sunbeam—marred by no shadow—you can almost forget what has just happened! That is the second movement!—Then, when you awaken from this nostalgic dream and must return to life's confusion, it may easily occur that this perpetually moving, never-ending, ever-incomprehensible hustle and bustle of life becomes *eerie* to you, like the movements of dancing figures in a brightly-lighted ballroom into which you gaze out of the dark night—from so far off that you *do not hear the dance-music* any more! Life becomes senseless to you then, a ghastly apparition from which you, perhaps, recoil with a cry of disgust!—This is the third movement! What follows it is already clear to you! [10] —

We shall have more to say later about "what follows." For the present, Mahler's comments on the first three movements (the purely instrumental portion of the symphony) and the music itself give us a wide field for further commentary.

The first movement, to be performed *mit durchaus ernstem und feierlichem Ausdruck,* begins in a manner strongly reminiscent of the typical Bruckner symphonic opening. We already have observed such a phenomenon in the First Symphony; and such specific examples as

[10] Mahler, *op. cit.,* pp. 188–89.

these should make us wary of categorical statements that Mahler really owed nothing to Bruckner or, on the other hand, that Mahler was not able to assimilate what Bruckner had to offer (the manner of formulating the premise depending on whether the commentator is pro- or anti-Mahler). Here are all the ingredients of the opening measures of a Bruckner symphony: the *tremolo* pedal-point of long duration, the long principal theme unfolded gradually (in individual segments) in the bass instruments. In these respects Mahler's Second Symphony could well be compared with Bruckner's Second, which is, coincidentally, also in C minor. There, however, the differences begin—for the stormy mood of Mahler's principal theme contrasts radically with the tender lyricism of Bruckner's. Both bass-theme and *tremolo* pedal-point are set forth in a broad, extended form; then a brief semi-thematic transition leads to the first statement of the subordinate theme, which is still accompanied by the triplet-rhythm of the first theme. Although this subsidiary theme has all the lyrical qualities noted in that of the Finale of the First Symphony, Mahler has protected it from the too strict isolation which separated the latter theme from the motivic life of the rest of the movement, by using an accompaniment derived from the first theme. We are now prepared for a full unfolding of the lyrical theme, but just as it reaches its climax, Mahler cuts it off and backtracks to the *tremolo* on G and a variant of the first theme. Superficially, this is the procedure which he followed in the first movement of the First Symphony; but here we do not feel that the return to the beginning represents a stoppage of movement. It is, rather, as though the E major passage represented a brief interlude after which the mood of the beginning continues as though it had never been interrupted.

The section which now follows may be considered either as a second exposition or as the first part of the elaboration. The manner in which the first theme is re-developed, as well as the more extensive development of the second theme-group in C major and then in E major, would seem to justify the contention that this is rather a new and more detailed exposition of the principal thematic groups than a modulatory elaboration. On the other hand, the introduction of new thematic complexes, such as are often found in sections of elaboration, might well support the opposite view. An interesting thematic episode, which serves the function of "standing on the dominant" in preparation for the entrance of the subordinate theme in C major, is founded on a bass motive closely related to the First Symphony. These interrelationships between one symphony and the next are not uncommon in Mahler's work, as we shall have occasion to observe later. Here, the thematic relationship implements Mahler's own assertion that the Second Symphony is in a spiritual sense the logical continuation of the First.

The most important of the new thematic complexes, which begins as though it were to be a simple continuation of the E major (or minor) section of the subordinate theme-group but which soon discloses a developmental character that removes it entirely from the realm of the exposition, is related in spirit to the first theme and also resembles it rhythmically. Accompanied by a figure the derivation of which from the first theme is obvious, the new theme, stated by the English horn and bass clarinet in octaves, begins with a chorale-like simplicity of rhythm which foreshadows the important "Dies irae" motive. The developmental section which begins with this theme elaborates both principal and subordinate motives in modulatory fashion, and terminates in a clear B major after which the sudden irruption of the principal theme in E flat minor comes as the greatest possible surprise. Just as in every other instance of the appearance of this theme in the movement, the beginning of a new section is marked by its entrance. This section may be regarded as still another "elaboration"; it serves the purpose of presenting another new theme, which may be styled the "Dies irae" motive, although its similarity to the Gregorian "Dies irae" theme (already used by so many composers) ends with the opening phrase. It is significant that, just as Mahler used a familiar motive ("Frère Jacques") in the First Symphony, he feels the need of referring here to one almost equally familiar. Yet another proof of the spiritual relationship between the First and Second Symphonies!

The formal analysis of this movement thus far indicates that Mahler is not attempting to fill out an accepted pattern of "symphonic form." The classical tripartite pattern is present only in approximation, for the major sections of the movement are at least five in number— counting the recapitulation, which begins with the characteristic principal sixteenth-note motive, restates the subordinate theme in E major (curiously enough, the same key in which it appeared in the first exposition), and plays towards the end with that shift from major to minor which is one of Mahler's most trenchant mottoes. The novel construction of the movement goes far to confirm the principle that each symphonic entity must be built up as a separate world. Mahler has used constructional techniques already familiar to us from the First Symphony (e. g., the persistent tendency to return to the tonic and to the principal theme) but has handled them with more confidence and conviction here.

"Here follows," writes Mahler at the close of the first movement, "a

pause of at least five minutes." Five-minute pauses are surely unusual
in symphonic performances; but the reason for this indication on
Mahler's part is not far to seek. Ostensibly, the detailed program given
by Mahler might be accepted as sufficient justification for such a procedure. But the plain fact is that the musical material of this second
movement, while in itself charming and developed with finesse, is not
of sufficient weight to follow the ponderous and somewhat sinister first
movement. This is equally true of the *Ländler*-like first theme, with its
strong overtones of Bruckner and Schubert,[11] and of the *scherzando*
second theme. With characteristic intellectual honesty, Mahler admitted this musical deficiency in a letter to Julius Buths, a conductor
and the director of the Düsseldorf Conservatory, who was planning a
performance of the Second Symphony for April 2, 1903:

> . . . a definite pause for organization is necessary after the first movement
> *also*, because the second movement does not achieve the effect of contrast, but
> is merely a discrepancy after the first movement. This is my fault, and not due
> to any lack of understanding on the listener's part. . . .
> While the first, third, fourth, and fifth movements hang together themati-
> cally and spiritually, the second movement stands alone and interrupts, in a
> sense, the stern and inexorable sequence of events.[12]

As for the form of this disputable movement, it is of the simplest
nature—in rondo-like fashion, the first theme always returns with variations—and so does not require further discussion.

With the third movement, we return to a type of composition already familiar to us from the First Symphony—the character-piece
based on a song. The song in this case is a setting of a *Wunderhorn*
text, *St. Anthony's Sermon to the Fishes,* which expresses symbolically
the same restless and futile motion that we feel instinctively in the
orchestral score even without knowing the song text. This *Wunderhorn* poem describes the tribulations of St. Anthony in most amusing
fashion. The hapless saint, who finds it useless to preach in church
because no one comes to hear him, goes to the river in despair, not
to drown himself, but to preach to the fishes. The shining carp listen
in attitudes of gravest attention, with mouths wide agape. Crabs, tor-
toises, eels, and codfish join the throng; and all aver that never was a
more pleasant sermon heard. But, as soon as the sermon is over, the
fish go about their business—and return to their several sins. The
crabs still crawl backwards and the carp are just as greedy as before.
"The sermon was clever, but they're the same as ever!"

With the exception of a solo kettledrum passage added at the be-

---

[11] Mahler himself called the movement "schubertisch."
[12] Mahler, *op. cit.,* pp. 315–16.

ginning to separate the new movement from the preceding idyll, the opening pages of the movement follow the pattern of the song strictly. It is curious, however, to observe that the vocal line is not transposed into the orchestra; this procedure is different from that followed in the First Symphony, where the vocal lines of the songs *Ging heut' Morgen übers Feld* and *Die zwei blauen Augen von meinem Schatz* are of the utmost thematic importance. Here, Mahler has considered the original accompaniment-figure sufficiently significant and characteristic to stand as a theme in its own right. (Ten measures after number 30 in the full score, however, the vocal melody begins to figure in the orchestral score as well.)

The first 131 measures of the song are followed strictly; then development and modulation set in, and a significant new section begins with the vocal *Predigt* theme in major, intoned ponderously by the 'celli and basses. The music rapidly modulates to D major, and then to E major, in which latter key a new theme is set forth by the trumpet. The unusual choice of the trumpet for a *cantabile* instrument is enhanced by the sharply contrasted accompanying instruments— harps and muted violins. Passages like this show vividly how different Mahler's conception of the orchestra is from Bruckner's or Wagner's. Bruckner, as we have already seen, liked to build his scores with juxtaposed, unmixed color-groups of homogeneous instruments which resembled in tone-quality the stops of organ-registration rather than the mixed doublings of the Wagnerian orchestra which Bruckner's disciples tried to transplant into his scores. In Mahler's scores, there is no lack of numerous and varied instrumental doublings, nor of the juxtaposition of homogeneous instrumental groups (a procedure of which the beginning of the fourth movement of this symphony, with its alternation of strings and brass, is an excellent example); but in addition we find an element which proves to be of great historical significance—a subtle appreciation of the possibilities of heterogeneous solo instruments balanced against each other. The wide variety of such possibilities is fully exploited by Mahler in a way to give pause to those who would see in him only the protagonist of a baroque monumental instrumentation; it was Mahler's experimentation in this field which gave inspiration to Schoenberg and to all those who, following his example, began to write for esoteric chamber groups rather than for a giant orchestra.

Further detailed formal analysis of the third movement is not necessary; it is more important here to discuss the problem—now posed for the first time in Mahler's work—which is offered by the introduction of the human voice in the fourth and fifth movements.

Historical analysis of the function of the human voice in the symphony is not as simple a task as it might seem. It is easy enough to say that Beethoven was the first to introduce the choral group and the solo voice into symphonic structure and that subsequently composers like Spohr, Berlioz, Mendelssohn, Liszt, and Mahler copied the procedures of Beethoven. But it is harder to ascertain whether the conception of the purpose of the human voice in the symphony was the same for all these composers. Offhand, the imagination would be inclined to suggest that it was not. Analysis tends to confirm this impression in some cases and to contradict it in others. Beethoven's conception, which it is most important to establish correctly here since it has often been misapprehended, is a rigidly and abstractly musical one. The formal principles and thematic material of the Finale of the Ninth Symphony are laid down along instrumental symphonic lines before the voices appear; we are presented with a finale in variation-form which (with the exception of the recitative) would be of equal validity as a purely instrumental piece. The way in which the voices are handled can be explained logically in this way alone. Much has been said about Beethoven's not knowing how to write for the human voice; but it is palpably absurd to accuse Beethoven of being unable to learn techniques which can be mastered by any adept student of composition. Beethoven did not approach the problems of this movement from the vocal viewpoint; had he done so, the history of the Ninth Symphony and of its subsequent influence would have been a far different one.

The Ninth Symphony suffered even more than the rest of Beethoven's work from that unfortunate misapprehension of the Romanticists, who wanted to make him the father of the romantic era in music and thus lost sight of his true position at the culminating point of classicism. This misunderstanding was especially acute in France, where Berlioz was the arch-offender in re-interpreting Beethoven's classical music according to the gospel of romanticism. (It is indeed possible, though far-fetched, to build a complete theory of French romanticism on the French interpretation of Beethoven, as Schrade has done in *Beethoven in France*.) So far as the problem of vocal music in the symphony is concerned, Berlioz went so far in this re-interpretation of Beethoven's intent that he felt it imperative to explain, in the preface to his *Roméo et Juliette,* the impossibility of expressing everything in terms of vocal music, and the resultant necessity of having some symphonic movements in which the voice is not used. That it should be necessary to explain in this way the presence of purely instrumental music in a symphony, the great instrumental form *par excellence,* speaks for itself as to the magnitude of the error which had been made in assessing the contribution of Beethoven. In the philosophical realm, this error was perpetuated by Wagner, who believed and proclaimed that Beethoven turned to the human voice because he had exhausted the possibilities of expression inherent in instrumental music. Up to a point, Mahler was strongly influenced by this conception of Wagner, as he himself indicated in his letter to Arthur Seidl on February 17, 1897:

When I conceive a great musical idea, I always come to the point where I must make the "word" the bearer of the idea.—That is what must have happened to Beethoven in his Ninth—only that era could not yet furnish him with appropriate material. For, basically, Schiller's poem is not fitted for the expression of the unheard-of conception which was in Beethoven's mind. Furthermore, I recall that Wagner says this somewhere in quite uncompromising fashion. What happened to me with the last movement of the Second Symphony is simply this: I really looked through all the world's literature, even the Bible, to find the redeeming Word—and was finally forced to express my feelings and thoughts in my own words.

The way in which I received the inspiration to this act is very indicative of the true nature of artistic creation.

At that time I had long planned to introduce the chorus into the last movement, and only hesitated in fear that this might be interpreted as a superficial imitation of Beethoven. Just then, Bülow died, and I attended his funeral here [in Hamburg].—The mood in which I sat there and thought of the departed one was exactly that of the work which occupied me constantly then.—At that moment, the chorus, near the organ, intoned the Klopstock chorale "Auferstehn!" It struck me like a bolt of lightning, and everything stood clear and vivid before my soul. The creator waits for this bolt of lightning; this is his "Holy Annunciation." [13]

It may be questioned whether or not Beethoven would have subscribed to Mahler's interpretation of his intentions and of the success with which he had fulfilled them. In some ways, Mahler's conception of the Ninth Symphony was far more romantic than classic, as witness his reorchestration of certain passages in the last movement according to nineteenth-century ideals of *Klangfülle.* But we must not make the mistake of assuming that Mahler's musical realization of Beethoven's ideal distorts the original model. As a matter of fact, Mahler displays a good grasp of two essential Beethovenian principles. The first of these has to do with the treatment of the text. Since, in a symphonic structure, the "setting" of a strictly established text in cantata-like fashion must be eschewed in favor of a more flexible handling of the words conformable to the needs of the music, the composer must be willing and able to reconstruct and rearrange the text

[13] *Ibid.,* pp. 228–29.

which he has chosen, even adding new lines of his own if the music requires it. In principle, Mahler would have been the first to subscribe to Wagner's theory that the word is more important than the music. In actual fact, just as Wagner was unable to create a word-drama which could stand alone, but wrote music which, when played in purely instrumental form, rivals and even surpasses the greatest symphonies in concert-hall popularity, Mahler, instinctively sensing the essentials of Beethoven's procedure, handled Klopstock's text with freedom equal to that with which Beethoven treated Schiller's *Ode*.[14] Beethoven, as is well known, wrote the words of the famous recitative, "O Freunde, nicht diese Töne!" himself, and freely selected and rearranged those stanzas of Schiller's poem which he needed for musical reasons. He did not hesitate to change the poet's wording, as, for example, in the line "Was die Mode streng geteilt" ("Sundered by stern Custom's ban"), where he substituted *frech* (bold) for *streng* (stern). In the same way, Mahler added poetry of his own to the basis of Klopstock's ode: thus, he wrote the deeply moving lines, "Believe, my heart, believe: naught hast thou lost! Thine is what thou hast longed for, what thou hast loved and fought for! O believe; thou wert not born in vain! Thou hast not lived in vain, nor suffered!" [15]

Just as important as a free handling of the text in accordance with musical principles is a logical derivation of the thematic material of the vocal sections from that of the preceding instrumental passages, so that the vocal sections do not give the impression of being nonfunctional additions. Beethoven solved this problem by incorporating the vocal sections into a set of instrumental variations which could be worked out on the same level without the use of the human voice; it is significant that he did this not only in the Finale of the Ninth Symphony but also in the Choral Fantasy.[16] Mahler does not bind himself to the variation device, but he does relate his vocal themes to his preceding instrumental themes, and uses many of his instrumental motives as vocal motives without changing them at all. This practice gives the required logical continuity to the vocal-instrumental complex.

The functional significance of Mahler's use of the chorus is further differentiated from Beethoven's by the introduction of a frankly theatrical element which reminds us anew how close Mahler is to Wag-

[14] Mahler had already resorted to such procedure as early as the *Lieder und Gesänge*, in some of which he combined various *Wunderhorn* texts with the greatest freedom.

[15] Mahler, *Second Symphony*, pp. 193–95.

[16] The text for the *Choral Fantasy* is by Christian Kuffner. The principal theme of the variation section shows definite similarities to the *Ode to Joy* theme.

ner's *Gesamtkunstwerk*. In the previously quoted letter to Buths, Mahler indicates this himself when he describes what amounts to a stage-effect for the Finale of the Second:

> May I be permitted to tell you about my experience with reference to the *a cappella* chorus in the last movement?
>
> So far I have noticed that it is impossible to avoid a disconcerting commotion when the singers of the chorus rise, as is customary, at the moment of their entrance. Our concentration is strained to the utmost and sharpened by the trumpet fanfares, and now the mysterious sonority of the human voices (which enter *ppp* as if on the furthest horizon) must come as a *complete surprise*.— I recommend that the chorus (which has been seated up to that moment) should continue to *remain seated* and should only be allowed to rise at the E flat passage "Mit Flügeln, die ich mir errungen" (basses). This has always been surprisingly effective.[17]

It is in this conscious exploitation of the purely human mass-effect of a large chorus on the stage that Mahler's conception of the "Choral Symphony" differs from Beethoven's. Doubtless it is significant that this conception did not come to him at the beginning of his career as a symphonist, but entered his consciousness only after he had undergone many difficult years of operatic experience. Perhaps only an opera conductor could have come to so just an appreciation of the sheer dramatic value of the chorus; but only a creative genius could have fused dramatic and abstract-musical values so convincingly. It cannot be too often reiterated: Bruckner and Mahler, neither of whom ever wrote an opera,[18] possessed eminent, if latent, gifts for music-drama; in them the nineteenth century and its symphonic music-drama lost two potentially great practitioners of the art.

When we have comprehended the musical and dramatic reasons for the introduction of the chorus into the Finale of the Second Symphony, we must still explain the use of a solo song for the fourth movement. Here, reasons both musical and philosophical must be taken into account. A plausible musical reason is the advisability of introducing a single human voice as preparation for the chorus to come. In this connection, it may be noted that Beethoven does the same thing—within the confines of a single movement, it is true—when he makes "O Freunde, nicht diese Töne!" a *solo recitative*. But such an explanation fails to take into consideration the immense (and not purely quantitative) difference in sonority between a single voice and a large chorus. By using first the solo voice and then the chorus, Mahler seems to be trying to sharpen the contrast already inherent in his literary program—the contrast between the destruction of a single

[17] Mahler, *Briefe*, p. 316.
[18] If we do not count Mahler's unfinished *Rübezahl*.

(though symbolic) individual—the inescapable symphonic "Hero"—and the vast drama of all mankind's resurrection. If such philosophical concepts seem too much of a burden to absolute music, it must be remembered that the abstractions of an ideal may be assimilated with the abstractions of music when the specifically pictorial details of an elaborate program may not.

It is far more important to grasp the essential purpose of these last two movements than to analyze them from the point of view of "form"; since "form" here is—as it should always be—something created by the pressure of the musical ideas and not imposed upon them, little would be gained by dissecting the thematic or instrumental content of each measure. But many interesting details of structure and orchestration should not be neglected. We come at once upon a striking refutation of the statement that Mahler owes but little of his inspiration to Bruckner. We have already spoken of the "blocked" orchestration of the beginning of *Urlicht* which is so vividly reminiscent of Bruckner's use of the orchestra. This resemblance to Bruckner is not a matter of orchestration alone. The sturdy diatonic *choralmässig* harmony is absolutely in the spirit of Bruckner; and of exceptional psychological interest is Mahler's own tempo-designation for this movement, *Sehr feierlich, aber schlicht*. One wonders whether it was by accident or by design that he hit upon Bruckner's favorite direction, *feierlich*—a word which, it has been said, could well be used as the *leitmotiv* of all Bruckner's creation, and which Wagner, too, had known well. It is certain that, in this particular passage—and, indeed, in the whole movement—Mahler comes as near to the naïve childlike faith of Bruckner as a man of his complex nature ever could come, although even in this simplest of movements there are undertones of the struggle which was Mahler's whole life: "Oh, then came an angel fair and would turn me aside! . . . Ah no! I would not turn aside! . . . I come from God, must return to God!" The relationship of this type of musical expression to that of Bruckner furnishes one more proof of that great continuity of Viennese musical tradition the demonstration of which is the chief purpose of this book.

The Finale displays astounding virtuosity as a purely instrumental-symphonic composition, quite aside from the fact that it is Mahler's first choral movement. Every detail is at once dramatized and functionalized. The opening pedal-point on C, although sixty-one measures long, does not deaden the musical "action," because of the variety of its treatment. (In the opening section, *Wild herausfahrend*, which bristles with frenetic harp arpeggios and string tremolos—it is noteworthy that Mahler uses the same "surprise" beginning for this Finale as for that of the First Symphony, a *fff* following without interruption upon the *ppp* ending of the preceding movement—the pedal-point is vigorously rhythmicized in the kettledrums.)

Two features which appear early in the Finale are of great significance for the ultimate development of the instrumental portion of the movement. The first of these is the horn-call which suddenly interrupts the C major pedal-point already referred to:

The most important thing about this horn-call is the direction for its mode of performance: "The greatest possible number of horns, played forcefully and placed at a great distance." The idea of offstage music need not be accounted for by any notion so complicated as Schaefers' concept of the expansion of absolute music into a new spatial dimension.[19] Rather, it is, like the mass stage-effect of the rising chorus, of purely operatic derivation: one need only remember Beethoven's off-stage *Leonore* trumpet to be convinced of this.

The chain of trills in the violins which follows so closely upon this horn-call is the first suggestion in this symphony of a motive from nature which attains symbolic significance in Mahler's work—bird-song. (Oddly enough, its value for him was only symbolic; actually, he found the singing of birds around his *Komponierhäuschen* in the summertime so disturbing as to be intolerable, and even used to shoot some of them to discourage their fellows.) It is bird-song which Mahler uses, just before the entrance of the chorus, to symbolize the last living sound of a mortal world about to be dissolved. Combined with the distant calls of trumpets and horns, in rhythmically free fashion, the trills and flourishes of the flute and piccolo arise from the débris of the symphonic world-structure. This miniature tone-drama is the *grosse Appell*, the trumpet-call of Resurrection. Here is one of the most striking examples of Mahler's art of combining esoteric groups of solo instruments, in contrast with his more celebrated *Monumentalinstrumentation* as exemplified in the closing pages of the Second Symphony. The triumphant key of E flat major, victorious over the funereal C minor of the beginning (the first example of tonal progression from beginning to end of a symphony), is apotheosized on the last page "mit höchster Kraftentfaltung" by two flutes and two pic-

[19] Today, with the growth in the concept of "spatial music," we may hear this passage differently.

colos, four oboes, five clarinets, three bassoons and a contra-bassoon, ten horns, six trumpets, four trombones and a tuba, two kettledrums, two tam-tams, three large bells of indeterminate pitch, a full complement of strings, and an organ. Further than this the expansion of external orchestral means could hardly go; the "Symphony of a Thousand" and Schoenberg's *Gurre-Lieder* are already adumbrated here, and after those twin triumphs of musical externalization, no more progress in the same direction was possible—unless Berlioz' use of multiple bands were really put into effect!

As background for the composition of the grandiose Third Symphony we are fortunate in having not only Mahler's own utterances in his letters, but also the reminiscences of his good friend Natalie Bauer-Lechner, second violinist of the Soldat-Roeger female string quartet. To her we owe the accounts of many fascinating conversations with him, which she recorded faithfully in a journal. The first comments of interest to us come in the summer of 1895, when she was visiting him in Steinbach am Attersee:

Mahler has scarcely arrived here, and already he is at work on his Third Symphony. "I hope to earn applause and money with this one," he said to me in fun on one of the first days; "for here's humor and jollity, a tremendous laugh to overspread the whole world!" But already on the next day he contradicted himself: "Look here, the Third won't make me any money either! For people at first won't really understand or admit its happy mood; it still hovers *above* that world of struggle and sorrow in the First and Second, and could only be produced as a result of that world.

"It is really inadequate for me to call it a symphony, for in no respect does it retain the traditional form. But to write a symphony means, to me, to construct a world with all the tools of the available technique. The ever-new and changing content determines its own form. In this sense, I must always learn anew to create new means of expression for myself, even though (as I feel I can say of myself with justification) I have complete technical mastery." . . .

" 'Summer Marches On' will be the Prologue. Right away I need a regimental band to get the crude effect of the arrival of my martial boon companion. Really, it will be just as if the city band were on the march. A raggle-taggle mob such as one seldom sees is crowding around.

"Naturally, they don't get by without a battle with the opposing force, Winter; but he's soon thrown out of the ring, and Summer, in his full strength and superiority, soon seizes undisputed leadership. This movement, as an introduction, is humoristically conceived throughout, in a baroque manner.

"The titles of the Third will be, in order, as follows:
1. Summer marches on.
2. What the flowers in the meadow tell me.
3. What the animals in the forest tell me.
4. What Night tells me (Mankind).
5. What the morning bells tell me (The Angels).

6. What Love tells me.
7. What the child tells me.
"And I'll call the whole thing 'My Joyous Learning'—for that's what it is!" [20]

To Anna von Mildenburg, with whom he was very intimate at this time, Mahler wrote about the progress of his work on the Third Symphony during the next summer, 1896. Thanks to his letters to her and to the further notes of Frau Bauer, we are able to follow the composition of the symphony practically step by step. Not only the totality of the musical conception, but that of the philosophical idea became ever clearer to him as the work progressed. However, he was still planning a seventh movement (never to be composed) when he wrote to Anna on the first of July:

. . . the symphony is concerned with another kind of love than that which you imagine. The motto of this movement (no. 7) reads
"Father, gaze on my bed of pain!
Let no creature be lost again!"
Do you know what this is about? It is supposed to symbolize the peak, the highest level from which one can view the world. I could almost call the movement "What God tells me!"—in the sense that God can only be comprehended as Love. And so my work is a musical poem embracing all stages of development in progressive order: It begins with inanimate Nature and rises to the love of God! Men will have to work a long time at cracking the nuts that I'm shaking down from the tree for them. . . .[21]

The plan of a seventh movement was not carried out; but the apotheosis of love was transferred to the sixth movement, with its tender reminiscences of Beethoven—and, perhaps, of Bruckner as well.

As the great work neared its completion, Mahler became more and more nervous, morose, and excitable. Though he was devoting but four hours a day to the actual composition, his mind was constantly filled with the music. Often, when on a walk, he would stop suddenly and scribble something in the little sketchbook which he always kept by him. The grandiose conception of this music weighed upon his mind even in his dreams. One particular passage had given him great trouble, "but then," he told Natalie as they bicycled down to the lakeside village of Unterach on July 10, "a voice called out to me as I slept (it was Beethoven's or Wagner's—I don't keep such bad company at night, do I?): 'Let the horns come in three measures later!' And—I couldn't believe my eyes—there was the most wonderfully simple solution of my difficulty!" [22] (How strangely reminiscent of Ignaz Dorn's appearing to Bruckner in a dream with the theme of the Finale of

[20] Natalie Bauer-Lechner, *Erinnerungen an Gustav Mahler*, pp. 19–20.
[21] Mahler, *op. cit.*, p. 161.
[22] Bauer-Lechner, *op. cit.*, p. 48.

the Fourth Symphony!) [23] And at last, on July 28, 1896, Natalie was able to write in her journal, "What joy, what relief: Mahler's Third is finished!" [24]

Thanks to an unusually complete documentation we are enabled to view closely Mahler's creative processes during the period of the Third Symphony. It would be difficult, indeed, to approach the actual music without some knowledge of these creative processes, for of all Mahler's symphonies it is this one which is hardest to comprehend from the point of view of purely musical logic. This is not only because of its vast extent, but also because of the wide diversity of the several movements, which have little thematic material in common with each other. [25] Up until this time Mahler had used cyclic form exclusively, and his departure from it in a work of such huge proportions was a daring step, which can be explained only by his desire to keep the various levels of development, as represented by the various movements, strictly separated.

About the final Adagio, the most characteristic mood of which we have already commented on, Mahler himself has made the most pertinent remarks. As he said to Natalie,

> In adagio movements, everything is resolved into quiet being; the Ixion's wheel of outward appearances finally becomes still. But in fast movements, in minuets and allegros (even in andantes, these days) everything is flow, movement, change. So I end my Second and Third, contrary to custom—although, at the time, I myself was not conscious of the reason for it—with adagios, as with a higher form in contrast with a lower. [26]

Perhaps he is a little too disingenuous in disclaiming knowledge "at the time" of the reasons for his choice of adagios as suitable last movements; for this is a lesson which he surely learned from Bruckner. No one who was as profound a student of the works of the *Adagio-Komponist* as Mahler could ignore the special significance of the Adagio. All this is part of the growing tendency to place the center of gravity of the symphony in the finale—a tendency which has been pointed out by Paul Bekker in his treatise *Gustav Mahlers Sinfonien*. This practice is in marked contrast to the usage of the classic era, when most symphonies ended with a lively *Kehraus-Finale* which was

---

[23] Ignaz Dorn was a theatre conductor at Linz, Kitzler's successor. H. F. Redlich gives a different version (*Bruckner and Mahler*, p. 278): "Bruckner used to relate that Dorn had appeared to him in a dream and had given him the principal subject of the first movement of Symphony VII."

[24] Bauer-Lechner, *op. cit.*, p. 49.

[25] The first movement is briefly quoted in the Finale.

[26] Bauer-Lechner, *op. cit.*, pp. 50–51.

deliberately written in a light vein. The center of gravity of a symphony by Haydn or Mozart is rather in the first two movements—the opening Allegro and the Andante or Adagio—than in the latter two. For this reason, no greater contrast can be imagined than that between a Haydn Rondo-Finale and a Finale such as that of Mahler's Second Symphony.

Although in the two preceding movements—the story of man and of the angels—Mahler has introduced first a solo contralto voice, then a combination of women's and boys' chorus, in the Finale the human voice is absent. The reason for this has, perhaps, something to do with the carrying out of the planned program. The single voice expresses the hopes and fears of humanity, while the women's and boys' chorus portrays the purity of the angels; what, then, is left to describe the love of God? Mahler may well have felt that such a wonder transcended the powers of verbal expression; but at least—less self-conscious than Berlioz in this regard—he did not put himself in the anomalous position of apologizing for the presence of purely instrumental music in a symphony.

Before analyzing the two vocal movements any further, let us retrace our steps to the two movements which treat of the life of flowers and animals, respectively. The first of these (composed at Steinbach in the summer of 1895) is a delightful minuet which may well be compared with the *Ländler*-like second movement of the Second Symphony. The succeeding movement, headed "Comodo. Scherzando. Ohne Hast.," invites comparison, in much the same way, with the Scherzo of the Second Symphony. The identity of key might be dismissed as mere coincidence; less easily dismissed is the fact that both movements are based on animal-fantasies from *Des Knaben Wunderhorn*. In the Second Symphony we heard a tale with a wry moral; the song which furnishes the source-material for the movement now under consideration, *Ablösung im Sommer*, is far less susceptible of grimly philosophical interpretation.[27]

The cuckoo fell to its death on a green meadow! So who shall keep us amused all summer long? Ah! that task falls to my Lady Nightingale who sits on a green bough! The little dainty nightingale, the sweet, beloved nightingale! She hops and sings; she's full of joy when other birds are silent. We wait for Lady Nightingale, who lives in the green hedgerow; when the cuckoo's day is done, then she begins to sing![28]

The first section of this *scherzando* movement follows the song literally from beginning to end, with two unimportant exceptions (the

[27] But for a possible philosophical/religious interpretation, see Dika Newlin, "Alienation and Gustav Mahler," *Reconstructionist*, May 15, 1959.

[28] Clemens Brentano and Achim von Arnim, *Des Knaben Wunderhorn*, III, 111.

symphonic movement has four measures of introduction as compared with only two in the song, and the closing measures of the instrumental postlude in the song are altered slightly in the symphony, so as to avoid an unwanted final cadence). Two motives, the first, or "Cuckoo," theme, with which is associated an amusing accompaniment-figure characterized by the upward leap of a fifth, and the second, or "Nightingale," theme, in C major, dominate this section. The complete exposition of the song materials is followed by the introduction of a new, contrasting motive in 6/8. This 6/8 section, which is 52 measures long, never modulates away from the tonic-dominant region of C major, and contains no serious thematic development. Here, perhaps, is a case in which we might feel that the new section had been introduced merely to fulfill the requirements of a form into which the original brief song has been, more or less suitably, expanded. The difficulty which Mahler experiences at first in escaping the tonic-dominant complex for any length of time, even in the free restatement of the "Cuckoo" and "Nightingale" themes where some roving harmony is introduced, would seem to confirm this view. But, when F minor appears (cue number 12), we realize that the movement has entered upon a freer phase. Mahler, always in his element where the fantastic is concerned, makes the most of the romantic possibilities of the episode now following. Hitherto, we have listened only to the mysterious small sounds of the forest; now, suddenly, a new human element enters upon the scene. From a great distance, the call of the postillion's horn is heard, and there ensues a charming alternation between the motives of the animals and the horn-call, which, with its carefully gradated effects of distance (*Wie aus weiter Ferne; wie aus der Ferne—sich etwas nähernd; sich entfernend*), strongly suggests the three-dimensional effects of the Second Symphony. Another F minor section, *Mit geheimnisvoller Hast!* leads to a cheerful new theme in F major. The rhythms of the first thematic complex, introduced into the accompaniment figures of this episode, logically prepare the entrance of the "Weiden!" rhythm (four sixteenths and a quarter-note) after cue number 22. A comical metamorphosis of the "Nightingale" section, in its original key, begins at cue number 23; its dissimilarity to the original version may be gauged by the orchestration—the "Nightingale" motive is taken over by six horns playing *fff*, which are accompanied by 'celli and double-basses at the same dynamic level supported by three bassoons and the contrabassoons playing *ff*. "Roughly!" ("Grob!") writes Mahler, to reinforce the effect still further. Scarcely has the climax of this passage been reached when, after a brief transition in *diminuendo,* the horn-call (which has been lost sight of for a long time) returns, once more in F major—"frei, der

Empfindung folgend. . . ." Its motive is reechoed tenderly in the
strings, "as if listening," Mahler says, thereby giving the dimensions
of life to his forest creatures. But the tender mood is soon abandoned;
lively stirrings begin once more, and a simple but striking modulation
leads back to the tonic major. In this brief coda section, tiny motivic
fragments and fanfares are tossed from instrument to instrument, only
to culminate in complete thematic liquidation—stubborn repetition
of the C major chord (without the third) swelling from *p* to *fff*.

It is surprising that a movement of such variety and scope should
have been created from a simple bi-thematic song. Such a weakness
as a certain lack of tonal differentiation may be attributed to the
source-material; but on the whole the movement tends to confirm the
view that, once Mahler had mastered the art of using his song-themes
instrumentally only in middle movements of suitable dimensions, the
resulting instrumental lyricism could offer no bar to his development
as a symphonist. Except for the tripartite beginning, which is a little
stiff because of the thematically uninteresting 6/8 section in C major,
the formal development is in no way stereotyped. Considering this, it
is significant that Mahler felt the entire symphony to be very close to
the spirit of classical form. Just before he finally finished work on the
first movement, he said of it,

> To my surprise—and likewise my delight—I see that in this movement, as in
> the whole work, there is the same structure and the same foundation (without
> my having wanted it or even thought about it) which is found in Mozart or,
> in a more highly developed form, in Beethoven, but which was really devised
> by old Haydn. It must be established according to profound and eternal laws,
> which Beethoven observed and which I find again in my own work as a kind
> of affirmation. Adagio, Rondo, Minuet, Allegro, and within these the tradi-
> tional structure and the familiar periodization—only that in my work the
> order of the movements is different, and the variety and complication within
> the movements is greater.[29]

We have already compared this Scherzo to that of the Second Symphony. Perhaps still another comparison is possible, for the romantic
suggestive power of the horn-call episode reminds us of many a passage
in Bruckner's Fourth Symphony, particularly in the well-known "Hunting Scherzo." But the form of Bruckner's Scherzo follows an externally
imposed pattern far more than does that of Mahler's.

Beyond the realm of inarticulate plants and animals, we come at
length to the worlds of man and of the angels. More subtle appeals
than were used in the preceding movement are to be found in the
Nietzschean invocation *O Mensch!*, which begins with a reminiscence

---

[29] Bauer-Lechner, *op. cit.*, p. 49.

(perhaps unconscious) of *O Röschen roth!* The single germinal motive of this movement is derived from the motto in seconds which occurs at the beginning. The descending second immediately appears in the second violin part of the "O Mensch!" chordal passage; thereafter, it becomes the chief structural element of the vocal part, which is written in short, widely separated phrases. As in so many other movements of both Mahler and Bruckner, the harmonic background of this composition is dominated by a pedal-point. In this case, the pedal-point always consists of two notes (D–A) and is executed by the 'celli in an even rhythm of fourteen (or twenty-one) eighth-notes to the bar. Occasionally rhythmical complications on several levels are introduced. The longest uninterrupted pedal-point passage in the movement lasts, it may be of some interest to note, for thirty-nine measures.

The fifth movement, *Three Angels Sang a Sweet Song,* with its carefully calculated naïveté of harmony underlined by a fresh and novel orchestral apparatus (no violins, but four flutes, four oboes, four bells, and a glockenspiel, in addition to two harps, three horns, five clarinets including the bass-clarinet, three bassoons, and the lower strings) and by the original use of a boy's choir singing the syllables "Bimm Bamm," [30] is noteworthy for its use, as a refrain, of a simple cadential formula, marked by the free use of parallel fifths and octaves, which was later to serve the same purpose in the Finale of the Fourth Symphony. This music first appears to the text "Ach, komm und erbarme dich!" The corresponding episode in the Fourth Symphony is likewise to be found in a movement based on a *Wunderhorn* text. The Third and Fourth Symphony texts display parallelism not only as to source but also as to subject matter: while that of the Third Symphony exemplifies the moral "Liebe nur Gott in alle Zeit! So wirst du erlangen die himmlische Freud!" that of the Fourth Symphony gives a naïve picture of the good life in Heaven. The conscious utilization of thematic relationships between one symphony and the next is not, of course, Mahler's own invention; perhaps the idea was originally suggested to him by Bruckner's "reminiscences" in the Adagio of the Ninth Symphony. Beethoven had bound together his last great quartets in a super-cycle by means of inter-thematic suggestion, but there may be some question as to whether this process took place consciously or unconsciously. Bruckner's reminiscences are rather of a sentimental than of a functional kind. Mahler, however, seems to have made a deliberate effort to organize his first four symphonies, at least,

[30] Mahler gives the following instructions for performance: "The tone is to imitate the peal of a bell; the vowel is to be attacked sharply, and the tone is to be sustained by humming the consonant M."

into some kind of inwardly unified structure. We have quoted remarks of his which hint at definite connections between the First and Second Symphonies, and also between the Second and Third; there is every indication that he felt each of these symphonies to be the logical continuation of its predecessor. When we add to this literary evidence the testimony of the music itself—the hints of thematic similarity between First and Second Symphonies, the partial parallelism of certain movements in the Second and Third, and the direct quotation of the Third in the Fourth—there can be no doubt that the unification of these four works under but a single heading is justified. They might be called the "Wunderhorn-Sinfonien," for it is scarcely necessary to repeat that the Second, Third, and Fourth Symphonies contain, not only *Wunderhorn* vocal pieces, but also (in the case of the Second and Third) orchestral movements based on *Wunderhorn* songs; and the First Symphony, even though it contains no material from the *Wunderhorn*, may be considered a logical prologue to the later works because of its utilization of self-created folk-like material.

We must still consider the cornerstone of the symphonic colossus which is Mahler's Third—the vast first movement, which has not been analyzed until now because, though it was the basis for the original conception of the symphony, it was the last portion to be completed.

The opening, powerfully intoned by eight horns, sets the tone of the whole. It is important to note that Mahler has used here the melody of an Austrian marching song; this and the "Frère Jacques" theme in the First Symphony are the only popular melodies thus far traceable in the symphonies, although the folkloristic element is, in more general formulations, well-nigh inescapable, as he himself testified: "The Bohemian music of my childhood homeland has found its way into many of my works. It influenced me particularly in the 'Fischpredigt.' The national style-characteristics included there may be heard, in their crudest form, in the piping of the Bohemian musicians." [31]

The basic conflict in the movement is between the minor theme with its sequel of sombre drum-beats and heavy trombone chords, which represent the inertia of nature, and the major theme, which represents the life and light of dawning summer. The antagonism between major and minor modes is an important concomitant of this thematic conflict, and, indeed, becomes a symbol of the philosophical content of the entire movement; for, just as the burgeoning forces of spring and summer vanquish the inertia of the frozen earth, F major

[31] Bauer-Lechner, *op. cit.,* p. 11.

triumphs, at the end, over the D minor with which the movement began. The "Life" theme, which appears only tentatively in the intro· duction (after cue number 11), at first in the oboe in D flat major and then in the solo violin in D major—and, still later (after cue number 18) in the 'celli and basses, once more in D flat major—finally makes its definitive appearance after a cheerful F major variant (cue number 23) of the ponderous "Inertia" theme in the first horn. Immediately it continues in a more militant guise; its dotted rhythm comes from the march-like strains of 'celli and basses which marked the transition from introduction to exposition (cue numbers 20–23).

The thematic development goes on in this vein, and reaches an impressive climax in D major, only to be interrupted (and herein lies the conflict) by a recurrence of the "Inertia" theme-complex, in its original key of D minor. All its component elements are there; the vast horn-theme and its concomitant, the trumpet flourish, play an important part. What we have here is the development on a much larger scale of a device which we have already observed in the First Symphony. There, Mahler repeated the long introduction to the first movement between exposition and elaboration; however, he was un- able to make this process completely convincing from the point of view of symphonic form. In the Third Symphony, he has evaded this issue to a certain extent, first of all by expanding the dimensions of the basic form to such an extent that discernment and comparison of the individual sections do not necessarily follow upon hearing the music, and then, on a more abstract level, by associating the recur- rence of the "Inertia" motive with a positive poetic-philosophic idea.

The "Life" ideas are briefly recalled, as in the parallel passage of the introduction, after cue number 35. The true development section does not begin until cue number 39, and is signalized by a modulation to G flat major. It begins in a rather sentimental and peaceful mood, as though the opposing forces were temporarily in a state of suspended animation. A reminiscence—perhaps unconscious—of the fourth-motive of the First Symphony appears in the flutes; *pianissimo* arpeggios in the first harp and first violins maintain the stability of the mood. But this state of affairs does not last long. A modulation to B flat minor brings us to the actual dramatization of the conflict proper. The "Life" forces march upon the scene in battle array. The opposing themes clash against each other boldly in C major (cue num- ber 49); then the absolute dynamic climax of this whole development comes in a furious upsurge of sixteenth-notes—a motive which, after two brief appearances in the introduction, finds its logical apotheosis here. From this high point of the struggle, a martial passage for the side-drums leads back to a partial recapitulation of the old introduction. Here, the logic of the musical form gains the upper hand over any extra-musical demands of the "program," which would seem to call for the immediate supremacy of the "Life" motives as the outcome of so titanic a struggle. But, after the introduction has been recapitulated in abbreviated form, the "Life" motives hold undisputed sway (from cue number 64 onwards). The bright key of F major is constantly in the foreground until the final flourish and last crashing chord. As for the "Inertia" motives, they are made to take on the pace and the spirit of the forces which (figuratively) conquered them, and they join eagerly, as it were, in the final optimistic affirmation of this recapitulative section.

Of what follows this first movement, we have already spoken. But before we leave the Third Symphony it will be advisable to take note of what Mahler has really accomplished in its most significant portion. He is justified, to a certain extent, in his statement that he unconsciously preserved the essential outlines of classic symphonic form; but he subtly—and perhaps not altogether wisely—changed the emphasis on the component parts of that form. The second, or F major, theme-group becomes of far greater importance than the "principal," or D minor, theme-group—so much so, indeed, that the initial D minor section is rather an introduction than part of an exposition. The predominance of the second theme-group usually denotes excessive lyricism; but that is not so here, because neither theme-group is lyrical. Subtleties and ambiguities of this kind have thus far been in evidence in all the Mahler symphonies which we have observed. After approaching such problems rather tentatively in the First Symphony, Mahler learned to handle them with greater security and confidence; but his own genius could not prevent them from being pitfalls for those who would succeed him—in other words, his solutions were only validated by the vitality of his personality as expressed in his "style," and could not be successfully copied by others. Small wonder that the era of the romantic Viennese symphony died with him; small wonder, too, that his greatest successor, Schoenberg, wisely chose to apply Mahler's moral precepts to new problems rather than to follow in the gigantic footsteps of his spiritual master.

After the great strain which he had imposed upon himself in the Third Symphony, Mahler could well afford to write a less pretentious work. He had attained the ultimate in that style which is represented by the grandiose utterances of the Second and Third Symphonies; he might now feel entitled to compose a comparatively unproblematic symphony, in which the sureness of hand which he had acquired during the unremitting toil at the earlier works would serve him in good stead, but in which he would not feel the compulsion to multiply those difficulties, both technical and spiritual, which had furnished the impetus for the First, Second, and Third Symphonies. Assured of his mastery, he no longer had to prove it to himself by attempting tasks of unusual magnitude. This change of attitude comes to light in a conversation of his which took place at the time when the earliest ideas for the Fourth Symphony were germinating in his mind. Natalie Bauer-Lechner is once more our source for this conversation; according to her, it was at the summer resort of Aussee, during the last week of July, 1899, that Mahler expressed himself on the subject of consciously cultivated "originality" as follows:

> Formerly, I liked to adorn my compositions with unusual details, and to make them completely unconventional as to external form; even so, a young man likes to dress conspicuously, whereas in later life he is glad enough to be average and inconspicuous in outward appearance, so long as what is within sets him far apart from the others. So, today, I am satisfied when I can pour my music into the customary molds somehow or other, and I eschew all innovations unless they are absolutely necessary. Formerly, for example, if a piece began in D major I would try to end in A flat minor; on the other hand, I now take a great deal of trouble to end in the same key with which I began.[32]

This little statement is quite revealing in more senses than one. For one thing, the remark about pouring music into unconventional molds strikingly illuminates the cleavage between form and content which had begun in the post-Beethovenian era and which was about to bring the romantic symphony to an end as soon as its last great exponent, Mahler, was no longer present to guide its destiny. As Mahler's youthful idealism was tempered by realism, he became ever more conscious of this situation, and so was moved to put his feelings on the subject into words. Nevertheless, what he says here must be taken with a grain of salt. It would be easy to misinterpret it as a profession of purposeful academicism, and no greater misunderstanding would be possible. Mahler, like every great Viennese artist who preceded him and like his great successors, had a boundless respect for the musical traditions which had nourished him. Nevertheless he could not deny his own originality or modernity, nor would he if he could. The psychology of this statement is the same as that of Schoenberg's remark "I am a conservative who was forced to become a radical"; both Mahler and Schoenberg may have clung to tradition in their hearts—but

---

[32] *Ibid.*, p. 120.

Mahler still ends his G major symphony in E major, and Schoenberg still progresses from post-Wagnerianism to atonality.

It was during the next summer (1900) that Mahler resumed work on the hasty sketches which he had made the year before. Never had he written a work with less pleasure—and this in spite of the basically cheerful, humorous tone of the whole of this Fourth Symphony. But, when it was completed, he felt that the bad mood in which he had composed it had not harmed it at all. This taught him a profound artistic truth: "Perhaps it is not always necessary or even desirable for a work to spring out of inspiration like a volcano. Rather, in place of inspiration, there must be reliable craftsmanship; that is the real art, which is always at the fingertips of its possessor and which helps him over all obstacles, even his own disturbed state of mind." [33]

Mahler had not at first intended this work to be a full-length symphony, but, rather, a "symphonic humoresque." However, just as he had planned, in his Second and Third Symphonies, works of conventional length, which grew to three times the normal symphonic dimensions, his "symphonic humoresque" turned into a forty-five-minute symphony. Nevertheless, there is still much of the humoresque about it, particularly in the first movement. Mahler cleverly remarked that this movement begins "as if it couldn't count to three," and indeed this description catches very well the spirit of the pleasant, Biedermeierish first theme. But, in spite of the simplicity of the basic form (it is, says Mahler, "built up with the greatest, well-nigh academic regularity"), greater complications come to light, especially in the dramatic development section.

The Scherzo belongs to the same class as the Scherzos of the two preceding symphonies. (Mahler evidently did not have the "animal-piece" of the Third Symphony in mind when he composed it, although he did say that it was the only composition of his which was modelled on one of his previous works, the Scherzo of the Second Symphony.) Though it received no identifying title—"I know the most wonderful names for the movements," he remarked, "but I will not betray them to the rabble of critics and listeners so that they can subject them to banal misunderstandings and distortions" [34]—its theme is the gruesome Dance of Death, led by a figure of popular demonology, "Freund Hain," with his mistuned fiddle, which is heard at the very beginning. The identity of key and metre with the Scherzo of the Second Symphony is self-evident. Mahler himself has given the best description of the *Stimmung*:

[33] *Ibid.*, p. 146.
[34] *Ibid.*, p. 144.

What I envisioned here was uncommonly hard to picture. Imagine the unvarying blue of heaven, which is harder to reproduce than all changing and contrasting hues. That is the fundamental background of the whole. But often it becomes dark and ghostly and frightening; it is not the heavens, though, which are clouded, for they shine on, eternally blue. It is only a sudden grisly feeling which comes over us, just as one is often panic-stricken in broad daylight in the sunlit forest. The Scherzo is so mysterious, confused and supernatural that your hair will stand on end when you hear it. But in the following Adagio, where all this passes off, you will immediately see that it was not meant so seriously.[35]

Mahler was indeed right in assuming that any lingering feelings of discomfort engendered by the supernatural theme of the Scherzo would be quickly dissipated by the ineffable peace of the Adagio.[36] He thought it the best slow movement he had ever written—perhaps even his best work in any form. Although, as an individual composition, it has not attained the popularity of the *Adagietto* from the Fifth Symphony, Mahler's own evaluation of it seems to be an unusually fair one. It is outstanding, not only for the mastery of the double-variation form (variations on two themes) which it displays, but also for the dignity of its style, the sweetness of which never deteriorates into saccharinity. Mahler found many pictorial similes for this pure and exalted mood. Once he told Walter that the recumbent stone images on sarcophagi in a cathedral had inspired him to the representation of the eternal peace in which they dwelt. But his explanation to Natalie was a different one; he was trying to depict St. Ursula, he said, and, when asked whether he knew the legends about her (it was a reference to her in the *Wunderhorn* text of the last movement which had brought her into the picture), he replied, "No, otherwise I certainly would not have been able to paint so clear and splendid a picture of her." But the smile of St. Ursula merged into another, different smile—a smile seen only through a veil of deep sorrow—and the composer looked back into childhood memories to see the tearful face of his own mother—the gentle Jewish girl, Marie Hermann, who limped a little and so was considered only too lucky to be able to marry the stubborn, hard-headed Bernhard Mahler, when she really loved someone else; who bore and buried child after child, who suffered poverty, ill-health, and neglect, yet whose loving, forgiving nature remained unaltered through it all. Her image passed over into

35 *Ibid.*, p. 143.

36 Its correct tempo designation is now *Ruhevoll, poco adagio*. However, at the time of composition he referred to it indiscriminately as *Adagio* or *Andante*. When Natalie questioned him about this, he replied that it could just as well be called *Moderato, Allegro,* or *Presto,* because there was a little bit of everything in it! *Ibid.*, p. 144.

the realm of ideality, and he wrote the music which symbolizes her and St. Ursula, and the recumbent statues of the long-dead: "a divinely joyous and deeply sorrowful melody . . . you will laugh and cry when you hear it." [37]

Though, as befits the double-variation form, there is a second motive, it is the first G major theme, in its many permutations, which dominates the whole. It is interesting to note that Mahler changed his original conception after the composition was finished, in one small detail. At the time of its completion, he told Natalie, "In this movement, as in the whole symphony, there is not a single *fortissimo,* on account of the nature of the subject-matter—the gentlemen who always aver that I use only the most extreme means will be sorely puzzled by that!" [38] As a matter of fact, he employed the *fortissimo* whenever he wished; it is particularly in evidence at the E major climax of the Adagio, where (figuratively and thematically) the heavens open to give us a momentary glimpse of the delights of the last movement. However, he stuck to his resolution not to use the trombones anywhere in the symphony, although he would have liked to have them for those few measures. The impressive climax subsides quickly into a subtly but simply harmonized closing passage which Mahler referred to as "sphere-music . . . almost a Catholic religious mood." [39]

The final D major chord of this Adagio is the logical upbeat-harmony to the charming, celestial pastorale theme which opens the Finale. The *Wunderhorn* text, *Der Himmel hängt voll Geigen,* which is the basis of this movement (composed, incidentally, before any of the others), gives an amusing and tender picture of the musical and culinary pleasures to be found in Heaven. The soprano is particularly directed to sing without parody, for nothing could be easier than to emphasize the absurd elements of the poem to the detriment of its sincere feeling. The cyclic form-principle is manifested not only in the persistent refrain-like return of the opening measures of the first movement, but also in the repeated quotation, already referred to, of a characteristic harmonic progression of the Third Symphony (probably suggested by the reference to St. Peter, who figures in both symphonies). This thematic reference symbolizes the position of the Fourth Symphony as the culmination of a unified cycle—a position which it also attained, in Mahler's opinion, by reason of its special merits. He felt that it was his most finished creation, and that in its composition he had demonstrated his powers at their highest. Poster-

[37] *Ibid.*   [38] *Ibid.,* p. 145.
[39] *Ibid.*

ity has tended to confirm his judgment, although perhaps not for reasons of which he would have approved; in this country, for example, the Fourth is one of his more frequently performed symphonies because it is not of unusual length and does not demand an extravagantly large orchestra or a chorus. Taking all this into consideration, it is strange to note that it was by no means a popular work with Mahler's contemporaries. In a letter to Julius Buths, Mahler speaks of it as a "luckless stepchild." [40] His pessimism was motivated by a series of strikingly unsuccessful performances, of which—characteristically —the most unsuccessful took place under his own direction in Vienna. It was on January 12, 1902, that the notoriously conservative audience of the Vienna Philharmonic assembled to hear a "new" symphony. Their reception was most unfavorable, but Mahler could afford to ignore the barbs of criticism. Secure in the feeling that he had attained perfection in one symphonic *genre,* he had voluntarily abandoned this security in order to begin the ascent of a new, and steeper, path.

Early in 1902, Mahler married the girl whom he had known and loved for only four months, Alma Maria Schindler. On November 3, their first child was born. And in the early fall of that year, the Fifth Symphony was completed. Thus, if only through coincidence, the fulfillment of a radical change in his mode of life came at the same time as the change to a new style of symphonic composition. It is through the sympathetic eyes of Frau Alma that we must view the birth-pangs of Mahler's later symphonies.

That first summer of married life in Maiernigg was a quiet one. Alma, for the sake of her husband's work on the symphony (already completely sketched and partly worked out in detail), had to devote much of her time to copying out the full score as fast as he finished composing it. It was nerve-wracking work for a young woman not in the best of health; but she had her reward when, in the fall, he played the completed symphony for her. Proudly they walked arm in arm to the *Komponierhäuschen,* and so, for the first time, Mahler played a new work for his wife. Her immediate reactions are interesting:

> When he had finished I told him everything about this splendid work with which I had fallen in love at once, and at the same time mentioned my doubts about the closing chorale. This churchly, uninteresting chorale! He objected, and said, "But what about Bruckner!" I retorted, *"He* can, you can't!" And, while we walked back through the forest, I tried to make clear to him the difference between his nature and Bruckner's. I felt that his forte was anything but the working-out of a religious chorale.

40 Mahler, *op. cit.,* p. 317.

There, I sensed a rift in his personality. It often brought great inner conflicts to him. Catholic mysticism attracted him, and this tendency was encouraged by those friends of his youth who allowed themselves to be baptized and changed their names. But his love of Catholic mysticism was completely genuine. [41]

How accurately did the sensitive Frau Alma put her finger on a problem so important in Mahler's life! It is beside the point whether or not her criticism was justified from a musical point of view; for to us the triumphant quality of the chorale seems altogether consistent with the busy optimism of the fugued rondo which is the last movement; and that optimism, in turn, is a logical climax of the hierarchy of moods which is an important part of the structural basis of this symphony—from funereal despair (first movement) to struggle and defiance (second movement) to superhuman energy (Scherzo), with a brief rest in the calm recesses of the past (Adagietto) before the final energetic apotheosis of the joy of living (Finale). Indeed, in spite of its obvious function of furnishing an interlude and a respite between those two immense movements in D major, the *Adagietto*—not unlike part of an earlier work, the *Andante grazioso* of the Second Symphony—seems more inconsistent with its surroundings than the chorale theme could possibly be said to be. The *Adagietto* is, in fact, one of those rare symphonic movements—a true character-piece within itself —which can be removed from its environment and still make perfectly good sense. Actually, it is more often heard separately than not. The reason for its comparative popularity is not far to seek; for its sweet lyricism, not untinged with sentimentality, presents no difficulties to the comprehension of the average cultivated lover of music. Its mood, as has been indicated in a previous chapter, is not dissimilar to that of the song "Ich bin der Welt abhanden gekommen"; the tone is set by the tender melody of the principal lyrical theme, with its gently chromaticized harmony.

However, let us return from the question of the *Adagietto* to that problem which we had already begun to discuss—the role of Catholicism (as represented by the Brucknerian chorale) in Mahler's musical psychology. Though the chorale as such is a Protestant symbol, the *Kirchenlied*—whether Catholic processional or Protestant chorale—is a universal symbol of Christianity. Certain it is that, as Frau Alma (herself reared in the Catholic faith) realized, the Catholic element definitely symbolizes a rift in Mahler's personality. While the modern, forward-looking, restless part of his nature ceaselessly questioned,

---

[41] Alma Mahler, *Gustav Mahler, Erinnerungen und Briefe*, p. 63.

doubted, and tried to solve insoluble problems, the traditionalistic side of his character sought refuge in that mysticism which belongs to Catholicism. Of course, Mahler had also been converted to Catholicism for purely practical reasons, since an orthodox Jew would not have been acceptable as director of the Imperial Opera House. But his interest in mysticism (and in chorale-like themes) antedates his conversion (as witness the Finales of the First and Second Symphonies). The conflict, if conflict it be, between the chorale theme of the Fifth Symphony and such forward-looking elements of that work as its "progressive tonality" [42] (from C♯ minor in the first movement to D major in the Finale) reflects once more Vienna's perpetual struggle between convention and revolt—just as Mahler proclaimed his desire to be conservative in the Fourth Symphony, and yet progressed ever onward into new realms.

The disputed chorale-like motive really appears twice—in that D major section which is a momentary ray of light in the turbulence of the second movement (cue numbers 27–30 in the full score) and at the close of the Finale, as already indicated (cue numbers 32 ff.). Like the so-called Brucknerian chorales which Mahler had in mind as a model, it is not so much a real chorale as an isometrically harmonized diatonic melody preferably intoned by the heavy brass. The construction of such a motive is not particularly complicated; more interesting here is a possible key-symbolism—for D major seems to have a very special significance for Mahler. It is the key of energy, of optimism, of high seriousness or of superhuman triumph, or of the utmost love; in all these capacities we have already seen it in the First and Third Symphonies, and now here in the Fifth. (Thus its later use, in the first movement of the Ninth Symphony, to express a mood of gentle resignation and regretful contemplation of past life has a peculiar poignancy.) The symbolic value of the individual tonality, so important in the classic era, still lived in Mahler, and, indeed, could not entirely disappear until it was absorbed in the levelling process of "pantonality." But this time was not yet; the art of emotionally suggestive modulation, as well as the symbolism of the individual key, was still tremendously important to Mahler. Nothing could bring out to better advantage the tireless energy implicit in the busy counterpoint of the Rondo, with its baroque bass-passages of uninterrupted eighth-notes, than the frantic modulations which take place after cue number 6.

---

[42] The concept of "progressive" (vs. "concentric") tonality, first introduced in this book, has since been extensively used by Hans Keller in many articles (in *Music-Survey*, *Music Review*, etc.).

From D major to B flat major; back to D major again; on to B major, G major—seven measures of D major!—then A major, C major, B major, D flat major (on the dominant)—again D major, B flat major, C major—round and round the treadmill goes, with yet more modulations to come. Never was Mahler closer to Reger (with whose work, by the way, he was quite out of sympathy) than in this Rondo.

How far is all this healthy tonal and rhythmical activity from the brooding beginning of the symphony, in C♯ minor! Might Mahler have been thinking of the beginning of another Fifth Symphony when he wrote the opening fanfare of this *Trauermarsch?* A stark brass fanfare at the beginning of a symphony is strikingly effective; Mahler had already proved that in the Third Symphony. It was a lesson he had learned from the Bruckner of the "Romantic Symphony"—only Mahler does not break the impact of his horns and trumpets on a soft cushion of *tremolo.* His is the more modern, the more realistic way. And this observation may fittingly bring us to more general remarks on the orchestration of the Fifth Symphony. Mahler, having written only "vocal symphonies" (though many instrumental movements) since the period of the First Symphony, found himself confronted with new problems here. He himself said that he had to start over again as the veriest beginner, and when he first heard the Fifth Symphony he found the orchestration so full of faults that he insisted upon revising it. But, in its final form, there is nothing unfinished or tentative about the orchestration, which is chiefly of the "monumental" kind and employs all the resources that Mahler had denied himself in the Fourth Symphony—including three trombones and a full complement of percussion instruments. However, the chamber-music-like elements of orchestral style, which often lend lights and shades to Mahler's work where the casual observer sees only an unrelieved mass, receive their apotheosis in the *Adagietto.* While, at important climaxes, the dynamics are frequently (if not always) vertically homogeneous, in the conventional manner, there is no lack of examples of that nervous gradation of dynamic levels which is a characteristic feature of Mahler's compositional technique; as—to take but one of many such instances—at cue number 10 in the second movement, where 'celli and bassoons *fortissimo* double the fourth trumpet *forte* and three oboes *piano,* to the accompaniment of second violins and violas *piano.*

The sketches for the Sixth Symphony were begun in the summer of 1903. It was a quiet, peaceful time; Mahler and Alma took long walks in the woods, and he could dance and sing by the hour with

his tiny daughter Maria—"he was so young and light-hearted then." [43]
One day, after he had finished the sketch of the first movement, he
came to Alma with an offering born of love: "I've tried to picture
you in a theme," he said to her, "but I don't know whether or not
I've succeeded. You'll just have to like it, though!" It was the subordinate theme of the first movement to which Mahler referred; and, in
truth, Alma had no cause to be displeased with this musical portrait
of herself. The lushly beautiful, slightly Italianate melody in F major
is one of Mahler's most "romantic" inventions.

The summer of 1904, during which the Sixth Symphony was completed, was as happy and conducive to relaxation as the previous one
had been. A new joy had come to the family in June with the birth
of a second daughter, Anna. Mahler was now inseparable from the two
children, with whom he spent many hours daily. Frau Alma avers that
in the Scherzo (eventually the third movement of the symphony, but
originally the second) he wanted to give another homely vignette of
family life—to picture the two little children vigorously disporting
themselves in the sand before the summer-house. But something went
wrong with the picture. In spite of reassuring directions like "Altväterlich," more alarming things than children at play seem to come
to light in this Scherzo; we can easily see that its vigor is not untinged
with that mood of tragedy, of dark foreboding, which dominates the
entire symphony (with the exception of the second movement). Alma,
who was already much perturbed because her husband insisted on
composing the last three *Kindertotenlieder* during that summer of
1904 which was outwardly so "beautiful, peaceful, happy" (she said:
"I can't understand how one can sing of the death of children when
one has hugged and kissed them, well and happy, not half an hour
ago,") found the Scherzo *schauerlich;* "those children's voices become
ever more tragic," she writes, "and at the end a smothered little voice
whimpers." [44] Of course, considering the misfortunes which befell the
Mahler family in later years, the temptation to read prophetic significance into the Sixth Symphony as well as into the *Kindertotenlieder*
is a very great one. But there can be no doubt that even at the time
he composed it Mahler felt that its tragedy held some special personal
significance for him. "No other work of his ever came so directly from
his heart as this one," wrote Frau Alma. "At that time [i. e., when
Mahler first played it for her] we both wept." [45] How ironic that
Mahler's happiest work, the Fourth Symphony, should have been com-

[43] Alma Mahler, *op. cit.,* p. 77.   [44] Alma Mahler, *op. cit.,* pp. 89–90.
[45] *Ibid.,* p. 90.

posed in a discontented mood, whereas the Sixth, of all his symphonies the most encumbered with all the outward appurtenances of tragedy (it is the only one which ends in a minor key) was written at a time when the composer was "cheerful, fully conscious of his great work, and flourishing like the green bay tree"! [46] (It is interesting to note that the same had been true of Mozart, who wrote calm and joyous works like his great E flat major symphony and the *Jupiter* symphony during one of the most miserable periods of his life.)

The only part of the Sixth which completely reflects Mahler's contentment in this period of his life is the second movement.[47] This *Andante* portrays a spiritual state of peace as deep and lasting, and perhaps more unworldly, than that depicted in the *Adagietto*. (Once again the mood of *Ich bin der Welt abhanden gekommen!*) But, whereas the *Adagietto* is orchestrated in true chamber-style, here Mahler has denied himself none of the resources of his most opulent orchestra. In fact, he even introduced a special effect—a set of cowbells. But far from his thoughts was any suggestion of a crude realism. Rather, the cowbells are a symbol, just as the bird-song on Judgment Day is in the Second Symphony. Mahler wishes to express such feelings as one has on a distant mountain-top, far from the hurly-burly of humanity. The last earthly sound which one hears in these higher regions is the tinkling of the cowbells of some wandering herd. And so, the bells (used here for the first time in musical literature, so that Mahler had to invent his own notation for them!) first figure in an E major passage which displays a marked similarity with the great E major climax of the third movement of the Fourth Symphony (perhaps Mahler was consciously recalling the "heavenly" symbolism of that passage and applying it here?), and again at the dynamic high-water mark of the *Andante* (cue number 59 ff.).

But when we leave the realm of sublime calm embodied in this slow movement, and leave out of account such momentary passages of contentment as the "Alma" theme in the first movement, and the "Altväterlich" passages in the Scherzo, we are confronted everywhere with a mood of grim determination, of "do-or-die" defiance. We have already encountered such a mood many times in Mahler's works, for it is one of his most characteristic mental attitudes; but here it receives quintessential expression—nowhere more than in the sturdy, square opening theme of the first movement.

[46] *Ibid.*

[47] Mahler originally intended the Scherzo to appear in second place, the Andante in third. This order has been restored in the Critical Edition (cf. introductory *Revisionsbericht* by Erwin Ratz).

This first movement, however, does not express that ultimate pessimism with which the symphony closes. At least outwardly, it climaxes in the triumph of the "hero" (to lapse for a moment into the symbolic language beloved of Mahler and of his commentators)—for it ends brightly in A major. But, in the last movement, defeat is inescapable. Its symbol is a clear, unmistakable motto, which has already appeared in less definite form in other works of Mahler (e. g., the first movement of the Second Symphony). The major triad sinks to the minor triad; no harmonic process could be simpler—none more expressive of the final expiration of hope.[48] Then comes the true opening of the exposition, with its significant reminiscences of the principal theme of the first movement—octave leap and dotted rhythm. Mahler no longer erects a bulwark of artificial conservatism (as he did in the first movement with the double-bar and repeat sign at the end of the exposition) to maintain equilibrium in his struggle. All his usual thematic types appear in battle-array—the march-like and chorale-like motives with whose essential nature we are already familiar through the preceding symphonies—but some new, and highly significant, details have been added. Chief of these is the hammer, whose sharp blows (Mahler specifies that they should be "short, powerful, but dull in sound . . . *not* of metallic character") mark not only major emotional climaxes but also minor formal divisions. The first hammer-blow, *fff*, points up a modulation (achieved by a deceptive cadence in D major) and immediately precedes an important statement of the major-minor motto in G (six horns). The second blow, *ff*, coincides, once more, with a modulation (from A major to B flat major), and also with the reintroduction of one of the more significant thematic forms of this movement (based on the octave, which figures so prominently in other themes of the symphony). The third and final stroke comes at that critical point in the coda (a partial recapitulation of the introduction) where A major, which seemed for a while about to win out as it did in the first movement, finally disappears from view with a vigorous asseveration of the fateful motto. This hammer-stroke is, like the preceding one, marked *fortissimo* in the full score [49]—a fact which detracts, not only from Strauss' rather ill-timed criticism of this finale, "I can't understand why Mahler deprives himself of such a wonderful effect in the last movement—why, he wastes his greatest strength at the beginning and then becomes weaker and weaker!" but

[48] Mahler learned this device from Schubert, who used it with no such philosophical implications. Cf. the opening of the G major quartet, op. 161.

[49] This final hammer-stroke is not found in the Critical Edition (p. 260).

also from Frau Alma's spirited defense of her husband: "He [Strauss] never understood Mahler. Here, as always, his theatrical nature betrayed itself. That Mahler had to make the first blow the strongest, the second weaker, and the third (the death-blow to the expiring hero) the weakest, is clear to anyone who has the slightest understanding of the symphony." [50] But such misunderstandings were inevitable when feelings ran as high, emotions were as intense, as at that première of the Sixth Symphony at the festival of the *Allgemeiner Deutscher Musikverein* at Essen, in June, 1906. Strauss, as was his wont, had already distinguished himself through incredible tactlessness. After the dress-rehearsal, Mahler was so deeply affected by his own music that he broke into sobs and frantic gestures, stalking up and down the artists' room the while. Just at the wrong moment, Strauss burst noisily into the room and called out: "I say, Mahler, tomorrow you must conduct a funeral overture, or some such thing, before the Sixth Symphony— the mayor here just died! That's the custom here—why, what's the matter with you? What seems to be the trouble? Oh well—" And out he went, leaving Mahler, Frau Alma, Gabrilowitsch, Julius Buths, and Oskar Fried all standing there, fairly petrified with shock. After this unpleasant incident, Mahler regained control of his nerves; but the next day, says Frau Alma, he "conducted the symphony *almost* badly, because he was ashamed of his excitement, and was afraid that his emotions might break out of bounds during the performance. He did not want to reveal the truth of this most frightening last movement with its dreadful anticipation!" [51]

As for the form of this last movement, it has elements of what is conventionally known as "sonata-form," but the music does not follow a set pattern to the detriment of free development of the themes. Thus, "expositional" treatment merges directly into the type of contrapuntal and modulatory writing appropriate to "elaboration" sections (the modulations rival in frequency and trenchancy those already signalized in the last movement of the Fifth Symphony); the beginning of the principal theme-group is recapitulated in C minor rather than in A minor, and the C minor chorale theme (*Schwer, Markato*) of the exposition is never recapitulated at all. So much for the outward mould in which Mahler chose to cast his "dreadful anticipation"—if one should use the term *mould* for a form which *follows*, rather than *determines* the contours of the thematic material.

In September, 1908, we find Mahler in Prague, preparing for the première of the Seventh Symphony. To Alma, in the days before she

[50] Alma Mahler, *op. cit.*, pp. 124–25.   [51] *Ibid.*, p. 124.

came to join him at the final rehearsals, he writes, half amused and half annoyed, all the commonplace and cumbersome details of his stay. The city is noisy, he complains, and overcrowded with conventions of one sort and another; parts have to be corrected, and, he says, in the midst of all this confusion "I have to figure out how to make a sausage-barrel into a drum, a rusty funnel into a trumpet, and a beer-garden into a concert-hall." [52] Even at the final rehearsals, Mahler was still nervous and perturbed. He was constantly altering the orchestration (just as in the Fifth Symphony), spent as much time as possible in bed resting, and tried to avoid the society of musicians (though he was unable to avoid a long visit with the artist Emil Orlik —"the inescapable Orlik, whom I meet everywhere I go"—whose fine etching of the Master is familiar to all Mahler's admirers). But, bit by bit, things improved. Mahler's best friends were there—men like the physicist Arnold Berliner and Gabrilowitsch—and young people like Berg, Bodanzky, and Klemperer helped him with the corrections in score and parts. Too, he had the satisfaction of knowing that he was truly esteemed in Prague. The Czech Philharmonic orchestra, under the direction of Dr. Zemanek, gave a very successful performance of his Fourth Symphony, on September 22; though Mahler himself was unable to be present at the performance, Bodanzky and his other friends assured him that it had been "superb"—which he could well believe.

How Mahler's life had changed since the première of the Sixth Symphony! His five-year-old daughter had died of diphtheria; his relationship with the Vienna Opera had finally been broken, and he had lived through the first of those strange years which he was to spend in New York. Never again would he see the scenes which had witnessed the composition of the Seventh Symphony in 1904 and 1905. The house at Maiernigg had been sold; it would have been spiritually impossible for him to return to that place after the little girl's tragic death there. . . .

At length, the day of the Prague première arrived. Since the orchestra was "very good and willing," [53] and the audience contained so large a proportion of Mahler's friends, there was every reason to expect an outstanding success. But Frau Alma says unequivocally that the symphony met with only a polite reception, and that the public scarcely understood it at all. [54]

What difficulties of comprehension might the Seventh Symphony have presented to a musical and conventionally sympathetic audience

[52] *Ibid.*, p. 408.   [53] *Ibid.*, p. 409.
[54] *Ibid.*, p. 177.

in 1908? The tonal problem may, of course, have been one of the stumbling-blocks; for in this symphony Mahler returns to the ideal of "progressive tonality" which he had abandoned in the Sixth. The first movement itself progresses from B minor (introduction) to E major, while the brilliant Rondo-Finale (reminiscent in spirit of the corresponding movement in the Fifth Symphony) is in C major. Also, the size of the symphony may have been, then as now, a deterrent to comprehension. Once again, Mahler has reverted to the five-movement form, which he had put aside in the Sixth Symphony. In this instance, the two end movements are the cornerstones of the symphonic structure; the space between is filled with two *Nachtmusiken* (a title straight from Eichendorffian romanticism), and a mysterious scherzo-like movement, marked *schattenhaft,* which, with the flighty triplets of its opening theme, vaguely recalls the elfin Scherzo of Bruckner's Sixth Symphony. The *Nachtmusiken* are fascinating romantic character-pieces of a kind dear to Mahler since the days of his first instrumental movements based on *Wunderhorn* themes. The provocative title *Nachtmusik* within a symphony is an open invitation to program-making; but Mahler has conceived no detailed program here, either as a basis for his own work or as a guide to his audiences. However, the giving of a title is a definite hint that the imagination of the individual listener may range widely without violating the musical intentions of the composer.

The first of the *Nachtmusiken* (the second movement of the symphony) begins with a bit of romantic tone-painting by two horns, which certainly owes some of its inspiration to the pastoral episode of Berlioz' *Fantastic Symphony.* One may also recall the post-horn passage in the Third Symphony, though the external similarity is not great. The essential structural element here is the direct and telling juxtaposition of major and minor, the special significance of which for Mahler we have already noted in the Sixth Symphony. Mahler makes full use of the possibilities of this contrast—in the curious cross-relations of the first theme, the biting dissonance implicit in a concomitant C minor motive, and the final frank statement of the Sixth Symphony major-minor motto. (Incidentally, this last passage is a striking example of Mahler's art of dynamic gradation. While the flutes, playing the motto chord-combination, increase from *piano* to *forte,* the trumpets (doubling the flutes) simultaneously diminish from *fortissimo* to *piano.* Meanwhile, the *pizzicato* melody of the first violins is being played *fortissimo* against a *pianissimo* trill in the second violins.)

Between this *Nachtmusik* movement and the next one is interposed the Scherzo. That contrast and juxtaposition of parallel major and minor which was the motivic basis of the preceding movement is also present here, in a somewhat different form. The first Scherzo section in D minor already contains a contrasting motive in D major, and the "consequent" phrase of the D major trio theme is definitely ambiguous as to mode, in the characteristic Mahler manner. It is in this Scherzo that the 'celli and basses are asked to play *pizzicato fffff* (four bars after cue number 161) with the direction, "Attack so sharply that the strings rebound against the wood." Such a remark typifies Mahler's tendency, emulated by Schoenberg, to demand the utmost (if not the impossible) from his instrumentalists—a tendency which was also paramount in his career as a conductor. How well this is illustrated by Frau Alma's story of the immense hide-covered sounding-box which he had made especially for the last movement of the Sixth Symphony, to replace the bass drum! At a rehearsal with the Vienna Philharmonic before the Essen première, Mahler grew more and more impatient as the luckless drummer, although he put all his energy into his efforts to play the monstrosity of an instrument, was able to produce only the feeblest of sounds. Finally, Mahler grabbed the hammers from the drummer's hands, swung with all his might—and practically no sound at all resulted! (The bass drum, which Mahler had discarded as insufficient, subsequently turned out to be exactly what he wanted for the passages in question.) [55] Such an uncompromising attitude towards the individual instrumentalist was to become as characteristic of Schoenberg as of Mahler; has not Schoenberg said—even if only in fun—that his violin concerto called for a new type of six-fingered violinist?

The second *Nachtmusik*, *Andante amoroso*, presents no formal or tonal complications, and is novel only in its orchestration. In choosing instruments proper to the serenade-style, guitar and mandolin, Mahler has, whether consciously or not, recalled the very beginnings of the Viennese symphonic style, which, in the days of the Monns and the Manns, was so close to the style of the divertimento, the cassation, and the serenade. But the use of the guitar and the mandolin in serious music was something new to the Viennese tradition. It was not, however, to remain unimitated (cf. Schoenberg's *Serenade*).

The opening bars of this movement might almost have been written by Schumann; the reference to *Träumerei* seems clear. Surely this unconscious reminiscence reflects Mahler's immense admiration for Schumann the lyricist, of which he spoke so vividly to Natalie Bauer-

55 *Ibid.*, p. 123.

Lechner: "Schumann is one of the greatest song-composers, worthy of being named in the same breath with Schubert. No one is a more consummate master of the rounded song-form, complete in itself, than he; his conception never exceeds the bounds of lyricism, and he does not demand anything beyond its realm. Suppressed emotion, true lyricism, and deep melancholy fill his songs. . . ." [56]

But the happenings in the three central movements are of secondary importance to the symphonic structure as compared to those in the two outer movements. The truly symphonic elements, as contrasted with those of purely lyrical-romantic nature, naturally find their expression in movements of large form. This fact simply confirms our observation made with respect to the symphonies of the "first period"; after the First Symphony, Mahler no longer used *themes derived from songs* in movements of major form. But that does not mean that lyricism in the broader sense is absent from such movements—indeed, it underlies all of Mahler's musical thought. Like that of Mozart, his instrumental style was nourished by vocal music, particularly by the opera—the Italian opera as well as Wagner's *Gesamtkunstwerk*. For example, a melodic line such as that of the C major subordinate theme of the first movement of this Seventh Symphony (which has a strong family resemblance not only to the "Alma" theme of the Sixth Symphony but also to the principal theme of the *Adagietto*) could not have existed without operatic inspiration. No greater contrast could be possible than that between this *ausdrucksvoll* melody and the "first theme" of the Allegro (following upon a long, slow, and brooding introduction in B minor, somehow reminiscent of the corresponding section of the Third Symphony in character and function) with its strong flavor of Bruckner's trumpet-motives. This contrast, however, is far better assimilated than it was in the comparable instance of the Finale of the First Symphony. Once again, Mahler had, simply by his skill in creating an impression of unity through movement, solved a symphonic problem in a satisfactory manner. But the solution was valid in the practical realm alone—not in the abstract and well-nigh extra-musical realm of *principle;* that is, it was a product of Mahler's own personal ingenuity and as such enabled him to make his individual symphonic structures convincing in themselves, but it could not permanently eliminate the basic problem of the ever-increasing rift between dramatic and lyrical elements in the symphony (that is, between the characteristics of principal and subordinate themes).

We have encountered one Rondo-Finale previously in Mahler's work

[56] This was in 1910. Bauer-Lechner, *op. cit.*, p. 161.

—that of the Fifth Symphony. In another symphony which belongs to the same period of Mahler's creative activity (for it has already been suggested that the Fifth, Sixth, and Seventh Symphonies may be classed as a more or less homogeneous group), it is not surprising to find that another Rondo-Finale bears certain important resemblances to its predecessor. It conveys the same impression of untrammelled energy, not only because of its vividly expressed major tonality (C major comes with doubly brilliant effect as a strong root-progression from E minor, the principal tonality of the first movement) but also because of the vigorous nature of its themes. Whereas the Rondo of the Fifth Symphony began in rather tentative fashion and continued for a while in an almost pastoral vein, this one opens directly with a stirring fanfare of drums and horns. The promise of the brave beginning is amply fulfilled by the principal theme, a bold trumpet melody, and its continuation in the strings and horns. Some of the alternating episodes provide the relief of quieter moments; but the rousing *fff* ending, climaxed by a quotation from the principal theme of the first movement (thus reaffirming the principle of cyclic form maintained by Mahler in every symphony we have thus far studied), reflects precisely the mood of the beginning and so rounds out the form dynamically.

On June 21, 1906, Mahler wrote "in greatest haste" to his old friend Dr. Friedrich Löhr ("Fritz"),

1. Translate the following for me:
   Qui paraclitus diceris
   Donum Dei altissimi,
   Fons vivus ignis caritas
   et spiritalis unctio.
2. How is *paraclitus diceris* to be accented, or scanned?
3. Translate the following:
   hostem repellas longius
   pacemque dones protinus
   ductore sic te praevio
   vitemus omne noxium.
4. All this is from *"Veni creator spiritus."* Is there a good (preferably rhymed) translation of it?
   Please send me the information *immediately special delivery!* Otherwise it will come too late. I need it in my capacity as creator and creature! [57]

With such prosaic inquiries as these did Mahler lay the groundwork for one of his most astonishing and certainly one of his most publicized compositions—a work which is, however, interesting to us not

[57] Mahler, *op. cit.*, pp. 290–91.

because the impresario Gutmann chose to style it the "Symphony of a Thousand," or because Stokowski said that audiences wept at its American performances under his direction (1916), but because it opens a new phase of Mahler's creativeness. This phase was never repeated, and found no continuation in Mahler's subsequent work, but that does not lessen its significance.

A special glamor has always surrounded the Eighth Symphony ever since the eventful day of its world première, under Mahler's leadership, on September 12, 1910. That day marked the high point of Mahler's career; but it marked, too, something more fateful. Beneath the tumult and the shouting of the gala occasion graver undertones might be sensed. Within the year, Mahler would be buried at the little cemetery in Grinzing. The enthusiastic audience, who had risen from their seats in awe-stricken silence when Mahler mounted the podium on this greatest day of his life, could not know that a doomed man stood before them. The more perceptive among them might, however, have been able to realize a more profound truth—that they viewed, not the end of a man's life, but the symbol of the end of an era. For how would it be possible to go any further in the monumentalization of the symphonic style than Mahler had gone in this work? He had exhausted all the possibilities; others, unless they wished to create a merely epigonous (and hence comparatively unprofitable) art, would have to strike out in new paths.

How many difficulties had been overcome for the sake of this première! The concert-manager, Emil Gutmann, with whom Mahler had been in communication from New York since the beginning of 1908, had obtained Mahler's permission for the performance by cabling him that rehearsals were already under way and that the parts were printed, when such was not the case. Mahler, discovering that even the Universal-Edition piano score was not yet ready, and that the *Riedelverein* of Leipzig might be substituted for the *Wiener Singverein* which he had wished to have for the choruses, was annoyed, confused, and frantically anxious that the performance should be called off. Fortunately, it was not; but even after Mahler's return to Europe at the close of his New York season, there were still many causes for bitter argument with the over-ambitious concert-manager. For example, Gutmann wanted to dispense with the third day of final rehearsals because he was sure that the enthusiasm of the *Singverein* would make up for the lack of extra time. Mahler disposed of this idea in no uncertain terms: "Please, now, *once and for all!* Either you stick to our agreement in every respect—I get the promised *three days* in their entirety without any limitations (the *minimum* of what is necessary, by the way)—or you accept my final resignation herewith. I beg to be excused from any further discussion of this matter." [58]

Mahler arrived at Munich in time for the final rehearsals in a state of exaltation. The letters which he wrote to Alma in the days before she came to join him for the première are among his most impassioned avowals of love; for the work—which he had finally decided to dedicate to her—kept his emotions in a constant state of pleasurable turmoil. But even at this last moment there was unpleasantness to be endured. Mahler was not satisfied with the work of the concertmaster of the Munich orchestra, and proposed that his brother-in-law Arnold Rosé, concertmaster of the Vienna Philharmonic, be engaged in his place. The ensuing scandal is best described by Frau Alma, who had in the meantime arrived in Munich:

Before the first general rehearsal, something painful had occurred. The arranger had, at Mahler's request, taken over the duty of informing the orchestra that Rosé wanted to play in the Eighth Symphony as honorary concertmaster. However, out of cowardice he had neglected to pass the word along. Mahler thought the whole matter was arranged, and telegraphed Rosé, who immediately came from Vienna. All unsuspecting, we went to the rehearsal with him. The orchestra felt that its concertmaster had been insulted, and the moment that Rosé started to sit down, they all got up and left their places. Mahler stood motionless.

Rosé got up slowly, begged Mahler not to disturb himself, and gravely walked away from the podium with his violin, down to where we were sitting. This was a demeaning action, and so blameworthy; but the noble feelings which he revealed thereby immediately put the fault on the side of the others. [59]

But such disagreements as these could not mar the ultimate triumph of September 12. An unforgettable experience for anyone privileged to be there, as Thomas Mann and Stefan Zweig and Max Reinhardt could testify; unforgettable, too, the festivities which followed—the gay party in the big banquet-hall reserved for the composer's friends and guests; the gradual break-up of the happy and congenial group, and the wonderful dialogue between husband and wife afterwards, which lasted far into the dawn. Never again would Mahler see a night quite like this one.

What manner of music was it, then, which could produce such powerful emotional responses? And what place are we to assign to the Eighth Symphony, not only in Mahler's own career as a symphonist but also in the music of its period?

[58] *Ibid.*, p. 379.   [59] Alma Mahler, *op. cit.*, p. 222.

We have already said that it represents, historically, the end of an era—a position which it may honorably share with that other great essay in monumentalization, Schoenberg's *Gurre-Lieder*. In a sense, too, it is the ultimate consummation of certain tendencies already present in Mahler's earlier works. Spiritually and musically, it is a pendant to the Finale of the Second Symphony, displaying (especially in the *Faust* section) a striking parallelism, not only in tonality, but also in philosophical content (resurrection as compared with Faust's transfiguration), to that work. The similarities even extend to orchestration —for what else is the final page of the Eighth Symphony but a heightened, accentuated version of the corresponding passage in the Second Symphony? On the whole, the orchestra of the Eighth Symphony is similar to that of the Second, although somewhat enlarged (particularly by the addition of a special brass choir). The final brass chorus of the Eighth Symphony—quite aside from its purely dramatic (not programmatic) significance—serves the purpose of heightened thematic emphasis; for it is the apotheosis of the "Veni, creator spiritus" theme, which is the cornerstone of the entire symphony. Mahler may have found the Schalk version of Bruckner's Fifth Symphony, wherein a special brass group is added for the final statement of the great chorale theme of the Finale, very suggestive in this respect; however, the question of precedence is not especially important. Regarding the use of groups of isolated instruments in the Second and Eighth Symphonies, we may conclude that in one respect at least these groups serve the same function, that of adding a sense of physical space to the music. When we introduce the concept of physical space, we are very close to the concept of stage music; and, indeed, Mahler as an original composer [60] is (with the exception of *Das klagende Lied*) never closer to opera than in the Second and Eighth Symphonies. Discovering this increases our regret that we may never know the dramatic works of Mahler's youth, which he destroyed. We must construct (or reconstruct) Mahler's dramaturgy on a symphonic basis alone. When we do this, we shall discover that what Mahler has created in the Eighth Symphony is in reality a new kind of *Gesamtkunstwerk*, liberated from the distractions of the stage which is (as Appia so truly said in *Die Musik und die Inscenierung*) the most imperfectly realized part of Wagner's grand design.

In spite of the exclusively choral character of the Eighth Symphony, it would be hard to justify the application of the term "cantata" to

---

[60] His arrangement and completion of Weber's *Die drei Pintos* was the only compositional venture into the operatic field which he allowed to stand. A recording of it is now available (RCA Victor PRL 3-9063).

it, for it completely lacks that freedom of structure which characterizes the cantata. Every scrap of thematic material is worked out symphonically, and the intersectional thematic relationships are never lost sight of. The detailed thematic analysis given by Richard Specht in his brochure *Gustav Mahlers VIII. Symphonie* (which, like the same author's corresponding pamphlets on the Sixth and Seventh Symphonies, was written at the composer's request) brings all of these relationships clearly to light; since the brochure is available to serious students of the subject in both German and English, it is needless to repeat an analysis which has already been done so thoroughly. So tightly woven is this symphonic web that we might well find it entirely adequate for a purely instrumental work (and in this it brings Beethoven's Ninth Symphony to mind). But then we would be forgetting compositional elements which are just as important as the thematic structure. For, fundamentally, in spite of its orchestra which glows with all the vivid colors of post-romanticism, and in spite of its peculiarly symphonic style of development which could never have existed without the achievements of the Viennese classic era, the Eighth Symphony is in spirit a *baroque* composition. The grandiose *élan* of its opening chorus has the quality of a Handelian oratorio; and yet it would be impossible to confuse the form of the symphony with the form of the oratorio. The literary form of any oratorio must of necessity be a narrative one; in the Eighth Symphony, on the other hand, we are confronted with the triumph of musical logic over verbal logic, the combination of texts in two different languages (German and Latin). No symphonist had yet dared to combine two different languages in a choral-symphonic work; that Mahler could do it without sacrificing unity is a striking tribute to the strength of his musical structure. (It is, however, noteworthy that in *Das Lied von der Erde* he turned to a completely different form of textual organization, treating the texts in the manner of a song-cycle and so making them a contributing factor to musical unity rather than a conflicting force against it. The mere contrast between those two works brings forcibly to our attention how different Mahler's whole conception of symphonic form was from that of Bruckner with his rigidly established post-classical formal precepts.)

In connection with what we have already said about operatic elements in the Eighth Symphony it is important to keep in mind that in the second part of the work we are dealing with *drama*—the final scene of *Faust*. Needless to say, Mahler has taken full advantage of the dramatic possibilities of his material, and the imaginative listener (placed in a receptive mood by the long atmospheric introduction, with its 164-bar pedal-point on E♭) may well visualize the scene laid before him at the beginning:

> *Forests are waving here,*
> *Rocks their huge fronts uprear,*
> *Roots round each other coil,*
> *Stems thickly crowd the soil;* . . .[61]

It is when we come to the closing *Chorus mysticus,* "Alles Vergäng-liche ist nur ein Gleichnis," that we find the opportunity for a valua-ble comparative study in styles, since Liszt had already used the same text in the final *Andante mistico* section of his *Faust* symphony. Ex-actly what are the significant similarities and differences between the two settings? First of all, the chorus serves a completely different func-tion in Liszt's music; whereas Mahler brings it as the logical musical and emotional climax to a complete choral work, Liszt simply adds it at the end of the Mephistopheles movement and has even written a special ending so that the entire choral section can be dispensed with if desired. (Only if one tries to imagine Mahler writing a special end-ing for the Second Symphony so that the *Aufersteh'n* chorus could be omitted if no choir happened to be available can one fully com-prehend the magnitude of the psychological gulf between these two composers.)[62] Furthermore, the choral setting of Liszt (tenors and basses only, with tenor solo) is markedly different from that of Mahler (two mixed choruses, a choir of boys' voices, and seven solo voices). Liszt's orchestral setting does not even approach the size of Mahler's, although Liszt ends his symphony with a triumphant blaze of glory in C major (*fff*) which is, surely, comparable in function to the closing pages of Mahler's work. An interesting detail in the orchestration of Liszt's setting is the use of the organ (for which the harmonium may be substituted) which may well have inspired Mahler's use of organ *and* harmonium (not to mention the piano!) in the same context.

When all the differences are taken into account, there still remain some notable similarities between the two settings. A comparison of the opening bars is particularly instructive. The rhythmical declama-

[61] *Faust,* Part II, Act V, 11, 805–8, tr. by Anna Swanwick.
[62] Mahler evidently felt this discrepancy of natures keenly. During a conversation with Natalie Bauer-Lechner at Steinbach am Attersee in the summer of 1893, he mentioned his disagreement with Strauss on the subject of Liszt. "When we last got together," he said, "he [Strauss] told me that he used to have as low an opinion of Liszt as I do, but that he later came to value his works very highly. This I will never do. When one examines his music closely, its meager content and specious hack-work are as obvious as the frayed and scratchy threads of a badly woven garment after a few wearings." (Bauer-Lechner, *op. cit.,* pp. 16–17.) But in connection with a per-formance of *Die Heilige Elisabeth* Mahler described that work as the most wonderful *Stimmungsmusik* that it is possible to imagine. So kaleidoscopic were his changes of opinion! (*Ibid.,* p. 175.)

tion of the text is identical, except for small details. This would not
necessarily prove that Liszt's version influenced Mahler, for the text
naturally suggests such a declamation, although of course still other
modes of rhythmical setting would have been possible. But it is remarkable that both composers should have turned to a five-bar phrasing; this coincidence cannot be accounted for in terms of the text,
since it would readily permit (and would, indeed, most naturally suggest) a four-bar phrasing. Certainly the deduction is clear that Mahler
was definitely influenced by the conception of Liszt. This deduction is
confirmed by additional similarities—the presence in both settings of
a melodic motive composed of repeated notes, and of a chromatic bass-
motive which may easily be extracted from the scores:

Furthermore, the phrase "Das Ewig-Weibliche zieht uns hinan" is
treated soloistically in both versions; Liszt gives it to a tenor solo
which alternates with the chorus, while Mahler gives it to two solo
sopranos against a choral background.

If we admit that the repeated-note pattern and the rhythmical pat-
tern ♪ ♩ ♩ ♩ | ♩ ♪ ♩ may have been suggested to Mahler by Liszt's version
of the *Chorus mysticus*, we shall immediately find that these important
elements underlie not only Mahler's *Chorus mysticus*, but the whole
symphony. The dotted rhythm (in diminution) combined with the
repeated-note idea appears immediately in the first theme of the first
movement:

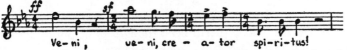

Ve- ni ,   va- ni, cre - a- tor   spi-ri-tus!

the dotted rhythm (undiminished) in the second theme, the rhythm
(foreshadowing the *Chorus mysticus* melodically as well) in the fourth
bar of the introduction to the Second Part, and both repeated notes
and rhythm in the "love" theme of the *Pater ecstaticus*, which of all
the themes thus far mentioned is the closest to the *Chorus mysticus*. The
tracing of such motives, frequent in all music, to a single common
source may at first sight appear to be hair-splitting; but in the last
analysis, when the rigidly logical interrelationships of practically all
the themes in this symphony are taken into consideration, it is really
not too far-fetched to assume such a common origin.

The question of the comparative merits of the two settings is one which must, perhaps, be decided in the long run by personal preference alone. But certainly Mahler's music is the more grandiose (and convincingly so) in gesture; and, to the present writer, the intensely expressive melody with which Mahler has invested the opening lines of the *Chorus mysticus* conveys far more of musical and philosophical value alike than does Liszt's simple C major triad.

In the "Symphony of a Thousand," Mahler had created a new type, the music-drama-symphony. Now, in *Das Lied von der Erde,* he created still another type, the solo-song-symphony; for this work, even though Mahler hesitated to include it among his numbered symphonies because of his well-founded superstition that the composition of a Ninth Symphony would bring his death, was considered by Mahler as a symphony, and was even given the sub-title "A Symphony" by him. In other words, just as the Eighth Symphony is the sublimation of that type of choral writing represented by the Finale of the Second Symphony, *Das Lied von der Erde* is the sublimation of the song-cycle idea as originally exemplified by works like *Lieder eines fahrenden Gesellen* and *Kindertotenlieder;* but it is more than that, for it is the final synthesis of the symphonic spirit and lyricism. Ever since his First Symphony Mahler had striven for such a synthesis. We have followed him through his first phase, wherein he tried to solve the problem by introducing song elements into symphonic form; through his second, wherein he rigidly eliminated all song elements and concentrated on the purely instrumental symphony; through the Eighth Symphony, wherein he forcibly freed himself from all voluntary limitation to purely orchestral means in order to rise to hitherto undreamed-of triumphs of monumentalization. Now, in *Das Lied von der Erde,* he was ready to attempt his synthesis from a new angle. Previously, he had attempted to introduce lyrical elements into symphonic form. Now he reversed the process by introducing symphonic style-elements into a form which had hitherto been thought of as purely lyrical, the song-cycle. When he introduced song elements into major symphonic movements, as in the first movement of the First Symphony, he ran the risk of forcing lyricism into a too prominent position in a form where, though always present, it had not always been paramount; later, by banishing the instrumentally transcribed song elements to the inner movements, he avoided this danger but diminished the possible perfection of his synthesis. Also, no matter how carefully the transition might be motivated, there was always a certain inconsistency between vocal and instrumental movements. But when all the movements are vocal a whole new field of possibilities is opened up. What these possibilities are, and what use Mahler has made of them, we shall now see.

It is unfortunate that the unnamed author of the preface to the English edition of *Das Lied von der Erde* has dismissed such an important problem with a few misleading sentences:

> The expression "symphony" is here conceived in a rather broader sense. When writing a symphony the composer usually intends to express a complex idea by complex means; he employs a variety of movements which permit the development of various moods, thus presenting different and contrasting aspects of the one idea. . . . The subtitle of Mahler's work "A Symphony" implies that its contrasted sections are to be considered as a unity.

But such elementary unity as this belongs as well to the simple song-cycle as to the symphony, to *Kindertotenlieder* as to *Das Lied von der Erde*. A less superficial observation of the structure is necessary, if we are to discover its secret.

A unified poetic idea is commonly considered necessary to the song-cycle—that is, it must consist of verses written by the same poet, or at least of verses of a single kind; and these verses are ordinarily arranged in such a way as to tell a story, or to convey some kind of total impression. Mahler has taken this basic principle in *Das Lied von der Erde* and has made it serve as a principle of symphonic unity. It may seem strange that never before in a symphony (with the exception of the Fourth which has only one text) had Mahler used the verses of one poet only. In the Second Symphony, he had combined the *Wunderhorn* and Klopstock; in the Third, the *Wunderhorn* and Nietzsche; and in the Eighth, he had used the most disparate combination of all —Latin hymnody and Goethe's *Faust*. He was the first choral symphonist to follow such a procedure, and it is but logical to assume that he had a definite reason for doing so. It may well have been that the procedure was the consequence of his interest in the ultimate expression of a musical or philosophical idea rather than in the conventional setting of texts; but, whatever the cause, the result was certainly to make symphonic unification even more difficult than it was already. Thus the unification of text-material was a great step forward in Mahler's fulfillment of his own symphonic ideal. He still retained, however, the freedom to deal with the text as he chose, which had always marked his vocal writing; for he added words and sentiments of his own to the original text of the last movement, and combined two separate poems for that text.

The multiplicity of sections required by the song-cycle is nothing new to Mahler's symphonies (one need only remember the Third, which has more movements than either of Mahler's real song cycles), so there was no adjustment necessary in this respect in order to make one form correspond to the other. Some analysts have tried to accommodate *Das Lied von der Erde* to the conventional four-movement pattern by lumping the movements "Von der Jugend," "Von der Schönheit," and "Der Trunkene im Frühling" together as a Scherzo section; but this is a purely academic procedure without value for the true understanding of the work.

If the problem of the major formal outlines was thus easily solved, the problem of length and musical unity was something else. No song-cycle had ever been extended to the length of an hour, which had become Mahler's minimal symphonic unit. In order to impose upon the lyrical framework an architecture compatible with such dimensions, he employed two devices. The first, and most important, is the basic motive—the assertion of the fundamental principle of cyclic form. Such a principle had never been consistently applied in the song-cycle before. Schumann had rounded off his cycles *Dichterliebe* and *Frauenliebe und Leben* with piano postludes which recapitulated earlier song material, but this is far different from the introduction of the same basic motive into each and every song.

At the very beginning of the first movement, *Das Trinklied vom Jammer der Erde,* the bounding interval of the basic motive, a fourth, is outlined,

and is immediately followed by the basic motive itself:

This motive is a very pliable one. It can be inverted and still remain recognizable; the size and relative position of the two component intervals can be altered; it forms an important part of the pentatonic scale with which Mahler plays in the third movement for coloristic reasons; and it can even be used harmonically.

The penetration of nearly every significant theme in the entire work by this basic motive represents far more than a simple extension of the cyclic principle. It is the first step in that development which eventually led to the formulation of the tone-row idea. That this is so is indicated by one detail in particular: the use of the basic motive as a *vertical* principle in the final chord. (The freedom to use a given fragment of the row vertically or horizontally at will is one of the most important tenets of the theory of the "twelve-tone scale.")

Having now found a unifying principle, which is combined with the progressive principle of tonality (to which he had returned after dispensing with it in the Eighth Symphony), Mahler had next to devise a means whereby his lyrical forms, once they had achieved the requisite unity, could be convincingly extended to the requisite length. The obvious solution to this problem was the introduction of long instrumental interludes, which, far from serving the mere purpose of relieving the singer, actively carry on the important themes in true symphonic development. Then, as in most of Mahler's other symphonies, the Finale was made the focal point of all development and, furthermore, became the longest movement, with a thematic structure comparable to that of a normal instrumental symphonic movement. Thus, after the long central instrumental section in C minor which serves not only a musical function but also a poignant dramatic one (it actualizes the period of sorrowful waiting suggested by the important text-words "I wait for him, to say the last farewell," and provides the necessary dimension of space which must separate the two distinct poems, with two different viewpoints, of which the text is composed), the opening recitative "The sun is setting far behind the mountains" is recapitulated, still in C minor, to new words: "Dismounting now, he offered him the drink of sad farewell." Here, musical structure has won precedence—as nearly always in Mahler—over the mere setting of words. But there is nothing stiff about the thematic recapitulation, which has all the flexibility of the emotions that the music expresses. The F major section which functioned more or less as "second theme" in the first part—"The brook sings, sweetly sounding through the darkness"—recurs here as "I wander toward my homeland, there to rest me"; but this recapitulation is brief as compared to the corresponding episode in the first section, and leads quickly to the C major coda which is the culmination, not of this movement alone, but of the whole symphony. Not only musically but also emotionally, it is peculiarly fitting that the message of beauty and hope conveyed by the closing lines "The earth so sweet blooms everywhere in spring, grows green anew!" should be set to a transfigured variant of the passionate music which climaxed the first section: "I long tonight, O friend, to be beside you, delighting in the beauty of this evening. . . . O Beauty! O world, drunk with eternal love and life!" As for the sevenfold repetition of the word *ewig* at the very end—a repetition which takes the word completely out of the intellective realm into a world of symbolic-musical expression—it reveals Mahler's characteristic attitude towards the text-word, which always has more value as a symbol, as an outlet for the ultimate content of the music, than as the conveyor of an immediate and practical meaning.

Mahler never attempted to reduplicate the synthesis which he had accomplished so brilliantly in *Das Lied von der Erde*. Had he lived longer, would he have followed the instrumental Ninth and Tenth Symphonies with a return to this field, which he had made so particularly his own? The question is a tempting one, even though it does not admit of a positive answer. But it is unlikely that he would have wished to reproduce so personal and individual an expression in the same terms a second time. As it now stands, the *Lied* is unmistakably a farewell to the world. The depth of pessimism expressed therein moved some to condemn Mahler for a "decadence" which he never professed. Instead of acknowledging such accusations, let us accept *Das Lied von der Erde* for what it is: a striking and novel solution of the symphonic problem, a distillation of the essence of Mahler's personality, and one of the most significant works of the twentieth century—as inimitable, and as epoch-making in its way, as *Pierrot Lunaire*.

In a sense, it is unfair to the Ninth Symphony (1908–09) to consider it as a mere appendage or postlude to *Das Lied von der Erde,* for the work is well fitted to stand on its own merits. But, since its composition occupied the same summer months which were devoted to work on the *Lied,* it is only natural that it should have absorbed a certain amount of the spiritual atmosphere of the latter piece. Indeed, the first movement begins with clear reminiscences of the basic motive of the *Lied.* Still another familiar motive, the "Gib Acht" theme of the fourth movement of the Third Symphony, is recalled to us by the melody of the second violins in this same passage. The Ninth Symphony in general, as a matter of fact, displays a tendency towards reminiscence which, even though we have encountered it in Mahler's symphonies before this, seems somehow to be the special property of a last work (cf. Bruckner's Ninth). The quotation from *Das Lied von der Erde* is probably deliberate; other reminiscences may be unconscious. Among these latter are the citation from the second movement of the Fifth Symphony, noted by Stiedry, in the *Burleske,* which is in the same key as the abovementioned movement and is not unlike it in spirit,

and, in the same movement, a passing reference to the "Life" theme of the Third Symphony:

There is an even more subtle similarity between the last movement of the Ninth Symphony and its counterpart in the Third Symphony. It is not only that both are Adagios in the great Brucknerian tradition; it is a certain likeness of mood which goes deeper than the likenesses of surface form. Both movements start from the premise of God's love; but—as befits the immense difference in the periods of Mahler's life when they were composed—while the Third Symphony closes triumphantly, the Ninth ends in a mood of gentle resignation. In keeping with the reminiscent spirit which pervades the whole symphony, this movement, written in the twentieth century, looks back to the nineteenth century more than do some of Mahler's other works. The visible symbol of this backward-looking tendency may be seen in the numerous "Wagner turns" which dot the score. And it is shown in other ways as well—in the insistent fugato writing of the *Burleske* (the fugato was always the preferred refuge of the puzzled nineteenth-century symphonist, although the skilled treatment accorded it by Bruckner and Mahler raised it above that level) and in the similarity in mood between the opening *Ländler* of the second movement and the sturdy Scherzo of the First Symphony written so long before—but how much more subtlety, more variety, has been brought to the realization of the *Ländler* idea in the Ninth Symphony! Whatever nineteenth-century ideals may exist in this work, they do not destroy its forward-looking elements. Many a passage—as, for example, the closing page of the first movement—reminds us anew that it was Mahler, in spite of his well-earned reputation for monumentality, who, with the refinement of his soloistic and semi-soloistic orchestral passages, gave the impetus to that movement which eventually produced such works as Schoenberg's *Kammersymphonien* and *Pierrot Lunaire*. And, at the end of his career as a symphonist as at the beginning, we find him clinging to the principle of "progressive tonality" (for this symphony begins in D major and ends in D flat major) which, it cannot be sufficiently emphasized, was the first step in the dissolution of tonality into "pan-tonality" that made the system of the twelve-tone scale possible.

It was in America that Mahler came upon one of his most striking ideas for the Tenth Symphony.[63] The incident in question was a slight but touching one. One day (in 1907) when Mahler, Frau Alma, and a friend of hers, Marie Uchatius, were all in the Mahler apartment in New York on the eleventh floor of the old Hotel Majestic, overlooking Central Park, they heard a great commotion on the street. Looking out, they saw a huge crowd watching an approaching funeral procession. It was that of a fireman who had died heroically in line of duty. The procession stopped in front of the hotel; the captain of the fire brigade spoke a few words, almost inaudible on the eleventh floor; and then—"Short pause, then a stroke of the muffled drum. All stand in complete silence—and then proceed. The end." [64] The scene might almost have been staged for the benefit of those interested listeners. Frau Alma anxiously looked towards the window of her husband's room —and he was leaning out, his face wet with tears, overwhelmed by a sensation of tragedy. He recaptured the same emotion when he ended the fourth movement with a single stroke of the muffled bass drum, and then wrote after the double-bar, in a big, sprawling handwriting which grows almost illegible towards the bottom of the page, "You alone know what it means! Oh! Oh! Oh! Farewell, my gentle lute! Farewell, farewell, farewell—Oh! Oh! Oh!" This superscription was written with his wife in mind; in these last years of his life he had felt a deepening of his love for her, and expressed it not in his music alone, but in an almost adolescent effervescence of love-poetry and little messages of affection. Now that he felt death approaching, he realized that he had lived much of his life with insufficient regard for the human values—"Ich habe Papier gelebt!" he once said—and was trying to make up for it.

A special glamor always seems to attach itself to a major unfinished work of a great composer, especially when a legend can be associated with it. It is not merely fanciful considerations, however, which attract us to Mahler's unfinished Tenth Symphony. Any true admirer of Mahler could not resist the opportunity to see the composer in his shirtsleeves, as it were, to gain new light not only on his art but also on his personality; hence we owe a debt of gratitude to Alma Mahler for allowing a facsimile edition of the manuscript to be published—a step which must have caused her many doubts and

---

[63] The unfinished Tenth Symphony has appeared in several "performing versions." The best-known is that of Deryck Cooke. His final realization was published in 1976 by AMP/Faber Music; a recording by the New Philharmonia conducted by Wyn Morris is available (Philips 6700-067).

[64] Alma Mahler, *op. cit.,* p. 166.

heartaches, in view of the personal and emotional nature of Mahler's marginal remarks. Even so, her sacrifice was not as much appreciated at the time (1923) as it might have been; there were not wanting those who attributed to her selfish motives for wanting the manuscript published, as well as those who insisted that it should have been burned as Mahler wished (even though he contradicted this wish several times), and those who questioned the validity of the reconstruction of the first and third movements by Křenek, Franz Schalk, and Berg. But eventually the party in favor of the publication won the day. [65]

The Tenth Symphony as we have it is in five movements; but what the final order of these movements would have been, or whether they would all have found a place in the definitive version, are questions which must remain undecided. Specht thinks the second, fourth, and fifth movements are so much alike that Mahler might later have discarded one of them. This, however, is problematic. Nevertheless, it seems fairly certain that Mahler finally decided to put the Adagio (clearly marked I. in blue pencil) in first place. This Adagio is written out in a score-form sufficiently complete so that, with suitable reconstruction, it may be performed—which would seem to be a convincing argument in favor of Mahler's having thought enough about it to know definitely what place he wanted it to occupy in the symphony. But, as far as the arrangement of movements goes, after the first movement Mahler obviously went through a period of great uncertainty. The second movement receives the bizarre designation of "Scherzo-Finale"; and the fourth movement has a really dramatic title-page—it has first been designated as "2. Satz," then as Finale (which appellation has been vigorously crossed out with the same black ink with which it was written), then as "1. Scherzo (I. Satz")"; finally Mahler has crossed all this out with blue pencil, and, after a last stab at the idea of using this movement for a Finale, has left it designated as fourth movement only. To top off all this, there is the programmatic title, "The Devil dances with me," and the well-nigh delirious exclamation which follows upon it: "Madness, seize me, the accursed! Destroy me, that I may forget my existence! That I may cease to be! That I may for—" The unfinished word gives eloquent testimony of the disturbed state of the composer's mind; these comments were certainly never intended for the public eye, and even the descriptive title

[65] A more extensive facsimile, including subsequently discovered pages, was brought out by Erwin Ratz in 1967 (Verlag Walter Ricke). Noteworthy in Ratz' editorial comments is his vehement denial of the possibility of performing the complete Symphony, in which he even brings the dead Schoenberg to testify on his behalf.

would probably have been suppressed by Mahler, had he lived to see the work published and performed, as being too conducive to irresponsible program-making on the part of listeners and commentators alike. The same holds true for the title of the third movement, *Purgatorio*.

The preliminary version of the opening Adagio, which is also included in the facsimile, gives us a fair idea of Mahler's methods of work. The music is written out in simplified score fashion, with the instruments cued in on four- or five-line systems. This score, which is certainly not a first sketch, is very close to the "final" version for the most part; in the later form, the order of the variants of the first theme at the beginning has been changed, certain measures (clearly crossed out in the preliminary version) have been omitted, and, most important, the ending has received a more elaborate development (in the preliminary version it exists in two different forms, both fragmentary). In addition to this preliminary version of the first movement there exist further, more fragmentary pages of sketches for other movements. The first page of this material belongs to the second movement; the second through seventh pages are a more or less rough sketch for the "Teufel" movement, while the last page definitely belongs to the Finale. These sketches, as well as the incomplete score itself, offer far more material for comment than can be covered in a general study of this kind—nor does Specht's working analysis come anywhere near exhausting the possibilities. Suffice it to say here that, in the light of such things as the beginning Adagio which, with its recurring instrumental recitative in the violas, recalls the final Adagio of the Ninth Symphony, the similarity between the accompaniment-figure at the beginning of the *Purgatorio* and that used in *Das irdische Leben,* and the presence of the three scherzos or semi-scherzos which might be thought of as a grim counterpart to the central *Nachtmusiken* of the Seventh Symphony, the Tenth Symphony does not seem to add anything new to Mahler's style; but for all that it should become better known, to the extent that this is possible with a work in such unfinished condition.[66]

And now that we have followed Mahler's career as a symphonist to its conclusion, we must, before we move on to fresh fields, take the

[66] For more on the still-controversial problem of the work's performance, see Deryck Cooke, "The Facts Concerning Mahler's Tenth Symphony," *Chord and Discord,* 1963, pp. 3–28. Dika Newlin reviewed the world première of Cooke's first version in "A Final Musical Testament," *The New Leader,* September 14, 1964. Her "Conversation Piece: Mahler and Beyond," concerning the first two movements only (not Cooke's version) appeared in the program booklet of the New York Philharmonic, January 14–17, 1960 (reprinted in *Chord and Discord,* 1960, pp. 117–20).

precaution of orienting ourselves historically with respect to his creations. Therefore, let us sum up a few of the conclusions which have been drawn by inference in the main portion of our discussion.

We have already signalized the conservative and the forward-looking elements in the work and personality of Bruckner. Though far less conservative than his great predecessor, Mahler is, to an even greater extent than Bruckner (for Bruckner's career did not unfold itself at such a critical moment in musical history), an end and a beginning. Often, he has been accused of composing obsolete, nineteenth-century, overblown music in the midst of an age of musical progress. This superficial criticism hides a part of the real truth about Mahler. His historical position is in some respects analogous to that of Bach. Like the great contrapuntist, he was destined to be the last great exponent of a style and form which had been created by others but which, in his hands, expanded in new, unforeseen directions. Bach, writing gigantic baroque fugues and intricate polyphony in the era of the burgeoning German Rococo, is as much—or as little—of an anachronism as Mahler writing the "Symphony of a Thousand" in 1906. But, whereas Bach's works exerted little or no influence in his lifetime, and scarcely received public attention until Mendelssohn's celebrated *Gewandhaus* performance of the *St. Matthew Passion*, Mahler's songs and symphonies influenced young composers and gave impetus to new developments while he himself was still in his prime. If these developments were sometimes of such a nature as to puzzle, if not to displease, their instigator, that was only a natural part of the inevitable evolution—more natural, perhaps, in Vienna than anywhere else in the world. Fundamentally, Mahler was in sympathy with the most important new movement which sprang up under his aegis. But that is another story, and one to the telling of which we must now proceed, as we enter upon the last phase of our history.

BOOK THREE

SCHOENBERG AND BEYOND
DECADES OF DECISION

CHAPTER I

1874-1899

IN 1874, Emperor Franz Josef was ruling paternalistically over his Dual Monarchy, which was outwardly at peace with other nations, but inwardly riven by inter-racial dissension. The seeds of the revolt which was eventually to smash Austria's polyglot Empire had been sown as far back as the Thirty Years' War. Now these seeds were burgeoning: the Pan-Slav movement, which had been established by the Czechs during the revolution of 1848, was growing ever stronger, to the dismay of both Hungarian and German elements in the Dual Monarchy. To add to the general uncertainty, a severe financial depression in 1873 had seriously shaken the liberal ministry. Fundamentally, Austria had not really changed since the aftermath of 1848—and that was her tragedy. "Modern improvements" and other such outward signs of progress had been grafted on to a political body which was unbelievably conservative. The elements of convention and revolt which had always co-existed in Austria were now coming into ever sharper conflict; here, at least, political history and musical history might be said to run parallel.

It was into this politically turbulent world that a son was born on September 13, 1874, to Samuel Schoenberg, a merchant with an amateur's interest in music, and his wife, born Pauline Nachod. The boy's early history was not very different from that of many another talented Viennese youth in straitened circumstances. He went to school, where he learned quickly what he chose to learn, although he felt most at home in heated discussion with his schoolmates before or after classes; lost his father at an early age; began to take an interest in music, to play the violin and viola, to participate in informal chamber music with his young friends, and to write little trios for use at such casual gatherings. All this might not necessarily have indicated that Arnold Schoenberg would follow music as a calling. As Stefan Zweig remarked in his autobiography, many boys and young men of that era, who prided themselves on their romantic interest in poetry and music during their school days, and often produced works of astonishing talent, settled down, later on, to respectable if somewhat stodgy careers in engineering, medicine, or the law, and would have blushed to be reminded of their youthful excesses. But at some point in the boy's life there came into being that high seriousness of purpose which was to guide his career thenceforward. It was this which sent him again and again to those performances of Wagner the influence of which was so decisive for his early music. He and his friends had a game all their own which they played with *Tristan*. Already over-familiar with its most celebrated strains—the "plums" which an intelligent listener might have for the picking—they delved deeper into the structure of the work, seeking for new melodies; and at every performance more and more of such melodies came to light. The analytical habit of mind which brought listening to such a peak of refinement is but the reverse side of the thinking processes which governed the young man's composition. Richness of thematic material and interrelationship between the various themes became of paramount importance to him. A publisher to whom he brought a promising early quartet remarked shrewdly, "You must believe that if the second theme is a retrograde inversion of the first theme, that automatically makes it good!" or words to that effect. Such a comment made at the time of Schoenberg's earliest serious attention to composition deserves consideration. A popular misapprehension of Schoenberg, unfortunately fostered by far too many widely read books on music, pictures him as an unsuccessful imitator of Wagner, who, disappointed at his inability to write acceptable music in the post-romantic idiom, suddenly decided to make a name for himself by irresponsible innovation. But, on the contrary—as the casual criticism shows—his musical intent was consistent from his first beginnings as a composer until the present day. And not only was he consistent with himself; he was also consistent with the traditions which had produced him.

In Vienna of the closing decades of the nineteenth century, one could still be a *Wagnerianer* or a *Brahmsianer* if one chose. Young Schoenberg, though enchanted by Wagner, considered himself rather a follower of Brahms. The duality of direction is important; the eroticisms of Wagner and the intellectualism of Brahms join in a new blend in Schoenberg. Approaching the idol from Hamburg was, however, a different matter. One did not come to Brahms for advice lightly. Hans Rott, Mahler's sensitive and talented school-friend and pupil of Bruckner, had tried it, with—literally—fatal results. Brahms, completely out of sympathy with the influence of Bruckner on the young conservatory students, told Rott that he had no talent and advised him to give up music. Mortally wounded by this blow, the young man, his constitution already severely undermined by the privations of poverty, went insane and died shortly thereafter. Brahms and Bruckner had both been present at his funeral, and Bruckner had been sorely tempted to say harsh things to Brahms—things which remained unsaid because Bruckner, the man of God, still was too greatly humbled by the presence of the man he referred to as "verehrter Herr Präsident" to speak out all that was in his heart. The terrible example of Rott could have come to Schoenberg's ears. In any event, he admired Brahms from a distance—the distance being considerably diminished on a day, noteworthy in young Schoenberg's life, when, as he stood in the back of a crowded concert-hall, Brahms came in and found a place next to him. Schoenberg made himself as small as he could, duly overawed by the Master's proximity. But he was not to have—and was always to regret not having—the opportunity to hear Brahms' opinion on his first major work, *Verklärte Nacht*. Death came to Brahms, as to Bruckner, three years before *Verklärte Nacht* was completed in 1899. Encouragement from Brahms would have meant a great deal to Schoenberg; but one wonders whether he would have received such encouragement on the strength of a work so deeply influenced by Wagner as was *Verklärte Nacht,* or whether Brahms would have approved of the transfer of the concept of the symphonic poem to chamber music. (Here Schoenberg was immediately an innovator; for, though Smetana had produced the first "program quartets" in his *From my Life* [1876] and its less familiar sequel [1882], written as a description of the sensations of total deafness—a work, incidentally, which Schoenberg greatly admired [1]—Schoenberg was the first to write a piece of chamber music in the style of a symphonic poem.)

Verklärte Nacht had been preceded by other significant works.[2] A string quartet in D major (not the one that he had completed in a week's time on a bet) was well-liked when the Fitzner Quartet played it in public during the 1897–98 concert season; but it was not published or preserved.[3] On the other hand, the songs of Opp. 1, 2, and 3 were later published by Berlin's Dreililien-Verlag. Op. 1, made up of

[1] Zdeněk Nejedlý, *Frederick Smetana*, p. 132.

[2] See Josef Rufer, *The Works of Arnold Schoenberg;* also Dika Newlin, "The Schoenberg-Nachod Collection; A Preliminary Report," *Musical Quarterly*, October, 1968, pp. 31–46.

[3] Schoenberg did not contradict this statement. But the manuscript was found in his legacy to the Library of Congress. The score was published by Faber Music in 1966; see Dika Newlin, "Schoenberg's Quartet in D Major (1897)", *Faber Music News,* Autumn 1966, pp. 21–23. A recording by the LaSalle Quartet is in their album of Schoenberg's, Berg's, and Webern's quartets (DGG 2720-029).

two songs, *Dank* and *Abschied* (settings of rather diffuse poems by Karl, Freiherr von Levetzow) already displays the style-characteristics of the early Schoenberg: rich, complex harmony (always tonal) and a vocal line which is bold but which does not strive for the extreme effects of the later works. The piano writing is full and sonorous, with many conventional octave-doublings in the left hand, and shows the influence of Brahms. All these characteristics are likewise present in the songs of Opp. 2 and 3. In Op. 2 (four songs) we find settings of the works of two Berlin writers, Richard Dehmel and Johannes Schlaf. Schlaf was the close friend and literary collaborator of Arno Holz, who was rather indirectly associated with the *Überbrettl* movement wherein Schoenberg was later to play a small part. As for Dehmel (who also wrote the poem of the same name on which *Verklärte Nacht* is based), the admiration which he and his wife felt for Mahler, and their association with him as attested by documentary material in Alma Mahler's memoirs, are noteworthy as a further illustration of that constant interchange among literary, musical, and artistic circles which was of such importance to men like Schoenberg and Mahler. Schoenberg's treatment of a short Dehmel poem, *Erhebung* (also taken as a text by the talented Erich Wolff) is lushly romantic in keeping with the sentimental quality of the words, but at the same time has a subtlety which keeps it from degenerating into *Kitsch*. The single Schlaf setting in this group, *Waldsonne* ("In die braunen, rauschenden Nächte"), has a pleasant, innocuous quality which is rare enough even in early Schoenberg. Its fresh charm is evident in the little piano postlude, with its subtle harmonic turn three measures from the end:

Op. 3 (six songs) contains Schoenberg's first setting of a *Wunderhorn* poem, *Wie Georg von Frundsberg von sich selber sang.* It would not be altogether accurate to ascribe his choice of such a text to the influence of Mahler. On the one hand, it is true that Mahler's settings had more or less put this poetry back into musical circulation; but, on the other hand, familiarity with the *Wunderhorn* need not denote favorable knowledge of the Mahler songs, and, actually, Schoenberg was not yet an admirer of Mahler. Several of the other songs of Op. 3 breathe that bold, defiant spirit so characteristic of the composer's personality. The text of the last one of the group, *Freihold* (written at the same time as Op. 1), somehow seems prophetic of the opposition which was to beset Schoenberg throughout his life:

> I stand alone, yes, all alone,
> Even as the roadside stone.

But the closing lines triumphantly asseverate the proud, aloof philosophy which was Schoenberg's own:

> Lightnings, write upon this stone:
> "Would you go free, walk alone!"

and the music reflects, and even surpasses, the defiance of the text.

All this, however, is only a prelude to the young Schoenberg's first major achievement, *Verklärte Nacht*. Few works have led to more misunderstandings about their composers than this one. Considered disgracefully radical when it was first performed (1903), it was soon viewed in its proper historical perspective, as a late bloom of romanticism. But this change in viewpoint did not really help matters, for as soon as the harmonic-melodic idiom of *Verklärte Nacht* became as acceptable as that of *Till Eulenspiegel* or *Don Juan*, there was the great danger that, his works in the post-romantic vein being most popular and most frequently heard, Schoenberg would be viewed as a romanticist *manqué* who had found himself unable to compose anything but epigonous Wagnerian music until he deliberately made up his mind to be "different" and write "modern" music. As far as the average American musical public is concerned, that is exactly what happened. Too often, no attempt has been made to bridge intellectually the gap between *Verklärte Nacht* and "atonality"; in the public eye Schoenberg becomes a symbol of one phase of his development or of the other, but insufficient familiarity with the works of the transition period (and with the background from which he sprang) has made it hard for us to view his development as a whole. Be that as it may, the music of *Verklärte Nacht* has become sufficiently familiar, and has been sufficiently analyzed in the past, so that we need not repeat the details of its well-known program or outline all of the themes which symbolize the poetically conceived characters of the little drama. Let us not fail, however, to call attention to an important detail of harmonic structure which, while it must always have been latent in Schoenberg's mind, did not come to him as a consciously formulated concept until years after the composition of *Verklärte Nacht*.

One night, unable to sleep after a performance of the work which he had conducted in Barcelona, he thought the music through and through again, and suddenly hit upon the idea which (though he had not realized it when composing) is the true structural basis of the work's profound inner logic. The fundamental tonality is D minor or, later, D major—a key which seems to have been especially dear to Schoenberg in this period of his career (cf. the early D major quartet and the official "first" quartet, Op. 7, in D minor). One of the most important themes in that tonality is that which begins the "fourth section" of the tone-poem, as indicated by Wellesz (corresponding to the lines of poetry "Das Kind, das du empfangen hast, Sei deiner Seele keine Last")[4]—a theme which, incidentally, contains in the second 'cello part a progression in open parallel fifths of a kind most unusual in the puristic Schoenberg part-writing, but apparently used here for the sake of the rich sonorities of the low double-stops on the 'cello. Schoenberg now had the very logical idea of approaching this focal point once from a half-step above (E flat minor) and again from a half-step below (D flat major). It is this second approach which builds the grand climax of the whole work, and rightly so; for it satisfies not only our logical sense of form (as the proper counterpart and answer to the approach from above) but also our sense of emotional fitness, as the final assertion of a theme which is associated with words of reassurance. Our tonal sense is satisfied, too, in a very special and subtle way. The approach to the first appearance of the D major theme is as near to "impressionistic," non-functional harmony as the logical-minded Schoenberg ever comes: a diminished seventh chord surmounted by a flourish of pure tone-painting in the first violin, followed by the E flat minor triad (first circumscribed by the lower D natural and then simply repeated). Schoenberg then takes advantage of the enharmonic change G flat–F sharp; but as the significant tone is the *third* of the chord in each case (E flat–G flat–B flat–D–F♯–A) there is no feeling of forcible progression. On the other hand, the second appearance of the theme is prepared by a really functional modulation; and, furthermore, the basic harmonic progression itself belongs to the super-strong root-progressions (D flat–F–A flat–D–F♯–A— no common tone between the two successive chords). In this modula-

---

[4] *Eulenburgs kleine Partitur-Ausgabe*, p. 26.

tion, too, enharmonic values are utilized; for the dominant of D major—A–C♯–E—may also be understood as the altered sixth degree of D flat major—B double flat–D flat–F flat, in place of B flat–D flat–F (a procedure analogous to the formation of the Neapolitan sixth chord on the lowered second degree of any scale). On such subtleties of technique as these is a passage of such highly charged emotional content based; and those who accept the "romantic" Schoenberg while rejecting his later works as the arid products of a purely mathematical mind would, therefore, do well to remember that the young Schoenberg is as inexorable and logical a technician as the old one, and that the differences between this music and, let us say, the Third Quartet—to choose a work written strictly in the twelve-tone method—are more differences of medium and scope than of basic musical thinking. This question has a reverse side; for there also exists the type of mind which welcomes the cerebral qualities of the twelve-tone music while deliberately, and somewhat scornfully, rejecting the sensuous emotional appeals of Schoenberg's post-Wagnerian period. But to take such an attitude is really to be *plus royaliste que le roi*, for Schoenberg himself rates *Verklärte Nacht* high among his works and considers that it was a remarkable achievement for one of his youth—contrary to the practise of so many composers who made a fetish of destroying the works of their early years, as did Mahler.

It is significant that *Verklärte Nacht* should have been written as a string sextet, rather than as a quartet; this fact, coupled with the novelty of the idea of writing a symphonic poem for a chamber ensemble, is a clear indication of that phenomenon which we have already had so much occasion to remark upon—the penetration of orchestral idiom into chamber music. Schoenberg, thanks to the atmosphere of devotion to chamber music in which he had spent his young years, was not unacquainted with the great traditions of Viennese chamber music, and so was protected from making too great errors of tact or taste in his own essays in that field. It is not as if *Verklärte Nacht* were his first chamber work; as we have already seen, he was experienced in the writing of duos, trios, and quartets. Nevertheless, at this stage of his development, Schoenberg was a child of his time in that his chamber music possessed a certain orchestral orientation. He himself has given further confirmation of this in one of those revealing moments of self-analysis which so often illuminated his classroom teaching. Speaking of the evolution which he had undergone between the composition of the First and Fourth string quartets, he said that in the First Quartet he still (influenced perhaps by Brahms) wrote in a "thick" style, with few rests for the instruments, but that in each successive quartet he came nearer to the Mozartean ideal of "transparency" in chamber music style by thinning out some of that forest of motivic work (much of which is far more obvious to the eye than to the ear) which blackened the pages of the First Quartet, and replacing it with rests which are so necessary to the clarity and comprehensibility of the finest chamber music. Translated into terms relating to our problem of the moment, this simply means that an ideal of full and rich (i. e., orchestral) sonority has been transformed into an ideal of spare, economical part-writing. On a lesser scale, it is the same difference that exists between the score of the *Gurre-Lieder* and that of the first *Kammersymphonie*. It must be remembered, incidentally, that the *Gurre-Lieder,* though not completed until much later, were really begun in the same period as *Verklärte Nacht*. The latter work had been completed during three weeks in September, 1899; and already in March, 1900, Schoenberg was at work on the *Gurre-Lieder* in Vienna. The *Gurre-Lieder* had originally been planned as a simple song-cycle with piano accompaniment (in this form it was designed as an entry in a prize contest, but was not completed in time for the deadline); however, this has no bearing on the grandiose final version of the work. Keeping all of these facts in mind, it is well to qualify—or at least to apply to a somewhat later period of Schoenberg's creativeness—Wellesz' significant and basically true statement:

> Now it is interesting to notice how Schoenberg's youthful predilection for chamber music became the foundation of all his creative work. Most young people of his generation were inspired to become musicians by hearing a music-drama of Wagner or a symphony of Bruckner; this led to a sort of *al fresco* music-making and to a neglect of the basic necessities of craftsmanship. But even in his great orchestral works Schoenberg had remained true to the chamber music style; he tries to give every voice its own direction and its own life, and finds his most spontaneous expression in passages where he can build upon the polyphony of string-quartet writing.[5]

After all, the influence of "hearing a music-drama of Wagner" upon Schoenberg should not be, and cannot be, minimized. (Naturally, Wellesz shows himself thoroughly cognizant of this phase of Schoenberg's development in his description of the impassioned Wagner discussions of the young intelligentsia of the Café Griensteidl or the Café Landtmann.)

It would be impossible to close any survey of the years during which Schoenberg's earliest serious development as a composer took place without mentioning the name of a man whose lasting influence upon

[5] Egon Wellesz, *Arnold Schönberg*, pp. 17–18. (Kerridge, in his translation [p. 11], makes "a symphony by *Beethoven*" the determining influence upon Vienna's young musicians—thus obscuring an important factor in Vienna's musical development.)

him began during that period. Alexander von Zemlinsky died at
Larchmont, New York, on March 16, 1942. At that time a statement
of Schoenberg's about him was recalled by many: "It is not necessary
that his works should enjoy a great success. He can wait. Zemlinsky's
work will not die. Zemlinsky was my teacher, my friend, later my
brother-in-law, and when I wanted advice, my guide." All this, and
more, Zemlinsky (only two years older than his friend) had been to
Schoenberg; Zemlinsky, who had been more fortunate than Schoenberg in that he had met Brahms and had, luckily, captured the old
man's imagination to the extent that Brahms actually secured the
publication of some of Zemlinsky's music. The young man was a student at the Vienna Conservatory at the time; even in Vienna's atmosphere of intense musical toil his diligence was legendary—when
he was copying music by the hour to make a living, he would use the
few moments that each inked page took to dry to snatch a few precious
minutes for piano practising. Through a mutual acquaintance who
had been profoundly impressed by the promise of the younger composer's talent, Schoenberg came to Zemlinsky for a few months' instruction in counterpoint—the only formal instruction, it cannot be
sufficiently emphasized, which Schoenberg ever had. The more formal
relationship quickly ripened into friendship. Schoenberg, a self-taught
'cellist, played 'cello in Zemlinsky's orchestral society *Polyhymnia*.
They went on vacations together in the mountains; and Schoenberg
made a piano reduction of his friend's prize-winning opera *Sarema*
during one of these summer trips (1897). Favors were mutual, for it
was Zemlinsky who played the piano part in the first performances of
the songs *Dank, Abschied,* and *Freihold* (dedicated to Zemlinsky) by
Eduard Gärtner. The marriage of Schoenberg and Zemlinsky's sister
which was to make this bond of friendship even stronger had not yet
taken place at the time of the completion of *Verklärte Nacht,* which
was written during the summer vacation with Zemlinsky in 1899. It
was not marriage alone which would change Schoenberg's life in a
very short time. New financial pressures and new obligations would
appear, bringing with them their own problems. And the life of the
world Schoenberg lived in would soon undergo profound changes—
many of them unforeseen, however, as the turn of the century approached.

CHAPTER II

1900-1907

IN SEPTEMBER, 1900, there was published in Berlin a slender
volume of verse by several authors, entitled *Deutsche Chansons (Brettl-
Lieder)*, which was issued under the supervision of the popular poet
and novelist Otto Julius Bierbaum. This pocket-anthology had a definite purpose behind it, and Bierbaum explains, in his prefaces to the
several editions through which the work went, just what this purpose
was. His slogan, and that of the group which followed his ideals, was
"applied lyricism." What this concept meant is made clear in Bierbaum's own words:

> Art for the variety theater! But isn't that a shameful profanation? Are we
> not playing an unseemly joke on the muse of lyric poetry when we send the
> children that we owe to her favor out on the vaudeville stage? How can cabaret
> tinsel and lyricism be made to fit together? . . . But I must confess that we
> have very serious ideals too, even though we place our art in the service of
> vaudeville. For we have the notion that life in its entirety must be imbued
> with art. Today, painters make chairs and are proud of the fact that these
> chairs are not mere museum-pieces . . . so we too want to write poems which
> are not intended merely to be read in a quiet room, but which may be sung
> before a crowd anxious to be amused.[1]

This was the philosophy of the organization known as the *Überbrettl* (founded by Bierbaum) which drew into its orbit many of
Berlin's musicians and literati. To those unfamiliar with the term
Überbrettl, it may be explained that the word means simply "something on a higher level than ordinary variety entertainment"—such
ordinary entertainment being implied in the word *Brettl,* a deprecat-
ing diminutive of "die Bretter," or what we would call, in stage par-
lance, "the boards." Percival Pollard, who has written of the *Überbrettl* movement in his book *Masks and Minstrels of New Germany,*
suggests that the term be translated as "artistic variety." However, for
the sake of convenience, we shall continue to refer to the *Überbrettl*
by its original name.

[1] Otto Julius Bierbaum, *Deutsche Chansons (Brettl-Lieder)*, pp. IX–X.

Let us see who were some of the important contributors to the collection of *Brettl-Lieder*. Richard Dehmel is represented there by a variety of lyrics, including a translation from Li-Tai-Po which, though Dehmel calls it simply *Chinesisches Trinklied,* is the same poem used by Mahler (in Bethge's translation, under the title *Das Trinklied vom Jammer der Erde*) for the opening movement of *Das Lied von der Erde.* Frank Wedekind, one of the most prominent members of the *Überbrettl* group, not only contributed much verse to the *Brettl-Lieder* but also sang his own songs, to the accompaniment of the lute, in the *Überbrettl* and its Munich counterpart, the cabaret of the *Elf Scharfrichter.* After 1904, he gave performances in Max Reinhardt's Berlin theater, acting in his own sensational dramas *Frühlings Erwachen* (a grim study of the problems of adolescent life and love) and *Erdgeist.* This latter play, written in 1895, and its sequel, *Die Büchse der Pandora* (which first stirred and shocked Percival Pollard in the magazine *Die Insel* where it was printed in July, 1902), are of especial interest to us as the source material for Alban Berg's *Lulu.* Lulu, the apotheosis of physical woman who lives only for the glorification of her own body, was perhaps Wedekind's most powerful single character-creation, the very summing-up of those qualities inherent in all of his plays.

Wedekind had always led a life of fascinating eccentricity. He had been intended by his father for a career in law, but, even when he was presumably a law student in Munich, most of his attention was devoted to the society of artistic people of his own kind; and later, when he transferred the field of his activities to Zürich, he founded the modernistic "Ulrich Hutten" group, which was joined by many significant personalities. One of these was Otto Erich Hartleben, the high-living, spirited writer of comedies and harmless anecdotal sketches. It was he who revealed to the German public, in 1892, the moonstruck verses of the decadent Belgian, Albert Giraud. Writing to Arno Holz, in May, 1892, he speaks of the wonderful things in *Pierrot Lunaire;* and in an undated letter of the same year to his friend Heilmann he speaks of enthusiastic public reaction to the verses.[2] Indeed, Hartleben had not made a bad guess as to the taste of an artistic public, judging from the number of musical settings of his *Pierrot* translations—for not only Schoenberg, but also Josef Marx and the less-known composers Vrieslander and Kowalski used them. Stefan George knew the Hartleben translation, but what he thought of it has not been recorded. Bierbaum, also, has left no opinion of the translation; however, in his journalistic novel *Stilpe,* wherein he first hinted at the

[2] Otto Erich Hartleben, *Briefe,* p. 161.

plan of the *Überbrettl* under the name of the Momus Music Hall, he satirized the translator as "that fat German beersoak . . . that Pilsener-Goethe. . . ." [3]

The *Überbrettl* included also Ernst von Wolzogen, the best-known librettist of Strauss (*Feuersnot*) next to Hugo von Hofmannsthal and Stefan Zweig; in fact, he was one of the most active members of the group, and manager of the *Buntes Theater* in which its ideas were carried out. Says Pollard,

In the Überbrettl' period it was he who literally fulfilled the old troubadour simile, chanting himself, to his own music, upon his own instrument, in a theater of which he was manager, songs which he had written himself. The centuries had reversed the figures a little, that was all; of old a ragged minstrel, a thing of shreds and patches, sang in the marble halls of barons; in this Überbrettl' day of ours was a Baron von Wolzogen singing to such rag-tag and bobtail as might compose a music-hall audience.[4]

Wolzogen was the author not only of popular songs and of libretti, but also of more solid books, among them a novel based on the life of Liszt at Weimar (*Der Kraft-Mayr*) and a collection of essays entitled *Ansichten und Aussichten,* in which latter work (1908) he devoted a whole chapter to "Das Überbrettl." After outlining, in the first part of this essay, his idea of bringing "artistic variety" in the French manner to the attention of the cultivated German taste, he goes on to tell the causes of the failure of the venture. His conception of the reasons for this failure is different from that of Bierbaum. The latter had said, in 1902, "In Berlin the Überbrettl began as a joke, and went to pieces when the joke grew stale. Every effort seriously to realize the truly fine idea of a lyric theater in music-hall form, was bound to fail there, because the notion of a literary hoax was too closely allied to it." [5] Wolzogen, in a more sinister mood, attributes the failure to the lack of idealism of the Jewish business-men who were associated with the venture and who cheapened it for their own profit; yet, ironically, he had to admit that the Jewish element had by his own choice furnished many of the movement's most valuable poets and composers. Among these (though not mentioned by Wolzogen) was Arnold Schoenberg.[6]

For Schoenberg, having married Mathilde von Zemlinsky on the

[3] As quoted in Percival Pollard, *Masks and Minstrels of New Germany,* p. 138.
[4] *Ibid.,* p. 216.   [5] As quoted in Pollard, *ibid.,* p. 14.
[6] For a good account of Schoenberg in the *Überbrettl,* Stuckenschmidt, *Schönberg: Leben–Umwelt–Werk,* pp. 44–57, Seven Schoenberg *Brettl-Lieder,* as well as the Brettl song *Nachtwandler* for soprano, piccolo, trumpet in F, snare drum, and piano, were published by Belmont Music Publishers. The recording of these and other early songs by Marni Nixon and Leonard Stein (RCA Victor ARL 1-1231) received a Grammy nomination in 1977.

seventh of October, 1901,[7] went with her to Berlin in December of that year. Already he was embittered by the dire financial need which had forced him to interrupt the composition of the *Gurre-Lieder* (of which he had completed the first two parts and the beginning of the third) in order to make a living by orchestrating other composers' operas and operettas. (Wellesz says that in this painful period of his life Schoenberg had orchestrated over six thousand pages of such works.) [8] A brighter future seemed to beckon in Berlin, so there he was, conducting *Überbrettl* music in the *Buntes Theater* and even composing some of it himself. Schoenberg's personal history was already beginning to be cast in a familiar mold; of course it could be foreseen that his esoteric talents—somewhat akin to those of Stefan George, whose poetry he was later to set to music, although, even at his most abstract, Schoenberg has more emotion to offer than the chill, manneristic George—scarcely belonged in the world of "O.J.B." and the *Lustige Ehemann*:

> *Ringelringel Rosenkranz*
> *Ich tanz mit meiner Frau,*
> *Wir tanzen um den Rosenbusch,*
> *Klingklanggloribusch. . . .*[9]

The orchestration of the *Gurre-Lieder* was recommenced in Berlin, but had soon to be abandoned in favor of operetta-instrumentation; the lack of a possibility for performance also discouraged the composer from finishing the work at this time. Besides, there was much else to be done. *Überbrettl* work was time-consuming, and soon there was another job too—an instructorship at the Stern Conservatory in Berlin, obtained through the intercession of the powerful Richard Strauss, who had also secured the Liszt fellowship for Schoenberg (at that time his good friend). In fact, it was Strauss who inspired Schoenberg to the composition of the tone-poem *Pelleas und Melisande* (the "forty-minute wrong note" as an irate critic once called it). Strauss would have liked to see Schoenberg write an opera on the subject, but the latter, perhaps fortunately, decided in favor of a symphonic poem instead. So, at this period of Schoenberg's life (*Pelleas* was composed in 1902 and its orchestration was completed in 1903 before Schoenberg's return to Vienna in July), we must realize that the influence of Strauss upon him preceded that of Mahler.

Neglected in America in comparison with the symphonic poems of Strauss, *Pelleas* might well appeal to the same public which devours

[7] Slonimsky, in his *Music since 1900*, gives the month and day, but erroneously quotes the year 1911.

[8] Wellesz, *Arnold Schönberg*, p. 22.

[9] Bierbaum, *op. cit.*, p. 4.

Strauss with avidity—even though its greater length might be a deterrent to immediate and willing comprehension, and the degree of contrapuntal complication is far greater (and that of superficial externalization correspondingly far less) than in the work of Strauss. Episodes of Maeterlinck's drama are clearly outlined in the music, but the actual literary form is not so closely followed as in the case of *Verklärte Nacht*. The harmonic-melodic style is richly chromatic; one feels the background of Wagner, Liszt, Strauss (even, perhaps, Bruckner, in the cantabile F major mood of the important theme

although there is more sensuality here than in much of Bruckner— certainly more than in the opening of the F major quintet which it recalls)—and yet Schoenberg's originality is everywhere, too. It was typical of Schoenberg to write a real symphony in one movement, not a fragmentary episodic work. Some passages were dictated by the taste of the time, there is no doubt; such are the two violent measures immediately preceding the theme quoted above, with their sharp pizzicato chords in the strings—"breaking dishes," Schoenberg once said humorously—and rushing chromatic passages in woodwinds and trumpets. Strauss liked to call this sort of thing "al fresco music," written not so much for the sake of the notes as of the noise; and even Schoenberg later permitted himself to smile at it, although there is really nothing meretricious about it. It is no criticism to say that the charming waltz-like theme in A major associated with Melisande (quoted below), surrounded as it is by all sorts of gracious accompaniment-figures in the winds (and in the strings as well, the viola having an especially pleasing figure), smacks more of a slightly rococo *Alt-Wien* than of the mysterious forests of Northern France. There is no reason why this should not be so, for the free treatment of the Pelléas theme by composers of varying nationalities shows that it has truly universal qualities in addition to those peculiarly French characteristics so inimitably underlined by Debussy. As a matter of fact, the sudden intrusion of a

Viennese atmosphere into this music gives us yet another indication of the unbreakable continuity of Viennese tradition which we have striven to emphasize. In connection with this, it might be noted that Schoenberg, at the time he composed *Pelleas*, was unfamiliar with the trends of Debussy; nor, indeed, had he ever been much concerned with musical trends that were not specifically German or Austrian—that is to say, French or Russian music, to say nothing of the more regional types (for example, Czech, Norwegian, or Finnish), never exerted an appreciable influence on his development. Whatever is national in Schoenberg is Austrian, and this national element takes precedence over the racial (Hebrew) element, which, though Nazi critics might have tried to find it in "degenerate" atonality, really exists only in works of racial inspiration like the modernization of the *Kol Nidre* or the opera *Moses and Aaron*.[10] However, not only because of Schoenberg's personal genius but also because so much of the music on which he was nurtured—Mozart, Haydn, Beethoven, Schubert—belonged to the world rather than to Austria alone (in spite of its folkloristic elements which almost completely disappear in Schoenberg although vigorously maintained by Bruckner and Mahler), his art is not merely national, but truly universal. This is no contradiction of the existence of a "Viennese school," the development of which we have tried to trace. All the composers of whom we have spoken were universalists first and nationalists second, but the national elements play an important role in binding them together historically. Nevertheless, they learned from each other in matters universal as well; and nothing could be more futile in studying these composers than to pursue "national influence" into its most infinitesimal subdivisions of province, township, and village.

10 For a later view, see Dika Newlin, "Self-Revelation and the Law: Arnold Schoenberg in Religious Works," *Yuval I* (Studies of the Jewish Music Research Centre, Jerusalem, 1968), pp. 204–20.

The most famous passage in *Pelleas* is the scene in the vaults under the castle, where, to the accompaniment of muted drumbeats, of flutes flutter-tonguing in their lowest register, and of 'celli bowing *tremolo* and *sul ponticello pppp,* the muted trombones then execute their mysterious chromatic *glissandi* up and down. It is typical of Schoenberg that at the time he wrote this passage he did not really know whether it was technically possible according to the standards of the time or not, but invented his own technique for its performance, which he carefully explained in a footnote. Such procedures were always to expose Schoenberg to many criticisms, just as when a learned phonetician, writing in the German journal of speech studies, *Vox,* tore the preface of *Pierrot Lunaire* (and hence the esthetic principles of the music itself) to pieces on the ground that Schoenberg's explanation of the processes of the human voice was unscientific.[11] But his comments could not destroy the effectiveness of *Pierrot Lunaire;* and by the same token it is not surprising to find that the trombone passage is not only playable, but provides an unusually appropriate orchestral coloring for this scene. Not experienced in the ways of orchestras through extensive conducting, as Mahler was, Schoenberg was nevertheless led to the composition of passages of this kind by the irrefutable instinct of the musician's inner ear.

Back in Vienna in the fall of 1903, Schoenberg sketched another string quartet, which was never finished, but which, Wellesz says, foreshadowed in its style the D minor quartet, Op. 7; he also worked at parts of another choral composition. But more important than all this was the meeting with Gustav Mahler. The man whom Schoenberg had once openly characterized as an incompetent composer first met the young revolutionary at Rosé's rehearsals of *Verklärte Nacht* in 1903. Rosé had called Mahler's attention to the significance of the work, which he was preparing for performances in the *Wiener Tonkünstler-Verein* and in a concert of his own. (It was at one of these concerts that the Rosé players responded to the furious hissing of the audience after *Verklärte Nacht* with bows and smiles quite as if they had received the most enthusiastic ovation, and when the audience persisted in its protests they calmly sat down to play the complete work a second time!) Rehearsals were being held in a spare room of the opera-house, and so one day Mahler dropped in to see how things were going. Thus began the significant friendship between Mahler and Schoenberg.

It was hardly to be expected that two such temperamental musicians would find themselves in perpetual agreement. Though Schoenberg

[11] W. Heinitz, "Die Sprechtonbewegungen in Arnold Schönbergs Pierrot Lunaire," *Vox,* I, 1925, 1–3.

and Zemlinsky were frequent visitors to the Mahler apartment, their visits would often break up in fireworks. But, whatever the differences of opinion between Mahler and Schoenberg might be, they were at one in that they strove to follow the highest ideals of modern musical art. Hence it was fitting that Mahler should have been asked to be honorary president of the *Society of Creative Musicians* (*Vereinigung schaffender Tonkünstler*) which was summoned into being by Schoenberg and Zemlinsky during the season of 1903–04, although it was active only during the concert season of 1904–05. Characteristically, the society was organized at a meeting in the back room of one of Vienna's cafés. Kurt Schindler, who was present on that occasion, never forgot the meeting; he wrote about it in 1914, in a brochure designed to introduce the Flonzaley Quartet's New York première of the Schoenberg quartet Op. 7. Erich Wolff was in the *Vereinigung*, and so were, of course, Schoenberg and Zemlinsky; there were figures less familiar, too, such as Gustav Gutheil, Oskar Posa, Franz Schmidt, Karl Weigl, and Josef Venantius von Wöss, the devoted transcriber of Bruckner and Mahler for piano.

The *Vereinigung* had a short but distinguished career. Mahler conducting the Viennese première of the Domestic Symphony—what could have been a more brilliant beginning for any concert season? Then there was a chamber music evening featuring Pfitzner's piano trio, songs of Kurt Schindler, and songs of Rudolf Stephan Hoffmann. This was followed by the second orchestral evening, with its own special sensation, *Pelleas und Melisande,* under the composer's leadership. Of the public reception of this work, Paul Stefan says: "A sort of rage came over the audience. Many simply left . . . many more created disturbances. A very few felt the promise of this new music, had some inkling of its message. . . . Among these were several young men, our friends and helpers—above all, Anton von Webern, Heinrich Jalowetz, Karl Horwitz: pupils of Schoenberg, carried away by the teachings of the Master. . . ."[12]

Mahler's *Kindertotenlieder* and *Wunderhorn-Lieder* were highly successful when performed in their orchestral version at a *Vereinigung* concert. Schoenberg, too, was now the composer of orchestral songs, inspired, perhaps, by the influence of Mahler—at least one finds a stirring *Wunderhorn* song, *Das Wappenschild,* in the *Sechs Orchesterlieder,* Op. 8. For the first time the tender melancholy of Petrarch

[12] Stefan, *Arnold Schönberg: Wandlung–Legende–Erscheinung–Bedeutung,* pp. 54–55. Many of these young people, Erwin Stein and Egon Wellesz among them, had been, oddly enough, led into the Schoenberg fold by the influence of a musicologist—Guido Adler, Mahler's friend since the early days in Iglau, and director of the University of Vienna's Institute of Musical History.

finds expression in Schoenberg's work, in three songs of this group. The last of these, *Wenn Vöglein klagen,* is particularly touching and beautiful. The orchestral introduction, with its discreet tone-painting (later imitated in the voice) sets a mood in masterly fashion. Schoenberg's harmonic style is now more and more involved in chromaticism, while the vocal line becomes ever more extravagantly expressive, especially through the use of large intervals—sevenths and ninths are particular favorites. A quotation at random may suffice to illustrate this trend:

These songs were already completed in 1904. And then, in the summer of that year, at the Viennese suburb of Mödling, Schoenberg began a new work which he was to finish on the banks of the Traunsee in the summer of 1905. It was the "First" String Quartet, Op. 7. With the exception of his strictest works in the twelve-tone system, there exists no other work of Schoenberg in which the principles of thematic logic are more inexorably carried to their inevitable conclusion. It has often been said that there is not a scrap of non-thematic material (not derived from the principal motives) in the entire composition, and while this cannot be literally true—after all, "filler" parts are sometimes required by the nature of instrumental ensemble polyphony—it is certainly ideologically true; there is no waste material, for example, in the "first theme" (measures 1–14 of the score). In this work Schoenberg has combined several different principles of form. The ideal of the one-movement symphonic structure, created by Liszt in the B minor piano sonata and adumbrated in Schoenberg's own work by *Pelleas und Melisande,* is here definitively fulfilled. The First *Kammersymphonie,* though intended to fulfill the same ideal, is far more concise in form than is the quartet, which rests on a base of truly Mahlerian breadth, as is only proper to a work wherein the exposition of the first theme alone (complete with a development and recapitulation within itself) is nearly one hundred measures long. Schoenberg carries out his conception of the one-movement form by interweaving the other traditional movements (Scherzo, Adagio, Rondo-Finale) with sections of development of material belonging to the "first movement" ideas—a process which is neither difficult nor unnatural, since the themes of all four movements are interrelated. In such a theme, it is sometimes hard to determine where "exposition" leaves off and "development" begins. But this is already characteristic of the late quartets of Beethoven; and, indeed, Schoenberg himself feels that his style of string-quartet writing (as represented in the development from First to Fourth Quartets) is the continuation of tendencies inaugurated by Beethoven in those late quartets, especially in the *Grosse Fuge.* In fact, he once said that certain portions of the latter work could easily pass as his own composition if presented to the average musical audience under his name. While this statement is obviously meant as a good-natured exaggeration, there is a kernel of truth in it.

The influence of Beethoven upon Schoenberg's First Quartet is even more strikingly demonstrated by the fact that Schoenberg deliberately modelled the first major development section of this quartet after the development of the first movement of the *Eroica* symphony. The visible parallelisms here are remarkable. Perhaps the most notable of these is the correspondence between the great "liquidation" section, with its ever more closely-spaced *sforzati,* of the Beethoven work (I, 248–80) and the liquidation through intensified repetition of the sixteenth-note figure (previously stated in *tremolo* quarter-notes, then rhythmically diminished to eighths and to sixteenths) in Schoenberg (pp. 23–24 of the score). But the resemblance extends to even smaller de-

tails than this. There is a short introduction to the development in
Beethoven—and in Schoenberg. The first motive of the development
in Schoenberg, itself derived from a part of the subordinate theme,

displays a definite rhythmic similarity to the motive found at the
corresponding place in Beethoven (also, by the way, derived from
one of the exposition's subordinate themes).

Then, in Schoenberg, comes a motive which belongs to the first theme,
being a diminution of its counterpoint; and at this point in Beethoven we find the principal theme itself entering the development—but
it was preceded by a scalewise motive which is not dissimilar to
Schoenberg's theme:

Beethoven:

Schoenberg:

This comparison could be carried out in even further detail, but we
have observed clearly enough how his form is modelled on Beethoven's.

Does it seem to be a contradiction in terms to pattern a section of a
string quartet after a tremendous symphonic work? If so, that is merely
a reflection of the general *rapprochement* between chamber music and
orchestral music which, as we have seen, had already begun in the
post-Beethovenian period. Consistent with this symphonic treatment
of the form is Schoenberg's use of "orchestral" effects of a coloristic
kind in the First Quartet, as, for example, the *tremolo sul ponticello*,
which is the basis of a remarkable passage *con sordino* in the Adagio

(p. 65 in the score). Such devices fit into the orchestral texture of the whole work, to which we have referred previously.

The First Quartet completed, Schoenberg turned to the composition of other works, some of which were finished, others not. A piece for male chorus, *Georg von Frundsberg* (a sequel to the already-written *Wunderhorn* song on the same subject) remained unfinished, as did a string quintet. But the eight songs Op. 6 were written, among them the charming *Enticement* (*Lockung*) which, though nominally in E flat, manages to avoid the tonic completely, with the exception of an insignificant passing-chord, till the very end. Schoenberg was still a tonalist (as the emphatic D major coda of the First Quartet, to choose one example, surely proves), but he was attaining ever greater freedom within tonality and ever greater skill in the unhackneyed use of its means. Other outstanding songs of this opus include *Dream-Life* (*Traumleben*), a Dehmel setting, and *Ghasel* (after an old Persian verse-form, by Gottfried Keller), both of which are characterized by a fruitful and functional chromaticism, integrated tone-painting, and a rich harmonic background complemented by extremely expressive vocal intervals (cf. the opening bars of *Traumleben*); the longest and most ambitious of the songs, *Der Wanderer,* is based on a text by Nietzsche (which immediately brings us back into the Mahler-Lipiner sphere of influence).

We need not dwell upon the two *Ballads,* Op. 12 (1906), which, though finely conceived and executed, add nothing new to our knowledge of Schoenberg's pre-atonal vocal style. His interest in the different modes of expression of vocal music now led him to try his hand at opera for the first time, with some sketches based on Gerhart Hauptmann's play *Und Pippa tanzt.* These sketches were abandoned, however—even as Berg's later plans for a work on the same subject were to be shelved—and so Schoenberg's next important work (1906) was the First *Kammersymphonie,* Op. 9.[13]

Formally, this "chamber symphony" represents still another application of the principles of "portmanteau" symphonic structure—all movements in one—and hence may be regarded as a continuation of the First Quartet. However, there are important differences between the two works. For one thing, Schoenberg has achieved a greater degree of concision in the *Kammersymphonie;* this is important because it marks a trend in his work which will eventually lead to the utmost

[13] On August 1, 1906, Schoenberg began to write a Second *Kammersymphonie,* in two movements. However, it was put aside, to remain unfinished for thirty-five years until the composer completed it on a commission from the New Friends of Music.

compression of the musical idea in epigrammatic form, the *Six Little Piano Pieces*, Op. 19. For another, Schoenberg, through the use of a motto in fourths which is employed both harmonically and melodically as a source for thematic material and for chord-progressions, which stands at the very opening of the work, and which serves as a transition to the slow movement of this symphony (the order of the inner movements is the same as in the First Quartet, Scherzo-Adagio), has achieved, despite the unmistakable E major tonality of the composition, an approach to tonality which adumbrates the system of the tone-row; this complex of fourth-chords, which can be used not only in a harmonic sense but also in a melodic sense, is the logical predecessor of the tone-row, which possesses these same characteristics. This indicates that a more comprehensive knowledge of the works of Schoenberg's transitional period (among which this *Kammersymphonie* may certainly be numbered), and particularly of those where, as in the Second Quartet, tonality really begins to break up, is necessary for us to bridge the gap between *Verklärte Nacht* and, say, the wind quintet.

Schoenberg did not confine his formal experimentation to the combination of all symphonic movements into one, but also contributed his own solution to the ever-intriguing problem of the recapitulation in "sonata-form" (a question which has two aspects: how may mechanical repetition be avoided and how may a transition from tonic first theme to tonic second theme be effected convincingly?) by reversing, in the final section, the order in which the two themes are recapitulated. In addition to this, a problem is posed in the very name of the composition. Schoenberg's work for fifteen solo instruments, the arrangement of which upon the stage is carefully prescribed in a special diagram attached to the score, is apparently the first existing *Kammersymphonie* so titled. This is symptomatic of the *Zeitgeist*, of the turning away from dreams of Wagnerian grandeur to more practicable forms (this, though Mahler had not yet achieved his great triumph with the Eighth Symphony and the *Gurre-Lieder* were as yet incomplete! But both these works represented rather the highest possible development of a kind of music already existing than the first burgeoning of a new species). One is reminded of the state of affairs which characterized the beginnings of the symphony, when it was very difficult, at times, to distinguish chamber music from orchestral music (cf. Stamitz' "Orchestertrios," to use the felicitous term of Riemann). But, after all, this particular *Kammersymphonie* is easily distinguishable from chamber music in our modern sense. A trace of the old ambiguity returns, however, in the fact that Schoenberg made orchestral versions of the *Kammersymphonie* and *Verklärte Nacht,* though in each case he preferred the chamber music version, for reasons of sonority.

When we remember that the trend towards soloistic treatment of instrumental bodies was, as previously indicated, well under way in Mahler's mature works (cf. the score of the *Kindertotenlieder*) we may not find it without significance that during the period of the composition of the *Kammersymphonie* Schoenberg's relationship to Mahler was becoming ever closer and warmer. Already in 1904, Schoenberg, the one-time unbeliever, had written to Mahler, on the occasion of the performance of his Third Symphony, a fervent tribute which throws additional light on Mahler's deep influence upon the younger composer:

12.XII.1904

Honored Herr Direktor! In order to do any sort of justice to the unheard-of impressions which I received from your symphony, I must speak, not as musician to musician, but as man to man. For I have seen your soul naked, stark naked. It lay before me like a wild, mysterious landscape with its frightening crevasses and abysses—and, beside these, sunny meadows gay and pleasant, idyllic nooks of repose. It struck me with the force of a phenomenon of nature —terror and evil, then the transfiguration of the peace-bringing rainbow. What difference does it make that, when I was told the "program" of the music afterwards, it seemed to have little relationship to my impressions? Does it matter whether I am a good or bad interpreter of the emotions released in me by an experience? Must I understand correctly, when I have experienced and felt? And I think I have felt your symphony. I sensed the battle for illusions; I experienced the grief of the disillusioned one, I saw the forces of evil and of good struggling with each other, I saw a man, deeply troubled, fighting for inner harmony; I perceived a man, a drama, *truth,* truth with no reservations!

I had to get this out of my system—forgive me. There are no intermediate emotions with me; it's either—or! [14]

The letter of July 18, 1906, written at the Tegernsee in Upper Bavaria, is not so emotional, but indicates that a new stage of the friendship has been reached. Schoenberg writes:

Nothing could have made me happier than your saying that we have come nearer to each other. I take more pleasure and pride in this than if you had praised a work of mine—although I have the greatest regard for your judgment. Personal sympathy is, to me, the most important element in the relations of human beings among themselves, and I do not think that anything else could come to its full fruition without this sympathy. [15]

Schoenberg was too busy to do much composing during the fall of 1906, but later (March 9, 1907) he finished the chorus *Friede auf Er-*

[14] Alma Mahler, *Gustav Mahler: Erinnerungen und Briefe*, p. 329.
[15] *Ibid.,* pp. 355–56.

den, Op. 13, written to a Christmas text by the Swiss poet C. F. Meyer.
This *a cappella* chorus, for which Schoenberg provided the possibility
of a modest orchestral accompaniment in case of difficulties of intonation, is a strongly-knit, tonal work, which builds its vocal complexes
(noticeably in the refrain, "Friede, Friede auf der Erde") on clusters
of parallel thirds and sixths. One hardly feels that it is a work of controversial nature; and in this respect it differs from most of Schoenberg's other creations, as was soon to be demonstrated—not for the last
time—in this year of 1907.

For one of the most resounding scandals in the history of the recep-
tion of Schoenberg's work occurred at the first performance of the
First String Quartet by the Rosé organization, which took place on
February 5, 1907. It is almost impossible to read a book about musical
Vienna of this epoch, about Schoenberg, or about Mahler—or to en-
counter a musician who lived through this time in Vienna—without
hearing, in one version or another, the story of that famous occasion.
Alma Mahler, who was present at the concert, describes it as follows:

> The critic K. [Korngold?] yelled "Stop it!" when the audience was register-
> ing quiet but unanimous amusement. An unpardonable error! for his shouts
> were followed by such a whistling and racket as I have never heard before or
> since. A fellow parked himself in front of the first row and hissed at Schoen-
> berg, who insisted on coming back for innumerable bows, cocking his head—
> the head of a Jewish Bruckner—this way and that, as though asking pardon
> and at the same time unobtrusively pleading for consideration. Mahler jumped
> up, stood beside the man, and said, "I'd just like to get a good look at a fellow
> who hisses!" Upon this, the other made as if to strike Mahler. Moll saw this,
> ran through the disorderly audience like a streak of lightning, and separated
> the quarreling men, much to their astonishment. He chased the cowardly
> bourgeois right out of the *Bösendorfersaal,* and the latter, intimidated by
> Moll's greater strength, let himself be driven out. But at the exit he screwed
> up his courage and shouted, "Don't worry, I hiss Mahler's symphonies *too!*" [16]

Mahler had still another opportunity to defend his colleague publicly, on the occasion of a performance of the *Kammersymphonie* (also
by the Rosés, supplemented by wind-players of the opera orchestra)
which followed closely upon the première of the D minor quartet.
On this occasion, the unruly audience was commanded to silence by
Mahler, who, after the performance, stood up ostentatiously in his
box and, leaning as far over the edge as he could, applauded loudly
until the last of the troublemakers had left the hall. Afterwards, talking over the evening's events at home, Mahler was deeply concerned
with the problems of Schoenberg's music. "I don't understand his

[16] *Ibid.,* pp. 138–39.

work," said he, "but then, he's young and he may well be right. I'm old and perhaps I don't have the ear for his music." [17] It is a tribute to Mahler's integrity that, in spite of these mental reservations, he vigorously supported Schoenberg in public.

[17] *Ibid.,* p. 139.

CHAPTER III

First Steps in Atonality: 1907-1911

THE YEARS 1907–11 proved to be important for Schoenberg's fate as a composer. During this period there were written a whole series of works which mark the transition from the last frontiers of tonality to the most outspoken "atonality" [1] which would be surpassed in Schoenberg's evolution only by its final and systematized synthesis, the tone-row scheme. The Second Quartet, composed between March, 1907, and August, 1908; the songs of Op. 14, succeeded by Stefan George's *Book of the Hanging Gardens*—for Schoenberg, ever more aloof from the public and its misunderstandings of what he was trying to do, felt a strong bond with the aristocratic nature of George at this time; the *Three Piano Pieces,* Op. 11, composed in February and March, 1909; the *Five Orchestral Pieces,* Op. 16, also written in 1909, and—as that year's most startling production—the monodrama *Erwartung,* which was completed in two weeks' time. Then, the beginning of the pantomime *Die glückliche Hand,* continuing work on the *Gurre-Lieder,* the first sketches of the *Harmonielehre*—indeed these were significant years in Schoenberg's life. He might well have attached a symbolic value to those words of George which he had used as a text for the last movement of the Second String Quartet, *I feel the breath of other planets blowing.* For in truth he had crossed into a new world.

The Second Quartet does not display so intense an integration of structure as the First. The tight contrapuntal network has been somewhat loosened, and more frequent rests bring light and air even into the visual picture of the score. In place of the one-movement symphonic form we have the "classical" four-movement grouping which is to remain standard in Schoenberg's subsequent quartets. Cyclic form, achieved through the quotation of the principal theme of the first movement in a rhythmically altered guise and in a different key

[1] Schoenberg, I am well aware, abhorred this word because of its negative connotations. However, since his preferred term "pantonality" never gained wide currency in the sense in which he used it, I have used the more commonly understood "atonality." For more on this, see pp. 260–61.

(E flat minor) at the beginning of the third movement, the *Litanei,*
brings about unity in spite of the problems of organization created
by the presence of instrumental movements and vocal movements in
one and the same composition. Schoenberg could well have learned
this lesson from Mahler—or from Beethoven! But the spirit of Mahler
hovers even more persistently over the Scherzo, with its bizarre quotation (in the Trio section) of "O, du lieber Augustin," a quotation
which reminds us of the bitterness of *Frère Jacques* (or *Bruder Martin*
as the Germans would have it) in Mahler's First Symphony. Bitterness
is the keynote here too, and not heedless humor—the crackling dissonances with which Schoenberg has counterpointed the innocuous melody would make this clear enough even if his own words did not.
"*Alles ist hin,*" read the writer's own notes on this passage, made during Schoenberg's classroom discussion of it; "*not* ironical—a real emotional significance." Perhaps we glimpse here another "secret program" such as the composer himself had already postulated but not
revealed for the First Quartet. [2]

True atonality manifests itself first in the Finale, that famed movement of the "other planets," *Entrückung.* The mysterious muted arpeg-
giated figures of the opening of this movement are the very *Urform*
of so much that is familiar to us in Schoenberg's later style—of *Pierrot,* of the piano pieces. It is true that the piece ends with a tonal cadence on F♯ major, but that should not mislead us as to the intentions of innovation embodied therein, which were already sufficiently
indicated by the absence of key-signature. The opening vocal phrase,
too, in spite of its unequivocal octave-leap, is imbued with a vague
and neutral quality which expresses the underlying emotion of the
text perfectly:

ich   füh-le   Luft   von   an-de-ren Pla-ne-ten—.

The songs of the *Hanging Gardens,* with their pulsating, well-nigh
hysterical emotionality born of a union between the exciting new
musical style and the carefully contrived exoticism of the George texts,
logically follow the George movement of the quartet. Of the *Hanging
Gardens,* Schoenberg said (in connection with the concert at which, in
addition to the première of this song-cycle, the piano pieces Op. 11
were first publicly played by Rudolf Réti, future organizer of the
ISCM):

2 Clearly so, in view of the problems with Schoenberg's marriage at this time.
See Stuckenschmidt, *Schönberg: Leben–Umwelt–Werk,* pp. 87–90.

In the George *Lieder* I have succeeded for the first time in approaching an ideal of expression and form that had hovered before me for some years. Hitherto I had not sufficient strength and sureness to realize that ideal. Now, however, that I have definitely started on my journey, I may confess to having broken off the bonds of a bygone aesthetic; and if I am striving towards a goal that seems to me to be certain, nevertheless I already feel the opposition that I shall have to overcome. I feel also with what heat even those of the feeblest temperament will reject my works, and I suspect that even those who have hitherto believed in me will not be willing to perceive the necessity of this development.[3]

That last was unfortunately all too true. Even friends could misunderstand the new Schoenberg, as is tragically evidenced by Busoni's ill-starred "concert arrangement" of Op. 11, no. 2. For, after all, the new piano music offered enough technical difficulties—leaving the musical ones, for the moment, quite out of the matter—without benefit of any "editing." It was from the Brahms piano style, bristling with thick chords and thunderous left-hand octaves, that Schoenberg's instrumental idiom in this music was derived. Though this derivation is less superficially obvious than was the case in the accompaniments of the early songs, we often have the weird feeling of listening to what Brahms' piano music would have been if it were atonal; this feeling is especially strong in such passages of Op. 11, no. 2, as this, which has even the visual aspect of Brahms' music, except for the forest of accidentals,

and in the entire Op. 11, no. 3, which of all the group presents the most purely technical difficulties. However, the most interesting feature of pianistic technique, a real innovation of Schoenberg's —the use of "harmonics" on the piano (an effect achieved simply by pressing down a tone or tones soundlessly with one hand and then, while holding these, having the same tones struck audibly in another octave)—occurs on the opening page of the first of the three pieces.

Perhaps the most easily assimilable of the pieces of Op. 11 is the second (which was composed first, on February 22, 1909). The recurring pedal-point on D and F, which associates itself with two different thematic complexes,

and

is perhaps helpful to the listener in organizing his comprehension of the music; but it must be emphasized that there is no real feeling of "tonality" in a conventional sense bound up with its recurrence. It represents a transitional stage of the development of atonality, wherein Schoenberg felt the need of a certain point of vantage to which he could return without creating cadential obligations, but had not yet discovered the "tone-row."

The liking for groups of small pieces now extended itself to the orchestral field, and so came into being the *Five Orchestral Pieces*, Op. 16. Originally given broadly descriptive names like "The Past," or "Presentiments," the pieces were later left untitled because Schoenberg, even as Mahler, found that the use of titles confused rather than enlightened the audience, accustomed to the Liszt-Strauss type of program music.[4] But in one instance the knowledge of the program which Schoenberg had in mind is helpful in understanding the intentions of the music. This is the third of the orchestral pieces, once known as "The Changing Chord," which has been described as picturing the changing colors of sunrise over a lake. The superficial descriptive pattern is less interesting than the real structural idea on which

[4] For more on this, see Schoenberg, *Berliner Tagebuch*, pp. 13–14. (Translation by Newlin in Rufer, *The Works of Arnold Schoenberg*, p. 34.)

the piece is based and for which the descriptive pattern is only an excuse. Alma Mahler reports a conversation (undated) between Mahler and Schoenberg "in which Schoenberg demonstrated the possibility of creating a melody merely by allowing *one* tone to be sounded by different instruments . . . a possibility which Mahler strenuously denied." [5] The outcome of this conversation was the "Changing Chord" idea. Schoenberg does not carry his theory to its ultimate consequences, for the harmonies change throughout the composition, as do the instrumental combinations; but the harmonic changes are more often than not motivated by the instrumental shifts, and the compositional approach is clearly not melodic or contrapuntal, as is evidenced by the presence in the solo contrabass parts of parallel-fifth passages which would never be tolerated by Schoenberg in his normal part-writing. This kind of musical pointillism was to find its most ardent imitator in Anton von Webern, who used it in his chamber music, in his orchestral music, and even in orchestrating Bach.

Experimentation appeared in still another guise in the *Five Orchestral Pieces*. The half-bracket marks which occur at strategic points in the last piece are the first form of the marks H⁻ and N⁻ (*Hauptstimme* and *Nebenstimme*) which are used in Schoenberg's subsequent scores as a guide to performers and conductors. These marks reflect the insistence on accurate interpretation which characterizes Schoenberg's scores even as Mahler's; for Schoenberg has just as many detailed messages for the performer in his score as has Mahler, and, in fact, even more. But, whereas Mahler often gave every part a different dynamic marking in his efforts to attain plasticity and clarity, Schoenberg says himself that he found this system too cumbersome and so substituted the unequivocal H⁻ and N⁻ signs.

Songs, chamber music, piano music, orchestral music—all had now felt the breath of the new atonal style. One great *genre* remained untouched: opera. And Schoenberg, striking boldly where Bruckner, the Wagnerian, and Mahler, the opera director, had feared to tread, escaped the shadow of Wagner to create something new in this field as well. It was the unique music-drama for one performer, *Erwartung*.

We say that this work "escaped the shadow of Wagner" and this is indeed true from the point of view of the music alone. As we have seen, Schoenberg's style grew out of Wagner, but the important thing to remember is that his music developed *from* Wagner and did not

---

[5] Alma Mahler, *Gustav Mahler: Erinnerungen und Briefe*, p. 223. Schoenberg's idea has since received unexpected realization in a number of "minimal" works (of lengths ranging from an hour to a week!) based on a single tone: Corner, *Elementals;* Newlin, *Atone*, and others.

remain fixed at a stage of development only slightly beyond Wagner's, as was the case with Pfitzner and Schreker. Certainly to the ear, and even to the eye (in spite of the immense orchestral score with its impressive longitudinal dimensions), there is nothing even superficially Wagnerian about the esoteric atonal sonorities of this music which was dashed off at white heat in a fortnight. But the basic idea of the drama is something else again, for the entire picture of the emotions of a woman on finding the dead body of her lover in the forest is but an intensification, far more morbidly expressed, of the *Liebestod* idea. (This plot, by the way, is Schoenberg's own, having been suggested by him to the actual librettist, Marie Pappenheim.) [6] Not only does this derivation hold true for the broader scheme, it also applies to details. For example, when, after the long and tortured night, the dawn comes: "Silence," read the stage directions, "dawn in the east, clouds far on the horizon, pale light with the yellowish tinge of candlelight." This is surely the same dawn which brought betrayal and tragedy to Tristan and Isolde. The subsequent words of the heroine (designated, in typical expressionistic fashion—see the dramas of Georg Kaiser and others—simply as "Frau") would seem to bear this out. Night, and not day, had been the friend of Wagner's lovers; "Let daylight defer to death," Tristan had sung—and the conflict between night and day, death and life, had become the psychological basis for that whole music-drama, and the premise on which Appia based his complete concept of its staging. Even so, Schoenberg's heroine sings: "Beloved, beloved, morning is dawning . . . what shall I do here all alone? . . . In this endless life . . . in this dream without limit or shadow . . . *morning parts us . . . always morning. . . . Another endless day of waiting. . . .* Oh, thou wilt never awaken again. . . ." [7] The connection is unmistakable. Paul Bekker called attention to the links between *Erwartung* and *Tristan* in his program-notes to the performance of *Erwartung* which took place at Wiesbaden, on a double bill with Busoni's *Turandot,* on January 22, 1928. Fortunately, however, he brought out not only *Erwartung's* connection with the past, but also its importance for the future, in words which deserve all the more attention, since the music itself has been, on account of its difficulties, so unwarrantedly neglected as far as performance is concerned. "Even including the most striking creations of the youngest generation—Hindemith's *Cardillac,* Křenek's *Orpheus* and *Jonny,* Berg's *Wozzeck*—nothing has yet been written that—so far as stylistic formulation of

[6] In personal interview, Marie Pappenheim-Frischauf stated (1951) that the idea of the monodrama, and its plot, were her own.

[7] Marie Pappenheim, *Erwartung* (libretto), p. 17. (Italics are the present writer's.)

the vocal part and of the orchestral score, development of harmony, and intensity of the complete emotional organism are concerned—was not already contained in Schoenberg's *Erwartung*. This work is one of the fundamental manifestations of modern operatic composition."

But in 1909 the riddle of *Erwartung* had not yet been propounded in public. Schoenberg's *Harmonielehre* had not yet been written. Nor had that tragic event occurred which was to bring to an end an exciting and significant era of Viennese musical life.

CHAPTER IV

1911-1915

GUSTAV MAHLER was dead. That was the important event in musical Vienna in the year of 1911.

Even when he had returned from his last journey to America, a mortally sick man, he had still cherished hopes of renewed life and work. The first day in Paris had begun gloriously with plans for a vacation trip to Egypt and for a restaging of Cornelius' *Barber of Bagdad;* but, by the time that day was over, all knew that Mahler would not live long. He was brought to Vienna more dead than alive; though everything possible had been done for him, the end finally came at midnight on the eighteenth of May.

Frau Alma lay, herself dangerously ill, in her own bed in Heiligenstadt. Dr. Chvostek, who had so faithfully attended Mahler during his last illness, came to her; "You must take care of yourself now," he admonished, "otherwise you'll follow him all too soon!" She lay there, listening to the tolling bells, and wanting nothing more than to "follow him all too soon." It was raining in Grinzing, where he was to be buried that day beside the grave of his little daughter, beneath the ivy-twined but unadorned gravestone of his own wishes: "Nothing should be on it but the name 'Mahler.' Those who are looking for me know who I was, the others don't need to know." [1] But, at the very moment when the coffin was lowered into the grave, a ray of sunshine burst through the clouds in momentary transfiguration. All of this is represented with the utmost sensitivity in the few brief measures of one of Schoenberg's most haunting compositions, the last of the *Six Little Piano Pieces,* Op. 19 (1911), wherein the bells are heard, but so vaguely as to be only a memory, a faded leaf from a sad past, the equivalent in tones of Stefan's nostalgic book-title *Das Grab in Wien*—for it was Mahler's grave that was meant.

Schoenberg had planned that his *Harmonielehre* should be dedi-

1 Alma Mahler, *Gustav Mahler: Erinnerungen und Briefe*, p. 241.

cated to Mahler, and had discussed the dedication with him when they last conversed together before Mahler's final trip to America. But Mahler's death changed everything; and so the *Harmonielehre* had to come out with the following inscription:

> This book is consecrated to the memory of Gustav Mahler. The dedication was to have brought him some slight pleasure during his lifetime. It was to express respect for his work, for his immortal compositions; it was to furnish testimony that this work, which cultivated musicians have shrugged off and scornfully passed by, is worshipped by one who is, perhaps, possessed of some slight understanding.[2]

Schoenberg expressed these and similar sentiments on many other occasions—notably in a speech given in memory of Mahler, wherein he frankly admitted that formerly he had been a non-believer in Mahler's art, but that now, having been converted from a Saul to a Paul, he felt that he had even more right than most to defend the work which he had once attacked. Mahler, for his part, had left Schoenberg with good reason to be grateful to him. In his last days he had often been heard to speculate about what would happen to Schoenberg in Vienna after he was gone; Frau Alma, interpreting his wishes rightly, established a fund (over which Walter, Gabrilowitsch, and Busoni were custodians) the income of which was to be turned over to a deserving composer each year, and which Schoenberg was the first to receive.[3]

The impact of the *Harmonielehre* upon the musical world was, by the very nature of the work, not so sensational as the public performance of a new piece of music by Schoenberg would have been; in music, at least, a textbook usually causes fewer riots than a symphony. Nevertheless, it created no inconsiderable stir among friends and foes of Schoenberg. The younger generation took to it with enthusiasm; in later years he himself used to tell how, during the war, he received "fan mail" from boys who had carried the book to the trenches with them. But others, no admirers of Schoenberg's modernism, professed to be disappointed that he had not written a handbook of so-called "modern harmony." Hugo Leichtentritt could see nothing in the work but a stale rehashing of every other harmony textbook. Jalowetz, on the other hand, was much concerned lest the book should fail to reach two classes of people: those "who already have confidence in the name of Schoenberg, but are alarmed by the title 'Manual of Harmony,' because they do not realize that this work is a profession of faith which speaks to all," and those "who may be looking for a harmony

---

[2] Arnold Schoenberg, *Harmonielehre* (1911), dedicatory page.
[3] The Mahler essay in *Style and Idea* is a moving testimonial to Schoenberg's feelings about his great forebear.

textbook but are alarmed by the name of Schoenberg, because they believe those poisoners of public opinion who, seeing that some of Schoenberg's pupils write dissonances, draw the false conclusion that their teacher demands this of them." [4]

Actually, the *Harmonielehre* is that very unusual thing, a textbook which is strict without being academic. But it is considerably more than that, for many of its most interesting sections are concerned with extra-musical subjects. Schoenberg's active mind roves into the fields of physics and philosophy, and, even if his theorizing on these subjects is not always based on the most scientific information, his speculations add immeasurably to the value of the book as a personal document. (Yet it is precisely these extra-musical elaborations, many of which are of an abstract nature that lends itself far better to formulation in Schoenberg's flexible German than to rendering in English, which have, to date, made the problem of translating the *Harmonielehre* into English such a difficult one.) [5]

Schoenberg's justification of atonality rests directly on the overtone system. For him, there is no traditional division into "consonances" and "dissonances," since those sound-combinations which we conventionally term "dissonances" result simply from the use of tones more remote in the overtone-series, and so differ in degree only, not in kind, from the familiar fifth, third, or sixth. By the same token, there can be no tones "extraneous to the harmony," for the chordal combinations produced by passing-tones have as good a right to be used independently as any other harmonies. A tone can only be extraneous to a given academic harmonic system, never to harmony itself.

Schoenberg always prided himself on not being a student of harmony manuals and music histories, and so his approach to the problems of harmony teaching remained fresh and creative. With the exception of some chorale harmonizations, he discarded the harmonization of given melodies and also that of figured basses, because he wished to develop the creative impulse in his pupils even in the construction of simple harmonic sentences wherein "bass" and "melody" are not separate entities but the complete harmony is logically conceived at one time. And yet, when we come to his doctrine of the root-progressions (expounded not only in the *Harmonielehre* but also in his classroom teaching and in the later textbook *Models for Beginners in Composition*), we may clearly discern the influence of an academic theoreti-

---

[4] Heinrich Jalowetz, "Die Harmonielehre," in *Arnold Schönberg*, p. 57.

[5] Robert D. W. Adams' translation for Philosophical Library eliminated all the extra-musical discussions and concentrated on the harmonic pedagogy. A complete translation of the book by Roy E. Carter will be published in 1978 by Faber & Faber.

cian; for, as previously indicated, it is to Simon Sechter, the teacher of Bruckner, that Schoenberg returned for this theory.

Schoenberg classified root-progressions into strong ("ascending") weak ("descending"), and super-strong progressions.[6] At the head of the list of "strong" progressions we are not surprised to find Sechter's basic rising fourth (or falling fifth); the descending third is also strong. "Weak" progressions are simply the strong progressions in reverse, i. e., the rising fifth and rising third; and there is a hint of the theory of intermediary roots in the idea that these progressions are best used in combinations which will add up to a "strong" progression. Thus the weak progression I–V, when followed by VI, produces I–V⌐VI. Here, I–VI is the basic progression and the weak V is almost an intermediary root, although in a different sense from Sechter's. As for the crucial steps of a second up or down, Schoenberg did not use intermediary roots to explain them, but put them in the special category of "super-strong" progressions, also called "deceptive" progressions because they can be used for deceptive cadences.

If all this terminology suggests a sufficient acquaintance with Sechter's theory, the explanation of the terminology suggests it still more strongly. It will be remembered that Sechter explained the strength of the basic progression V–I by pointing out that the root of V became the fifth of I. Here again, Schoenberg transposed a theory of Sechter's into his own terms with stimulating results. The V–I progression is strong because the root of the first chord, its strongest element, is *conquered* by the second chord; that is, the second chord, I, converts the previously strong root into its weakest element, the fifth. Similarly I–VI is a strong progression because the root of I is forcibly converted by VI into a weaker element, the third. It is this element of "forcible conquest" which makes a progression strong. On the other hand, I–V and I–III are weak progressions because, in each case, a tone which was of lesser importance in the first chord becomes the root of the second chord; the fifth of I becomes the root of V, the third of I the root of III. The "super-strong" progressions are in a category by themselves, since chords involved in such progressions have no tone in common (e. g., I–II).

To this there must be added an additional parallel between Schoenberg and Sechter: the theory of the diminished seventh chord as ninth chord with omitted root. Schoenberg used this idea with great effect in his writing and teaching. He believed that tying the diminished seventh down to a definite root gives it a functional place in harmonic

---

[6] It should be understood that "ascending" and "descending" are not meant literally. For example, a root-progression of a third *up* is "descending."

progressions, and discourages its use as an easy way of modulating quickly or as a mere color element—an "aspirin harmony" as he wittily termed it. Such an attitude towards the diminished seventh chord was even more necessary in 1911 (and all the more so in 1946) than it was in Sechter's time, when the unfortunate harmony had not been quite so much abused by legions of minor romantic composers and Protestant hymn writers.

Some composers turn to the field of theory only when their creative inspiration is gone. Not so Schoenberg; for the period following the *Harmonielehre* was to bring forth some of his most significant works. The *Six Little Piano Pieces*, Op. 19, were of particular importance because they started a Viennese vogue for the composition of short musical aphorisms which, while they might at times present an "impressionistic" appearance superficially, were worlds removed from the truly impressionistic utterances—extended and improvisatory in form—of a Debussy. As so often in past epochs of musical history, the new style had come into being on the piano. Beethoven and Schubert had always indulged in more formal experimentation in their piano sonatas than in any other type of music; "romanticism" had first burgeoned in the short character-piece for piano as written by W. A. Mozart the younger, Tomašek, or Voříšek; and every refinement of the Wagnerian orchestral style had been foreshadowed in Liszt's piano music. Even as in these previous instances, the aphoristic style did not remain confined to its original medium—as witness Berg's *Four Pieces for Clarinet and Piano* and Webern's minuscule groups of tiny pieces for 'cello solo, string quartet, and orchestra. Many other figures in Viennese musical life (Toch, Křenek, and Wellesz among them) paid tribute to the trend with groups of piano pieces; and Schoenberg himself returned to this form at various times throughout his career.

Considering how closely the Viennese musical and literary cultures have always interlocked, it is by no means surprising to discover that the tendency towards musical aphorism has its distinct literary parallels. Arthur Schnitzler, for example, wrote aphorisms; and, when it comes to the short literary sketch, which is also in its way a parallel to the musical form that we have in mind, we must immediately think of "Peter Altenberg" (Richard Engländer). This lovable and quaint Viennese figure, a good friend of Alban Berg and of Berg's wife, the former Helene Nahowska whom he had married just two weeks before Mahler's death, immortalized many delightful passing moments of Viennese life in his brief atmospheric sketches, some of them no more than a few lines long. He had paid glowing tribute to Helene Nahowska in three sketches of his book *Neues Altes,* which also contains those "Texts for Picture Postcards" that Berg set to music with such telling effect. These songs, performed under Schoenberg's direction on March 31, 1913, in a concert that also included the *Kindertotenlieder,* orchestral pieces of Webern, songs of Zemlinsky, and Schoenberg's own *Kammersymphonie,* provoked one of the most unpleasant concert-scandals of Schoenberg's career, which even led to the haling into court of some of the participants on charges of disorderly conduct.

Schoenberg, now removed to Berlin (Zehlendorf) for the second time, was still busy, in 1911, finishing the composition of *Die glückliche Hand* and the orchestration of the *Gurre-Lieder.* He found time, too, to return to the inspiration of Maeterlinck, which had already served him well in one work, *Pelleas und Melisande.* The new composition was *Herzgewächse (Feuillage du Coeur),* a setting (for "high soprano," harmonium, celesta, and harp) of a poem from Maeterlinck's volume *Serres chaudes.* "High soprano" is no exaggeration, for the voice is asked to reach F above high C in a passage of enormous range within a short space.[7]

But, more than this, the lower limit of the voice is G sharp below middle C, and immense flexibility is required of it in all registers. Such writing calls for a virtuosity that brings to mind the celebrated achievements of seventeenth-century castrati and nineteenth-century divas; yet the technical difficulties here are in no way external ornamentation, but are an essential part of the musical conception itself.

It is interesting that Schoenberg, so completely Viennese in background, should have been, at this time, much concerned with the composition of texts translated from the French; for now came his next big work, undertaken at the instigation of the actress Albertine Zehme,[8] and based on that Hartleben translation of the Giraud verses already mentioned in an earlier chapter—the inimitable *Pierrot Lunaire.* "Inimitable" one may well say; for the texts were set by other German composers of the twentieth century, Josef Marx among them, and yet the settings of Marx (for example) present no opportunities for

---

[7] No novelty in Schoenberg! Cf. the famous skip of two octaves plus a half-tone in
[8] For Zehme's career, see Stuckenschmidt, *Schönberg: Leben–Umwelt–Werk,* especially pp. 179–99.

comparison with Schoenberg's creations. Never before had there been any sonorities quite like this new combination of the bizarre *Sprechstimme,* neither speech nor song—already used by Schoenberg in the third part of the *Gurre-Lieder,* but not to this extent—with a flexible accompanying ensemble that changes its components for each successive recitation, using alternating instruments (piccolo instead of flute, bass-clarinet instead of clarinet, viola instead of violin) so that in only a very few numbers need the same combination be reduplicated. This idea of the very small and specialized ensemble is a logical outgrowth of the renewed interest in chamber music; Schoenberg himself credited such works of Brahms as the horn trio and the clarinet quintet with stimulating his own interest (and that of his circle) in specialized combinations.

It was not Schoenberg alone among the Viennese composers who was strongly drawn to *fin de siècle* French poetry, or to poetry that became generally known towards the end of the century; for Alban Berg chose to set three poems of Baudelaire to music in his "concert aria" *Der Wein.*[9] The choice of such subject-matter might seem to lend color to the charges of "decadence" brought against these composers by their opponents. It is true that by this time both French and Austrian cultures were in that state of exhaustion which preceded the cultural destruction of our day. But that did not prevent their bringing forth some remarkably vigorous manifestations, of which *Pierrot Lunaire* is surely one of the most individual. It was never successfully imitated and never repeated; to us, by reason of its subject-matter and the treatment of that material, it seems so uniquely of its time and place that it is difficult for us to imagine how generations yet unborn might react to this work were it to be "rediscovered" by musicologists. And yet, for all the esoteric expression, the musical values are universal ones. Let it not be forgotten that Schoenberg's art, however morbid some of its surface manifestations may be, is fundamentally a healthy art of strong ancestry. Berg's comparison (1930) of Schoenberg to Bach (certainly one of the least "decadent" of all composers!) is fully justified by the Schoenbergian technical accomplishments. Berg could well speak (cleverly demonstrating that only a few phrases of one of Riemann's dicta on Bach need be changed in order to make it apply to Schoenberg) of his master's "inexhaustible fund of healthy melody," his rhythm, "so varied and pulsing with so much life," and his harmony, "so refined, so bold and yet so clear and transparent."[10]

---

[9] Berg used the translation of Stefan George in addition to the original text.
[10] Alban Berg, "Credo," *Die Musik,* Jhg. XXIV, Heft 5 (January, 1930).

It requires no straining of the imagination to discover all these characteristics in *Pierrot,* a score of far greater fantasy than most music produced in the twentieth century. Beside the uncompromising originality of its music, the minor question of the selection of second-rate texts pales into insignificance.

Pierrot was completed on September 9, 1912, the "Crosses" (fourteenth of the recitations) being the last number to be written; for the twenty-one pieces are not arranged in order of composition, but in groups of seven according to categories of mood and subject-matter. Even during the composition of the work, rehearsals (with Frau Zehme reciting, Schoenberg conducting, and Eduard Steuermann officiating at the piano) had begun; and the première took place in Berlin that fall. This was the performance which James Huneker saw and which shocked him so profoundly as a manifestation of "decadence." Of it, he wrote as follows:

A lady of pleasing appearance, attired in a mollified Pierrot costume, stood before some Japanese screens and began to intone—to cantillate, would be a better expression. . . . What did I hear? At first, the sound of delicate china shivering into a thousand luminous fragments. In the welter of tonalities that bruised each other as they passed and repassed, in the preliminary grip of enharmonics that almost made the ears bleed, the eyes water, the scalp to freeze, I could not get a central grip on myself. It was new music (or new exquisitely horrible sounds) with a vengeance. The very ecstasy of the hideous! . . . Schoenberg is . . . the cruelest of all composers, for he mingles with his music sharp daggers at white heat, with which he pares away tiny slices of his victim's flesh. Anon he twists the knife in the fresh wound and you receive another horrible thrill. . . . What kind of music is this, without melody, in the ordinary sense; without themes, yet every acorn of a phrase contrapuntally developed by an adept; without a harmony that does not smite the ears, lacerate, figuratively speaking, the ear-drums; keys forced into hateful marriage that are miles asunder, or else too closely related for aural matrimony; no form, that is, in the scholastic formal sense, and rhythms that are so persistently varied as to become monotonous—what kind of music, I repeat, is this that can paint a "crystal sigh," the blackness of prehistoric night, the abysm of a morbid soul, the man in the moon, the faint sweet odours of an impossible fairy-land, and the strut of the dandy from Bergamo? . . . There is no melodic or harmonic line, only a series of points, dots, dashes, or phrases that sob and scream, despair, explode, exalt, blaspheme.[11]

And now, for the first time, Schoenberg's fame was beginning to spread to foreign lands; despite the difficulties which his compositions offered to listener and performer alike, he had by no means to wait as long for the propagation of his works abroad as had, for example, Bruckner. On September 3, 1912, Sir Henry Wood had conducted

[11] James Huneker, *Ivory, Apes and Peacocks,* pp. 92–96.

the première of the *Five Orchestral Pieces*—". . . music," as the program-notes had it, which "seeks to express all that dwells in the subconscious like a dream; which is a great fluctuant power, and is built upon none of the lines that are familiar to us; which has a rhythm, as the blood has its pulsating rhythm, as all life in us has its rhythm; which has a tonality; which has harmonies, though we cannot grasp or analyze them, nor can we trace its themes"[12]—on a Promenade Concert in Queen's Hall. *Pierrot* was taken on tour, that same fall, to many cities in Germany and to Prague and Vienna, too. This was the first of Zemlinsky's successful seasons in Prague as director of the Philharmonic—seasons which, it would later be said, recalled Mahler's triumphant years in the Vienna Opera, and which might also have brought to mind his brief but brilliant activity as conductor in Prague. Schoenberg had visited that city in February, 1912, to conduct *Pelleas und Melisande*. It was particularly appropriate that his next invitation to conduct this work should come from Amsterdam, the traditional seat of an intense Mahler cult, where Mengelberg[13] had brought the *Concertgebouw-Orchester* to ever greater perfection. Nothing speaks better for the musical education that Mengelberg had given his Amsterdam public than the fact that they, trained to a genuine appreciation of Mahler through repeated hearings of his major works, also took the work of his spiritual successor Schoenberg to their hearts and accorded it the enthusiastic reception which it had not met with in Vienna. Even Tsarist St. Petersburg, which one would not think of as a particularly fertile ground for Schoenberg's music, seems to have received *Pelleas und Melisande* quite well in 1912—that is, if a criticism by one Ernst Pingoud (whom Wellesz is happy to quote as an antidote to Vienna's somewhat carping attitude towards his master) can be considered typical.

As a further symptom of Schoenberg's growing reputation there appeared, also in 1912, the first of those volumes of essays which were, in years to come, to mark successive milestones of his life. The "birthday books," with their persistently adulatory tone which tends on occasion to obscure essential facts, are in general a characteristically German phenomenon. This first commemorative volume for Schoenberg (not strictly a "birthday" book in the sense of the 1924 and 1934

---

[12] As quoted in Nicolas Slonimsky, *Music since 1900*, pp. 127–28.

[13] The later tragic defection of Mengelberg from the ranks of democracy ought not to dim our appreciation of the things which, in an earlier day, he did for Schoenberg and Mahler, both of whom paid him tribute with good cause. The Amsterdam Mahler Festival of 1920, the first big international musical event after World War I and one of the most successful of such events in our time, could not have existed without Mengelberg.

publications) contains contributions by many devoted disciples. Webern is represented there by concise analyses of Schoenberg's compositions, including *Verklärte Nacht,* the *Gurre-Lieder, Pelleas und Melisande,* the First and Second Quartets, the First *Kammersymphonie,* the
Three Piano Pieces, Op. 11, the *Five Orchestral Pieces,* and *Erwartung;*
he also contributes a significant page to the article "The Teacher"
wherein a group of Schoenberg pupils—Wellesz, Erwin Stein, Jalowetz, Karl Horwitz, Berg, Webern, and the less well-known figures
Paul Königer, Karl Linke, and Robert Neumann—all have their say
about their master's pedagogic activity. Jalowetz (as mentioned above)
writes about the *Harmonielehre,* while Karl Linke tries to give the
reader a spiritual introduction to Schoenberg, the painter-writer-
composer.

It is most interesting to observe that, in this comparatively small
volume, two entire articles are devoted to Schoenberg's activity as a
painter. He had done most of his work in this field during the years
1907–10; quite untaught in art, he had found his way to that expressionistic technique wherein the artist represents the outside world
only by expressing its workings within himself, rather than by setting
down its momentary impressions upon his retina. This technique produced, in Schoenberg's case, portraits of a most uncompromising and
unacademic kind (many self-portraits among them, one of the most
striking of which is a rear view of the artist proceeding up a dark
street), as well as some landscapes and "visions" of weird faces never
seen save in the artist's own mind. It is informative to compare Schoenberg's self-portraits with the portraits of him done by such prominent figures in the Austrian art-world as Oskar Kokoschka and Schoenberg's good friend Egon Schiele. Both these artists followed expressionistic lines in their modernism, and Schoenberg's work is comparable to theirs in approach and technique.

When the paintings had been exhibited, beginning on October 8,
1910, at the bookstore and art-gallery of Hugo Heller, they had, naturally, created a sensation. This was not altogether to the good, for,
as Wellesz puts it, "even people who had nothing to do with music,
on the strength of the impression they gained from the exhibition,
now believed they had the right to express an opinion on Schönberg the composer." [14] But, on the other hand, a chosen few "felt the
inner necessity that urged the solitary artist to express himself visu-
ally, and were thus able to penetrate more deeply into his music." [15]

[14] Wellesz, *Arnold Schönberg* (tr. Kerridge), pp. 27–28.
[15] *Ibid.,* p. 28.

Wassily Kandinsky, the revolutionary Russian "non-objectivist," became a staunch admirer of Schoenberg, and defended him, not only in his general writings about art but also in a special study written for this 1912 volume. Kandinsky defined the aim of painting as the presentation of an internal impression in an external, visible form. He felt that few contemporary pictures satisfy this definition, for too much art is cluttered up with unnecessary details which contribute nothing to the achievement of this essential aim. Schoenberg, on the contrary, paints "not in order to paint a 'pretty' or 'charming' picture, but in an effort to set down his subjective 'emotions' *alone* in permanent form. Scarcely thinking about the picture itself while he paints, and dispensing with objective results, he uses *only* those means which, at the moment, appear to him to be indispensable. Not every professional painter can boast that he creates in this way! Or—in other words—infinitely few professional painters possess the power, the heroism, the strength of renunciation which would enable them to leave alone all the diamonds and pearls of the painter's art or to reject them even when they force themselves of their own volition into the artist's hand. Schoenberg goes directly towards his goal, or through his goal proceeds only to that result which is necessary in this specific instance." [16] Or, as Kandinsky put it more concisely a little later on, Schoenberg's painting may best be termed "only-painting," that is, art without frills, furbelows, non-essentials, or "social significance."

All this is clear enough. Unhappily, the other contribution in this volume to the study of "Schoenberg the Painter," written by one Paris von Gütersloh, is considerably less lucid. Its confused philosophizing on the psychological development of the artist hardly impresses us as being particularly applicable to the case of Schoenberg, though doubtless it found its appreciative readers at the time. A far more valid contribution to the solidarity of artists and musicians was made by such a publication as *Der Blaue Reiter*. Originally intended as a periodical, it was designed by its editors, Kandinsky and the German painter Franz Marc, to be "a gathering-place of those movements, so vigorously active today in all fields of art, the basic tendency of which is the extending of the previous boundaries of artistic expression." [17] And so, in the first (and only) volume, put out in 1912, one found articles on many phases of modern music and art, including a discussion by Schoenberg of "The Relationship Between Composition and Text," and reproductions not only of good modern art (Cézanne,

16 Wassily Kandinsky, "Die Bilder," in *Arnold Schönberg*, p. 60.
17 From an advertising prospectus of *Der Blaue Reiter*.

Matisse, Picasso, Kokoschka, Henry Rousseau, Kandinsky—and Schoenberg), but also of compositions by Schoenberg (*Herzgewächse*), Berg (the Altenberg picture-postcard songs) and Webern—altogether, a stimulating survey of modern tendencies.[18]

In his article for the 1912 Schoenberg volume, Webern made a demand which was soon to be fulfilled. Speaking of the *Gurre-Lieder*, he said,

> Schoenberg wrote this work in 1900, and up to now it has not received a complete performance. Only the first section was performed in 1909(!) in Vienna with piano(!!). It is the greatest duty of those whom I have in mind to bring this work to a worthy performance. It is true that this would make great demands, but such tasks have already been fulfilled in the past; why not in this case, as well? [19]

Webern's query was answered on February 23, 1913, with a brilliantly successful performance of the *Gurre-Lieder* in Vienna under the direction of Franz Schreker, composer of many operas in a post-Wagnerian idiom (*Der ferne Klang, Die Gezeichneten*), teacher of many musicians—Ernst Křenek among them—and good friend of Schoenberg. Even in spite of Schreker's sympathetic direction and the presence in the cast of many fine musicians, the preparation of the performance had brought its heartaches. There was, for example, the incident of the first horn-player, who, in a sudden access of fury during one of the rehearsals, leaped from his place in the orchestra and tried to attack Schoenberg with his instrument. Schoenberg, unconscious of what was going on around him, absorbed in his score, was only rescued from serious injury by the intervention of his disciples. The maddened player, still storming and shouting "I refuse to play any such music as this!" was ordered to leave by Schreker, and he did so, carrying his part under his arm, only to return later to beg the composer's forgiveness for his misunderstanding of the music, which had led to so ill-considered an act. Since Schoenberg accepted the apology in the spirit in which it was meant, it may be assumed that the converted horn-player took part, after all, in the first performance.

The audience (containing, no doubt, many of the same people who had once hissed the First Quartet and even *Verklärte Nacht*) sat spellbound as the "new" score unfolded. The beautiful love-songs of Tove (*Nun sag' ich dir zum ersten Mal, Du sendest mir einen Liebesblick*) and of Waldemar (*So tanzen die Engel, Du wunderliche Tove*), almost operatic in their vividness of dramatic expression; the tragic revela-

---

[18] A modern documentary edition, edited and with an introduction by Klaus Lankheit, was published in English translation in 1974 by the Viking Press as part of its series *The Documents of 20th-Century Art*.

[19] Anton von Webern, "Schönbergs Musik," in *Arnold Schönberg*, p. 25.

tion of the Wood-Dove following the climactic symphonic transition from Tove's last outpouring of love; Waldemar's violent rejection of God in some of the most intense pages of the entire work; the "Wild Chase of the Summer Wind" with its unusual orchestration; the long monologue of the Speaker (in which the technique, if not the spirit, of *Pierrot Lunaire* is already foreseen) ending with the words, "Awake, awake, ye blossoms, to bliss!"—all these seemed but to lead to the dynamic climax of the whole, the triumphant C major outburst of the eight-part chorus, "Behold the sun!" At this moment the audience rose, as of one accord, and remained standing till the very end. Then came a torrent of applause, and shouts of "Schoenberg! Schoenberg!" But Schoenberg was nowhere to be seen. Finally he was discovered seated inconspicuously in an upper gallery, ignoring the tumult of the audience completely. With great difficulty he was induced to come to the stage; but then, to the amazement of all, he bowed only to Schreker and the orchestra and took hasty leave without once acknowledging the enormous ovation which was greeting him from the hall.

Why had Schoenberg behaved so strangely? This, as much as the overwhelming grandeur of the music which had just been heard, was the subject of seemingly endless discussions in the coffee-houses and on the streets after the performance; and, as befitted the gravity of the occasion—for this was one of Vienna's notable premières of the year —many an argumentative group did not break up until past dawn. Schoenberg himself provided an answer to the question, an answer which was a scathing indictment of the public attitudes that had poisoned this triumphant occasion for him. "For years," he said, "those people who cheered me tonight refused to recognize me. Why should I thank them for appreciating me now?"

The fact that the composition and orchestration of the *Gurre-Lieder* spread over more than a decade of Schoenberg's life naturally led to certain small discrepancies of style, particularly of orchestration, which the composer himself freely admitted, but which he had allowed to stand because he felt that tampering with the earlier part of the work would even more seriously impair the total unity. But these discrepancies should not disturb our sense of the historical position of the work as a whole. Like Mahler's Eighth Symphony, the score of the *Gurre-Lieder* stands at the peak of the development of the giant orchestral style, and it would be difficult to surpass the lavishness of its instrumentation. Eight flutes, five oboes, ten horns, six trumpets, four Wagner tubas, seven trombones, and a veritable percussion orchestra including a brace of heavy iron chains—these do not necessarily bespeak the influence of Mahler, but their use certainly furnishes a perfect historical parallel to Mahler's use, for example, of the cowbells in the Sixth Symphony.[20] In its fusion of types, too, the work was characteristic of the era; just as Mahler combined symphony and song-cycle, or symphony and cantata, in the *Gurre-Lieder* the song-cycle merged into the cantata—and almost into the opera, though at least there is no hint of the symphony here to add to the complexity (even though the long orchestral passages between songs are characterized by that type of logical, consequent thematic development which we often call "symphonic"). It might be intriguing to draw a parallel between *Das Lied von der Erde* and the *Gurre-Lieder* on the basis of the alternation of solo songs for male and female voice, and the use of long symphonic interludes within a lyric framework, which take place in both works; but actually, of course, the two compositions present no parallels in technique or in spirit, for the broken-hearted Mahler who wrote *Das Lied von der Erde* was far removed from the grandiose world of the *Gurre-Lieder*—or of his own Eighth Symphony.

It is almost needless to point out that the *Gurre-Lieder* were composed under the spell of Wagner. This is evident not only in the music itself (e. g., in a martial theme of Part II, "Lord God, I too am a ruler," which is strongly reminiscent of a well-known theme in the third act of *Tristan und Isolde,* and in a brass passage at the opening of Part III, *The Wild Hunt,* which might have come from many a page of the *Ring*), but also in the subject-matter of the work, which is partly legendary, although based upon the life of a historical character, the Danish king Valdemar the Great (1157–82). The star-crossed lovers, Waldemar and Tove, doubtless could not have existed, in Schoenberg's interpretation, without Tristan and Isolde, even though the fate of the Danish lovers, in Jakobsen's adaptation of the old story, is a different one from that of Wagner's protagonists—for it is Tove who dies first, poisoned by Waldemar's jealous wife Helwig, while the spirits of Waldemar and of his men are condemned to ride forever in the "Wild Chase of the Summer Wind," in punishment for the king's blasphemy of God.

Far removed from the twilit Wagnerian world of the music of the *Gurre-Lieder* is Schoenberg's next finished creation, *Die glückliche Hand.* This work, though begun in the same period as *Erwartung* (and a sister composition to *Erwartung* insofar as both works are dramatic experiments of a new and unusual kind) was not completed till November 18, 1913. It would be difficult to imagine a greater contrast

---

[20] The use of the percussion instruments was later a separate cult, represented by Edgar Varèse's *Ionization.* In 1977, the independent percussion ensemble is an accepted feature of musical life.

than that between the music of *Die glückliche Hand* and that of the *Gurre-Lieder,* to say nothing of the dramatic aspects of both works; but at the same time it bespeaks the logic of Schoenberg's personal development, as well as the soundness of his growth from a previous tradition, that it is possible to find links connecting the two works not only with each other but also with a common ancestry. For *Die glückliche Hand* is equipped with orchestral means comparable to those of the *Gurre-Lieder.* Even if Schoenberg is now using only four flutes instead of the eight required by the earlier work, his battery of percussion instruments is just as formidable now as before. The large orchestra has, however, to fulfill different functions in *Die glückliche Hand* from those for which it served in the *Gurre-Lieder.* Instead of accompanying and lending additional force to mass choral scenes such as those of Part III of the latter work, it must, in its great variety, provide many different colors (especially those of solo instruments) for the subtle delineation of psychological nuances. Further differences of orchestral treatment must of necessity be brought about not only by the shift from tonality to atonality but also by the immense differences between the two dramas (for the *Gurre-Lieder* must be thought of as a drama, even though not staged). Whereas the drama of the *Gurre-Lieder* is rather melodramatic and old-fashioned, that of *Die glückliche Hand* is a characteristic specimen of modern expressionism, imitating the expressionistic plays of its period even to the extent of using only abstract, categorical names for its characters—"Man," "Woman," "Gentleman."

In spite of the vast differences between the two dramas, it may accurately be stated that both are legitimate descendants of Wagner— the *Gurre-Lieder,* as already indicated, on account of their legendary subject-matter and Wagnerian musical idiom, *Die glückliche Hand* on account of its development of the *Gesamtkunstwerk* idea. Schoenberg, here for the first time his own librettist, now conceived his own staging and lighting effects, an integral part of the whole artistic structure, far more vividly than Wagner ever did. Adolphe Appia had, in his remarkable treatise *Die Musik und die Inscenierung* (so familiar to Roller and Mahler), promulgated the idea that Wagner's views on staging were—in spite of Bayreuth!—the least perfectly realized part of the *Gesamtkunstwerk,* because they were not "ahead of the times" as his music was, and so were not consistent with the rest of the *Gesamtkunstwerk* conception. Schoenberg did not make this mistake, for his stage effects are not only of great boldness, but are perfectly correlated with the music. Especially is this true of the lights, which play a particularly important role in *Die glückliche Hand.* One of the most dramatic effects of the work is the crescendo of light—indicated in the score by means of an elaborate system of cue-figures—from pale red through brown, dirty green, blue-grey, violet, dark red, blood-red, and orange to brilliant yellow, which accompanies a corresponding crescendo in the music that is further supplemented by theatrical wind-effects. This deliberate correlation of colors and music reminds us of Scriabin and his mystic desire to blend harmony, color, and even perfume into one vast creation; but here is only the parallelism of isolated thoughts existing in men of uncommon imagination who worked quite independently of each other.

One feature of *Die glückliche Hand* which deserves special mention is the "Sprechchor" of six men and six women. Part of the time this bizarre chorus really sings, but mostly the twelve performers are called upon for a *Sprechstimme* technique of the kind already familiar in *Pierrot Lunaire* and first used in the *Gurre-Lieder*. This was the first time that Schoenberg used such a technique in choral parts. Its presence here bespeaks anew his constant preoccupation with new ways of using the human voice, reflected in his later works as well (cf. the *Ode to Napoleon* which was first performed on November 23, 1944).

Before *Die glückliche Hand* was finished Schoenberg had begun another work, the *Four Orchestral Songs*, Op. 22. To be exact, the first of these, *Seraphita*, a setting of a poem by the English poet Ernest Dowson (translated into German by Stefan George, whose name we are not surprised to find once more associated with Schoenberg's creation), had been composed on October 6, 1913. What a gulf between this and the earlier *Orchesterlieder!* Here for the first time Schoenberg applies his atonal techniques to the specific *genre* of the orchestral song, and displays his customary skill in exploiting this new musical material both motivically and coloristically (for certain parallel-fifth passages which appear in violins and 'celli on the very first page of *Seraphita* are hardly "functional" in a harmonic sense). It is in these songs, too, that Schoenberg uses for the first time his "simplified score" scheme, in which the score is written in the smallest possible number of lines with the individual instruments "cued in" on these lines as they appear. One disadvantage of the system cannot be gainsaid—it makes the individual instrumental line very hard to follow. But, on the other hand, it is far easier to get an overall view of the complexities of a Schoenberg score in this form (particularly since all instruments become non-transposing!) than in a giant score like that of *Erwartung* or *Die glückliche Hand*. Schoenberg further simplifies the picture by his consistent use of the H- and N- signs and his complete renunciation of Mahler's dynamic scheme. With a certain amount of exaggeration, he explains his reasons for this in the informative preface to the songs:

> I find this manner of indication [with H⁻ and N⁻] better than the exaggerated gradations of dynamics. With the latter method, it can happen that one instrument is marked *ff*, and one *p*, and a third *pp*. The purpose of this is to equalize the general dynamics. But it is the tendency of instrument-makers and performers alike to develop instruments and their technique to such a point that I am scarcely exaggerating when I say that finally all instruments will be able to play equally loud and equally soft. So if the general dynamics of a given passage cannot be deduced from a score and the former relationships between instruments have once been forgotten, conductors of the future, confronted with such a score, will not know what to do. Therefore I think it is better to indicate the general dynamics. [21]

Schoenberg's new work was not destined to be completed in a world at peace. Already armies were mobilizing, and events were building to the inevitable catastrophe of June 28, 1914, and the declaration of war one month later. On August 28, Schoenberg set to music Rainer Maria Rilke's *Premonition*, wherein the sensitive might already discern a forecast of dark days to come:

> I feel the winds that come, and must endure them
> While things on earth still rest in utter stillness.
> The doors close softly, in the rooms is silence;
> The windows yet unmoved, the dust is heavy.
> But I live the storm—I am stirred like the sea—
> I stretch forth my arms—am thrown back on myself—
> I cast myself forth—and remain all alone
> In the greatest of storms. [22]

[21] Arnold Schoenberg, "Die vereinfachte Studier- und Dirigier-Paritur," Preface to *Vier Orchesterlieder*, Op. 22 (U.-E. No. 6060).

[22] Rainer Maria Rilke, "Vorgefühl," in *Das Buch der Bilder*, p. 55. (Schoenberg, Op. 22 no. 4.)

CHAPTER V

To the "Twelve-Tone Scale"—and After

SCHOENBERG was now indeed to "live the storm." In December, 1915, he was drafted into the ill-starred Austrian Army, but not before he had been able to begin the poem which was later printed as *Die Jakobsleiter* (*Jacob's Ladder*). This work had a checkered career. As far back as 1910 Schoenberg had planned a great three-part oratorio of which the first section was to be based on a poem by Richard Dehmel. Then the text of the second section, *Totentanz der Prinzipien* (*The Death-Dance of Principles*), was written down on January 15, 1915. *Die Jakobsleiter* would now have been the finale of this trilogy; but Schoenberg soon found that the material permitted independent development and so allowed the text to be printed as a separate entity. The composition, however, was another matter. Begun during these war years, it was of necessity interrupted during the composer's two periods of military service (December, 1915–September, 1916, and July–October, 1917), and was later taken up and discarded many times.[1]

The study of the text of *Die Jakobsleiter* reveals to us still another Schoenberg, one whom we have not yet considered: the philosopher, moralist, and mystic. This work shows no special preoccupation with questions of religious creed, although such questions have always been of more than academic interest to Schoenberg; for he was once converted to Lutheranism [2] but later returned to Judaism when destruction threatened the Hebrew world. Rather, the poem is an expression of the author's personal philosophy, through the allegory of the souls on Jacob's Ladder. From the most earthbound of souls—the rationalists, the cowards, the skeptics, the cynics, the cunning ones, the

---

[1] See Dika Newlin, "Die Jakobsleiter: Its History and Significance," and Leonard Stein, "Die Jakobsleiter: The Music," both in the Royal Festival Hall program booklet of the BBC Third Programme broadcast (British première), November 8, 1965.

[2] Schoenberg entered the Lutheran church on March 21, 1898 (see Stuckenschmidt, *Schönberg: Leben–Umwelt–Werk*, p. 33).

journalists, and the unclean ones—to those nearest to Heaven—the daemons, geniuses, stars, Gods, and Angels—all are represented here. The spokesman of the author's own ideas is, however, the Angel Gabriel. It is he who opens the drama with a telling statement which has been quoted by Wellesz as typical of Schoenberg's attitude towards life, and which may well be quoted here also:

Whether right or left, whether forward or backward—one must always go on without asking what lies before or behind one.

That should be hidden; you ought to—nay, *must*—forget it, in order to fulfill your task.[3]

Again, in moving words, Gabriel urges the souls to pray:

Learn to pray; for "he who prays has become one with God." Only his wishes separate him still from his goal. But this union must not cease, and will not be invalidated by your faults. The Eternal One, your God, is no jealous God of revenge, but a God who reckons with your imperfections, to whom your inadequacy is known, who realizes that you must falter and that your road is long.

He listens to you, protects you on your way; you are eternally in His hand, guided, watched over and protected in spite of your free will, bound to Him in spite of your evil desire for sin, loved by Him—if you know how to pray.

Learn to pray:

Knock, and the door will be opened unto you! [4]

And it is the united response of the souls to this plea which closes the work:

> *Lord God in Heaven,*
> *Hark to our weeping,*
> *Pardon our trespass,*
> *Have pity on us,*
> *Attend to our prayers,*
> *Fulfill all our wishes,*
> *Give place to our wailings,*
> *Grant us love and bliss in eternity.*
> *Amen!* [5]

It was somewhat later than the beginning of *Die Jakobsleiter* that a new principle of composition first appeared in Schoenberg's work. Having incalculably enriched his musical resources by the adoption of atonality—or "pantonality," the synthesis of all tonalities, as he preferred to call it—he now sought for a means of organizing this new wealth in a systematic manner. Thus was born the much-maligned "twelve-tone scale." Few methods of composition have been more universally misunderstood than this one, about which misinformation is

[3] Arnold Schoenberg, *Die Jakobsleiter*, p. 3.   [4] *Ibid.*, p. 29.

[5] *Ibid.*, p. 32.

the order of the day. And yet, the actual processes involved in twelve-tone composition are less complex than one might suppose. All twelve-tone music is based on the premise that each of the twelve tones of our chromatic scale is of equal value, no further division into fundamental (diatonic) and auxiliary (chromatic) tones being admissible. For each composition, a special arrangement of these twelve tones, known as the tone-row, is constructed; and this row, in all its possible variants, must furnish all the material of the composition, so that not a single tone of harmony or melody is non-thematic. In the statement of the tone-row, each tone may be repeated *successively* as many times as desired; but, in the strictest twelve-tone writing, it is not customary to *return* to a previously used tone until all the other tones of the row have been traversed. This principle is designed to prevent any one tone from attaining the prominence of a temporary tonic.[6] It is also to avoid any unwanted associations with tonality that (again in the strictest style, which is far from being the only manner of twelve-tone writing practised by Schoenberg and his followers) the consonant harmonic intervals are customarily relegated to weak beats and the octave is usually avoided.

Actually, the system of the tone-rows as understood by Schoenberg is neither so mysterious nor so complicated as too much explanation has often made it seem.[7] The constant accusations that music written according to the twelve-tone system is purely "mathematical" and devoid of the ability to express emotions are uttered by critics who are ignorant of the issues involved. For such a viewpoint as theirs, historical validity cannot be claimed. It is when the mechanical means of composition—the transpositions, the inversions and retrograde inversions, the divisions of the tone-row—are described that the impression of an unspontaneous and unmusical method of composing is all too often given. Such an impression is far from the truth. Composing in the twelve-tone system was, to Schoenberg, as natural a process as composing "tonal" music. This is as it should be, for spontaneity should be promoted by the greater variety of resources available to the composer who knows how to use atonality intelligently. Atonality and

---

[6] The idea has often been misstated in would-be popular explanations of the system (which are usually opposed to it). One such avers that the opening bars of Beethoven's Fifth Symphony would be quite impossible in the twelve-tone technique because of the repeated tones. This is untrue, but even if true would obviously tell us nothing about the merits or demerits of the system.

[7] This situation is even worse in 1977, thanks to some writers for such publications as *Die Reihe* and *Perspectives of New Music*. We should never forget Schoenberg's own statement: "my works are twelve-tone *compositions*, not *twelve-tone* compositions." (Rufer, *The Works of Arnold Schoenberg*, p. 142.)

tonality are not mutually exclusive any more than "consonance" and "dissonance" are; and here is where the term "atonality" shows itself to be an inadequate and deceptive definition of the musical phenomena which it purports to describe. "Pantonality," the term which Schoenberg preferred but which has received no wide popular circulation, is a far better description of his music, inasmuch as it emphasizes the merging of *all* tonalities in one larger complex. This merging process becomes particularly clear in works where "atonal" and "tonal" techniques have been combined or exist side by side. Berg, freer than his master in the handling of the system, furnished notable examples of this latter type in such representative works of his as the *Lyric Suite,* in which the beginning of *Tristan und Isolde* is quoted, and the violin concerto, which climaxes in the Bach chorale *Es ist genug* from the cantata *O Ewigkeit, du Donnerwort.* Schoenberg, too, has demonstrated once and for all that "atonality" and "tonality" need not be two separate, incompatible concepts, in so late a composition as the *Ode to Napoleon,* which employs all the techniques of "atonality" but ends in a clear E flat major. Works of this kind have a greater flexibility and variety, it must be admitted, than those compositions which belong to the "classic" period of Schoenberg's twelve-tone composition, when he was taking his first steps in the new system and so felt impelled to a greater rigidity in the application of its "rules." In fact, the works of this period, which is to say the *Five Piano Pieces,* Op. 23, the *Serenade* (for clarinet, bass-clarinet, mandolin, guitar, violin, viola, 'cello, and bass or baritone voice), Op. 24, the piano suite, Op. 25, the wind quintet, Op. 26, the *Four Pieces* and *Three Satires* for mixed chorus, Op. 27 and 28, and the septet for piano, three clarinets, violin, viola, and 'cello, Op. 29, seem to be more academic than anything previously created by Schoenberg. Particularly is this true of the two groups of mixed choruses; dry and mordant music accompanies cold moralizing or satire which is more distinguished for bitterness than for wit. Charm, wit, and humor are certainly present in the *Serenade,* the rococo dance movements which make up the piano suite, the "Waltz" of Op. 23, and the "Dance Steps" of the septet; but in other works of this period, the powerful emotional values which characterized works like *Erwartung* and *Pierrot Lunaire* were shelved in favor of a more intellectual, restrained style. This was Schoenberg at his most remote and unapproachable; and there may well be those who prefer him in other guises. But we condemn our own time when we use the word "cerebral," in connection with this music, as an unpleasant epithet and mode of attack. Since when has the greatest music of all centuries not been a product of cerebration, and why should our century take upon itself the right to reverse this process.[8] Ought not those devices of inversion and crab-canon, of augmentation and diminution (which Schoenberg used in his "tonal" works as well as in his "atonal" ones, but which seem to be closely associated in the public mind with the rather unpleasant ideas of "atonality" and "dissonance") to be taken for granted as a part of the normal technical equipment of every creative musician, rather than considered as *tours de force,* the comprehension of which is not for everybody? These are questions which we must seriously ask ourselves; but, when they have been asked, the best thing to do is to throw aside all preconceptions with regard to this twelve-tone music of Schoenberg's and to listen to it exactly as one would listen to any other music, whether by Palestrina, Bach, or Wagner. It is not even a matter of great import if one does not discern the tone-row on the first hearing, any more than it is necessary to be uninterruptedly conscious of the theme of a fugue. However, knowledge of the tone-row of each composition is important to the analyst and also to the performer. (Schoenberg was to learn, with the first performance of his one-act opera *Von Heute auf Morgen* [*From Today Till Tomorrow*] that the singers found it much easier to memorize their parts when they had familiarized themselves with the tone-row.) And in the future it may well be that the musical ear will assimilate the tone-row as readily as it now extracts the scale of C major from a composition in that key.

With the systematization of "atonality" came a new classicism in form. Of Schoenberg's quartets, the Third, first to be written in the new idiom, is also first to follow the formal model of the classical quartet—four separate movements (complete with Rondo-Finale); no more assimilation of all movements into one, no more introduction of the human voice! The same was already true of the wind quintet, the gay rondo of which is a veritable Haydnesque *Kehraus-Finale* in spirit; while the use of the forms of the eighteenth-century dance suite in Op. 25 might suggest to us a picture of Schoenberg in a "Back-to-Bach" mood, did we not know that he was unalterably opposed to any such pseudo-classicistic movements, as a general principle.[9]

Everybody knows that this new music had no easy path; its path is still not easy, though today the most novel works of Schoenberg are heard, not only without organized protest, but even with a great deal

[8] See Schoenberg's "Heart and Brain in Music" in *Style and Idea.*

[9] He was once heard to say (in jest, of course, but with a serious thought behind the words) that people ought to be required to take out a license—for which special qualifications would be demanded—in order to admire Bach. This would do away with that indiscriminate worship of his name under cover of which all sorts of sins against music are committed.

of spontaneous enthusiasm.[10] Political aims were, of course, to enter into
the later German condemnation of "atonal" music as one of the more
virulent forms of *Kulturbolschewismus;* but what was *Kulturbolschewismus* in 1933 was already "musical impotence" in 1920. One of those
who called it so was Hans Pfitzner, the erstwhile friend of the Mahler
family, who was now writing against the heirs of the Mahler tradition.
His book *The New Esthetics of Musical Impotence; Symptom of Decadence?* brought him a sharp rap on the knuckles from Berg, in the
form of an article, "The Musical Impotence of Hans Pfitzner's 'New
Esthetics.'" This essay, under the pretext of attacking Pfitzner's failure to give a valid musical analysis of Schumann's *Traümerei* (which
Pfitzner had selected as a prime example of a "beautiful melody" that
cannot yield the secrets of its beauty to mundane analysis), manages
to undermine most of Pfitzner's pretensions.[11] Berg, in this as in other
articles, displayed a real talent for polemics; and he could, like his
master, defend his own work with vigor; this was fortunate, for Schoenberg and his followers really had need of sharp tongues and ready pens
in order to hold their own against bitter opposition from many quar-
ters. And yet, the situation of "modern music" was immeasurably better than in the pre-war years! In the very month of the Armistice, a
new musical organization had come into being in Vienna. The *Verein
für musikalische Privataufführungen* (Society for Private Performances
of Music) it was called, and, even in a community that bristled with
Vereine, musical and otherwise, it was not quite like anything that
had been organized before. Its rules, as promulgated on February 16,
1919, were strict in the extreme; for its purpose, the propagation of
new music without regard to cliques and in a non-commercial atmosphere, was felt to require regulations of a very special kind. Critics were not only not invited to the performances of this unique organization; they were forbidden to attend. No advance programs were
ever given out, for one of the chief aims of the organization was to
make modern works better known through repeated performances and
it was feared that if people knew that a work they had not "liked"
on first hearing was scheduled for repetition they would stay away,
thus defeating the whole purpose of the Society. Members and guests
had to come to the weekly concerts armed with identification cards
(complete with photograph) lest unauthorized persons should break

---

[10] Thus, *Moses and Aaron* has played to packed houses. (Admittedly, extra-
musical considerations—such as the Orgy Scene—may have helped here.)

[11] Alban Berg, "Die musikalische Impotenz der 'Neuen Ästhetik' Hans Pfitzners,"
Musikblätter des Anbruch, II, 11–12, June, 1920. (Reprinted in Willi Reich, *Alban
Berg*, pp. 181–92.)

in, bent on creating *Konzertskandale* like those that had attended Schoenberg's career in the "good old days" in pre-war Vienna.

Few would have had the courage to create such an organization, radical in its ideas and bold in its execution of these ideas, in normal years, let alone in these troublous times in Austria, when food was scarce, coal practically unobtainable, and the street-car ride to one of the Society's concerts cost more than the rent of the entire hall. It is not surprising that Arnold Schoenberg should have been the one to do it. This was no mere act of self-interest, since for the most part his works were conspicuous by their absence from the programs (although ten public rehearsals of the First *Kammersymphonie*, which were not followed by a performance, offered an excellent opportunity to those who wished to become better acquainted with the structure of the work), and, on the contrary, the works of composers whose directions were far different from those of Schoenberg—Debussy, Ravel, Reger— were well represented. Schoenberg's disciples were, naturally, eager participants in the scheme. It was to their advantage to assist it, for it brought them performances that they might not otherwise have had in such difficult times, at a period when the world was not yet reopened to Austria. Webern, Berg, and Pisk found representation there, and such minor figures, too, as Fidelio F. Finke. Berg, living since the middle of 1919 on his earnings as a teacher of composition in Vienna, gave much time to the organization, in his capacity of director of all the performances. (His own *Four Pieces for Clarinet* were played at its concert of October 17, 1919.)

A significant event in the musical Vienna of 1919 was Schoenberg's direction of performances of his two string quartets [12] by a string orches- tra—a practice which Berg, too, was to countenance later, for the sec- ond, third, and fourth movements of his *Lyric Suite* for string quartet (first played by the Kolisch Quartet on January 8, 1927) received a special performance in an arrangement for string orchestra, under the direction of Jascha Horenstein, in Berlin on January 31, 1929. It is amazing that writers on Schoenberg (Stefan, Wellesz) and Berg (Reich) pass over such events with no attempt at evaluation. What better proof could there be that the grandiose ideas of Mahler still lived in these men? We are no longer surprised when conductors arrange classical string quartets and baroque organ music for every conceivable orches- tral combination; Schoenberg also took part in this vogue, for he orchestrated Bach's great E flat major organ prelude and fugue (the "St. Anne"), Bach's two chorale preludes, *Schmücke dich, O liebe Seele*

---

[12] No orchestration of the First String Quartet has survived. The string-orchestral version of the Second String Quartet was published in 1929.

and *Komm, Gott Schöpfer, heiliger Geist* (at the suggestion of Josef Stransky, then conductor of the New York Philharmonic) and Brahms' G minor piano quartet (which he orchestrated because, as he said, "chamber music groups never play it right and I wanted to show them how it ought to sound"). But the dangers of such a proceeding are all too well exemplified by the typical remark of a Schoenberg pupil: "Since I heard the Schoenberg orchestration of the Brahms quartet I really can't listen to the original any more—it seems flat!" And it is when we see the composer himself voluntarily orchestrating his own chamber works that we realize how profound and harmful has been the influence of the grandiloquent nineteenth century upon the twentieth-century attitude towards chamber music—this in spite of the fact that the direction of Schoenberg and Berg was, as already indicated, rather towards the smaller chamber work and away from the use of the huge orchestra of Mahler as a constructive principle.

Modern music was trying to become international once more. New periodicals furthered its cause—*Anbruch* in Vienna, and *Auftakt* (first published on December 1, 1920) in Prague, which would now, in its position of new-found prominence as the capital of a young and ambitious country and no longer a provincial city in a decaying empire, reaffirm its rightful place as a center of modern, significant musical activity; there was Scherchen's *Melos,* too, founded on February 1, 1920. In June, 1920, Vienna's municipal music festival had brought highly successful performances of *Pelleas und Melisande* and of the *Gurre-Lieder.* But of broader significance than this was Amsterdam's Mahler Festival of May, 1920, which was simultaneously a celebration of Mengelberg's twenty-fifth year with the Concertgebouw Orchestra. This was the first really international musical event that had taken place since the war, and was joyously hailed by all participants as the start of a new era. The Austrian delegates were treated with particular respect and deference. Visiting prosperous Holland, where food was plentiful (and bestowed upon the visitors with generosity), was, for them, like entering a new world. Mahler had always been cultivated in Amsterdam; during this festival, his work triumphed in a series of finished performances attended by the élite of Europe's musical world. And, wisely, the Mahler concerts were supplemented by programs of representative modern chamber music.[13] The proceedings culminated in the organization of an International Mahler Society, of which Schoenberg was elected president—a fitting climax to a career which

---

[13] Oddly enough in a "Mahler Festival," a definite Regerian tinge crept into some of Amsterdam's musical evenings at this time with the presence of Adolf Busch and the ex-Schoenbergian Serkin.

had been spent in furtherance of the ideals that Mahler had upheld through his own lifetime.

The cult of Mahler was taking on a new aspect in these difficult, turbulent post-war years. Now he was made—and it would have come as a great surprise to him!—the apostle of socialism; his music was suddenly the very epitome of music of and for the "masses"—masses whom the Schoenbergians did not scorn to educate, for Webern would now conduct workers' concerts, and Pisk would teach, according to the methods of Schoenberg's *Harmonielehre,* in the Vienna People's Center (*Wiener Volksheim*). They might have taken the lead from their own master in this, for had he not directed workers' choruses in his youth? All such activity was directly in line with the Socialist policies of Vienna's new government, which were to bring the workers improved housing and other advantages.

While the Mahler Festival was hailed by many as symbolizing a new spiritual union between nations, it also stimulated fresh interest in music festivals both national and international. On July 21, 1921, the first of the Donaueschingen festivals, sponsored by the *Gesellschaft der Musikfreunde,* began. Schoenbergians were represented on its programs, as they would be in practically every international festival; songs of Karl Horwitz were performed, as well as the piano sonata of Berg. Next year, there was a second Donaueschingen festival, also at the end of July, and the Salzburg Festival which took place shortly thereafter (August 7–10, 1922) brought performance of string quartets by Wellesz and Webern, of songs with string quartet accompaniment by Pisk, and of Schoenberg's Second Quartet. There were songs by Rudolf Réti, too—and he, though his works (including some very poetical piano pieces) are scarcely known in this country, is of more than passing interest to us, since he was one of the prime instigators of the International Society for Contemporary Music which has played a significant role in modern musical life right up to our own day. Its first festival took place in Salzburg (August 2–7, 1923), four months after the League of Composers had been founded in New York, and included not only sacred songs by Pisk and Schoenberg's *Buch der hängenden Gärten,* but a highly successful performance of Berg's early string quartet Op. 3 by the Havemann Quartet. How far the musical world had come since the days of 1911, when the première of that same quartet, the last work which Berg had written under Schoenberg's guidance, had brought out but a single critic who felt impelled to write of it, "Under cover of the name 'String Quartet' that form is mishandled under the auspices of Herr Alban Berg!"[14] And a year

14 Willi Reich, *Alban Berg,* p. 11.

later, in Prague (May 31–June 6, 1924), the second ISCM festival brought the world première of *Erwartung,* on June 6. Indeed, it now seemed as though the fortunes of the new "Viennese School" might rise steadily for many years to come.

CHAPTER VI

Triumph, Catastrophe, Reorientation: 1924-1944

NINETEEN TWENTY-FOUR was a jubilee year for Schoenberg and his followers. The Master's fiftieth birthday was a landmark which could not be lightly passed over by him, by his friends, or by his community. It was quite in order (though it would not have been so in 1912) that Vienna itself should make a festive occasion of that significant September 13, with the mayor giving a ceremonial address and the chorus of the Vienna Opera singing *Friede auf Erden*. It was comparable to that great moment of Bruckner's life when the University of Vienna conferred the honorary doctorate upon him, and Adolf Exner said, "I, the *rector magnificus* of this university, bow down before the former country-school teacher of Windhaag!" [1] Quite natural, too, was the issuance of a special Schoenberg "birthday book" by the *Musikblätter des Anbruch*. Who could know that the next "birthday book," ten years later, would commemorate one absent in a far-off land; that, in fifteen years, a municipal celebration of Schoenberg's birthday in Vienna would be a political impossibility? The far-sighted might have guessed these things; but few seemed to care for far-sightedness, and so the tone of the little volume *Arnold Schönberg zum fünfzigsten Geburtstage: 13. September 1924* is a predominantly optimistic one.

The collection of essays begins, as the 1912 one did not, with a word by the composer himself. After telling humorously how he had been informed in advance that he was to be "surprised" with a special birthday issue of *Anbruch* (so that he could make his own contribution to the "surprise"), he goes on to pose the pertinent question of whether his creative abilities are diminishing with the onset of age. The answer is negative; but Schoenberg has to admit that he finds in himself one clear symptom of old age—"I cannot hate any more the way I

[1] Windhaag was the tiny Austrian hamlet where the young Bruckner's "teaching" duties had included the hauling of manure, a task at which he balked.

used to; and, worse yet, I can sometimes understand things now without holding them in contempt." [2]

Adolf Loos, the famous architect and good friend of Schoenberg who had, in 1911, been so bitterly attacked for his "functional" building on Vienna's *Michaelerplatz*, contributed to this symposium some sound and constructive thoughts on the continuity of Schoenberg's creativeness. Imagining an average music-lover considerably puzzled by the differences between the *Gurre-Lieder* and the latest twelve-tone works—differences which Schoenberg would not dispose of by a convenient repudiation of the *Gurre-Lieder*—he answered this individual and his kind in trenchant words which might still be used to answer their descendants of today:

> My honored public, you are in the wrong. No artist repudiates what he has created: neither the craftsman nor the artist: neither the shoemaker nor the musician. The differences in form which the public observes are hidden from the creative artist. The shoes that the master made ten years ago were good shoes. Why should he be ashamed of them? Why should he repudiate them? Only an architect could have said, "Just look at that pile of mud over there—that's what I built ten years ago!" But it is well-known that I do not consider architects to be people.[3]

The inseparable names of Berg and Webern, already prominent in the 1912 volume, are present here too. Webern has but a few words to say about the long friendship between him and Schoenberg; Berg, on the other hand, is represented by a long and carefully thought-out article, provocatively entitled "Why is Schoenberg's Music so Hard to Understand?" In order to answer this question, Berg chooses to analyze in detail the first ten measures of the First Quartet, with regard to their harmonic and rhythmic structure and their melodic periodization. This was a wise choice, for it enabled him to prove that (since the work he analyzed for its difficulty was a tonal one!) "it is *not so much the so-called 'atonality'*—a term used by so many of our contemporaries—*that makes understanding* [of Schoenberg's later works] *difficult*, but, here too, the other details of the structure of Schoenberg's music, the wealth of artistic means utilized . . . the synthesis of all compositional possibilities of music through the ages; in a word, its immeasurable richness." [4] Berg, though he says that practically any quotation from Schoenberg's music would have served his purpose

---

[2] This is quite in line with his statement in a letter to Paul Bekker: "I am no longer the wild man that I was." (August 1, 1924.)

[3] *Arnold Schönberg zum fünfzigsten Geburtstage: 13. September 1924.* Sonderheft der *Musikblätter des Anbruch*, Jhg. 6, August–September–Heft 1924, p. 271.

[4] *Ibid.*, p. 339.

equally well, could not have picked a more characteristic example of the "complicated" Schoenberg than this one, with its wealth of melody and counter-melody, the constant subtle shifting of its harmonies, and its "free" rhythm, "prose-like" as both Schoenberg and Reger (independently of each other!) liked to call the characteristic uneven rhythm of their music.

Berg and Webern were not the only Schoenberg disciples to pay tribute to their master on this occasion. Paul Pisk described the *Verein für Musikalische Privataufführungen*—already defunct at this time because of the financial crisis in Austria and Germany—praising those artists, Steuermann, Serkin, and Kolisch among them, who had helped to make the *Verein* a going concern, and expressing the hope (not to be fulfilled) that it would renew its existence in the not-too-distant future. Hanns Eisler, who would later turn completely away from the Schoenberg school in order to write "communistic" music, now contributed a handful of amusing anecdotes about Schoenberg the soldier, the teacher, the ruthless critic of his contemporaries, the "musical reactionary." Among the other contributors, Erwin Stein emphasized the newness of Schoenberg's formal principles in his extended article on the operation of the twelve-tone system (later to be reprinted in the volume of essays *Von neuer Musik*, to which Schoenberg and Bloch also contributed articles). Analyzing the *Five Piano Pieces*, Op. 23, and the *Serenade*, Stein demonstrates how the tone-row is used singly or in combination with other tone-rows, how it may be inverted and transposed, and how it may be made to consist of less than twelve or more than twelve tones.

A brilliant list of performing artists honored Schoenberg on this occasion. Two of the most faithful exponents of the *Sprechgesang* of *Pierrot Lunaire*, Marya Freund and Erika Stiedry-Wagner, paid tribute to him, as did Marie Gutheil-Schoder (whom Mahler had brought into the Vienna Opera, who had been one of his favorite singers in the organization, and whom Schoenberg had once called "the only possible singer in Vienna" for the last two movements of his Second Quartet). Fritz Stiedry was among the conductors represented on this roster, as was Hermann Scherchen; [5] in fact, some of the conductors were the most spirited of all the contributors in their appreciation of the man and the occasion. Paul Scheinpflug, one of the few conductors to have directed performances of all Schoenberg's orchestral and choral works in Western Germany, dubbed him "The Great Leader of our

[5] Scherchen's *Handbook of Conducting* is distinguished by the use of many examples of modern instrumental technique, including extensive quotations from Schoenberg and Mahler.

time," while Rudolf Schulz-Dornburg, another of the better-known German conductors, voiced even more lyrical praises. Artur Schnabel found well-chosen, if more moderate, words of admiration; and Rudolf Kolisch, whose sister Schoenberg had married that summer, gave a characteristic sketch of Schoenberg the conductor and interpreter of others' works (as well as of his own), the Schoenberg who knows how to inspire others to a performance in his own spirit, "spiritual and not *sentimental,* intellectual and not emotional." [6] Any instrumentalist or singer who has ever worked with Schoenberg cannot fail to recognize some of his most characteristic traits in this description. Few would forget his stress on musical nuances that transcend the technique of performance, or the telling analogies, usually well-spiced with wit and sarcasm, with which he knows how to bring a performer to a consciousness of his own shortcomings. Kolisch recollects his saying of someone who consistently played without any semblance of clear, distinct, structural phrasing, "He makes music the way a Czech cook speaks German!" [7]

Congratulations on present accomplishment and best wishes for the future needed a background of recollection of the past, even though this past had not always been a glorious one. Friends of Schoenberg had many pleasant things to recall: the help and advice proffered to Schoenberg in his youth by men like Josef Labor, the blind organist-composer, Richard Heuberger, composer and critic who had once drawn fire for his partially unfavorable comment on Bruckner published after the latter's death, and Josef Scheu, founder and sponsor of many Austrian workmen's choruses, who had secured for Schoenberg that much-needed job as director of the metal-workers' chorus in Stockerau; [8] the happy evenings at Zemlinsky's *Polyhymnia* (which had even given Schoenberg a prize for his *Schilflied,* written in 1893 to the words of Lenau), [9] when ambitious amateur soloists even sang the *Mir ist so wunderbar* quartet of *Fidelio,* and the self-taught 'cellist Schoenberg was determined to play the 'cello part in Dvořák's piano quintet. But there was no attempt to suppress the more discouraging moments of Schoenberg's artistic past, even if they were presented only as a contrast to the bright future of his friends' hopes. A quotation from *Das Grab in Wien* recalled that painful day when Rosé had presented the Second Quartet in one of his regular concerts; the

---

[6] Scherchen's *Handbook of Conducting,* p. 306.   [7] *Ibid.*

[8] David Josef Bach, "Aus der Jugendzeit," in *Arnold Schönberg zum fünfzigsten Geburtstage,* p. 319. The picture of Schoenberg directing workers' choruses somehow foreshadows the post-war emergence (already referred to) of Mahler as a "socialist" composer.

[9] A text also used by Berg in the *Sieben frühe Lieder.*

weather had been far more bitter than is usual at Christmas-time in Vienna (so much so, indeed, that Stefan vows some people were talking about "God's judgment on Vienna for the new *Walküre*"—for this was the period of Weingartner's "cut" performances), and the reactions of the audience had been equally bitter. Marie Gutheil-Schoder, confronting that hostile crowd, had wept tears far different from those which she had shed in the privacy of her own studio—for how often (she could, in 1924, good-humoredly admit it) had she cried out of sheer exhaustion after studying this music with its "unheard-of" difficulties, how often had she wished the unfortunate composer and his too large intervals and his innumerable notes a most unpleasant fate! Then, there was the *Konzertskandal* of 1912 that had greeted Webern's orchestral pieces and Berg's *Altenberg-Lieder* and had prevented the performance of Mahler's *Kindertotenlieder*. This, too, is recalled, in a quotation from a Viennese review of that day. Even Berlin, to which Schoenberg had always gone as an escape from Vienna, and which now, having invited him to a high position, was to be the scene of his successful career until the catastrophe of 1933, had furnished its quota of opposition. The critic Walter Dahms, writing an open letter to Schoenberg in 1912, was of no two minds about what should be done with this annoying composer. A performance of the piano pieces Op. 11 by Richard Buhlig,[10] which had been attended with much fanfare by Busoni and his friends, infuriated him (he said) to such a pitch that he could think of only three things required for the proper treatment of Schoenberg: some door-keys in good condition,[11] a few handy missiles, and a small collection (taken up, presumably, among embattled audiences) to pay for the speedy return of this "charlatan and humbug" to Vienna. Today we can look back upon these incidents with amusement; but, even so, we must not lose sight of the fact that every such crude attack inevitably left its mark upon the sensitive composer, a mark not to be soon forgotten.

It was appropriate that this jubilee year of 1924 should also see the publication of Stefan's panegyric *Arnold Schoenberg: Development—Legend—Phenomenon—Significance*. Three years before, the first full biography of Schoenberg (and the only one to be translated into English),[12] written by Wellesz, had made its appearance under the imprint

[10] Later a resident of Los Angeles.

[11] Whistling through these keys was a common means of expressing disfavor at concerts.

[12] Stuckenschmidt's first Schoenberg biography (1951) was published in English by Grove Press; a translation of his second one (1974) by Humphrey Searle is in preparation. Willi Reich's critical biography appeared in Leo Black's translation in 1971.

of the Universal-Edition. Wellesz' compact and serviceable volume had borne no dedication, though an appropriate motto had been selected from the *Harmonielehre*: "The laws of the nature of a genius are the laws of the nature of future humanity." But Stefan, with equal appropriateness, dedicated his book to Alma Mahler, "the most alive of us all." (She had, indeed, recently been honored with a far more distinguished dedication, that of Berg's *Wozzeck;* a dedication more than justified, not only for reasons of friendship, but also for practical motives, since it was she who had done the most to make it possible for Berg to publish his piano reduction of the opera.)

During the next years, Schoenberg, secure (as he thought) in his Berlin teaching position, was proceeding with the composition of new twelve-tone works. On September 19, 1927, the Kolisch Quartet gave the première of the Third Quartet (dedicated to Elizabeth Sprague Coolidge), that classic work of the twelve-tone style, in Vienna. A year and a day later, Op. 31 (the orchestral variations) was completed at the French vacation resort of Roquebrune; nor had it to wait long for performance, for on December 2, 1928, Furtwängler conducted its première in Berlin. Schoenberg had indeed come a long way from the days when the *Gurre-Lieder* had to wait so many years for performance —and this in spite of the increasing difficulty of his music! The next year, he finished his one-act, five-character comedy of modern manners, *Von Heute auf Morgen,* written to a libretto by one Max Blonda; [13] and 1930 saw the completion of his *Accompaniment to a Film Scene.* In 1929 and 1930 respectively, two more new works were published, neither of which represents any fresh trend in his creation. The piano piece Op. 33a, with its interesting beginning of chord-wise clustered tone-rows, belongs to the same sphere as the rest of the twelve-tone piano music; and the six *a cappella* pieces for male chorus, Op. 35, composed to Schoenberg's own words, are a pendant to the two groups of pieces for mixed chorus written earlier. The last of the six pieces, *Verbundenheit (Obligation),* is, however, different from all the others. Although it has no tonal signature, it operates with the more conventional triads as distinguished from the chordal structures based on fourths and sevenths which characterize Schoenberg's atonal harmony, and seems to have a tonal center of D major or minor. The unusual ending on a D minor six-four chord is but one of the many harmonic subtleties which make this perhaps the finest part of Op. 35,

---

[13] As this writer's name was unknown there were those who surmised that it was a pseudonym for Schoenberg himself. It was, in fact, the pen-name of his wife Gertrud.

although the humorous piece *Landsknechte* (*Yeomen*), with its gay refrain "Tumpuru, tuturu," represents an equal level of technical accomplishment in a far different vein.

It was on January 30, 1933, that the international catastrophe happened—Hitler came to power. While the infamous Nuremberg laws were not promulgated till 1935, measures against the Jews already began to take effect in April, 1933; so it was that Schoenberg and Franz Schreker were ousted from their state-sponsored Berlin teaching positions on May 30. It was a move which any intelligent observer of the national scene might have foretold, just as each catastrophic event of the years to come was foretold by many students of the international situation—to whom nobody listened; but even foreknowledge could not deaden the shock of having to tear up one's roots and begin a new life. In a man of Schoenberg's spirituality, the reconversion to Judaism was, perhaps, inevitable as a reaction against the vicious attacks on his race; and this reconversion did, in fact, take place at a special ceremony in Paris held on July 24, 1933. Even faith might not have protected a weaker character from some spiritual catastrophe induced by the shock of such an uprooting, but at least Schoenberg was fortunate in that plans were already in train to bring him to America, a land where he and his works were not entirely unknown. Boston's Malkin Conservatory had offered him a teaching post for the next year, and competition was keen for scholarships to study with him; one of his comparatively recent works, the *Accompaniment to a Film Scene* mentioned above, had just been performed in the Hollywood Bowl under the direction of Nicolas Slonimsky (July 24, 1933); and one composition of his, the piano piece Op. 33b (companion number to Op. 33a) had even been published in America.[14]

Schoenberg arrived in New York with his family on October 31, 1933. Thus began that difficult first year in America, when the somewhat bewildered composer was swamped with interviewers who wanted a look at Austria's famous "wild man" of music, honored in concerts, and weakened in health by the unaccustomed rigors of Boston's winter climate. He was to have made his first American appearance as conductor of the Boston Symphony Orchestra's concerts of January 12 and 13, 1934, but illness prevented him; however, he did conduct there on March 16, presenting to that city his own *Pelleas und Melisande*.

His sixtieth birthday was now approaching. How strange it seemed

14 *New Music*, April, 1932 (Vol. 5, no. 3).

to his friends in Austria to be celebrating it in his absence! Hard times were already upon them; Berg, for instance, had undergone considerable financial loss since 1933, since Germany would tolerate fewer and fewer performances of his works, because of his "modernistic" idiom which was considered "non-German." But somehow a commemorative volume was compiled, for which many of the contributors of former years—Webern, Wellesz, Stein, Stefan, Pisk, D. J. Bach—wrote articles, as did other friends in good standing—Zemlinsky, Alma Mahler, Darius Milhaud (who had put through the first French performance of *Pierrot Lunaire*), Alois Hába (the Czech composer and originator of the quarter-tone system), Apostel (the Berg pupil), and Willi Reich. Schoenberg himself was represented by his poem *Verbundenheit*, which he had set to music in Op. 35, and by a reprint of his Prague speech (1912) in memory of Mahler. Berg contributed an acrostic poem, *Glaube, Hoffnung, und Liebe;* but his greatest birthday present to Schoenberg, the new opera *Lulu* after the tragedies *Erdgeist* (*Earth-Spirit*) and *Büchse der Pandora* (*Pandora's Box*) by Wedekind, was still in the process of instrumentation.

By this time Schoenberg, unable to stand the Eastern winter, had moved to Los Angeles and was teaching at the University of Southern California. He was composing again, too; the new work, a *Suite for String Orchestra,* was completed on December 26, 1934, and received its first performance under Klemperer in Los Angeles on May 18, 1935. But something had happened to Schoenberg; here, in the middle of his most outspokenly atonal period, was a work not only in a key (G major) but even "In Olden Style!" There were those who insisted that this proved the invalidity of the twelve-tone method of composition—why, even its inventor and chief exponent could not stick with it! But Schoenberg's next two works, each a fine example of his "classic" twelve-tone manner—the Fourth String Quartet (completed July 26, 1936) and the Violin Concerto (completed September 23, 1936)—should have silenced that argument once and for all, though his subsequent returns to tonality brought it up once more.[15] Then there were those who said that the change might be attributed to Schoenberg's new life in this country. Of course it was inevitable that the move to a new land should entail certain alterations in mental attitude; that is exactly what we should expect in the case of a person with any flexibility and sensitivity. But a sixty-year-old composer does not change his whole approach overnight for a purely external reason—and Schoenberg's fundamental musical thinking was not changed. His friends had often

15 See his essay "On revient toujours," in *Style and Idea.*

commented that his manner of writing was not stereotyped, for each new work was always a little different from the one before and a little different from what one had expected. So the sudden reappearance of tonality in his music was not inconsistent with what had gone before in his development, all the more so since he had never lost his belief in the validity of tonality as a means of expression for the future. One looks at the movements of the *Suite for String Orchestra*—Overture with fugue, Adagio, Minuet, Gavotte and Musette, Gigue—and thinks of Reger. Schoenberg had always been interested in the music of Reger and had admired many things in it. Once this might have seemed inconsistent with his adoration of Mahler—for Mahler detested Reger's work and all it stood for—but with the passage of time it seemed as absurd to play one of these composers off against the other as to be unable to appreciate both Brahms and Bruckner. Hence compositions of Reger had appeared on the programs of the *Verein für musikalische Privataufführungen*, and Adolf Busch was inspired by a suggestion of Schoenberg's to complete his long-contemplated revision of Reger's violin concerto, a version which he first performed in New York on January 29, 1942. Certain phases of Reger's style are recalled by the music of the *Suite*, with its busily moving counterpoint and its strongly chromaticized harmony based on traditional foundations. In structure, it is an interesting counterpart to the piano suite Op. 25, because it shows Schoenberg's ability to handle the "old forms" with equal skill in the atonal and the tonal idiom.

In 1935, Schoenberg suffered the loss of one of his dearest friends and most devoted disciples. On December 24 of that year, Berg died, his last feverish thoughts occupied with his unfinished *Lulu*. At first it was said that the task of completing the third act—which was not in shape for publication, so that the *Universal-Edition* piano reduction by Erwin Stein had to be confined to the first two acts—would fall to Schoenberg; but unfortunately this plan was not carried out.[16] It would have been especially appropriate for more reasons than one; *Lulu* had been dedicated to Schoenberg in the first place, and then, too, Wedekind's brutally realistic dramas of the untamed *virtuosa* of love had a Schoenbergian association by way of the long-forgotten *Überbrettl*, memories of which lived for a brief moment in the final act when Berg introduced the melody of one of Wedekind's own songs to the lute, a simple C major ditty. It was a long time since the days of the *Überbrettl*; and thirty years had gone by since the original inspiration for *Lulu*—the première of the second *Lulu* tragedy, *Pandora's Box*,

[16] Since the death of Mrs. Berg in 1976, it appears that the complete *Lulu* will finally be made available. (Berg *had* virtually completed the last act.)

which had been presented in Vienna on May 29, 1905, through the efforts of Karl Kraus, that fiery advocate of social and cultural reforms whose periodical *Die Fackel* (The Torch) shed a bright light on many dark corners of the contemporary scene. Berg had never forgotten Kraus' introductory speech to the performance, in which the completely amoral Lulu is justified and defended; he entirely agreed with Kraus' explanation of her character, which would make her a female version of Don Juan. And it is thus that she will live on, in Berg's all too little-known opera.[17]

Schoenberg transferred his teaching activities to the University of California at Los Angeles, and so began a period of educational work which ended only in 1944 with his retirement at the age of seventy. Here was teaching of a different sort from that to which he had been accustomed in Europe. By its very nature, the music department of a state university has to cater to many who will never be composers; for these, the training given in Schoenberg's classes served an unusual and laudable purpose—"ear-training through composition"—even those incapable of original creative work learned a new appreciation of the classic form and idiom through their own carefully supervised writing in this vein. (It cannot be too much emphasized that Schoenberg never taught "atonal" composition either in school or privately.) On the other hand, he did draw individual pupils of talent and distinction, but they never had that tendency to coalesce into a homogeneous "group" or "school" manifested by those who had been his friends in Vienna during his first struggles towards prominence. Thus one of the more attractive features of his European teaching career failed to materialize in America, partly because of the differences between American and German educational concepts. But any pupil, talented or otherwise, who partook at all of what Schoenberg had to offer during these years of American university teaching could not fail to come away with a new-found respect for and a deeper knowledge of the Viennese composers—up to and including Mahler—whose works had been the life-blood of Schoenberg the composer.

Meanwhile, Schoenberg continued to turn out new works and to complete old ones, at a rate which suggested no flagging of his creative powers. The previously mentioned violin concerto, so distant, in its formal classic detachment, from the perfervid romanticism of Berg's violin concerto; the modernization of *Kol Nidre*, which represents Schoenberg's first use of frankly Jewish musical material; the comple-

17 Much better-known now; there are several excellent recordings. *Lulu* even invaded that museum known as the Metropolitan Opera House in March, 1977.

tion of a work of a much earlier period of inspiration, the two-movement Second *Kammersymphonie,* which was first performed in December, 1940 and revived in November, 1943; the new piano concerto, one of Schoenberg's most brilliantly executed works in the twelve-tone system, conceived in a truly "symphonic" style (akin to that of the concertos of Brahms) with the piano becoming an integral part of the orchestral texture rather than a superimposed virtuoso instrument; a revision of the string-orchestra version of *Verklärte Nacht;* the variations for organ and the G minor variations for orchestra (originally for band), wherein Schoenberg's second return to tonality is manifest in a harmonic style akin (especially in the "neo-baroque" organ music) to that of Reger; and still another of those works of Schoenberg wherein novel possibilities of the human voice are exploited, the *Ode to Napoleon* (originally intended for string quartet, piano, and solo reciting voice, but later rearranged for string orchestra instead of string quartet), in which the composer for the first time, by his use of Byron's poem with its suggestive parallels to current events, revealed in music his reactions to the world situation in our era; the first completed theoretical work since the *Harmonielehre, Models for Beginners in Composition*—all these bespoke the fact that Schoenberg's mind and pen were as active and vital as they had ever been. So it was fitting that his seventieth birthday, on September 13, 1944, should be an occasion not only for performing his most recent works and for recalling his past career, but also for looking forward to future accomplishments.

CHAPTER VII

The Seven Last Years: 1944–1951

As EVER, Schoenberg took delight in preparing a special letter in reply to all those who had sent him birthday greetings. On October 3, 1944, he wrote:

For more than a week I tried composing a letter of thanks to those who congratulated me on the occasion of my seventieth birthday. Still I did not succeed: it is terribly difficult to produce something if one is conceited enough to believe that everybody expects something extraordinary from you on an occasion like this.

But in fact the contrary might be true: at this age, if one is still capable of giving once in a while a sign of life, everybody might consider this already as a satisfactory accomplishment. I acknowledged this when my piano concerto was premiered and to my great astonishment so many were astonished that I still have something to tell. Or perhaps, that I do not yet stop telling it—or that I still am not wise enough to suppress it—or to learn finally to be silent at all?

Many recommend: "Many happy returns!"

Thank you, but will this help?

Will I really become wiser this way?

I cannot promise it, but let us hope.

Most sincerely with many thanks, yours

Arnold Schoenberg [1]

The seventieth birthday brought compulsory retirement from UCLA. This created problems. Because of the brevity of Schoenberg's tenure, his pension was minuscule.[2] To educate a lively young family, to maintain the large Brentwood house, and to continue the pleasant style of living which the Schoenbergs enjoyed, more money would have to be found.

---

[1] Schoenberg's original text, mailed to the author on October 18. The English version in Schoenberg, *Letters*, p. 225, is retranslated from the German translation of the English original (*Briefe*, p. 237).

[2] Stuckenschmidt (*Schönberg: Leben–Umwelt–Werk*, p. 426) gives figures of $28.50, $29.80, $38 per month, and finally (commencing on March 3, 1945) $40.38. Schoenberg's annual salary at retirement was $5400. These figures must, of course, be viewed in light of subsequent changes in the value of the dollar.

Two world premières gave Schoenberg pleasure in the closing months of 1944. On October 20, the orchestral version of the Band Variations, Op. 43B, was performed by the Boston Symphony Orchestra. And, on November 23, the New York Philharmonic presented the *Ode to Napoleon* in the string-orchestra version which Schoenberg had prepared at Artur Rodzinski's special request.[3]

Seeking financial support which might give him more time to compose and to finish his major textbooks, Schoenberg applied for a Guggenheim Fellowship. To Henry Allen Moe, the Foundation's secretary, he wrote, on January 22, 1945:

I have served the Guggenheim Foundation quite a number of times in writing opinions about potential candidates for Guggenheim awards—with more or less success, because, seemingly, not everybody considered me an authority of the same magnitude as did the applicants who longed for a good opinion of mine.[4]

Today I am writing on my own behalf, and I hope the powers to whose decision I submit my application will grant better credit to my creative accomplishments than they did to my judgment.

[Schoenberg describes the circumstances of his retirement and pension.]

. . . At present I still have private pupils and there is a chance that their number might increase. But considering the fact, that I [have taught] now for almost fifty years; that, while in Austria and Germany I taught exclusively the most talented young composers, with the best background (think only of Alban Berg, Anton von Webern, Hanns Eisler . . .), here I teach generally beginners; and though many are very talented and promising, the chances are not very bright that I could teach them for the five or six years I deem necessary for a real knowledge of an artist.

Can you understand that under these circumstances I am tired of teaching —at least temporarily?

I have done so much for my pupils, exhausted my powers, irrespective of my own interest, that I have neglected my own creative work.

I feel, as long as I am living I must try to complete at least some of the works which for a number of years wait for that.

I feel: my life task would be fulfilled only fragmentarily if I failed to complete at least those two largest of my musical and two, or perhaps three of my theoretical works.

The two musical works are:

a) MOSES AND AARON, opera in three acts, whose second act I finished (in full orchestra score) in March 1932—almost 13 years ago. (Performance time about 2 hours and 20'.)

---

[3] I attended this première; I can still feel the thrill which went through the audience as Mack Harrell stirringly declaimed Byron's closing lines, "Bequeath'd the name of Washington, To make men blush there was but one!" to Schoenberg's exciting and unexpected E♭ major cadence. It was a rousing success.

[4] I was one of these. Schoenberg succeeded no better for me than for himself. The composer Anis Fuleihan, on whose behalf he wrote on February 22, was also rejected.

b) DIE JAKOBSLEITER, an oratorio for soli, large choruses and large orchestra (performance time about an hour and 45'.) Half of this is composed already, much is outlined and sketched.

The completion of the opera might occupy me for about 6–9 months; but the oratorio would demand about one-and-a-half to two years.

The theoretical works include:

(1) A textbook on counterpoint in three volumes:
   I. Elementary Exercises
   II. Contrapuntal Composition
   III. Counterpoint and Semi-Counterpoint in the Music of the masters after Bach.
   NB. Nothing has yet been written about the subject of Vol. III.

Of this textbook I have written only Vol. I, while the other vols. exist only in an outline and number of examples. The completion of these books might take two years, but much of it can be done besides composing.

(2) A textbook: STRUCTURAL FUNCTIONS OF HARMONY, something very essential for future composers. This I could write in a few months.

(3) Either a textbook, 'Fundamentals of Musical Composition,' of which I had started the third draft already 4 or 5 years ago:

or

A textbook on orchestration, outlines of which go back to 1917!

I would like to apply for a Guggenheim Scholarship which enables me to devote all my time, or at least most of it, to the completion of my works, in order that I may renounce any income through teaching and other distracting activities as much as possible . . .[5]

Schoenberg's application was rejected. Composer-winners in 1945 were Samuel Barber, Elliott Carter, Norman Dello Joio, Lukas Foss, Dai-Keong Lee, Nikolai Lopatnikoff, and Juan A. Orrego-Salas; for 1946, William Bergsma, Henry Brant, Alberto Ginastera, Alexei Haieff, John Lessard, Gian-Carlo Menotti, Harold Shapero, Louise Talma, and John Verrall.

It is instructive to follow the subsequent history of the projects on which Schoenberg based his application:

a) *Moses and Aaron* was composed only through Act II. A complete libretto for Act III exists, but no music. Performances of the work have either comprised the first two acts only or have included a spoken presentation of the third act (sometimes with "background music" from other parts of the opera).

b) 685 measures of *Die Jakobsleiter* were more or less completed. With further realization by Winfried Zillig, it was performable, and received its première in Vienna on June 16, 1961.

(1) *Preliminary Exercises in Counterpoint*, I, was edited by Leonard Stein (who had to provide commentary for the last four chapters)

---

[5] Schoenberg, *Letters*, pp. 231–32.

and published by Faber and Faber in 1963. The other two parts of the proposed book were never written.

(2) *Structural Functions of Harmony* was finished in 1948, with my editorial help. It was published in 1954 by Williams & Norgate, London (in the U.S. by W. W. Norton), with editorial credit to Humphrey Searle. A revised edition with corrections by Leonard Stein appeared in 1969 (W. W. Norton).

(3) *Fundamentals of Musical Composition* was substantially complete, except for the final chapter, on Schoenberg's death. Edited by Gerald Strang and Leonard Stein, it appeared with Faber and Faber in 1967.

Schoenberg must have felt disgust and disappointment at being refused the award which would have made his life easier. However, this did not deter him from undertaking a new project in September. Nathaniel (Nat) Shilkret, composer and conductor of light music, had proposed, while manager of Victor Records, "the massive concept of setting to music the first chapter of the Bible. . . . He decided that so tremendous a project should be shared by leading contemporary creators and carefully selected and commissioned composers to expound the various subjects.

" 'My colleagues,' Shilkret declared,' have approached their task in a spirit of the most profound reverence. Their devotion is apparent in the music they have created.'

"The separate movements have been conceived in complete independence, the composers each proceeding with their individual portion without reference to or knowledge of each other's work. The sole connecting link is the narrator, Edward Arnold, who delivers the Biblical story." [6]

The movements and composers were as follows:

1. Creation (Nathaniel Shilkret)
2. Adam and Eve (Alexandre Tansman)
3. Cain and Abel (Darius Milhaud)
4. Noah's Ark (Mario Castelnuovo-Tedesco)
5. The Covenant (Ernst Toch)
6. Babel (Igor Stravinsky)
7. Postlude (Arnold Schoenberg) [7]

[6] Album notes to *Genesis Suite,* performed by Janssen Symphony of Los Angeles, Werner Janssen, conductor. Artist Records JS-10.

[7] While called *Postlude* in the first performance and recording, the work has always been known since as *Prelude.* Schoenberg conceived it as a Prelude to Creation.

Schoenberg's contribution cogently combines brevity and large orchestral forces. The row, as in many of his works, is of a hexachordal type. Its first hexachord is B♭–G♭–D–F–E–C; its second, B–G♯–C♯–D♯–A–G. The tones of the second hexachord, reshuffled, yield the inversion, a fifth below, of the first hexachord: i.e., E♭–G–B–G♯–A–C♯. The tones of the first hexachord have a similar relation to the last six tones of that same inversion. Such a technique makes many fascinating combinations possible. Note the predominance of thirds in the row. Thirds, inverted, give the upward-yearning sixths which characterize one of the work's most important motifs. After the brooding introduction, with its dark low-string and low-brass sounds, a fugal section, depicting order coming out of chaos, makes much play with the motif E♭–C♭–B♭–A, its transpositions and inversions. This particular melodic inflection, rising minor sixth followed by one or more falling ("sighing") half-steps, was a Mahler favorite (first theme, Sixth Symphony; first theme, Piano Quartet). We know it best, however, from the *Tristan* Prelude (A–F–E–D♯). Is it possible that these reminiscences passed subconsciously through Schoenberg's mind? Deryck Cooke, in his thoughtful book *The Language of Music*, associates such motifs with "a passionate outburst of painful emotion" [8]—one such emotion is certainly the suffering inseparable from an act of creation.

Another musical reminiscence is probably deliberate and can hardly be missed: in measure 66, Schoenberg introduces a wordless chorus (God had not yet created the word!) which sings the widely arched melodic lines that grow out of the sixth-motif. Beginning softly, the passage rises, by measure 82, to a brilliant, *fortissimo* climax on C. The approach in the melodic line is distinctly tonal (D–F–E–C); and the C is generously doubled in octaves, both in the chorus and in the orchestra, something which is not usual in Schoenberg's twelve-tone works. This would seem to be a clear reference to the radiant C major of Light after the chaos-depicting introduction to Haydn's *Creation*.

1946 was to prove a fateful—and almost fatal—year for Schoenberg. It began promisingly with his election as honorary president of the International Society for Contemporary Music. Harvard University had commissioned a chamber work, and the University of Chicago had invited him to give a series of lectures, which would combine a diverting trip with a most welcome honorarium. On January 18, he drafted the first of these, *Heart and Brain in Music*, which was later published in the University of Chicago Press compilation, *The Works of*

---

[8] Deryck Cooke, *The Language of Music*, pp. 137–38.

the Mind, and also in Schoenberg's *Style and Idea.* Two other lectures were already written, needing only some revision: *New Music, Outmoded Music, Style and Idea,* and *Composition with Twelve Tones.* On April 24, he prepared an English version, *Criteria for the Evaluation of Music,* of an older German lecture, *Kriterien musikalischer Werte.* All these, too, were later published in *Style and Idea.* The lectures were delivered at the University of Chicago between May 2 and 23.[9] Schoenberg subsequently gave Robert Maynard Hutchins, the University's chancellor, detailed advice on the organization of a music department. His ideas could well be used by a progressive department head or dean today.[10]

On June 6, Schoenberg started to sketch a tone-row for the String Trio, his Harvard commission. Work on the piece was desultory thereafter. It was kicked into finished existence by an unexpected happening, perhaps the only time in history that a composer has actually put to music his own death (rather than foreshadowing it, as did Mozart in his Requiem and Berg in his Violin Concerto). In Schoenberg's own words:

Now I must describe the extraordinary event which I call my "fatality." On August 2 [1946] our house-doctor tried a new medicament for my asthma: benzedrine. An hour or two later, during the midday meal I suddenly felt sleepy and went to bed, something very unusual for me. At about ten o'clock in the evening I woke up, jumped out of bed and ran to a chair which I have been using during asthmatic attacks. I began to feel fierce pains throughout my body, particularly in the chest and around the heart. After trying for half an hour to find a doctor, a friend sent Dr. Lloyd-Jones, our present house-doctor, who then saved my life. He gave me an injection of Dilaudid, to reduce the pains. This immediately helped; but ten minutes later I lost consciousness, and my heart-beat and pulse stopped. In other words, I was practically dead. I have never found out how long it lasted. All I was told was that Dr. Jones made an injection directly into my heart. It was three weeks before I recovered. I had about 160 penicillin injections; my heart and lungs were examined, X-rays taken, and there were sometimes three or four doctors there at once, discussing my case. . ."[11]

As soon as he could write, Schoenberg set about transcribing this unique experience into music. The work, as usual with him, went fast; he started composing on August 20 and finished on September 23. The Trio's three principal sections, the last of which functions as a condensed recapitulation, are separated by two "episodes." This

[9] Dates from "Sources and Notes" in Leonard Stein's edition of *Style and Idea,* pp. 515, 518, 523.

[10] Schoenberg, *Letters,* pp. 240–42.

[11] Schoenberg wrote a detailed history of his illnesses on August 2, 1950. This citation is from Willi Reich, *Schoenberg: A Critical Biography,* pp. 218–19.

"episodic" construction seems somehow particularly appropriate to the programmatic nature of the piece. Nearly every available string "effect" is used; the sound is phantasmagoric. Motifs are often short, fragmentary; an expressive recitative-like melody may arise, only to be brutally cut off. Dynamic contrasts are violent. Row-technique is flexible. As Oliver Neighbour pointed out in his useful article "Dodecaphony in Schoenberg's String Trio," there is not one twelve-tone row, but four groups of six tones, with their inversions; any group of six may be used with one of four other such groups to comprise a complete set of twelve.[12] Again, because of Schoenberg's choice of intervals, tonal-like melodies or harmonies may occur. Striking is the last measure (203), in which a curving melodic line (A–C♯–D♯) over A♭–G♭ in the other two instruments gives a sense of ending on an unresolved dominant thirteenth chord (A♭–E♭–G♭–B♭♭–D♭). "Life must go on!"

The Trio received its première at Harvard on May 2, 1947. Many who knew nothing of Schoenberg's illness nevertheless must have sensed that something extraordinary was going on in the piece. My own reaction, when I first heard the work broadcast on May 8, 1949, may have been typical. Knowing nothing of the foregoing events, I wrote Schoenberg: "My strongest impression was perhaps this: that it is a reflection of something shattering and terrifying in real life, the representation of chaos, *without* being in itself chaotic." I could not improve on this description today. Schoenberg was doubtless gratified that his "message" had been clearly transmitted and received. Thomas Mann, too, "got the message" in another way. After listening to Schoenberg describe the piece, he "lifted" its characteristics ("impossible but rewarding") for a piece by his Faustian hero Adrian Leverkühn, of whom more anon.[13]

In the closing months of 1946, Schoenberg sketched, but did not complete, an orchestral piece.[14] His health was definitely improving. The coming year would see the birth of a new masterpiece, *A Survivor from Warsaw,* and the conferring upon Schoenberg of a new honor.[15]

12 O. W. Neighbour, "Dodecaphony in Schoenberg's String Trio," *Music Survey,* IV/3 (June, 1952), pp. 489–90.

13 Thomas Mann, *The Story of a Novel: The Genesis of Doctor Faustus,* p. 217.

14 Josef Rufer, *The Works of Arnold Schoenberg,* p. 114.

15 A third circumstance brought both of us pleasure: the publication of the first edition of the present book. I had written it very much in his spirit (I hoped) but without consulting him at any point. Now I sent it to him, and sat back (not without some trepidation) to await his reaction. A friendly response was not long in coming. While he was unable to read the book himself because of his nervous eye-trouble, Mrs. Schoenberg read much of it to him, and he expressed himself "much pleased with that portion." He cautioned only that I should check up on a few dates

A great joy during this spring was the special thousand-dollar grant awarded to Schoenberg by the National Institute of Arts and Letters. Unable to attend their ceremonies, he recorded a grateful reply, a speech which contains some of his most characteristic thinking. It has been reprinted many times; [16] most famous, perhaps, is this bit of colorful phraseology:

> Personally, I had the feeling as if I had fallen into an ocean of boiling water, and not knowing how to swim or to get out in another manner, I tried with my legs and arms as best as I could.
> I did not know what saved me; why I was not drowned or cooked alive . . .
> I have perhaps only one merit: I never gave up.

Typical, too, is the Schoenbergian irony of the conclusion:

> Please do not call it false modesty if I say:
> Maybe something has been achieved but it was not I who deserve the credit for that.
> The credit must be given to my opponents.
> They were the ones who really helped me.
> Thank you.

The Koussevitzky Foundation had commissioned a new work from Schoenberg. A subject was ready to hand: news received directly and indirectly about the wartime horrors of the Warsaw ghetto inspired him to write a text based on such communications. Thus was produced one of his most trenchant and dramatic works: *A Survivor from Warsaw,* for speaker, male choir, and orchestra. He composed it quickly (August 11–23, 1947). The results reflect the intensity of the creative experience. Unforgettable is the shattering climax. The Jews are "counting off" at the harsh command of the German sergeant: "Abzählen!" Agitated broken triplets, beginning softly but rising to pulsating loudness, vividly illustrate the text: "They began again, first slowly: one, two, three, four; became faster and faster—so fast that it finally sounded like a stampede of wild horses—and, quite of a sudden, in the middle of it, they began singing the Shema Yisroel." The male choir bursts forth in a beautiful, dignified twelve-tone unison chant,

---

which I may have obtained from "imprecise minds like Paul Stefan." In retrospect, I believe that he was concerned with questions of his priority in musical discoveries—something which was beginning to be questioned by the adherents of Webern. It was as a direct result of this work of mine that he now would recommend me to perform other tasks for him. Chief of these would be the translation of René Leibowitz' *Schoenberg et son école* and the first edition of his own *Style and Idea,* both of which Philosophical Library would publish. My professional and personal contact with him remained cordial till the end of his life.

[16] The complete text is in Schoenberg, *Letters,* pp. 245–46.

using the text of the familiar traditional Hebrew prayer, "Hear, oh Israel . . ." The audience was stunned at the work's première on November 4, 1948, in Albuquerque, N.M., under the direction of Kurt Frederick. (Koussevitzky had, in the end, not cared to conduct the piece.) It was immediately repeated, and received, after a moment's silence, with thunderous applause. René Leibowitz, too, reported an equally emotional audience reaction at the Paris première which he conducted.

In 1948 could be heard the first rumblings of an affair which took up, during the next two years, much more of Schoenberg's creative energy than it should have. In late 1947, Thomas Mann's *Doctor Faustus* was published. Word soon got around that the book's "hero," the syphilitic and demon-possessed composer Adrian Leverkühn, was based upon the personality of Schoenberg—at least to the extent that this fictional composer invents the twelve-tone method! [17] Alma Mahler Werfel, mischievously, perhaps, saw to it that Schoenberg got wind of the affair. Mann added fuel to the flames by sending Schoenberg an inscribed copy dedicated "To A. Schoenberg, *dem Eigentlichen.*" To Schoenberg, this meant clearly that he was the *eigentlicher* (real) model for Leverkühn. Understandably, he did not care to have his twelve-tone method presented to the public as a gift of the devil (whom he didn't worship) and a result of venereal disease (which he didn't have). Alma conveyed to Mann Schoenberg's request that a note crediting him with the invention of the twelve-tone method be included in subsequent copies of the book. This was done, but still did not satisfy the composer, because of its placement (at the end of the book) and its wording (calling Schoenberg "a" contemporary composer and musician). Schoenberg's reaction to this was, "in two or three decades, one will know which of the two was the other's contemporary." [18] The whole sorry squabble finally erupted in public on the first day of 1949, when Schoenberg's and Mann's letters on the subject appeared in the *Saturday Review of Literature*. The quarrel—worthy of neither man—continued to fester in public and private until January 2, 1950, when Schoenberg wrote to Mann:

> If the hand that I believe I see held out is the hand of peace, that is if it signifies an offer of peace, I should be the last not to grasp it at once and shake it in token of confirmation.
> In fact: I have often thought of writing to you saying: Let us bury the hatchet and show that on a certain level there is always a chance of peace.

[17] Schoenberg told me wistfully, in the summer of '49, "If Mann had only *asked* me, I'd have invented a *special* system for him to use in the book!"
[18] *Saturday Review of Literature,* January 1, 1949.

(continued on the 9th January!)

I had intended making public this declaration of peace. It was pointed out to me, however, (and this is the reason why I did not finish the letter) that by so doing I would, as it were, stab in the back all those who supported me in this fight—friends, acquaintances, and strangers.

So I suggest an intermediate stage of neutrality. Some day one or the other [of us] will be celebrating his 'eightieth'—but it need not even wait till then—; a fitting occasion to forget all pettiness—finally.

. . . Let us make do with this peace; you have reconciled me.[19]

The public reconciliation never came to pass. This letter came to light only after Schoenberg's death.

Perhaps because of preoccupation with this affair, Schoenberg composed but little in 1948. From this year we have only the *Three German Folksongs,* Op. 49, based on melodies in old songbooks of the sixteenth century and set in a style befitting these. Even this was a reworking of settings which Schoenberg had already done for the *Volksliederbuch für die Jugend* (C. F. Peters, 1930). In returning to such old material, Schoenberg reflected thoughts which would be verbalized later that year in his essay *On revient toujours.*

Although he wrote very little music, Schoenberg was extensively occupied with his theoretical and literary works. Earlier, Serge Frank had been helping him with the editing of *Style and Idea.* Schoenberg, however, was deeply dissatisfied with his work, as a stern letter to him shows.[20]

On December 19, 1948, the essay *On revient toujours* was published in *The New York Times* music section. Later reprinted in *Style and Idea,* it became one of Schoenberg's most-discussed essays because of his explanation of the stylistic "returns to the past" which he had from time to time enjoyed in these later years. As previously mentioned, some critics had seen this as a confession of the bankruptcy of dodecaphony. Schoenberg, however, saw it differently:

Only a man who himself deserves respect is capable of paying respect to another man. Only one who knows merits can recognize the merits of other men. Such feelings might have developed in a longing once more to try to achieve, in the older style, what they [the classic masters] were sure they could achieve in their own more advanced style.

. . . To me stylistic differences of this nature are not of special importance. I do not know which of my compositions are better; I like them all, because I liked them when I wrote them.[21]

[19] Schoenberg, *Letters,* p. 278.

[20] *Ibid.,* pp. 250–82. I was to take over this task in 1949. In 1948, I helped with *Structural Functions of Harmony,* but because of publisher disagreements with Schoenberg's conditions, this work did not appear till after his death.

[21] Schoenberg, *Style and Idea* (1st ed.), pp. 212–13. This article stirred up a flurry of correspondence in *The New York Times,* with a negative reaction by Tibor Serly and my vigorous rejoinder thereto.

Vigorous work on *Style and Idea* continued for most of 1949. During the first five months of the year, many letters flew back and forth between Brentwood and Westminster, Maryland, where I was then teaching, and making good use of the English translation of *Harmonielehre*. We had many spirited arguments about the book's language. Schoenberg did not want one word of his original changed; I was of the opinion that some of his Germanic idioms in English would, for many readers, get in the way of his message. (This indeed proved to be the case, for certain critics at least.) We eventually solved the problem with fairness to both Schoenberg's unique idiom and my stylistic preferences by the inclusion of a prefatory note: "Schoenberg himself has elucidated his attitude towards his own manner of writing in English as follows: '. . . I do not plan to hide the fact that I am not born in this language and I do not want to parade adorned by stylistic merits of another person.' Obedience to this viewpoint has governed editorial activities throughout." [22]

This jubilee year brought important celebrations, commemorations, publications, and honors. Schoenberg must have found it faintly ironic to receive word that, on his 75th birthday, he had been given the freedom of his hated and loved Vienna, which had not been exactly hospitable to him in earlier years. It would have been only human to indulge in sarcasm, but Schoenberg achieved a gracious response to the Burgomaster of Vienna, speaking feelingly of the music created there "which I have always so much loved and which it was always my greatest ambition to continue according to the measure of my talents." [23] My translation of Leibowitz' book, *Schoenberg and His School*, had appeared earlier in the year. During my visit to Los Angeles that summer, he expressed pleasure with it, though he was concerned by the tendency of Leibowitz and other young composers to exalt Webern at his expense. Though he had sincerely mourned Webern's violent death on September 15, 1945, his attitude towards his disciple had long been ambivalent. "Webern," he said to me ruefully, "always exaggerated!"

Schoenberg's newest work, the Phantasy for violin with piano accompaniment, Op. 47, was completed in March of 1949 and was premièred by Adolph Koldofsky and Leonard Stein on Schoenberg's 75th birthday. It is a real violin virtuoso piece in which the piano plays a subordinate but indispensable role. (Schoenberg had composed the entire violin part first and added the piano part only later.) The vigorous work bears no signs of Schoenberg's age; the violin's opening flourish

22 *Ibid.*, p. v.
23 Schoenberg, *Letters*, p. 277.

(marked *passionato*) still stands today as "one of Schoenberg's most fiery and *youthful* thematic conceptions." [24]

This was to be Schoenberg's last completed instrumental work. Two choral works, one finished, the other not, were products of this year. *Dreimal tausend Jahre,* to a text by Dagobert D. Runes, director of the Philosophical Library, is a gently flowing lyrical *a cappella* piece (SATB), pleasantly evoking scenes and sounds of Jerusalem which presage "Gottes Wiederkehr" (God's Return). In contrast, *Israel Exists Again,* of which Schoenberg managed to complete only 55 measures, uses a large orchestra and has a dramatic, proclamative tone. Schoenberg's own text begins, "Israel exists again! It has always existed, though invisibly." Again, SATB is used. Both works are strictly twelve-tone, in keeping with Schoenberg's strong association between the twelve-tone row and The Law (*das Gesetz*).[25]

Once more it was time to acknowledge birthday greetings. In a moving letter to his friends, beginning "To gain recognition only after one's death . . . . !" Schoenberg reviewed his stormy career and compared it with those of Beethoven, Wagner, and Mahler. How, he wondered, had these men—and he—been able to go on writing in the face of so much opposition? "I know only one answer: they had things to say that had to be said. Once, in the army, I was asked if I was really the composer A. S. 'Somebody had to be,' I said, 'and nobody else wanted to, so I took it on, myself.'

"Perhaps I too had to say things—unpopular things, it seems—that had to be said." [26]

The last two years of Schoenberg's life can be summarized briefly.

He did not finish his two great religious works, *Moses and Aaron* and *Die Jakobsleiter.* Today we can see this as somehow inevitable. As he wrote in his great Mahler essay,

> It seems that the Ninth is a limit. He who wants to go beyond it must pass away. It seems as if something might be imparted to us in the Tenth which we ought not yet to know, for which we are not yet ready. Those who have written a Ninth stood too near to the hereafter. Perhaps the riddles of this world would be solved, if one of those who knew them were to write a Tenth. And that probably is not to take place.[27]

[24] Dika Newlin, "Schoenberg's New Fantasy," *The Canon,* III/2 (September, 1949), p. 84.

[25] For more on this topic, see Dika Newlin, "Self-Revelation and the Law: Arnold Schoenberg in His Religious Works," *Yuval I* (Studies of the Jewish Music Research Centre, Jerusalem, 1968), pp. 204-20.

[26] Schoenberg, *Letters,* p. 290.

[27] Schoenberg, *Style and Idea* (1st ed.), p. 34.

He, like Mahler, "was allowed to reveal just so much of the future; when he wanted to say more, he was called away." [28]

But he still had things to say, and said them. Contemplating his profound setting of Psalm 130 (*Out of the Depths*) or the texts of his *Modern Psalms*, "conversations with and about God," part of one of which he was still able to compose, one thinks of his words, inspired by Brahms' *Vier ernste Gesänge* (in particular, "O Tod, O Tod, wie bitter bist du"):

> If a man who knows that he will die soon makes his account with earth and with heaven, prepares his soul for the departure, and balances what he leaves with what we will receive, he might desire to incorporate a word—a part of the wisdom he has acquired—with the knowledge of mankind, if he is one of the Great. One might doubt about the sense of life if it then would be mere accident that such a work, a life-terminating work, would not represent more than just another opus. Or is one entitled to assume that a message from a man who is already half on the other side progresses to the uttermost limit of the still-expressible? Is one not entitled to expect therefrom perfection of an extraordinary degree, because mastership, a heavenly gift, which cannot be acquired by the most painstaking assiduity and exercise, manifests itself only once, only one single time in its full entirety, when a message of such importance has to be formulated?[29]

But Schoenberg might interrupt, as, in brief self-irony, he imagined Brahms interrupting *him*: "Now it's enough poetry. If you have to say something, say it briefly and technically without so much sentimental fuss." Technically, then—suffice it to say that in both works, *Psalm 130* and *Modern Psalm*, purest twelve-tone technique is once more placed at the service of God and the Law.

Schoenberg entered his 76th year with some trepidation. His longtime superstition concerning the number 13 was reinforced by his old friend, the numerologist Oskar Adler, who reminded him that 7 and 6 add up to 13. He would say to his friends, "If only I can pull through this year, I will be safe." [30] He could not. Death came, as he had somehow known it would, on a Friday the 13th: July 13, 1951.

Writing to Schoenberg's sister, Ottilie, on August 4, his widow Gertrud described his last night:

> On the 13th (he and I were terribly afraid of it) he insisted that I get a night nurse. It was a German doctor, not licensed to practise here. I was very tired, but stayed awake the whole time, and we had the light on.

28 *Ibid.,* p. 35.

29 *Ibid.,* p. 98.

30 Quoted by Walter Rubsamen, "Schoenberg in America," *Musical Quarterly,* XXXVII/4 (October, 1951), p. 488.

Arnold slept restlessly, but he slept. At a quarter of twelve I looked at the clock and said to myself: 'Well, another quarter of an hour and the worst will be over." Then the doctor called me. He [Arnold] rattled a couple of times, there was one more strong heartbeat, and it was all over. But I could not believe it for a long while afterwards. His face was so relaxed and peaceful, as if he were sleeping. No pain, no death-struggle. I had always prayed for such an end. Only not to suffer! [31]

Now he belonged to the ages. The future would tell whether his wry prophecy concerning his work would be fulfilled: "The second half of this century will spoil by overestimation whatever the first half's underestimation left unspoilt."

[31] Letter quoted in Stuckenschmidt, *Schönberg: Leben–Umwelt–Werk*, p. 474 (my translation).

Bibliography

I. SOME EDITIONS AND SOME PERIODICALS

There are now two critical editions of Bruckner, one put out by the Deutsche Bruckner-Gesellschaft under the general direction of Robert Haas, the other, later one published by the Internationale Bruckner Gesellschaft's Musikwissenschaftlicher Verlag in Vienna, under the general direction of Leopold Nowak. The latter edition represents a "deNazified" Bruckner, since Haas, Orel, and others were discredited for political reasons. One cannot always say that Nowak's comments on his earlier confrères' work, therefore, are objective. Noteworthy is his incorporation of findings from the Columbia University manuscript of Bruckner's Fourth Symphony. The newer edition includes an interesting piece of "juvenilia," Bruckner's String Quartet.

The late Erwin Ratz spearheaded the work of the Internationale Gustav Mahler Gesellschaft, Vienna, in preparing their critical Mahler edition. He was thorough and enthusiastic, but filled with fanatic prejudices, the most notorious of which is his mania (I can only call it that) concerning Mahler's Tenth Symphony. This led him to state, in his foreword to the new facsimile edition of the Tenth (Walter Ricke Verlag, Munich, 1967), that Mahler had given no indications of instrumentation for the Finale, when one can, in fact, clearly see such indications in the facsimile. He admitted only the first movement of the Tenth into the Critical Edition. It must be said, though, that the Critical Edition volumes are well prepared, attractively printed, and clear up many previous errors

An interesting separate Mahler publication is that of Mahler's Piano Quartet (1876), brought out by Edition Sikorski. Deryck Cooke's fine performing version of the 10th is now with Faber/AMP.

The Schoenberg Sämtliche Werke are coming out at slow and steady pace under the patronage of the Akademie der Künste, Berlin, under general editorship of Josef Rufer. (The Volkswagen Company has been a generous contributor to expenses.) Editors here have many annoying problems to deal with, for, because of the complex nature of the musical material, there were many proofreading errors in the original Schoenberg publications. Much of this, but not all, is cleaned up in the Complete Edition.

Belmont Publishers—a Schoenberg house company as the name suggests—has reprinted many of the Schoenberg works in handy performing editions and has brought out previously unpublished early works (e.g. the *Brettl-Lieder*). Their editions are nicely designed; the *Brettl-Lieder* have a cover decorated with Schoenberg's playing-card designs, colorful and original.

As to special magazines, two will not be overlooked by readers of this book. *Chord and Discord,* the publication of the Bruckner (now Bruckner and Mahler) Society of America is presently inactive. The character of contributions to it over some 35 years varied widely, from real "fanzine" stuff to solid analytical articles. The *Journal of the Arnold Schoenberg Institute* began publication in October, 1976. It has been carrying many reminiscences by longtime associates of Schoenberg and will also contain more strictly scholarly commentary.

II. BRUCKNER

Auer, Max. *Anton Bruckner als Kirchenmusiker.* Regensburg, 1927.
————. *Anton Bruckner, sein Leben und Werk.* 2nd ed. Vienna, 1934.
Bruckner, Anton. *Gesammelte Briefe.* 2 vols. Regensburg, 1924.
————, ed. Ernst Schwanzara. *Vorlesungen: Harmonie, Kontrapunkt.* Vienna, 1950.
Decsey, Ernst. *Bruckner: Eine Lebensgeschichte.* Berlin, 1930.
Doernberg, Erwin. *The Life and Symphonies of Anton Bruckner.* London, 1960.
Eckstein, Friedrich. *Erinnerungen an Anton Bruckner.* Vienna, 1923.
Engel, Gabriel. *The Life of Anton Bruckner.* New York, 1931.
Goellerich, August, and Max Auer. *Anton Bruckner.* 9 vols. Regensburg, 1922–36.
Haas, Robert. *Anton Bruckner.* Potsdam, 1934.
Halm, August. *Die Symphonie Anton Bruckners.* Munich, 1914.
Hruby, Carl. *Meine Erinnerungen an Anton Bruckner.* Vienna, 1901.
Klose, Friedrich. *Meine Lehrjahre bei Bruckner.* Regensburg, 1927.
Lach, Robert. *Die Bruckner-Akten des Wiener Universitäts-Archives.* Vienna, 1926.
Louis, Rudolf. *Anton Bruckner.* Munich, 1918.
Oberleithner, Max von. *Meine Erinnerungen an Anton Bruckner.* Regensburg, 1933.
Orel, Alfred. *Anton Bruckner: Das Werk—Der Künstler—Die Zeit.* Vienna and Leipzig, 1925.
Redlich, H. F. *Bruckner and Mahler.* London, 1963.
Schönzeler, Hans-Hubert. *Bruckner.* New York, 1970.
Simpson, Robert. *The Essence of Bruckner.* Philadelphia, 1968.
Wolff, Werner. *Anton Bruckner, Rustic Genius.* New York, 1942.

III. MAHLER

Adler, Guido. *Gustav Mahler.* Vienna and Leipzig, 1916.
Adorno, Theodor W. *Mahler: Eine musikalische Physiognomik.* Frankfurt, 1960.
Bauer-Lechner, Natalie. *Erinnerungen an Gustav Mahler,* Leipzig, Vienna, and Zurich, 1923. Tr. and ed. by Dika Newlin and Peter Franklin, in preparation, Faber & Faber.
Bekker, Paul. *Gustav Mahlers Sinfonien.* Berlin and Stuttgart, 1921.
Blaukopf, Kurt, tr. Inge Goodwin. *Mahler.* New York and Washington, 1973.
————, comp. and ed., with contributions by Zoltan Roman (various translators). *Mahler: A Documentary Study.* New York and Toronto, 1976.
Cardus, Neville. *Gustav Mahler: His Mind and His Music.* Vol. I. London, 1965.

De la Grange, Henry-Louis, *Mahler*. Vol. I. Garden City, 1973.

Engel, Gabriel. *Gustav Mahler, Song-Symphonist*. New York, 1932.

Gustav Mahler. Tübingen, 1966.

"Gustav Mahler-Heft," *Anbruch*, XII/3 (March, 1930).

"Gustav-Mahler-Heft," *Die Musik*, X/18 (June, 1911).

Gustav Mahler und seine Zeit. Exhibition catalog. Vienna, 1960.

Holbrook, David. *Gustav Mahler and the Courage to Be*. London, 1975.

Holländer, Hans. "Unbekannte Jugendbriefe Gustav Mahlers," *Die Musik*, XX (1928), 807–13.

Klemperer, Otto. *Meine Erinnerungen an Gustav Mahler*. Freiburg and Zurich, 1960.

Mahler, Alma, tr. Basil Creighton, ed. Donald Mitchell. *Gustav Mahler: Memories and Letters*. London, 1968. Expanded American ed., Seattle, 1975.*

Mahler, Gustav, *Briefe 1879–1911*. Berlin, Vienna and Leipzig, 1924. Tr. by E. Wilkins and E. Kaiser in preparation.

Matter, Jean. *Mahler le démoniaque*. Lausanne, 1959.

Mengelberg, Rudolf. *Gustav Mahler*. Leipzig, 1923.

——, ed. *Das Mahler-Fest*. Vienna and Leipzig, 1920.

Mitchell, Donald. *Gustav Mahler: The Early Years*. London, 1958.

——. *Gustav Mahler: The Wunderhorn Years*. London, 1975.

Newlin, Dika. "Alienation and Gustav Mahler," *Reconstructionist*, XXV/7 (May 15, 1959), 21–25.

——. "Conversation Piece: Mahler and Beyond," *New York Philharmonic Program Notes*, Jan. 14–17, 1960. Reprinted in *Chord and Discord*, II/9 (1960), 117–19.

——. "Mahler's Opera," *Opera News*, XXXVI/17 (March 18, 1972), 6–7.

Pamer, Fritz Egon, "Gustav Mahlers Lieder," *Studien zur Musikwissenschaft*, XVI (1929), 116–38; XVII (1930), 105–27.

Redlich, H. F. *Gustav Mahler: Eine Erkenntnis*. Nuremberg, 1919.

Roller, Alfred. *Die Bildnisse von Gustav Mahler*. Leipzig and Vienna, 1922.

Schaefers, Anton. *Gustav Mahlers Instrumentation*. Düsseldorf, 1935.

Schiedermair, Ludwig. *Gustav Mahler*. Leipzig, 1901.

Schreiber, Wolfgang (ed.). *Gustav Mahler in Selbstzeugnissen und Bilddokumenten*. Reinbek bei Hamburg, 1971.

Specht, Richard. *Gustav Mahler*. Berlin, 1913.

——. *Gustav Mahler: Nachgelassene Zehnte Symphonie*. Berlin, 1924.

——. *Gustav Mahlers VIII. Symphonie*. Leipzig and Vienna, 1912.

Stauber, Paul. *Das wahre Erbe Mahlers*. Vienna, 1909.

Stefan, Paul. *Gustav Mahler*. Munich, 1912.

——. *Gustav Mahler: Ein Bild seiner Persönlichkeit in Widmungen*. Munich, 1910.

——. *Gustav Mahlers Erbe*. Munich, 1908.

——. *Mahler für Jedermann*. Vienna, 1923.

Walter, Bruno and Ernst Krenek, tr. James Galston. *Gustav Mahler*. New York, 1941.

* The quotations in the text are from the original German edition (*Gustav Mahler, Erinnerungen und Briefe*, Amsterdam, 1940) in my translation.

Werfel, Alma Mahler, with E. B. Ashton. *And the Bridge Is Love: Memories of a Lifetime.* New York, 1958.
Wiesmann, Sigrid, ed., tr. Anne Shelley. *Gustav Mahler in Vienna.* New York, 1976.

IV. SCHOENBERG

Akademie der Künste, Berlin. *Arnold Schönberg.* Berlin, 1974.
Alderman, Pauline. "I Remember Arnold Schoenberg." *Facets* (University of Southern California, 1976), 49–58.
Armitage, Merle, ed. *Schoenberg.* New York, 1937.
Arnold Schönberg. Munich, 1912.
Arnold Schönberg—Franz Schreker. Briefwechsel, ed. Friedrich C. Heller. Tutzing, 1974.
Arnold Schönberg. Gedenkausstellung 1974, ed. Ernst Hilmar. Vienna, 1974.
"Arnold Schönberg und seine Orchesterwerke," *Pult und Taktstock.* Sonderheft März–April, 1927.
Arnold Schönberg zum fünfzigsten Geburtstage, 13. September 1924. Sonderheft der Musikblätter des Anbruch. Vienna, 1924.
Arnold Schönberg zum sechzigsten Geburtstage. Vienna, 1934.
Bach, D. J. "Notes on Arnold Schoenberg," *Musical Quarterly,* XXII/1 (January, 1936), 8–13.
Berg, Alban. *Arnold Schönberg, Gurrelieder. Führer.* Vienna, 1913.
———. *Arnold Schönberg, Kammersymphonie Op. 9. Thematische Analyse.* Vienna, 1913.
———. *Arnold Schönberg, Pelleas und Melisande. Führer.* Vienna, 1920.
Boretz, Benjamin, and Edward T. Cone, eds. *Perspectives on Schoenberg and Stravinsky.* Princeton, 1968.
Crawford, John C. "*Die glückliche Hand:* Schoenberg's 'Gesamtkunstwerk,'" *Musical Quarterly,* LX/4 (October, 1974), 583–601.
Dibelius, Ulrich. *Herausforderung Schönberg: Was die Musik des Jahrhunderts veränderte.* Munich, 1974.
Ehrenforth, Karl Heinrich. *Ausdruck und Form: Arnold Schönbergs Durchbruch zur Atonalität.* Bonn, 1963.
Felber, Erwin, "Schönberg und die Oper," *Oper* (1927), 67–70.
Gould, Glenn. *Arnold Schoenberg: A Perspective.* Cincinnati, 1964.
Heinitz, W. "Die Sprechtonbewegungen in Arnold Schönbergs Pierrot Lunaire," *Vox* (1925), I, 1–3.
Hill, R. S., "Schoenberg's Tone-Rows and the Music of the Future," *Musical Quarterly,* XXII/1 (January, 1936), 14–37.
Jalowetz, Heinrich, "On the Spontaneity of Schoenberg's Music," *Musical Quarterly,* XXX/4 (October, 1944), 385–409.
Keller, Hans. "Unpublished Schoenberg Letters: Early, Middle and Late," *Music Survey,* IV/3 (June, 1952), 449–72.
Krieger, Georg. *Schönbergs Werke für Klavier.* Göttingen, 1968.
Lautner, Lois, "Arnold Schoenberg in Kammern," *Juilliard News Bulletin,* VII/4 (January, 1969), 2–9.
Leibowitz, Rená. *A. Schoenberg, ou Sisyphe dans la musique contemporaine.* Liège, 1950.
———. *Schoenberg.* Paris, 1969.

———, tr. Dika Newlin. *Schoenberg and His School*. New York, 1949.

MacDonald, Malcolm. *Schoenberg*. London, 1977.

Maegaard, Jan. *Studien zur Entwicklung des dodekaphonen Satzes bei Arnold Schönberg*. 3 vols. Copenhagen, 1972.

Martens, Frederick. *Schönberg*. New York, 1922.

Meyerowitz, Jan. *Arnold Schönberg*. Berlin, 1967.

Milhaud, Darius. "To Arnold Schoenberg on his Seventieth Birthday: Personal Recollections," *Musical Quarterly*, XXX/4 (October, 1944), 379–85.

Neighbour, O. W. "Dodecaphony in Schoenberg's String Trio," *Music Survey*, IV/3 (June, 1952), 489–90.

Nelson, Robert U., "Schoenberg's Variation Seminar," *Musical Quarterly*, L/2 (April, 1964), 141–64.

Newlin, Dika. "Arnold Schoenberg as Choral Composer," *American Choral Review*, VI/4 (1964), 1, 7–11.

———. "Arnold Schoenberg's Religious Works," *Reconstructionist*, XXIV/19 (January 23, 1959), 16–21.

———. "C. P. E. Bach and Arnold Schoenberg: A Comparison," in *The Commonwealth of Music*, eds. Gustave Reese and Rose Brandel, 300–60. New York, 1965.

———. "A Composer's View of Schoenberg's Variations on a Recitative for Organ," *Organ Institute Quarterly* (Spring, 1956).

———. "The Role of the Chorus in Schoenberg's 'Moses and Aaron'," *American Choral Review*, IX/1 (1966), 1–4, 18.

———. "Schoenberg and Wagner," *Bayreuther Festspiele 1967 (Siegfried)*, 15–25.

———. *The Schoenberg Diaries*. New York, 1978.

———. "The Schoenberg-Nachod Collection: A Preliminary Report," *Musical Quarterly* LIV/1 (January, 1968), 31–46.

———. "Schoenberg's String Quartet in D Major," *Faber Music News* (Fall, 1966), 21–23.

———. "Self-Revelation and the Law: Arnold Schoenberg in His Religious Works," *Yuval*, I, Jerusalem, 1968, 204–220.

———. "Some Tonal Aspects of Twelve-Tone Music," *American Music Teacher*, III/2 (November–December, 1953), 2–3, 18.

———. "Why Is Schoenberg's Biography so Difficult to Write?" *Perspectives of New Music*, Fall–Winter 1973/Spring–Summer 1974, 40–42.

Payne, Anthony. *Schoenberg*. London, 1968.

Rauchhaupt, Ursula von, ed., tr. Eugene Hartzell. *Schoenberg–Berg–Webern: The String Quartets. A Documentary Study*. Hamburg, 1971.

Reich, Willi, tr. Leo Black. *Schoenberg: A Critical Biography*. New York and Washington, 1971.

Ringer, Alexander. "Schoenbergiana in Jerusalem," *Musical Quarterly*, LIX/1 (January, 1973), 1–14.

Rogge, Wolfgang. *Das Klavierwerk Arnold Schönbergs*. Regensburg, 1964.

Rosen, Charles. *Arnold Schoenberg*. New York, 1975.

Rubsamen, Walter H. "Schoenberg in America," *Musical Quarterly*, XXXVII/4 (October, 1951), 469–89.

Rufer, Josef, tr. Dika Newlin, *The Works of Arnold Schoenberg*. London and New York, 1962.

Schoenberg, Arnold, ed. Josef Rufer. *Berliner Tagebuch.* Berlin, 1974.
————, ed. Gerald Strang and Leonard Stein. *Fundamentals of Musical Composition.* London and New York, 1965.
————. "Further to the Schoenberg–Mann Controversy," *Music Survey,* II/2 (Autumn, 1949), 77–80.
————. *Harmonielehre.* Vienna, 1911. 3rd enlarged and corrected ed., 1922. 4th ed., 1949. Condensed tr. Robert D. W. Adams, *Theory of Harmony,* New York, 1948.
————, ed. Erwin Stein, tr. Eithne Wilkins and Ernst Kaiser. *Letters.* London and New York, 1964.
————. *Models for Beginners in Composition.* New York, 1943. Rev. ed. Leonard Stein, Los Angeles, 1972.
————. *Moderne Psalmen.* Mainz, 1957.
————, ed. Leonard Stein. *Preliminary Exercises in Counterpoint.* London and New York, 1963.
————, ed. Willi Reich. *Schöpferische Konfessionen.* Zurich, 1964.
————, ed. Humphrey Searle. *Structural Functions of Harmony.* London and New York, 1954. Rev. ed. Leonard Stein, London and New York, 1975.
————, ed. and tr. Dika Newlin. *Style and Idea.* New York, 1950. Second greatly enlarged ed. by Leonard Stein, including most of the foregoing. London and New York, 1975.
————. *Testi poetici e drammatici.* Milan, 1967. Includes only publication to date of *Der biblische Weg.*
————. *Texte.* Vienna, 1926.
"Schoenberg Returns to Jewish Faith at Paris," *The New York Times* (7/25/32), 6:2.
"Schoenberg To Complete Orchestration of A. Berg's Opera *Lulu,*" *The New York Times* (2/17/36), 21:1.
Schönberg–Webern–Berg: Bilder–Partituren–Dokumente. Catalog of exhibit in the Museum des 20. Jahrhunderts. Vienna (May 17–July 20), 1969.
Specht, Richard. "Arnold Schönbergs *Gurrelieder,*" *Der Merker,* IV/5 (1913), 161–64.
————. "Der Hass gegen Schönberg," *März,* 20/9 (1913), 417–22.
Stefan, Paul. *Arnold Schönberg: Wandlung–Legende–Erscheinung–Bedeutung.* Vienna, Berlin, and Leipzig, 1924.
Stein, Erwin. "Idées d'Arnold Schönberg sur la musique," *Revue musicale* (November, 1928).
————. *Praktischer Leitfaden zu Schönbergs Harmonielehre.* Vienna, 1923.
————. "Schoenberg's New Structural Form," *Modern Music,* VII/4 (1930), 3–10.
————. "Schönberg's Position Today," *Christian Science Monitor,* November 25, 1939.
Steiner, Ena. "Schoenberg's Quest: Newly Discovered Works from His Early Years." *Musical Quarterly,* LX/3 (July, 1974), 401–20.
Stuckenschmidt, H. H., tr. Humphrey Searle and Edith Temple Roberts. *Arnold Schoenberg.* London and New York, 1959.
————. *Schönberg: Leben–Umwelt–Werk.* Zurich and Freiburg, 1974.
"Toward the Schoenberg Centenary" (a series of articles), *Perspectives of*

New Music, Fall-Winter, 1972–Fall-Winter, 1974.

Wellesz, Egon, tr. W. Kerridge. *Arnold Schönberg*. London, 1925.

———. "Arnold Schönberg," *Cahiers d'aujourd'hui* (April, 1914), 520–29.

———. "Arnold Schönberg," *Zeitschrift der-internationalen Musikgesellschaft*, XII (1910–11), 342–48.

———. *The Origins of Schoenberg's Twelve-Tone System*. Washington, 1958.

Whittall, Arnold. *Schoenberg Chamber Music*. Seattle, 1972.

Wörner, Karl H. *Schoenberg's Moses and Aaron*. London, 1963.

V. BERG AND WEBERN

A. Berg

Adorno, Theodor W. *Alban Berg, der Meister des kleinsten Übergangs*. Vienna, 1968.

Berg, Alban. *Briefe an seine Frau*. Vienna, 1965. Abbreviated tr. by Bernard Grun, London and N.Y., 1971.

Carner, Mosco. *Alban Berg: The Man and the Work*. London, 1975; New York, 1977.

Jouve, Pierre Jean and Fano, Michel. *Wozzeck ou le nouvel opera*. Paris, 1964.

Redlich, H. F. *Alban Berg: The Man and His Music*. London, 1957.

Reich, Willi. *Alban Berg*. Vienna, 1937.

———, tr. Cornelius Cardew. *Alban Berg*. London, 1965.

———, ed. *Alban Berg, Bildnis im Wort. Selbstzeugnisse und Aussagen der Freunde*. Zurich, 1959.

———. *A Guide to Alban Berg's Opera* Wozzeck. New York, 1931.

B. Webern

Kolneder, Walter, tr. Humphrey Searle. *Anton Webern*. Berkeley and Los Angeles, 1968.

Moldenhauer, Hans. *The Death of Anton Webern: A Drama in Documents*. New York, 1961.

———, and Demar Irvine, eds. and comps. *Anton von Webern: Perspectives*. Seattle and London, 1966.

Die Reihe: Information über serielle Musik, ed. Herbert Eimert and Karlheinz Stockhausen. Vol. II: *Anton Webern*. Vienna and Bryn Mawr, 1955.

Webern, Anton, ed. Josef Polnauer, tr. Cornelius Cardew. *Briefe an Hildegard Jone und Josef Humplik*. Bryn Mawr, 1967.

———, ed. Willi Reich, tr. Leo Black. *The Path to the New Music*. Bryn Mawr, 1963.

———, *Weg und Gestalt. Selbstzeugnisse und Worte der Freunde*. Zurich, 1961.

Wildgans, Friedrich, tr. Edith Temple Roberts and Humphrey Searle. *Anton Webern*. London, 1966.

VI. ARTS, IDEAS, HISTORY, MISCELLANEOUS, THEORY.

Adorno, Theodor W. *Klangfiguren*, Musikalische Schriften I. Frankfurt, 1959.

———. *Philosophie der neuen Musik*. Tübingen, 1949.

———. *Quasi una Fantasia*. Musikalische Schriften II. Frankfurt, 1963.

Appia, Adolphe. *Die Musik und die Inscenierung.* Munich, 1899.

Bahr-Mildenburg, Anna. *Erinnerungen.* Vienna and Berlin, 1921.

Bekker, Paul. *Die Sinfonie von Beethoven bis Mahler.* Berlin, 1918.

Betti, Adolfo. *La vita musicale a Vienna.* Turin, 1899.

Bierbaum, Otto Julius, ed. *Deutsche Chansons (Brettl-Lieder).* Leipzig, 1902.

Brahms, Johannes. *Briefwechsel mit Heinrich und Elisabet von Herzogenberg.* Berlin, 1908–12.

Capellen, George. *Ist das System S. Sechters ein geigneter Ausgangspunkt für die theoretische Wagnerforschung?* Leipzig, 1902.

Carlson, Effie B. A *Bio-Bibliographical Dictionary of Twelve-Tone and Serial Composers.* Metuchen, N.J., 1970.

Graf, Max. *Legend of a Musical City.* New York, 1945.

Gregor, Hans. *Die Welt der Oper—Die Oper der Welt.* Berlin, 1931.

Gutmann, Albert. *Aus dem Wiener Musikleben. Erinnerungen 1873–1908.* Vienna, 1914.

Hanslick, Eduard. *Aus Meinem Leben.* Berlin, 1894.

———. *Musikalisches und Litterarisches.* Berlin, 1890.

———, tr. and ed. Henry Pleasants III. *Vienna's Golden Years of Music.* New York, 1950.

Hartungen, Hartmut von. *Der Dichter Siegfried Lipiner (1856–1911).* Munich, n.d. (unpublished thesis).

Herbeck, Ludwig. *Johann Herbeck: Ein Lebensbild.* Vienna, 1885.

Hevesi, Ludwig. *Rudolf Alt.* Vienna, 1911.

Hijman, Julius. *Nieuwe oostenrijkse muziek.* Amsterdam, 1938.

Huneker, James. *Ivory, Apes and Peacocks.* New York, 1915.

Janik, Allan, and Stephen Toulmin. *Wittgenstein's Vienna.* New York, 1974.

Jászi, Oszkár. *The Dissolution of the Hapsburg Monarchy.* Chicago, 1929.

Kandinsky, Wassily and Franz Marc, eds. *Der Blaue Reiter.* Munich, 1914. Documentary Edition by Klaus Lankheit, Munich, 1965. Tr. Henning Falkenstein, New York and London, 1974.

———. *Über das Geistliche in der Kunst.* Munich, 1912. Tr. Hilla Rebay, New York, 1946.

Karpath, Ludwig. *Begegnung mit dem Genius.* Vienna and Leipzig, 1934.

———. *Zu den Briefen Richard Wagners an eine Putzmacherin.* Berlin, n.d.

Leibowitz, René. *Introduction à la musique de douze sons.* Paris, 1949.

———. *Qu'est-ce-que la musique de douze sons?* Liège, 1948.

Loos, Adolf. *Trotzdem: 1900–1930.* Innsbruck, 1931.

McGrath, William J. *Dionysian Art and Populist Politics in Austria.* New Haven, 1974.

Newman, Ernest. *The Life of Richard Wagner.* 4 vols. New York, 1933–41.

Perle, George. *Serial Composition and Atonality: An Introduction to the Music of Schoenberg, Berg and Webern.* Berkeley, 1962. Rev. ed., 1974.

Pfitzner, Hans. *Die neue Ästhetik der musikalischen Impotenz: ein Verwesungssymptom?* Munich, 1920.

Pollak, Gustav. *Franz Grillparzer and the Austrian Drama.* New York, 1907.

Pollard, Percival. *Masks and Minstrels of New Germany.* Boston, 1911.

Powell, Nicolas. *The Sacred Spring: The Arts in Vienna 1898–1918.* Boston, 1974.

Reik, Theodor. *The Haunting Melody.* New York, 1953.

Rochberg, George. *The Hexachord and Its Relation To The Twelve-Tone Row.* Bryn Mawr, 1955.

Rufer, Josef. tr. Humphrey Searle. *Composition with Twelve Notes.* London and New York, 1954.

Schnerich, Alfred. *Messe und Requiem seit Haydn und Mozart.* Berlin, 1913.

Sechter, Simon. *Die richtige Folge der Grundharmonien.* Leipzig, 1853.

Seidl, Arthur. *Neuzeitliche Tondichter und zeitgenössische Tonkünstler.* Regensburg, 1926.

Slezak, Leo. *Meine sämtlichen Werke.* Berlin, 1923.

———. *Der Wortbruch.* Berlin, 1927.

Specht, Richard. *Das Wiener Operntheater: Erinnerungen aus 50 Jahren.* Vienna, 1919.

Steed, Henry Wickham. *The Hapsburg Monarchy.* London, 1914.

Stefan, Paul. *Das Grab in Wien.* Berlin, 1913.

———. *Neue Musik und Wien.* Vienna, 1921.

———. *Die Wiener Oper.* Vienna, 1932.

Stein, Erwin. *Orpheus in New Guises.* London, 1953.

Ursprung, Otto. *Die katholische Kirchenmusik.* Potsdam, 1931.

———. *Restauration und Palestrina-Renaissance in der katholischen Kirchenmusik der letzten zwei Jahrhunderte.* Augsburg, 1924.

Viertel, Salka. *The Kindness of Strangers.* New York, Chicago and San Francisco, 1969.

Von neuer Musik: Beitrag zur Erkenntnis der neuzeitlichen Tonkunst. Cologne, 1925.

Weingartner, Felix. *Lebenserinnerungen.* Zurich and Leipzig, 1928–29. Tr. Marguerite Wolff, *Buffets and Rewards,* London, 1937.

Wiesenthal, Grete. *Der Aufstieg.* Berlin, 1919.

Wolzogen, Ernst von. *Ansichten und Aussichten.* Berlin, 1908.

Zichý, Géza. *Aus meinem Leben.* Stuttgart, 1920.

Zuckerkandl, Berta. *My Life and History.* New York, 1939.

Zweig, Stefan. *The World of Yesterday.* New York, 1943.

Index